Spindles and Spires

A Re-Study of Religion and Social Change in Gastonia

spindles and spires

A Re-Study of Religion and
Social Change in Gastonia

BY

JOHN R. EARLE
Wake Forest University

DEAN D. KNUDSEN
Purdue University

AND

DONALD W. SHRIVER, Jr.
Union Theological Seminary in New York

JOHN KNOX PRESS
ATLANTA

The following acknowledgments are made for permission to reprint material:

The Gastonia Gazette. Gastonia, North Carolina. Used by permission.

Millhands & Preachers: A Study of Gastonia. Liston Pope. Introduction by Richard A. Peterson and N. J. Demerath III. New Haven: Yale University Press. Copyright 1942 by Yale University Press. Used by permission.

The Social Construction of Reality. Copyright © 1966 by Peter L. Berger and Thomas Luckmann. Reprinted by permission of Doubleday & Company, Inc.

The Gathering Storm in the Churches. Copyright © 1960 by Jeffrey K. Hadden. Reprinted by permission of Doubleday & Company, Inc.

The Scientific Study of Religion. J. Milton Yinger. London: Collier-Macmillan Limited. Copyright © 1970, J. Milton Yinger. Used by permission of Macmillan Publishing Company.

Library of Congress Cataloging in Publication Data

Earle, John R   1935–
  Spindles and spires.

  Bibliography: p.
  Includes index.
  1. Church and social problems—Gastonia, N.C. 2. Church and industry—North Carolina
—Gastonia. 3. Church and labor—Gastonia, N. C. I. Knudsen, Dean D., 1932–   Joint
author.   II. Shriver, Donald W., joint author.   III. Title.
HN39.U6E27   261.8   73–13461
ISBN 0–8042–0854–9

Dedicated To

THE NEXT GENERATION OF GASTONIANS

Also In Memory Of

LISTON POPE

And Three Other Southerners:

JAMES MCBRIDE DABBS
LUCIUS H. PITTS
JAMES R. PRESTWOOD

Contents

Acknowledgments

A study extending over ten year's time, undertaken by three scholars, utilizing the direct assistance of at least a hundred people, and focused on the inhabitants of an entire county, accumulates a long list of debts. Not all of the people to whom we are indebted can be personally recognized here—a limitation both ordinary and regrettable in the records of human projects.

The financial base of the study was dispersed among many interested agencies. Though we did not happen to work with the help of the massive budgets commanded by much social research these days, we were fortunate to have a larger budget than the one used by Liston Pope when he wrote the book that is predecessor to this one. (On his own account to us, Pope spent one thousand dollars in the data-accumulation stage of his study.) Our budget, we are glad to say, was considerably more generous than that, thanks to the following people and agencies.

The initial stages of the study owe much to the Mary Reynolds Babcock Foundation of Winston-Salem, North Carolina, which, first through the good offices of the late A. Hollis Edens and then through his successor as executive Secretary of the Foundation, Dr. William C. Archie, provided the funds that permitted Donald Shriver to spend the summer of 1965 in Gastonia and to devote part of his time as a faculty member at North Carolina State University to the study. Further support came to Dean Knudsen through a special summer grant, followed by a one year grant from the College of Commerce of The Ohio State University; to John Earle through the administration and the Graduate Council of Wake Forest University and the Piedmont University Center of North Carolina; and to Donald Shriver through the Research Committee of Emory University. Then, an accumulation of financial help was provided us from the following seven agencies and persons, who in a series of approximately equal small grants made possible a fund for carrying on our field surveys. Particular persons in the offices of the seven agencies took the cause of this research to heart; so we have listed these individuals in the parentheses following the agency-names: The Board of Homeland Ministries of the United Church of Christ, headquartered in New York (Dr. Huber Klemme); the Board of National Missions of the United Presbyterian Church in the U.S.A., New

9

York (Dr. David Ramage); the Board of Christian Education of the Presbyterian Church in the U.S., Richmond (Dr. John Evans); the Board of National Ministries of the Presbyterian Church in the U.S., Division of Research, Atlanta (Dr. Samuel Southard—this and the former Presbyterian Board are now combined in the General Executive Board); the Board of Education of the Methodist Church, Nashville (Dr. Robert Wilson); the Textile Workers Union of America, Research Department, New York (Mr. George Perkel); and the Division of Christian Social Concern of the American Baptist Convention, Valley Forge (Rev. Elizabeth Miller). All of these agencies and persons saw fit to invest in the project when it was still mostly an idea in the minds of the three investigators. For this widespread expression of confidence in us, we are exceedingly grateful.

In addition, there was a cluster of other scholars in the social sciences who rendered invaluable on-site assistance in the field-work stages of the study. Sister Mary Annella, of the Department of Sociology of Sacred Heart College in Belmont, N.C. and Mr. Frank Avesing, then of Belmont College and now of St. Louis University, were both the source of great assistance in the recruiting and training of persons who did interviewing for us among a sample of citizens in Gaston County. Dr. Samuel Byuarm, head of the Department of Sociology of Johnson C. Smith University in Charlotte, rendered similar assistance to us in our work with students of that university who did interviews among members of the black community in Gastonia. Dr. T. Edwin Boling, now of Wittenberg University, wrote his doctoral thesis in connection with the research and helped us in assembling and interpreting a large body of our data. Mr. Fred Rochte assisted John Earle in a variety of tasks in the summer of 1967, especially in the completing of interviews among certain groups of people in our sample of citizens; and Mr. David Buchdahl spent the summer months of 1966 assisting Donald Shriver in library research on economic change in Gaston County. Some thirty students of sociology at Belmont College and Johnson C. Smith University conducted over 400 interviews which were a major element in the study. Their services, too, not handsomely paid for, were essential and much appreciated.

Hundreds of persons in Gastonia, of course, were at the heart of our study but by the very canons of social science we must acknowledge most of them as anonymous helpers only. Their lives, like ours, are too short and their interests are too many for us to presume that the interview-hours they gave us were always as valuable to them as to us. Among the Gastonians whom we may mention by name, however, is Mrs. Barbara Heafner, Head Librarian of the Gaston County Public Library, who facilitated our access to the microfilmed version of thirty years of copy of the local newspaper, and who took more time doing this than could possibly be repaid in terms of the copies of the book we hope to give to her library, where, she tells us, Liston Pope's book on Gastonia is now receiving the attention largely denied it by a former generation of Gastonians.

A former resident of Gastonia and the chief reader of those thirty years of *Gastonia Gazette* on microfilm was Peggy Leu Shriver, wife of one of the authors. When the typing of hundreds of pages of first draft manuscript is added to the eye-wearing business of microfilm-reading, and when the lack of any remuneration for these months of labor is duly noted, a first-class illustration of male chauvinism will immediately be apparent. "Newspaper scanning," a deceptively simple-sounding term for one job social scientists may do, is a job requiring patience, sensitivity, and intelligence, and Peggy Shriver combines all these virtues in a way which makes her in reality one of the scholarly contributors to the work.

Among the other frequently underrated and all-too-anonymous contributors to books are typists and other office workers who attend to the "mechanics" of scholarship, again a deceptive term among scholars. The secretaries to whom we owe much are Mrs. Kay Lassiter and Mrs. Carolyn Yorke of North Carolina State University, Ms. Donna Bystrom and Ms. Sue Simmons of Purdue University, Mrs. Bertie B. Slate of Wake Forest University, and in the last stages of manuscript preparation, Mrs. Susan Brown and Mrs. Bobbee Norvell of Emory University.

Most heartily, we wish to thank our colleagues in these and other universities who over the years have properly encouraged, scrutinized, criticized, or otherwise contributed to the content of the study. In particular we are grateful to Russell Dynes of the Ohio State University, Gerhard Lenski of the University of North Carolina, Chapel Hill, and C. H. Patrick of Wake Forest University.

On its way to publication, the manuscript benefitted immensely from the careful, critical reading of Professor Max L. Stackhouse of Andover Newton Theological Seminary and Professor Charles W. Powers, then of Yale University Divinity School and now Director of Public Responsibility for the Cummins Engine Company of Columbus, Indiana. More than readers of this present volume can know, they are indebted to these two previous readers, who liked the manuscript enough to want it improved.

Next-to-last, what is both inevitable and appropriate for the beginning of any book whose authors are known to us, we wish to thank our three families, ten persons in all, who endured closeted fathers, absent fathers, messy desktops, and innumerable doubts that "the book" would ever be written. Now that it is written, we hope that their endurance of this particular project has a happy ending.

Finally, in all due gratitude, we want to thank each other. The work of conceiving, executing, and writing up the study was a marvelous mixture of labor-divided and labor-overlapping. Shriver was largely responsible for the final draft of the book; but in fact we are no longer sure how to distribute credit for the final product among the three of us—hence the alphabetical listing of our names on the title page. What is perhaps most remarkable about the project is that it has ended with the co-authors in a state of deepened friendship—an event worthy of public acknowledgment.

Preface

By Donald W. Shriver, Jr.

In the spring of 1967, one of the three authors of this book asked a favor of some half dozen managers of textile plants in Gastonia, North Carolina. We were beginning to write a sequel to *Millhands and Preachers: A Study of Gastonia,* written in 1940 by Liston Pope. I knew few of the six had read Pope, but their opinions about him would be valuable to us. I supplied them a copy and asked if they would read it and discuss it with me in a month.

Out of their *yes* to this request came an evening's conversation, a bit of which is reproduced below. It is as fair an introduction to the subject matter of this second book on Gastonia as our data in the 1940-1975 period is likely to provide any of our readers.

Midway in the conversation, one of the managers, son of one of the early "pioneer textile men" of Gaston County, said with considerable feeling:

"The big strike of '29 made a big impression on me. I was sixteen at the time and there was violence involved—and I didn't like it. I have remembered it ever since, and I think that the young men of my generation remembered it, and all of us have been anxious to see that that kind of situation was not repeated. I believe that policies followed among the textile mills and other industries in Gastonia have been designed to see that that kind of situation will not be repeated."

"What made the biggest impression on you?" I asked.

"Some of the things they did. The headquarters of the (union) group was next door to my home. I remember the night after Chief Aderholt had been killed, the police came up and went into this house and took the participants, I suppose, to jail. I had a 22-caliber rifle loaded and across my lap . . . that was a tense time. . . . I think the people were pretty upset that outside agitators had come in and were tearing the community to pieces. There were a lot of civic-minded people here then. They didn't like it, and they wanted to do something about it."

"What have they tried to do about it?"

"Organizing such things as a strong Boy Scout movement, encouragement of camps by civic clubs, activities for young people to make them better citizens, giving them a higher sense of values. I think there has developed a strong sense of civic consciousness.

13

That is borne out by the Junior Chamber of Commerce, Boy and Girl Scout work, the number of civic clubs we have—almost all of our young men seem interested in making a contribution in the community."

"I gather that the organization of churches has also been a matter of interest to the leaders of industry in the county. Is that so?"

"Yes, we want churches in the community. We want the spiritual leadership that it provides . . . not from the standpoint of controlling the program of the church, but just to be sure that there are churches in the community."

"What are some of your reasons for wanting this spiritual leadership?"

"We just feel that it makes a better community. From every standpoint: it teaches values, makes better citizens."

"Pope says that many ministers and millowners believed that religion helps make a man a better *worker*. Do you think that the churches make people better workers?"

"I would like to say better *citizens*. 'Workers' narrows it too much. We are interested not so much in good workers as in good parents that bring up sound families."

A second executive of the group chimed in: "To bring up good human beings. That's what we're after. The whole man."

And the other concluded emphatically: "I for one would not want to bring up my family in a community in which no church existed. I think we all feel that way."

Such statements provoke many a question. Here is a southern Piedmont county, just west of Charlotte, whose skyline (to the eye of any casual traveler down Interstate 85) is dominated by two sorts of buildings: spinning mills and churches. What is the "use" of each of these institutions to the other? Here is a county that became notorious in the spring of 1929 as newspaper headlines around the world trumpeted the news of "a communist-led textile strike in Gastonia." Do these industrial leaders correctly describe the lingering impact of this event in their community these forty years later? Here also is a community whose elite believe that their local society hangs together, functions, and has its being partly in terms of a certain "civic consciousness" shared by its citizens. Is there such a consciousness? If so, what is its content, who shapes it, and to what purposes? Finally, here is a locale which participates with countless others in a complex phenomenon narrowly and deceptively tagged "modernization," "globalization," or "rapid social change." What are the major social changes that have occurred in Gastonia in the generation since Pope's book? And, if one happens to be interested in the subject, what has been the role of religion and its institutions in the making of those changes?

Stated simply, these are the questions central to this study. In the next chapter, we want to portray our interest in Gastonia in some more sophisticated frameworks of the two disciplines, sociology and social ethics, represented in our team of three authors. But anyone who has written books knows that they do not always begin with sophisticated intellectual questions. Sometimes books begin with experience. An experience behind the beginning of this book was the job that one of us performed for three years in Gastonia in the years 1956-59. In mobile America getting a job is the most characteristic way by which people get introduced to a new community; and, in this case, the job was one of critical importance for the answering of the questions sketched above: I was the minister of a Gastonia church.

It is not customary for sociological studies to begin with snatches of autobiography. Some theorists would say that self-reported experience is of no intrinsic interest to the sociologist, though it may be of interest to the psychologist. Without arguing the matter here, we have to confess our bias that the study of society is a more personal enterprise, and the study of persons a more social enterprise, than many of the respective students admit. Those who are troubled by this statement will find much to dispute in what follows!

My Introduction to Gastonia

Towards the southern end of Gaston County are two high ridges of kyanite-quartzite: the one, King's Mountain, was the site of a battle in the American Revolution; the other, Crowder's Mountain, casts a long shadow in the direction of a reminder of the Civil War: Lincoln Academy, a high school for black youth established with Yankee church money soon after that conflict had ended. My first acquaintance with Gaston County was on the grounds of the Academy, where for a week in 1949 I attended one of the first integrated, ecumenical church youth conferences to be held in North Carolina. One of the two things which stands out in my memory of that week is a warning which was communicated to the conference by one of its leaders that we "should stay away from the town of Gastonia. They had a violent textile strike there twenty years ago, and some mean remarks about 'that mixed conference' were heard today in the Gastonia bus station." The second thing I remember best was the figure of the Reverend Lucius H. Pitts, a black Methodist minister, standing against the backdrop of Crowder's Mountain officiating at a communion service. In retrospect, I realize that I was here touching the fringes of two major issues of social change in the next twenty years in Gaston County history: labor-management relations and race relations.

It never occurred to me then that seven years later I would become the pastor of a small Presbyterian church in west Gastonia from whose porch one had a splendid view of Crowder's Mountain. The steps by which I arrived there as a young professional were gradual: a first reading of *Millhands and Preachers* which an astute philosophy professor at Davidson College had first called to my attention; a summer internship as a theological student in production-line work in a small factory in Chicago; a summer pastorate in a chapel near a mill village in a county neighboring on Gaston; a year of study at Yale Divinity School where I met Liston Pope and took a class under him; and finally, a phone call from Gastonia inquiring if I would be interested in having my first fulltime appointment in that city. My acceptance of that invitation was motivated by reasons that would probably have puzzled most members of my future congregation: (1) I wanted to know if the Protestant churches of the South had any important contributions to make to the "humanization" of an urban-industrial civilization, and a community as proud of both its mills and its churches as was Gastonia seemed a likely place to find out. (2) I wanted to do something to overcome the traditional split in southern Protestantism between "personal" and "social" religious consciousness, and I had every reason to believe that the split was abundantly represented among the churches of this town. (3) Finally, the very fact that a first-class study in the sociology of religion had been written about this county made it an appealing place to go. One could "see" Gastonia more quickly and comprehensively with the prior help of Liston Pope. And so, to Gastonia I went.

The congregation of some 100 members was seven years old when I became its second fulltime pastor. The building was located on the edge of the "new" Gastonia. An airplane view of old Gastonia would have appeared as a collage of amoebae: a collection of mill villages each huddled around its respective nucleus-factory. The majority of churches were in the midst of those huddles. The fifty houses comprising our immediate neighborhood, however, had been privately built just after World War II. Many of their occupants had begun their work life in the mills, but had since taken an economic step up to better jobs. This was the dominant social-economic characteristic of the families in our congregation: they were moving *away from* the mill village in every possible sense. During the next three years I was never to hear a parent express the hope that his or her child would go to work in a mill.

The people of my congregation reminded me again and again of the importance of this "upward mobility." On one occasion during my first few months, I made the mistake of remarking that so-and-so was a "mill worker." One of his friends corrected me saying, "I think he would prefer to be called a *textile* worker." On another occasion, when I casually referred to the fact that a woman "worked in the mill," she quickly reminded me that though she had once worked on the mill *floor,* now she worked as a clerk in the mill *office.* She had made the transition from overalls to white collar.

Actually only six or eight members of the congregation were textile workers. Another half dozen did skilled work in machine shops. One was a bricklayer, one a carpenter, one an accountant, three were agents for insurance companies, two worked for small loan companies. Only two were college graduates, one a junior college teacher, and the other a graduate of the state university engineering school who worked in a new chain-saw manufacturing plant. One other man ran a small machine shop in his garage in 1956; not formally trained in engineering, he possessed superlative technical and business gifts, and by the early sixties he had built a new plant in north Gastonia, a new home in east Gastonia, and thereby a new economic status for himself. More than anyone else in the congregation he embodied the spirit of individual "Progress," which, I was to learn, suffused Gastonian affairs.

How Does the Church Attract Members?

Religion was one of the prevailing winds in Gastonia. Any new arrival soon discovered that. Even abstainers from church membership were invariably interested in religion and could talk about reasons for their abstinence. As I made calls in the homes of my congregation and other families in the community, I discussed many religious questions—the miracles of the Bible, the sin against the Holy Spirit, the difference between Presbyterian and Baptist church government. But quite as readily I sat on front porches and talked about my new friends' memory of the Loray Strike, recent changes in work policy in the mills, and the prospects of labor unionism. To the surprise of some, I visited the mills or factories where they worked and made the acquaintance of their supervisors. Sometime during my first year I discovered that a segment of my congregation was upset with my incursions into these matters. Our church lay scarcely a mile from the old Loray Mill, but few persons in the community who remembered 1929 enjoyed recounting those memories to "the preacher." One of the leading churchwomen among our members worked in a textile plant where a local of the United Textile Workers had managed to survive for the past decade. I asked her one day if she was a member of the union. "No," she said abruptly, "I don't have much to do with them." Later I learned from another person in the congregation that the woman had privately and indignantly remarked that "it isn't any of the preacher's business whether or not I am a member of the union." This was one of my first concrete warnings that for many Gastonians mere talk of labor unionism was taboo. Had I not read some of the emotional signals correctly, I am sure that I would have launched into a discussion of the pro's and con's of unionism with this woman. Such a discussion was stronger medicine than she was prepared to take.

During my first year as pastor, I was eager to define my role in the congregation to touch all the bases of preaching, counseling, teaching, administration, and community action. I soon found that only the first and second activities were strongly affirmed by a majority of the congregation. My early attempt to turn the Wednesday night prayer meeting from being a third "preaching" service into a Bible study group, for example, came to much grief. A few of the younger members liked the idea, but one elder complained to me: "I used to get a spark of inspiration out of prayer meeting, but I don't now."

"You get more out of hearing me talk about the Bible than out of our studying it together?" I inquired.

"Yes, indeed," he said firmly, "I don't come to church to go to school again."

For all its painfulness, it was one of the most illuminating remarks ever made to me during my three years in Gastonia. Hardly half of the congregation had graduated from high school. School was one of my successes; it was one of their failures! Something else than "learning" brought them to church, some of them three times a week. What was it?

A theory of church attendance in Gastonia permeated Pope's book. But like many another young professional, I had discovered that there is a rocky road from reading about a thing to dealing with it personally. Why do "my" people come to church? The experience of that year, not my reading, said to me that they come

—because they have been hurt and need comforting. (Therefore the content of preaching and pastoral calling had to center on peace, forgiveness, and love.)

—because they are lonely and need company. (Therefore the activities of the church must include many informal social gatherings.)

—because they are often reminded in their work that they are relatively low on the social totem pole, and they want to enjoy a different status somewhere. (Therefore the church must remain enough insulated from the world of everyday work to make clear to every member that different standards of "success" obtain here, and competition between church members must be as muted as possible.)

—because almost anyone can participate in the control of the church. (Therefore, it is important to know that you can safely criticize the seminary-trained professional minister; if you can't, he is just like any other company boss.)

What then for the carryover of religion into the affairs of the mill, the insurance company, city politics, and the like? Alas: there is little energy left for such things; little experience to suggest that workers can influence managers; so many complex economic and social questions that seem foreign to the Bible, that it may just be useless to talk about such things.

Toward a Strategy for a Social Ministry

How then could a minister in Gastonia pursue his interest in the social meaning of religious faith, in spite of the apathy of many people in his congregation? The strategy, I decided, must take account of the following constraints:

(1) He will have to work hard to match his parishioners' expectations of him as a pastor. He must come across to them as a person who is ready to be their companion in sorrow, their helper in trouble. (2) He must accept the personal dimension as the highroad into the social; that is, he can whittle away at the insulation between the two by frequently interpreting personal problems in terms of their social origins. (3) He must be willing to work out a few professional insulations of his own, carrying on a ministry to institutions that does not fit neatly with his ministry to persons.

The latter strategy had several tactical expressions during my last two years in Gastonia. First, I learned to do special work with one or another *subgroup* in the congregation. One such group, young adults, was eager for discussion and reading on issues of ethics in industry, government, and the church. I studied books on these issues in a Sunday school class with them, invited community leaders like the local congressman to meet with them and pursued the same subjects with them on porches and in living rooms. Again, I found that certain social issues could be pursued on a *noncongregational level of church organization*. One such issue was race relations, as illustrated below. Finally, I discovered that among professionals in the community, few were as free as the minister to find time for *personal participation in nonchurch social structures*. One did have to work at it. As pastor of a church geographically and socially on the margin of Gastonia's life, I had few regular institutional pressures to impel me into the mainstream of town affairs. Nobody ever invited me to a meeting of the Democratic Party, the Chamber of Commerce, or even a civic club. The reason was easy to discern: in Gastonia a pastor shares the social status of his parishioners. With some exceptions, he is treated as they are treated. But in spite of this, the minister of a church of 100 members was free to move into many a self-chosen relationship with that society. The local textile industry and the structures of local race relations interested me the most; and so, for two years I worked at getting acquainted with them.

Race Relations and the Church

It was the first appearance of a puzzle that gives much impetus to this book: the contacts I began to have with *race* relations in Gastonia I had largely *through the church;* the contacts I began to have with *industrial* relations I had largely *outside the church*. It was to prove to be an enormously crucial clue to what the church is, and is not, in the total social fabric of Gastonia.

The years 1956-59 were the years of the Montgomery bus boycott, the desegregation of the Little Rock high school, and other early stirrings of the civil rights movement. The leaders of that movement included people like my friend Lucius Pitts. Since our communion service in the shadow of Crowder's Mountain, I had been determined to make such an occasion possible for young people in my own congregation. So, when the local Presbytery asked me in 1957 to direct its youth program, I planned a summer conference to be led in part by Pitts and James M. Dabbs. During the conference we asked the two of them to talk about race relations in the South. It was the first time some of our young people had ever heard the subject discussed with candor in a "mixed" setting. Back home, I knew that Pitts and Dabbs had changed the outlooks of some persons from our own congregation. Their parents, with hushed appreciation, told me so.

Locally I got to know a few black ministers through the Ministerial Association, and one Sunday evening the choir of a local black Methodist church took part in our congregation's service of worship. But a more profound "meeting" with the black community occurred in my attempts to bring race relations into my Sunday sermons from time to time. Here I encountered the relation of the races in Gastonia in the images, feelings, and experience of my all-white congregation. What astounded me from the beginning of these encounters was the careful attention accorded these sermons. Ministers, like all public speakers, develop a sense for the quality of an audience's listening. My congregation responded to my preaching on this subject with an intense, troubled patience: they could neither enjoy nor dismiss such preaching.

In the fall of 1957, for example, school desegregation came not only to Little Rock but also to Charlotte, North Carolina, twenty miles to the east of Gastonia. A September issue of *Time* showed Dorothy Counts, the first black student to enter Charlotte's Harding High School, being jeered by white parents and students on the sidewalks. My sermon on September 15 was based on the Cain and Abel story, and its main illustrations concerned the various ways humans murder each other. Miss Counts was quoted as saying that she wanted to attend Harding High because she "loved to make friends and meet new people." I suggested that this girl's readiness to make friends with white people was getting crushed, a bit of her selfhood murdered. I called attention to one nameless young man in the picture who ridiculed the girl by making monkey gestures at her. That young man, too, was suffering from the death of something human in him.

Over the course of three years, only one person (to my knowledge) was enough offended by what I said from the pulpit about race relations to use this as a reason for not joining the church. After such sermons people would make comments like: "That sure was preaching today." "We need to hear more of that." "They say the preacher isn't preaching unless he steps on your toes." This same impression was strengthened in 1958 when the local First Presbyterian Church asked me to conduct a study series on a recently published book by Liston Pope, *The Kingdom Beyond Caste,* an uncompromising assault upon the theory and the practice of racial discrimination in American society. (No church in Gastonia ever asked me to conduct a study series on Pope's "other" book, *Millhands and Preachers.* It was a significant omission.) The same troubled patience met me in that upper-class Gastonia audience. It was as if the Bible, American history, and half-conscious personal awareness were combining to inform these church members that racism and their religion had an uneasy fit.

Towards the end of my stay, I concluded that I had not spoken forcefully enough about race relations. It was an apparently quiet time in racial matters in Gastonia. We did not desegregate our local church during those years—some would say there was no "provocation" for it. But it was my strong intuition that both white and black people of Gastonia were ready for some changes in local race relations and their readiness was more than vaguely associated with their religion. Deep down many whites knew that the Bible provided no justification for the downgrading of any human being and that, a lot of social tradition to the contrary, segregated institutions were due for an overhaul.

Labor-Management Relations and the Church

Having visited a number of spinning mills in the county and having talked about current labor-management changes with some of my members, I knew that a great rumbling was afoot in the mills over the "stretch-out." New machinery, new management efficiencies (symbolized by the dreaded stop-watch of the industrial engineer), and new requirements for the number of "sides" each worker was expected to tend, all quickened the pace of work in the mills. Complaint was legion. The stretch-out thereby seemed a good issue by which to connect the issues of personal and social salvation; so for a Sunday evening service in June 1957 I arranged a panel discussion between two members of the congregation, both textile workers, and the personnel manager of a large plant of Burlington Mills, Inc. This man, a Presbyterian, was later to become executive secretary of the Gastonia Chamber of Commerce. He was an effective promoter of the new "human relations" approach to management that was gaining popularity among Gaston managers in the fifties. He explained the new approach to our congregation, and after a few polite questions from the other panelists, I asked: "Suppose there is a conflict of interest between what management wants and what a worker wants—or the worker thinks there is one? What recourse does the worker have?"

"He can appeal to the next highest level of management," said our visitor. "Right up to the president."

"Suppose that the worker does not believe he is getting treated fairly even by the president. Should he have no other recourse?"

"That is sufficient in almost every case that we know of."

"But maybe that comes down to saying that finally the worker should do what management says. Should the worker always do what management says?"

After some hesitation, the personnel director replied: "Yes, I could almost say that."

Three months later I preached a Labor Day sermon on the difference between autocracy, paternalism, and mutuality in the slave-master relationship as treated by Paul in Ephesians 6:5-9. I attempted first to interpret the biblical notion of sin in terms of the "me first" ethic that tends to dominate capitalistic theory since the days of Adam Smith. In the tragic conflicts of one personal or group interest with another, I said that brute power is sometimes the only protection that people have over against other brute power. In this context, I raised (for the first time) the question of labor unions, bargaining, and strikes. "When a union calls for a strike against management," I said, "this does not necessarily mean that the union member enjoys strife or damaging the profits of the company. But it may mean that he does not know any way of challenging injustice without resorting to such organized action." I went on to express my sympathy for any person who had the job of a personnel manager in a mill. He is a man caught in the middle between "management's desire for more work at less pay and the worker's desire for less work at more pay. These days the personnel handbooks tell the personnel director to be 'sincerely interested in the worker as a person'; but sincerity itself can be used chiefly to get more work out of people. Wouldn't it be difficult to be a conscientious personnel manager? Whose interests would you be serving most of the time?"

If my sixth professional sense is to be trusted, the attention accorded these reflections, biblically-derived or not, was unimpressive. It never occurred to me that through panel discussions and sermons the church could make a powerful impact upon labor-management relations in Gastonia, but it had occurred to me that the church could combine a pastoral concern for people suffering distress at their work with inquiry into the social sources of that suffering. The church—by my theological lights—was supposed to be a place where people are free to look at these issues, to talk about them in a nonthreatening atmosphere, and to be unintimidated by "the powers of this world." But the reach of this ambition was never grasped significantly in our congregation.

Talk about social *conflict* found little or no resonance here. Questions about industry's work policies dribbled away in discussion like water in one's hands. There was not even "troubled patience" at the mention of labor unionism. The latter was simply out-of-bounds. Why would a *preacher* want to deal with it? It was a door they were afraid to open, and anyone who tried to do so had to be a quizzical sort of chap.

The sum of this experience was: *inside my congregation, people were as open to change in race relations as they were closed to change in labor-management relations.*

Labor-Management Relations Outside the Church

At this juncture, my third strategy had to be invoked: a private pilgrimage for educating myself to the realities of labor-management relations in Gastonia.

In the fall of 1957, the Textile Workers Union of America (TWUA) began its organizing campaign in Textiles, Inc., the largest locally-owned chain of mills in Gaston County. In explanation of its reasons for the campaign—low wages and the stretch-out chiefly—Southern Director Boyd Payton sent out letters to the "Merchants and Businessmen of Gastonia." I do not know how many ministers received this letter, but I was one recipient. In response I wrote Payton expressing a desire to meet the two local organizers named in his letter. "My job," I said cautiously, "is not to organize unions, but I suspect that the ministry in Gastonia could be of some service to the community if it attempted to acquire a balanced view of unionization and communicated the same to congregations."

Soon after I received a telephone call from James R. Prestwood, one of the local organizers. He was a Gaston County resident, who owned a farm just to the north of the South Carolina line. About forty-five years old, he had spent most of his life as an organizer for the TWUA. He was a Presbyterian, a Sunday school teacher, and a thorough cynic about textile managers. By the time I met him he had spent some discouraging years trying to organize textile unions in the Carolinas. He saw Gaston County textile managers as the most effective opponents of unionism in the South. In his eyes, South Carolina was a land of union opportunity compared with Gastonia. The characteristic in him that impressed me the most was the hurt in his voice whenever he talked about the power of textile owners over workers. His father had worked in the old Cramerton Mill. "Immediately after Burlington took over Cramerton Mills in 1946," he said to me on one occasion, "my father thought that the new conditions were wonderful. Then a year later the increase in work load standards started coming down from the head office: 'Reduce employment 20%, up production 20%, increase the number of sides per worker.' He felt that he had been deceived. Finally he took forced retirement, and he died eight months later, not knowing what to do with himself. Some of my bitterness towards textile companies comes from this. Knowledge of many more such things comes with getting into the union movement. It gives you a crusading cause—it makes you want to go out and 'fight sin' like a preacher!"

Acquaintance with this man and his colleagues in Gastonia convinced me that the popular management-promoted local image of the union-organizer as a power-hungry outside agitator was seriously distorted. For one thing, the union organizer could be as local a resident as any other. For another, anyone hungry for union power in Gaston County was subject to starvation. Why would anyone keep plugging away at a career which apparently bore so little fruit? The only answer I could find was Prestwood's own: dogged devotion to "a crusading cause." We might be mistaken idealists, but we both were idealists. We both believed in fighting sin.

From time to time my discussions with Prestwood circled around the question of *where* the "sin" was located in the present structure of labor-management relations in the textile business. I contended that the mixture of good and evil would always be dense on both the management and labor sides and that I knew textile managers who were not the villains he tended to see. We agreed that the power-imbalance on their side was so large as to tempt them regularly to exploit workers, but we disagreed on the importance of seeing both greed and generosity on all sides of the organized economic system. Just before Christmas of 1957 he asked my opinion of a Christmas letter which his office was thinking of sending to local workers whom the TWUA hoped to organize in 1958. The letter stated that Jesus was a "working man," and that if he returned to earth today he would be "the friend of the working man." Yes, I said, "but as Christians, don't we have to make it clear that Jesus was the friend of all people, not only working men, that he is even the friend of millowners?" It was a reversion to ethical universalism on my part which seemed decidedly to blunt his cry for help from religion to serve the cause of social justice. Sympathetic to unions, I wanted to remain critically sympathetic. I am sure that Prestwood saw in me a noble example of his perennial problem with intellectuals and liberals! At the same time I saw in him a strange sort of prophet, cynical yet courageous, investing his life in a cause that paid few dividends. He did indeed love workers rather than managers; but in declining to repent of the preference, he haunted me with the reminder of something Jesus said about "the least of these my brethren."

Over the next fifteen months I had two other contacts with the union issue in Gastonia. One had to do with a strike at a local printing company, the other with a series of programs on community issues for which I was responsible in the local ministerial association.

The strike at the printing company began in the early months of 1959. Almost all employees of the firm (numbering about 100) were skilled or semiskilled. One of them, a pressman, lived on my block in west Gastonia. He was not a member of any church, and his family had been on our "contact list" for a long time. His two daughters joined our church just as the strike at his plant began. The issue of the strike was the organization of a Press Workers' union, which the plant owner vigorously opposed by continuing to operate the presses with untrained employees. At the beginning of the strike, my neighbor informed me that it was impossible to operate a print shop with untrained labor, and that he was confident that the strikers would win out. They had an advantage in their skills, he said, which gave them more power than that of the average textile worker. He knew that union-organizing was hard in Gastonia but felt that they could break the pattern where others could not.

During the strike I made a point of visiting the picket line on three occasions. (My "church-prospect" was out there, and it seemed as good a place as any to do pastoral calling.) It was obvious in these visits that the men on the picket line were glad to have a local minister sit down with them around their fire. "All of the men," confided my printer-neighbor, "really are glad to have their preacher come visit the picket line."

Since I had once met the owner of the printing company, I went in to see him during my first visit to the picket line. It was a brief visit, during which he informed me that he did not intend to yield to the strike, that he understood from one of the strikers that I was sympathetic to their cause, and that he did not see how a minister could support such a thing. (Later on, at second hand, I heard that he was saying to his friends in an uptown church that he assumed that I must be a radical.) I told him that I thought labor unions were sometimes a benefit to their members and even to the managers of an industry, but that, in any event, a family in our community was involved in the strike, and I had some responsibility to try to understand his interests. But this brief conversation was enough to make it clear to me that, when the die was cast for a strike in Gastonia, professionals such as ministers were not likely to enjoy the luxury of standing up for "both sides of the question." The idea of "critical sympathy" was hard for manager and striker alike to acclaim. When a strike was on, each side looked for allies, and looked out for enemies.

My neighbor had early expressed his optimism about the outcome of the strike by quoting the National Labor Relations Board's (NLRB) election-supervisor as saying privately to the union members that perhaps they had no alternative but to "use your economic power" by striking. I remember distinctly that this was the first time in two and half years that I had ever heard the phrase "use economic power" repeated by a Gastonia wageworker. But my neighbor's initial optimism soon faded. Two months of cold picketing and decreased plant productivity did not bring the printshop owner to heel. He imported less skilled workers, took the cut in output, and finally managed to train the new workers to take the jobs of the old. A colleague and friend of mine at another Presbyterian church said to me that industrial managers all over town were watching the printshop strike closely, for they felt that this was their battle too. Every occasion for voting "union" or "no union" in Gastonia was an event for the whole economic structure.

In late spring my neighbor was on his way to a new job in Florida. One of his last comments to me was: "I had made up my mind to join your church." In effect we lost four members when he moved. If he had won the strike and joined our church, I would have felt that a tiny breakthrough had been achieved between ministry to an individual and ministry to a social structure—so tiny as to underscore the very difficulty of such an achievement. But not even this was to be. My only wry consolation was that now I could inject into any discussion of strikes with ministers the thought-provoker that one price of a lost strike may be the loss of church members! It was not for me the ideal way to personalize a social problem.

A chance to get ministers to think in more astute terms about labor-management relations came my way at almost the same time. As a member of the program committee of the Ministerial Association, I suggested that we invite two union leaders and two local plant managers to discuss with each other the problems of management and labor in Gastonia. The two union leaders accepted the invitation at once. One of the two managers invited was from Burlington Mills, Inc. He first called to tell me that he would have to check with their Greensboro office before consenting to appear on the panel. He called again to say that Greensboro would not permit him to appear on the same panel with union leaders. The other manager, from a locally owned company, made the same response, so we planned two programs rather than one.

The most remarkable feature of this pair of programs was the difference in atmosphere that prevailed during the two discussions among the thirty or so ministers in attendance. The first discussion between managers and the ministers was cordial, easygoing, and full of chummy feeling. When asked what service the churches provided industry in Gastonia, the managers replied that the good character of workers was an important part of their employability, and the churches did much to build character. During the discussion the best known of Gastonia's independent revivalists stood up and said proudly that he had always worked closely with the management of the mills, and, among other services, he had "frequently reminded people in the mill villages to turn off their lights so as to save on the electric bills being paid by the mill." One had the feeling that this comment was greeted by most of the other ministers as an archaic voice from the mill-village past, but the spirit of affability between ministers and managers in the meeting was nonetheless very real.

This easy familiarity gave way to brittleness and near-hostility in the second meeting. The two union leaders made short statements about the relationship they thought appropriate between the union movement and the church. It was not the business of the church, they said, to take sides in a union election or in a strike. But hopefully the church and the minister could stand up for the right of a worker to vote freely for or against a union, and surely the pastor could treat anyone on a picket line as a human being rather than an outcast. During a strike the minister should, for example, visit his members involved in the strike and give them personal friendship during a trying time in their lives. I was aware that I had no occasion to feel righteous on this point, because I had been in Gastonia thirty months before a picketline visit scrambled onto my agenda; but I was unprepared for the barrage of hostile questions which greeted this suggestion: were the union leaders aware of how satisfied most of the workers in Gastonia were? is a picketline visit the only way to show concern for a man on strike? what about all the corruption in labor unionism in other parts of the country?

On the whole it was a discouraging experience for anyone who believed that though the church need not advance the interests of any single group of people, it should be a place where different interests communicate with each other. This pair of discussions demonstrated that few ministers in Gastonia wanted to hear from the union side of any argument. The nervousness and suspicion that attended the second meeting was emblematic of a great anxiety among ministers toward the whole question of power and counterpower in the economic realm. The experience convinced me that in the twenty years since Pope had written, the attitude of Gastonia ministers towards unions had changed little. Later, union leaders told me that among younger ministers like myself the tide of sympathy for the union cause was definitely on the rise. But at most they were hopeful that the church someday (a) would no longer actively oppose unions, (b) would stand for freedom of choice in the matter for the workers, and (c) would treat union leaders and union members as human beings. It seemed a modest enough hope.

Retrospect and Prospect:
Leaving Gastonia and Coming Back

Little attempt has been made in this prefatory narrative to give account of the pastoral relationships to which I was party during these years. Sickness, death, birth, marriage, divorce, mental illness, unemployment, and suicide all came to our congregation. All of us learned something, I think, about the helps of religious faith and simple human friendship in personal crises. Indeed, the better I got acquainted with the personal troubles of many a person in west Gastonia, the less I could blame such persons for their failure to inquire if there is a social gospel as well as a personal gospel. Their sheer endurance of "the thousand natural shocks that flesh and blood are heir to," filled me with awe on more than one occasion. If all of *that* had happened to me, I reflected, my interest in the problems of society might become simply an unaffordable luxury.

But the question of the connection between personal and social dimensions of religion as it is institutionalized in American society continued to intrigue me. And, largely because Gastonia had reaffirmed for me the pertinence of that interest, in mid-1959 I accepted the opportunity of doing further graduate work in social ethics and the sociology of religion. For me, Gastonia set some of the agenda of that study, which in turn set some new agendas for a study of Gastonia from a very different angle than one can study it as a local minister. When I left in 1959, I had no idea that five years later I would meet two colleagues in sociology who would hatch with me a "Re-study of Gastonia." The academic, intellectual perspectives that we decided to take upon Gastonia is the stuff of the next chapter. But, clearly, certain fundamental issues of the study entered the bloodstream of one of us through the experience just re-counted. At the very least, this experience undermined all simple answers to the questions raised at the beginning of this preface. Indeed, on the surface, the data of my professional tenure in Gastonia and the data from the dialogue of the textile executives quoted above are hard to reconcile:

In the "new Gastonia" of suburban rather than mill-village churches, of what "use" can religious and industrial institutions really be to each other? How can the churches as organizations have influence on broad social affairs when so much activity in the churches focuses on personal religion?

Would the impact of the Great Strike of 1929 be sufficient explanation of the low estate of labor unionism forty years after the event? Aside from the 1929 precedent, what do the churches contribute, if anything, to the community's way of dealing with unionism?

The industrial elite of the county prize "civic consciousness" as an antidote to the social poison of 1929; but, again, how can the churches contribute to civic consciousness, if the drift away from civic discussion in my congregation was typical of many other congregations in this community? If the churches are not a major source of such consciousness, does the latter really prevail in Gastonia? Or are the elite wrong in identifying the churches as one of the sources?

Finally, suppose that Gaston County, like many another small community around the modern world, has changed over the past thirty years in response to numerous forces from outside its boundaries. Do religion and its institutions help mold the adjustment of this local community to these forces, or are they increasingly irrelevant to the modern world of interconnected global systems?

These are the "enriched" versions of the questions raised, in simpler form, at the beginning of this preface. I have tried to show how the experience of being a minister in Gastonia for three years made for such enrichment. But the questions will not be adequately stated until we provide the reader, in a more technical way, the conceptual framework that will dominate the historical and descriptive materials of this book. If we are true to the method we mean to use in the entirety of our study, however, we will not drift very far away from concrete matters like those in the narrative above.

GENERATION GAP

An avalanche
of hungry mountain poor
  descended to the mills,
    their faces cleft,
      eroded as the slopes
      they left behind,
      bronzed as sunbaked crags,
      and lit by fierce, determined eyes
      that glinted waterfalls.

They hear their mountain tunes
of wind and rain and birds
  transposed into the hum
   of whirring spindles,
   slapping shuttles,
   singing threads,
     as doors slide shut.

The fiber hothouse,
  humid, stale, and huge,
    employs a team of gardeners
     for each slim strand.
While woven rolls
  of springtime flowers
   flourish on the looms,
workers breathe
  a sterile pollen,
   dusting lungs with death.

When whistles shriek,
  the workers shuffle,
    pale and weak-eyed
     into light,
like insects startled
  by a lifted stone.

They stretch and numbly shake
  monotony
by seeking frantic joy,
  or solace in hereafter's hope.

But mountain children
  have a present hope.
They see their parents' wretched bodies,
  prematurely aged,
and vow to ride their meager heritance
  away from upland slopes.
    away from mills.
          —Peggy Shriver

Spindles and Spires

A Re-Study of Religion and Social Change in Gastonia

Introduction

Society is a human artifact. Or so social science assumes.

Few social histories fortify the assumption more eloquently than Liston Pope's account of early Gastonia. As a political formality, the county of Gaston was established in 1846, but not until the 1880s did society-building start in earnest as cotton mills and Protestant churches began to dot the red-clay farmland. In essence Pope's book is a study of changing relationships between these two institutions in the sixty years from 1880 to 1940.

It may help introduce the reader to our perspective on a later Gastonia if we recapitulate Pope's perspective on this early, formative period.

The period, Pope found, was roughly divided into three stages: (1) institutional growth, (2) social control, and (3) cultural defense. In the first stage, lasting twenty or thirty years, the founding of churches proceeded as rapidly as the founding of mills, with the one contributing impetus to the other. Ministers and other churchmen helped amass capital for the mills, helped recruit workers to tend the spinning frames, and cheered on industrial development with the religious zeal of southerners who were as sick of poverty as of sin.

In the second stage, beginning with the First World War, great prosperity hit the textile industry; great wealth began to accumulate in the pockets of the pioneers of 1880; and the resulting expansion of markets, capital, and work forces produced new social problems for Gastonia. Gone now were intimate personal relations between owners and workers of the mills. Gone, too, was the modest difference in their income. A sense of mutual pioneering in one generation gave way to a sense of employer-employee relations, and the problem of assuring collaboration between the two increased. Here, said Pope, the managers of mills began to promote the cause of church-building with a zeal of their own for the sake of maintaining the industrial system now in place. Religion, many owners decided, helped to mold the character and outlook needed now more than ever among workers in the mills: regularity in their duties, cooperation with their superiors, ambition to improve their station in life, and contentment if it improved slowly. Ministers, church services, and religious activities were now perceived by the owners as useful to the productive enterprise. Hence arose the system of subsidized "mill churches," the mutual screening and supervision of workers by managers and ministers, and

33

the continued economic growth of the community without much loss of social wholeness—i.e., social control.

A third stage began with a rude challenge to these placid arrangements: in the spring of 1929, a strike erupted in Gastonia's largest textile mill momentarily gripping several thousand workers. Before the crisis ended, two people had been murdered, the name of Gastonia had been trumpeted around the world, the cause of unionism had come to be identified locally with communism, leaders of the strike had been convicted of murder, and some of them had fled to Russia.

The origins, dynamics, and results of that strike are the central stuff of Pope's study, which the reader may want to consult before going further here. It suffices for our purposes to note that the absence of strong religious commitments among its communist leaders impressed millhands, millowners, and preachers alike in Gastonia. In the 1930s many turned their attention to "cultural defense"—to the restoration of an overarching community order which was deemed essential to continued industrial productivity.

Throughout all three of these stages of social change, Pope concluded, the churches of Gaston County had been influential in building, maintaining, and restoring the local society. At the beginning, the churches had influenced the mills more than the mills had influenced the churches, but in the later two periods the reverse was true. Summarizing the total interactions of the two institutions over time, Pope portrayed six possible historical relations between them:

At various times and in diverse ways [the churches] have been both *source* and *product* of economic developments. Both *indifference* and *irrelevance* to economic affairs have been notable characteristics of their strategy. They have provided powerful *sanctions* for prevailing economic arrangements. Slight traces of *antagonism* to those arrangements have likewise appeared at times, though the churches have been less active in this mode of relationship than in any other.[1]

In short, as of 1940 it could be concluded that:

Partially a source of industrial transformation sixty years ago, the religious institutions have become increasingly a product of that transformation and a guarantor of prevailing economic arrangements.[2]

The Problem of the Pope Study

Since our story begins in 1940, we have no occasion to rewrite Pope's fine book, or to quarrel long with its perspective on religious institutions, economic arrangements, and the process by which one may become the guarantor of the other. Fundamentally Pope agreed with Max Weber and many other modern students of religious and economic institutions that neither can rightly be seen as merely a variable dependent upon the other. Institutional interdependence is the theme of this tradition in sociological analysis, and Pope's own study of Gastonia added impressive evidence of the pertinence of this very perspective.

At the same time, an inconsistency marked his study that is a provocation of this sequel. In his Preface, Pope stated:

> In the pages that follow, the focus of interest lies in institutions rather than individuals or in such imponderables as "religion" or "economic welfare." Particular, observable cotton mills and churches are the characters in the story to be unfolded.[3]

By and large, Pope kept faith with this intention. His book is laced with all sorts of "hard" institutional data: industrial and church growth, wages and investments, work schedules and outputs, police forces and labor unions, organized church worship services and ministerial associations. But this was not all. Especially as the book nears its conclusion, *Millhands and Preachers* betrays Pope's inability to avoid "such imponderables as 'religion' and 'economic welfare.' " Statements like these punctuate his last hundred pages:

> The Loray management had broken the cultural fabric by its emphasis on making good yarn at the expense, if need be, of making good people.[4]

> [The 1929 strike] became a struggle between the culture organized around paternalistic capitalism and an alternative culture proposed by the Communists.[5]

> Most of the ministers . . . appear to have been sincerely opposed to the strike apart from questions of personal advantage. They were constrained by general culture much more powerfully than they could have been by fear of financial self-interest. They shared the general presuppositions of the community as to proper industrial relations.[6]

> God and good roads and cotton mills and contented labor and legal justice were all closely connected in the culture of Gaston County in 1929.

> Whether justly or not, the trial of the Gastonia [strike] defendants turned into a heresy trial.[7]

Here Pope was attributing great power for social change and social stability to the ubiquitous reality of *culture,* a word which deserved closer scrutiny than he gave it.

What is culture? The question has perplexed sociologists and their cousins the anthropologists for many a year. Is "culture" just another name for "society"? Or is it the sum total of the subjective images of society that individuals carry around in their heads? Is it rather an objective something, a "fabric" that can be "broken," a "constraint" that can be "powerful"? Pope's use of the latter phrases suggests strongly that in some sense he thought of culture as an objective reality. In fact, in his most sustained attempt to describe "Gastonia culture"[8] he mingles many dimensions of Gastonia's history in a way that makes shreds of his intention to avoid imponderables. The decline in Piedmont agriculture, the individualistic outlooks of mountaineer textile-recruits, the "passion that built the mills," the legal institutions of property ownership, and "the political and moral rights of the manufacturer to dominate the entire community"—all enter into Pope's description of this local culture, which was organized, he concluded, around this proposition:

> that the interests of the community and of the textile manufacturer were identical, but the interests of the manufacturer, being more definite and concrete and powerfully represented, were taken as the standard in terms of which the welfare of the community was to be judged.[9]

On the face of it, this heavy dependence upon the concept of the *power of culture* poses some interesting questions that Pope never pursued systematically: what is more "concrete"—the *interests* of manufacturers, or the *proposition* that those interests are primary for the welfare of a community? can mere propositions have power? must interests be defined in terms of something concrete as money in the bank, or is even "money in the bank" powerful as an *idea* before a single deposit has been made?

In a word, Pope allowed much ambiguity to afflict his description of culture and his account of Gastonia history would have had greater conceptual clarity if he had given a few more pages over to unpacking the ambiguity. In particular, there were several ingredients of his concept of culture that deserved analytical attention: *power, interests,* and *standards*.

Power, Interests, and the Logic of Justification

As a social phenomenon, "power" is often defined as the ability of one agent to compel another to do his bidding, whether the other wants to or not. Slavery is frequently alleged to be an extreme example of social power. But the most cursory history of slavery as a form of human interaction suggests that a qualification must be added: the power of the master is effective *if the institution is working as it is supposed to.* Various interventions can ruin a master-slave relationship: the slave's sickness—real or successfully pretended, a legal arrangement that permits a slave to buy his freedom, a refusal of the master to act like a master, and the refusal of the slave to play his role to the hilt. And "to the hilt" includes *thinking* of himself as a slave. History suggests strongly that the last intervention has claimed a lot of attention from the beneficiaries of slave-systems. Masters have always demonstrated great interest in forging a final link in the chains of the slave, namely in the latter's mind. The power to compel another to do what he or she does not want to do, therefore, is limited power. Power is never so powerful as when it is *legitimate* power; it is seldom so vulnerable as when it is subject to being thought illegitimate. Even in a society that accords its leaders dictatorial powers, these leaders have more and less power, depending on the degrees of collaboration they achieve with their subjects. Not all of the Pharaohs built great pyramids; only some of them had the skill to mobilize the money, the labor, the organization, and the will of their respective societies around the purpose of pyramid-building.

Socially effective power, then, must be distinguished from violence in much the same way that Hannah Arendt distinguishes it:

Power is . . . the essence of all government, but violence is not. Violence is by nature instrumental; like all means, it always stands in need of guidance and justification through the end it pursues.[10]

If one is born into membership in some social group, the need for "guidance and justification" for that group's existence may be hard to detect. Children in normal families usually require fifteen years before they raise the question about the legitimacy of this group's claim on their loyalty! Similarly an age-old governmental organization may claim the loyalty of generation after generation of citizens who have learned to accept its legitimacy as part of "how things are." That is the general proposition that revolutionaries invariably attack first: "things" ought to be different, and they can be. Thus may begin a new system of "guidance and justification."

In American society the rational, revolutionary tradition has accustomed many citizens to the view that social organizations may be formed, reformed, and abandoned according to the willingness of people to support the purposes of the organizations. (The late Paul Tillich said that, soon after he arrived in the United States from Germany in 1934, it seemed to him that Americans assessed everything in terms of the question: "what is the purpose of that?") Examples of such organizations abound in this country, perhaps as in no other country in the world: stock companies, political parties, churches, athletic clubs, and neighborhood associations all are thought to depend upon voluntary individual support of the announced purposes—or values—served by the organizations. But this pervasive "voluntariness" in American society, noted over a century ago by de Tocqueville, has entailed severe social problems, the most obvious of which is the problem of large-scale *social cohesion*. The growth of Gastonia from 1880 to 1914, for example, took place in the hard-nosed atmosphere of competition between textile mills in the South and textile mills in the North; and the drastic economic decline of the latter was undoubtedly explained (among Gaston County textile managers) as "the way the competitive system works." When confronted in the 1960s, however, with the working of that system on an international scale, the next generation of these textile men was busy supporting a congressional lobby for "protecting American jobs from low-wage imports." It was to their economic self-interest, of course, to applaud the working of the market in the first instance and to decry it in the second. But the inconsistency should not be exaggerated. If one purpose of being in the textile business is to make money, a threat to moneymaking in your segment of the industry is a threat to one of your social values. To protect such a value, in this instance, one may appeal to one or more *other* values: e.g., national strength and survival.[11] This means appealing to some "good of the social whole" to substantiate a particular way of promoting a good of a social part. Even here, of course, the particular whole in question is one nation among some two hundred nations of the world. Anyone seriously tempted to accord priority to the industrial growth of non-American economies finds little resonance for this view in the Gastonias of America, though one might find some support among those several large multinational textile corporations whose own continued economic growth is taking place now precisely in these other countries.

We have here an illustration of a generic social problem faced by the leaders and the members of every historic human society: *the problem of relating particular and general interests*. Individuals have that problem every time they want something for themselves (a job, a raise, a child) and can only get it in collaboration with someone else. Social groups have the same problem in relation to other social groups. Hence arises in social negotiations the necessity of perceived mutuality of interests between all parties, and on all levels of any society such perceptions account for much of the cohesion enjoyed by that society. The *structure* of these mutual perceptions is apt to be very complex in modern societies. For example, when the interests of the textile industry in Gastonia "were taken as the standard in terms of which the welfare of the community was to be judged,"[12] something very critical, in terms of social power, was happening to an "interest": it was elevated into a *standard for judging total community welfare*. It began to share the status of "law," unofficial law, to be sure, but nonetheless powerful for promoting social stability and social change.

In the study to follow, we have a name for that cluster of unofficial propositions in a community's life that function as links, real or alleged, between particular and general interests: *ideology*. But before expanding on our notion of ideology, we must define another word for which the word "ideology" is frequently substituted in social-scientific literature: *religion*. And to say with precision what we mean by both words will require a brief but systematic excursion into social theory.

Religion and Ideology in the Perspective of the Sociology of Knowledge

Physical scientists speak with some pride about "the" scientific perspective on reality; and they sometimes note with unveiled contempt that the social sciences cannot yet claim to be real sciences, because they exhibit no unity in their theoretical perspectives on society. As we shall see, the demand for a single, unified perspective is itself *sociologically* interesting; but the fact remains that as a whole academic students of society in 1975 do not "model" their object of study in a unified way.

But there is some order in the brawl of social-scientific disagreement. A decade ago Gibson Winter identified four regnant schools of sociological analysis in a scheme that is still useful.[13] The four schools of thought may be named: (1) Behaviorism, (2) Conflict theory, (3) Functionalism, and (4) Intentionalism. Very briefly characterized, behaviorism (as in the writings of B. F. Skinner) accounts for the existence of society in terms of relations between external stimuli in the human environment and internal biologically-conceived mechanisms. Conflict theory (as in the writings of C. Wright Mills) sees society as a more or less brutal struggle between organized interest-groups, and as the exploitation of the unorganized by those groups. Functionalism (as in the writings of Talcott Parsons) presumes that both individuals and societies survive because they manage to fulfill functions or useful exchanges with their environments in terms of economic adaptation, group organization, intra-group integration, and philosophic "grounding" in some system of meaning. Intentionalism (as in the writings of Alfred Schutz) sees society as the cumulative outgrowth of a dialogue between human selves, who produce social structures and processes that can be understood adequately only in terms of the self-intentions of the producers.

The following re-study of Gastonia depends exclusively upon no one of these schools of thought. We are indebted to all of them, and our data is subject to being analyzed from the perspective of them all. But both the generation and interpretation of our data have heavier debts to the second and fourth of these schools—conflict theory and intentionalism—than to the other two; and of these two, our heaviest debt is probably to intentionalism as it is summarized in a very important book: *The Social Construction of Reality,* by Peter Berger and Thomas Luckmann.[14] Subtitled, "A Treatise in the Sociology of Knowledge," this book portrays a model of society close enough to our own model to merit a summary here. Readers inclined to favor one of the other models of society will thus know how we appropriate the Berger-Luckmann school of thought, and how we must be argued with theoretically.

Society-Building

You can glimpse the puzzle that sociology tries to unravel, say Berger and Luckmann, if you will start with yourself and your most immediate, present experience. There you are, reading this book. There we were, some months ago now, writing it. And here we are, concretely connected with each other through this object called a book. But the object is meaningless, actually indescribable, apart from its relation to subjects like ourselves and other objects that make books possible—language, printing presses, and the book business. Surely nothing is so much a mingling of objective and subjective realities as a book.

But in fact, upon similar reflection, almost everything of which humans are conscious in everyday life, almost everything we do, and even everything we *think* is such a mingling. Without words, the very insides of our minds would lack much furniture; something would be lacking even from our dreams. Words are inventions of other humans most of whom lived centuries ago, but we enjoy "society" with those minds every time we speak. That is so even with the gamut of objects in our homes, our workplaces, our countrysides, and our cities. We people, living and dead, are part of each other's experience; and how that comes to be so is the major puzzle of the science of sociology.

To put the question succinctly: how does the subjective become objective, and the objective intersubjective? (How does a mere idea for a book become print on a page, and that print become meaningful to another human being?) Berger and Luckmann's try at an answer runs as follows:[15]

Society "occurs" in a three-fold, mutually reinforcing process that may be called *objectification, institutionalization,* and *legitimation.* Human beings tend almost invariably to want to express their inmost experiences: they have done so, since time immemorial, with elementary shouts of hostility, cries of pain, and murmurs of affection. In time those sounds—and other gestures—acquired socially shared *meanings;* they became "typifications," signs, symbols which people used to express themselves and understand each other. Verbal language is a uniquely complex, powerful, and pervasive set of such typifications. Apparently no human tribe has survived without it. And in the larger sense, there is language *in* all those contrived, biologically uninherited things that comprise human culture, organization, and experience. Each of these contrivances bespeaks a human intention, a meaning that some human being has invested in it and that some other human being may recognize. All the artifacts of society from weapons and houses to marriage ceremonies and cemeteries are thus "meaningful"—in an ordinary, everyday sense. "Social structure is the sum total of these typifications and of the recurrent patterns of interactions established by means of them."[16]

But it happens that some of the shared expressions of human groups acquire wider, more generally sharable meanings than others. They acquire such wide acceptance by the group, such durability from generation to generation, and (finally) such apparently indisputable meaning that we call them *institutions*. "Institutionalization is incipient in every social situation continuing in time."[17] For example, any stable meaning attached to a single sound, makes that sound a "word," i.e., a part of the institution of language. But language is only one of the complex of institutions in every known human culture. Any set of "taken-for-granted routines" which two or more people observe over a period of time can be called an institution; activities as different as hunting, farming, praying, marrying, gift-giving, lawmaking, and dying can be subject to institutionalization.[18] The most enduring, dominant institutions of a culture are those that have been routines for so long among so many generations that they are now accounted as elements of "how things are." As such, institutions acquire a reality, an unchallengeable objectivity and power as "coercive fact" in the eyes of those who account themselves members of a society. (The obligation to perform rain dances at certain seasons of the year is not a coercive fact for non-members of the Navaho tribe; but, for that tribe, neither is diplomatic recognition of Russia a political necessity. Different groups in history have varied widely in what institutions they have seen as "inevitable"; but no human group persists long without some institutions.)

Institutional coercion takes the individual form of certain *roles* which social tradition pressures individuals to assume. A role is the individual's participation in an institutional pattern. All the most common relationships by which most humans identify themselves to other humans are role-relationships: child, spouse, parent, citizen, employee, expert, office-holder; and the like—a *numerous* set of "likes" in a society which has evolved many institutions, for many specialized purposes, in which many people can play roles. We are a society in which a single person may wear many "hats."

Even in early, premodern societies one person during a lifetime might play many such roles in as many institutions. One may expect to do so from the earliest moments of conscious life. But how does one see unity and coherence among personal roles? How does the society itself unify its institutions into a *social whole?* One answer is that some roles in the society are widely understood as more important than others, because these roles represent not only this or that institution, but the integration of all institutions in a meaningful *world*. An old man, in a culture that identifies wisdom with age, may occupy such an integrative role; a judge, in a society with a developed code of law; a king, in a society accustomed to see its unity in one ruler; a priest, in a society that openly constructs its "world" in religious terms. Indeed "historically, roles that symbolically represent the total institutional order have been most commonly located in political and religious institutions."[19]

Members of modern, highly specialized societies are likely to be skeptical about the necessity of symbolic integrative roles and integrating symbols themselves for the unification of their society. It may take events like the assassination or the impeachment of a President to evoke a sense of such a necessity among Americans, or the uniquely modern global terror of the nuclear stand-off among nations. Whether or not they have names for such roles and symbols, all human societies must find a way to "glue" their members, institutions, and generations together. If they don't do so, they stop being societies. They fall apart. Indeed, precisely in those historic eras when "things fall apart"[20] and the "center cannot hold," the wise and the desperate seek to recover the old center—or to invent a new one. But "center" may be too local an image for the thing required to avoid threatening anarchy: "stable symbolic canopy" is a better metaphor.[21]

The canopy image suggests that humans want to be *at home* somewhere. They want to know what their place is in a universe, and what universe there is to be at home in. This is not primarily a theoretical interest for the large majority of humans, though they may turn to theorists at critical junctures to supply a glimpse of an old or a new sacred canopy. The need for integrity—consistent meaning—in human affairs is as practical a need as the need for consistency in the use of words. A world of no permanent structures, no dependable purposes, no dams against chaos, is a mad world, inducing madness in its inhabitants. It has lost its *legitimacy,* and thereby its livability. To such a world human beings are likely to say: "Stop it, I want to get off!"

The objectifications and institutions of early societies all grew under some such general assertions of meaning, which legitimated the whole pattern of life in those societies. Insofar as these highly general comprehensive symbols of meaning could be distinguished from the rest of culture, they could be called *religious.* Most religions in history have been religions of low differentiation from the society as a whole; that is, sacred structures and their sacred, permanent meaning suffused all the institutions of the culture. Kinship and obligations, the sources of economic survival, the goods and evils of the natural world, and the phenomenon of death all had their relation to the myths, the festivals, and the roles associated (in a later day) peculiarly with religion. But in certain historic times and places, the old legitimations of societies have declined in their plausibility. At these junctures, prophets have sometimes arisen to reinterpret old integrating symbols or to announce inspiring new ones. Thus the possibility of a "new world" dawns upon a society or groups within it. The new worldbuilders may not call themselves religious prophets. Philosophers, scientists, or artists can be also perceived by their followers as bringing a new, livable world into being for them. In any event the meanings they bring are *ultimate*, world-ordering meanings: "scientific principle," "evolution," "the Unconscious," "the kingdom of God," "the Thousand-Year Reich" can all be the master-symbols of these new-worlds. Each may command a following among a few people over a relatively short time or may attract millions over millennia. Whether short or long-lived, the cultural creations of the new legitimators acquire supreme authority for their followers. The language, rituals, and associated institutions of the new worldviews may eventually yield "immense edifices of symbolic representations that appear to tower over the reality of everyday life like gigantic presences from another world."[22] The Islamic Empire, the Medieval European Synthesis, and the Civilization of the Mayans must have been such presences to all who identified with them. Inside these societies "*all* the sectors of the institutional order are integrated into an all-embracing frame of reference, which now constitutes a universe in the literal sense of the word, because *all* human experience can now be conceived of as taking place *within* it."[23]

With this description of the realm of "legitimation," one arrives easily, with Berger and Luckmann, at the summary assertion: persons and societies, ancient and modern, tend to acquire for themselves livable universes. They seek through some master-symbols, consciously chosen or thrust upon them, to organize their worlds. And since those symbols with the greatest power of organization are by definition religious symbols, all persons and societies, ancient and modern tend to acquire some version of religion. But they acquire it in particular historical circumstances, in relation to particular institutional traditions, and in relation to certain kinds of personal readiness. *Understanding that historical-institutional-personal context of the acquisition and the mainte-nance of a sacred canopy is the principal business of the sociology of religion.* In particular, such a sociology is intent to understand "the interrelations between institutional processes and the legitimating symbolic universes" that sustain institutional processes in all societies.

Eventually a single "science of society" would integrate both sociology and psychology, for the study of persons and their social contexts should be one study. In the meantime, the sociologist of religion must try to study the trialectic—the perpetual mutual qualifying—of symbols, institutions, and per-sons. He or she must refuse to reduce any one of these to the other, or to separate an understanding of the one from an understanding of the others. "Reality" (for the social scientist and all other humans) is symbolically, socially, and personally defined.

Social Change

The implications of this theory of social integration for a theory of social change are numerous. Berger and Luckmann state one of the implications as follows:

> To understand the state of the socially constructed universe at any given time, or its change over time, one must understand the social organization that permits the definers to do their defining. Put a little crudely, it is essential to keep pushing questions about the historically available conceptualizations of reality from the abstract "What?" to the sociologically concrete "Says who?"[24]

That is, legitimation structures and institutional structures are constantly interacting with each other; each exerts a "pull" on the other. "It is correct to say that theories are concocted in order to legitimate already existing social institutions. But it also happens that social institutions are changed in order to bring them into conformity with already existing theories, that is, to make them more 'legitimate.' "[25] Some element in the religion of Christianity, for example, may assist in the birth of new institutions like the textile mills of Gaston County; but the value of the mills to widening circles of people in the society exacts a toll from the religious consciousness and religious institutions of the society: the *meaning* of the "mill church" is not quite the same as the meaning of the "country church." Indeed, the more highly specialized the institutions and the individuals of a society, the more diverse is likely to be their particular worldviews. When personal or institutional interests diverge or conflict, competition over legitimacy-interpretation is a crucial dimension of the *power*-competition, because the leaders of institutions know that institutional power eventually requires articulation with the total social fabric; for that very fabric is probably most real *at the level of symbolic legitimation structures.* Who gets the right to *say* what is legitimate in the society is the basic question of politics and most social conflict.

If one wanted to change a society very profoundly, therefore, and could wait indefinitely, one would be well advised by this theory to change legitimacy structures and rules concerning who should enforce them. But such change is difficult in the shortrange, and few such changes have succeeded in history in the lifetimes of their originators. The social changes that most change-agents (a minority among humans) want to effect are seldom so all-encompassing anyway. One must be radically religious to seek truly fundamental legitimacy-changes. But one need only to be moderately religious to promote a new way of relating some *sector* of personal and social life to old legitimacy-structures. The sector may be the family, the economy, the polity. One may need just enough reinterpretation of the sacred canopy to stretch it over one's new endeavor. If successful, the new endeavor will in turn reinforce its own roofing. For nothing reinforces change so well as the assertion afterwards that all along it was in accord with traditional values. In this sense it is *equally* true that "might makes right" and "right makes might." Money, guns, and righteousness are at their most powerful when they are *combined*!

What name should be given to the "moderately religious" symbols by which traditionalists and innovators draw down "radically religious" symbols to their aid and comfort? In this study, with Berger and Luckmann, we have given these lesser-order symbols the much-disputed name of ideology.

> When a particular definition of reality comes to be attached to a concrete power interest, it may be called an ideology. . . . The distinctiveness of ideology is . . . that the *same* overall universe is interpreted in different ways, depending upon concrete vested interests within the society in question.[26]

Whether a given historical set of legitimating structures should be called "religious" or "ideological" is an important question in the empirical investigation of a society's structure, its power-groupings, and its symbolic leverages for change. It is important to know, for example, that the fury surrounding the 1929 strike in Gastonia was connected not only with a diversity of economic interests but also with a clash between theists and atheists. Pope's own account of that strike and its aftermath shows clearly that its Communist leaders never succeeded in allying the workers to an atheist vision of the human life-situation. Had they been able convincingly to interpret the interests of workers in terms of symbol-systems of the Bible, they might have exerted more power in the strike. They would have done so at the cost of a terrible theoretical compromise of their own "world," of course; for Communists in 1929, like Christians in 50 A.D., could hardly have remained faithful to their founding prophet if they had rejected so fundamental an arch in their own sacred canopy. The most radical conflicts in society, in this sense, are not between vested *interests* or even between *ideologies*, but between *religions*. It is about the structure, dynamics, and the impact for change characterizing these three elements of human society, that this study of Gastonia is written.

A Method for the Study of Religion and Ideology

The Berger-Luckmann account of the structure and evolution of human society poses great problems for the empirical study of religion and society. Granted that religion is ubiquitous in ancient and modern history—you find it in the Indonesian jungle, downtown Nairobi, and suburban St. Louis. But how does the scientist get his calipers around it? How, when the above account makes all too logical a sweeping definition of religion such as that of Dean M. Kelley:

> The subject matter of religion is *the entire life of man and whatever affects him*.[27]

This is a formidable definition. How does one study "the entire life of man and whatever affects him"? Science ordinarily uses its special tools to investigate special segments of reality; and the contemporary sciences, physical and social, are probably less enthusiastic than ever for the project of rendering *empirical* descriptions of the "entirety" of anything. How, in short, shall we study the role of religion in society, when religion's connections with society are likely to be pervasive but subtle, real yet fugitive?

What we offer below is not a conclusive answer to such methodological questions. Rather, here are the answers that we have adopted in pursuing this study and reducing it to writing. Of the loose ends of our method we are very conscious; we know that others will be at work in the future tying them up.

1. *Locating religion in the social structure.* Robert Bellah's summary definition of religion is close to that of Berger and Luckmann: " 'Religion is a set of symbolic forms and acts which relate man to the ultimate condition of his existence.' "[28] Where do you find these symbolic forms and acts in the recent history of Gastonia? Manifestly one may find them in the "organized religion" of the churches, but (as already suggested in Shriver's autobiographical preface above) an "ultimate condition" for *social* existence is not necessarily intended or effected by all of Gastonia's churches. Liston Pope lamented this very fact in the last paragraph of his book when he openly affirmed his interest in "religion" by saying:

> [Gastonia's] religious institutions can be a source of culture transformation only as they transcend the immediate culture in which they function. Their insistence that they already have a transcendence of this sort is largely unwarranted so far as economic and social standards are concerned. Unless they find economic standards, as such, other than those of the economic culture from which they draw immediate substance, they will not be able to stand in effective judgment or criticism.[29]

A refinement of his own definition of religion was implicit in this conclusion: *Religion is that part of culture which makes the strongest intrinsic claim to the right to be the evaluator of the rest of culture.*

Whether, when and how that right is exercised is an important set of observations for the empirical study of religion. Can the sociological investigator detect those occasions in a community's life when a "religious" evaluation of that life is present or absent? He—or she[30]—can indeed, if he will accept as evidence phenomena of the following kinds:

—In concrete controversies between interest groups in a community, he observes whether the representatives of formal religious institutions (churches) make public judgments upon the controversy, in terms of reference to religious symbols. Such evidence may be scattered in newspaper reports, other documents, pronouncements by leadership groups, the personal reports of witnesses, and secondhand-hearsay. The *absence* of any of these evidences strongly suggests that such judgment, if promulgated at all, was not very public.

—In a community's deliberation on some issue of social continuity or change, (in political, economic, social organizations and churches) he observes what use the participants make of some logic of justification; what general or "final" argument is used; whether this argument has reference to some traditional religious symbols; and whether there is any correlation between the use of such symbols and the users' affiliations with formal religious organizations. (The observation of these phenomena must presuppose that reference to religious symbols for social-action justification has some sociological significance whatever the latter correlation may be.)

—In quantitative terms, he observes how often a salient social question is discussed publicly in a community with reference to *ideological* terms over against *religious* terms; qualitatively, what distinction, if any, is made between the two levels of generalized legitimation. (To make the quantitative judgment, the observer must have some supportable notion about the content or typical concepts of both ideology and religion in the community. To make the qualitative judgment requires an educated intuition about the meaning of verbal and other symbols in given cultural contexts.)

The attempt to make all such observations impels the observer to look for "religion" *in the whole spectrum of the institutional life of a community*. He may be especially interested in finding socially-pertinent or socially-irrelevant religion in churches, but he does not expect it to be confined there.

2. *Interpreting religious symbolism contextually*. The interpretation of the meaning of religious symbols from the "inside" is the professed business of theologians or other specialist-members of religious institutions. When set against the background of the social theory outlined above, the task of the sociologist of religion is ambiguous, because he can neither wholly avoid nor wholly participate in the work of the theologian. For example, he cannot avoid assuming that he understands something of what the theologian means by statements like, "God is no respecter of persons." The statement suggests that ordinary distinctions of social prestige are seriously qualified or rejected by the

religious view of humanity. When he sees signs like, "Come Unto Me All Ye" on the front lawns of churches, he may rightly intuit that the controversy in churches over racial segregation is connected with such symbols; he is rightly curious about the other sources of the controversy in the churches' participation in the social arrangements of the community at large. His major interest, in fact, lies in the *boundary* or interface between theological symbol and social organization. Pope was demonstrating just such a boundary-interest in the last page of his book. Some social scientists would say that in doing this he was playing the role of "theological ethicist" rather than "social scientist." But the logic of our definition of religion and society forbid us to make such a rigid distinction in regard to the statement quoted above. It would indeed be a theological claim to say: Gastonia's religious institutions actually have a source of truth that transcends their immediate culture, and they should vigorously enter into the application of this truth to their culture. This is an "insider" claim. Pope's statement is more of an outside, scientific, "if . . . then" sort of claim. "*If* they believe that they have any source of guidance from a transcendent source, they will have to work at concrete connections between the religious symbols and the less general standards of guidance that a society usually requires for its change." To be sure, this degree of participation in the understanding of the inherent meaning of religious claims is only a beginning of the wider understanding at which the sociologist of religion must aim. In accordance with one of Berger and Luckmann's basic rules, he has to follow a perpetual dialectic between the religious symbols and the institutional (or other social) framework in which the symbols appear. In this sense, he lays himself open to the burden of a double skepticism, as he asks a characteristic pair of questions: do the institutions reflect the meaning of the symbols? do the symbols themselves show the impact of their institutional matrix?

A cluster of debatable epistemological assumptions is entailed in all this, but the most basic is this: *that symbols and their social contexts must be regularly understood in relation to each other.* Purist theologians and purist sociologists alike will dislike this assumption. It is one which we mean to operationalize in the chapters to follow.

3. *The interrelation of attitudinal, structural, and symbolic data.* The Berger-Luckmann model of society represents one attempt by social scientists to develop concepts for describing a society comprehensively. They demonstrate this comprehensive aim by giving attention to individual members of the society (e.g., in their use of the concept of role), to social structures (e.g., institutions), and to symbol systems (e.g., ideology and religion.) It is a large step, however, from speaking about this comprehensive model to the development of balanced, consistent, interrelated methods for investigating all three of these levels of any particular society.

Many sociological studies demonstrate this problem in their large dependence upon the method of personal interviews with a sample of a given population. A great deal can be learned about the impacts of institutions upon persons by this method, but what about institutional structure? Unfortunately institutions cannot be interviewed. What a random sample of individuals say about institutions is only one sort of data required here. Other sorts of data must be resorted to—formal constitutions or charters, documents published by the institution, formal and informal rules governing the conduct of constituents, the division of responsibility (the role structure) of the institution's leaders, and the perception of the institution by persons trained in certain observational skills.

Many sociologists prefer to concentrate their attention upon these latter categories of data. Psychology, they say, has its proper work investigating individuals; social structure and process is the focus of sociology. But alas, field work breeds inconsistency in us all: the principal investigators of a community study arrive in that community to commence their on-the-spot observing only to discover that data about institutions are most readily available in the recollected experience of individuals (e.g., workers and managers in a mill) or in the seasoned knowledge of a few unexpectedly insightful citizens. Furthermore, the commonsense of the investigator says that it will be a very abstract, partial picture of a community that does not include the recorded views of live individual human beings. He knows that exclusive dependence upon the interview technique as a source of data on a community and its history is very dangerous to a sociological investigation. No conceivable sample of people from the community at large will uncover its institutional structure inductively; and, indeed, many of the inquiries about a respondent's institutional relations presuppose some prior knowledge in the investigator about the institutions. (E.g., time spent on the pro's and con's of labor unionism in our interviews plainly presupposed our knowledge that this was an important issue in the history of Gastonia.) But the investigators cannot ultimately divorce their understanding of institutions from their understanding of a particular limited number of the institutions' constituents. Practically speaking, the two must interpret each other.

This problem comes in its most difficult form when interviews aim at tapping and interpreting personal *attitude* towards the institutionalized, symbol-rich realities of social ideology and religion. It is one thing to secure accurate information from people about the "demographic variables" (age, sex, education, occupation, family status, and the like); it is another to get similar accuracy concerning their views of religion and social welfare; and it is yet another to portray accurately the mutual impacts of personal attitudes, institutional structures, and symbols. One way to avoid the difficulty of all this would be to restrict one's interest and description to one of three levels—i.e., to be a "good" psychologist, a "good" sociologist, or a "good" philosopher. But the weakness shared by all such accounts of society is their abstractness—a criticism which many sociological studies have earned among many general readers in the public at large.[31]

No very satisfying solution to this problem is advanced in this study. We make use of certain important connecting concepts such as social role (an intervening variable between individual and institutional levels) and the concept of institutional charter or constitution (intervening between social structure and symbolic legitimation). But we are frank to say that the most operative connection between these three levels of society is our own minds. If there is any convincing synthesis here, it is a product of our immersion in various kinds of data: we asked individuals how they saw themselves in relation to a variety of institutions, values, and symbols; we drew upon other sources for describing the institutional structures of Gastonia; and on occasion we interpreted both the intrinsic meaning of symbols and their relation to individuals and institutions. The presumption here is perhaps forgivable if the study achieves any degree of its ambition: to introduce the reader to a tangible rather than an intangible Gastonia. That it may be the wrong Gastonia is the risk that the scientific spirit in us is bound to take.[32]

4. *Longitudinal and cross-sectional study.* The wholistic presumption is a risk classically dared by historians, who come closest, probably, to trying to study "the entire life of man and whatever affects him" over *time*. Historians are an embattled lot among academic people these days for just this reason. On all sides social science seems to be peeling off this and that layer of human history as its expert preserve. Historians have responded to this invasion either by embracing more fervently the depths of specialization or by resigning themselves to their status as "the last generalists." If it were within its power, sociology would probably rewrite history by conducting surveys, interviews, and institutional analyses of people and societies in all periods of the past. Sociology dreams of a future history of the twentieth century that will depend for much of its data upon the painstaking cross-sections of society which it has produced so impressively in recent decades. Characteristically, if history seeks to produce a movie about human societies, sociology seeks to improve the quality of the individual photographic frames of that movie. The suspicion that they need each other haunts both disciplines.

Our re-study of Gastonia could have been shorter and simpler if we had aimed only at a cross-sectional study. We could have written a "then and now" report of comparisons and contrasts between the Gastonia of 1939 and the Gastonia of 1969, the year most of our field work there came to an end. But again, the richness of Pope's own study would have then found little imitation in this one; for his insights into 1939-Gastonia gained much of their vitality through his historical research into events that had occurred ten to sixty years before. Like Pope, we are not professional historians, but we believe that the story of social change in a local community can be reconstructed with data that is accessible to any reasonably diligent scholar. The readily available economic, demographic, and political data; the newspapers, the local histories, the selective memories of the longtime residents; the sharper recollections of persons who were chief actors in key events of community change; and the accessory events of national and world import which were tangent to local events—all these sources of data about the past are open to any faithful inquirer. We believe that the mastery of such data from the past is a vast aid to both the construction and the interpretation of sociological surveys and institutional analyses, which in turn greatly illumine the historical past. Such mutual illumination is the aim of a method which combines a long view of Gastonia over several decades with an intensive view in one recent time.[33]

5. *The organizing focus of the study: issues of social change.* Like society itself, studies of society are also human artifacts, slanted towards the interests and intentions of their authors. In this study, if we have given ourselves license to attend to many levels of society and many kinds of data, we have also disciplined ourselves to organize the whole around the single formal interest of *significant social change* and the single substantive interest of the *role of religion and its institutions* in such change.

A definition of "social change" inheres in our model of society. The most significant, abiding changes in a society occur when a shift occurs in the content and relationship of two levels of its structure: *legitimation* and *organization. A society changes significantly when a part or whole of its value-canopy is redefined in relation to the organization of its various corporate interests.* By this definition a social change is minor, merely incipient, or tentative if it cannot be described as *both* a newly *legitimated* human activity and a newly *organized* activity.[34]

Such a definition obviously influences our choice of the issues in recent Gastonia history by which we further organize that history: labor-management relations and race relations. The first is a natural choice because Gastonia is still an industrial community and because Pope's study was itself organized around its greatest crisis in labor management relations. (His own major methodological assumption was that "reactions in a time of cultural crisis reveal fundamental relations, often unobservable in times of cultural peace, between institutions in a community."[35]) For better or for worse, no event approaching the trauma of the Loray Strike afflicted the 1940-75 history of this locale, and a more modest version of the method had to be adopted for this study. A crisis in labor-management relations did simmer throughout the period, however, as did a crisis in race relations. On occasion the simmering approached a boil.

Nothing illuminated the active, passive, and absent roles of the churches in Gastonia society so vividly as did these two issues of conflict over legitimacy and organization for the interests of two particular groups of local people. The book as a whole, therefore, moves toward an account of how the churches and the community related to each other around these issues.

The Plan of the Book

We begin with a broad-brush account of Gastonia's sacred canopy—that complex of religious and ideological symbols that exert normative appeal over many people and institutions there. That it in fact exerts such appeal may be taken as hypothetical, prior to much other data to follow. One major theme of the local ideology appropriately tags our initial description of change in the community over the past thirty years: the "progress" of industries and churches in terms of financial, numerical, and other forms of growth or decline.

Then, in a focus on that institution whose role in the community interests us the most, we look at the churches from other viewpoints than the statistical: conceptions of the normative roles of church leaders—ministers—held by them and a sample of church members; views of the actual and proper relation of religion and society held by both groups; and meaning-orientations embodied in the organized activities of the churches.

In Part II of the book we turn to trace the dynamic of the church's involvement in two issues of change: should the community allow the organization of labor unions? should it permit its black citizens certain civil and other rights? In the last numbered chapter, we return to assess, in a more comprehensive way than was possible in Chapter One, the interrelations of religion, ideology, religious institutions, and other institutions in contemporary Gastonia in terms of four "illuminating incidents" from the last decade of local history. In the final analysis, where does religion exercise its influence on community affairs now, if and when it does so? What are its potentials and its limitations for contributing to the shaping of the Gastonia of the future? Our summary answers to the two questions bring the study to a close.

NOTES

1. Liston Pope, *Millhands and Preachers: A Study of Gastonia* with an Introduction by Richard A. Peterson and N. J. Demerath III (New Haven and London: Yale University Press, 1942 and 1965), p. 332. Italics ours. Henceforth references to this book will be made simply by the initials, *MP*.

2. *MP*, p. 332.

3. *MP*, p ix.

4. *MP*, p. 237.

5. *MP*, p. 268.

6. *MP*, p. 278.

7. *MP*, p. 302. Even in the early pages of the work, Pope conceded that it was "hazardous but important" to attempt an assessment of the personal motives of the early textile entrepreneurs, because personal motivation "provides a nexus between economic and religious aspects" (p. 16) of Gastonia's industrial transformation.

8. The phrase is used in *MP* on p. 268.

9. *MP*, pp. 214-215.

10. Hannah Arendt, *On Violence* (New York: Harcourt, Brace, & World, 1970), p. 51.

11. In conversation with textile executives in the late sixties, Shriver found that this was one of the arguments resorted to for import-restrictions on non-American textiles. "If we got into a war," said several of these men, "it would be disastrous for us to be dependent upon foreign imports for one of our national life necessities."

12. Above, p. 36 in quoted material which has footnote number 9.

13. Cf. Gibson Winter, *Elements for a Social Ethic: Scientific and Ethical Perspectives on Social Process* (New York: The Macmillan Company, 1966).

14. Peter Berger and Thomas Luckmann, *The Social Construction of Reality* (Garden City, New York: Doubleday and Company, Anchor Books, 1967).

15. This attempt to put in a capsule the argument of the first 128 pages of their book avoids, after their example, lengthy quotations from these pages and numerous references to their own theoretical forerunners. Among the latter, as any student of the Sociology of Knowledge knows, are Karl Marx, Karl Mannheim, Emile Durkheim, Max Weber, Robert Merton, and Alfred Schutz.

16. Berger and Luckmann, p. 33.

17. *Ibid.*, pp. 55-56.

18. *Ibid.*, p. 57.

19. *Ibid.*, p. 76.

20. The title of a poignant novel by the modern African writer, Chinua Achebe, concerning this very cultural crisis in his own time and culture. (London and Ibadan: Heinemann Educational Books, Ltd., 1958.) The title itself is part of a poem by the English poet, W. B. Yeats, meditating on the same problem in his own country in the early twentieth century.

21. Berger and Luckmann, p. 86.

22. *Ibid.*, p. 40.

23. *Ibid.*, p. 96.

24. *Ibid.*, p. 116.

25. *Ibid.*, p. 128.

26. *Ibid.*, pp. 123-124. That the concept of ideology is "much disputed" in sociological literature, few readers of that literature will dispute. For an excellent, comprehensive overview of the various uses of the term in social analysis from the period 1940-60, see Norman Birnbaum, *The*

Sociological Study of Ideology: A Trend Report and Bibliography (Oxford: Basil Blackwell, 1962). Originally issued as Volume IX., No. 2 of *Current Sociology,* 1960.

27. Dean M. Kelley, *Why Conservative Churches are Growing: A Study in Sociology of Religion* (New York: Harper & Row, 1972), p. 136.

28. As quoted by J. Milton Yinger, *The Scientific Study of Religion* (London: Collier-Macmillan Co., 1970), p. 6. Quoted from Robert Bellah, "Religious Evolution," *American Sociological Review* 29 (1964): 358.

29. *MP,* p. 334.

30. In preparation of this text, the writers—all three of us male—have sought to place decent restrictions on the use of the generic "he," out of real respect for those readers who detect male chauvinism in such usage. If on occasion we have failed to use "one" or "person" or "she or he" in place of the generic masculine pronoun, it is because we felt such a substitution to be repetitious, inaccurate, or linguistically awkward. We agree, however, that the generic "he" is overused in common parlance implicitly to promote the interests of men, and in this sense functions ideologically. We have tried to avoid that sense and implication wherever possible.

31. One of the reasons why among the social sciences anthropology enjoys a relatively high general readership is the happenstance that its practitioners tended to start their work studying "primitive" societies where the intermixture of personal consciousness, social structure, and symbolic code was so dense that there was no pulling them apart. One had to move rather easily from one level to another and back again. Such movement is difficult both practically and theoretically for all those who want to study so-called modern, complex, highly differentiated societies. To describe these societies as a whole is an intellectual gymnastic which is difficult for both the member and the observer of the society, especially when member and observer participate in much the same cultural canopy. This, of course, is one of the more subtle epistemological problems of social science. How can the American scientist observe American culture, when he is so ineluctably influenced, in his perceiving apparatus, by that culture?

32. Further reflection on this problem, cf. Appendix B, "Data as a Social Variable."

33. The problem of how to make a study like this "up-to-date" is one that we leave unresolved. Our first interviews of Gastonia residents took place in the summer of 1965. Later surveys of various persons in the community took place in the period 1966-69, while some of the historical research was also being completed. Actual writing of the book has extended over three years. Though some data from recent months is included in the book, autumn 1974 is the effective cutoff date of the research.

34. This definition is in thorough keeping with the dialectical stricture that the proper work of the sociology of religion is to move between symbolic and institutional social structures.

35. *MP,* p. 273.

PART I

PROGRESS AND HARMONY:
An Overview of Industry and the Churches, 1940–1975

Chapter One

Religion and Ideology in Gastonia:
World War II and Beyond

War times are evil times. But they are good times for two very different human projects: the prosperity of the textile industry and the sociological investigation of religion and ideology.

Nobody who knew twentieth century history doubted, in 1940, that the coming of a world war meant a rapid ascent of the American textile industry from the depths of the Great Depression. R. S. Dickson, investment banker from Charlotte, North Carolina, spoke for all of his knowledgeable colleagues when he said in January of that year: "The history of cotton mill operations under war conditions has proven that cotton mill stocks are an ideal investment hedge against inflation created by the ravages of war."[1] One year later he could make some statistical predictions from actual ravages which had occurred in the meantime:

Cotton mills, rayon mills, and machinery manufacturing plants in England, France, Belgium, Germany, and Italy have been so ruthlessly destroyed by bombing . . . that it seems reasonable to assume that at least 20% of all the producing textile equipment in Europe has been destroyed to date, and that before the war can end at least 35% or more of such producing equipment will have been demolished.[2]

The ill wind of war was about to blow good upon Gastonia for the second time in twenty five years, but it would blow evil, too, and this mixture makes wartime an apt time to begin a study of religion and ideology. War confronts a society and its members with many ultimate, religious questions: will we live or die? what is worth dying for? worth living for? what is the meaning of our suffering? War also confronts a society with sharp questions about the relation of particular and general interests: is the survival of a society to be given priority over the lives of certain of its members? if so, whose lives should be chosen for sacrifice? who has a right to profit from the sacrifice of others? if one's own society is under attack, can a counterattack bestow significant good upon one's enemies too? how universal are the benefits resulting from the victory of one's own side in a war? These are ideological questions, for they concern the tortuous relationship of particular social interests and universal social values.[3]

In fact, the public statements of many leaders of the Gaston County community, during the years of World War II, demonstrated some acute consciousness of the illegitimacy of thinking and acting in wartime only in terms of financial interests. In these days that promise such prosperity for our industry, said one of the county's "pioneer textile men" in early 1941, we must put "country before profit";[4] and twelve days after Pearl Harbor, an industry-sponsored advertisement in the *Gazette* proclaimed that economic progress was "no substitute for justice and conscience," because this distinction was an issue at stake in the war.[5] In the same vein, three years later, when the tides of war were running strong in the nation's favor, attorney Basil Whitener, now a navy lieutenant, wrote home his opinion that after the war "our government should take its proper position as leader in a community of nations based on our national interests and in response to the Moral Law."[6]

There were two measures of justified political policy—interest and moral law: what if they did not coincide? Ironically enough, one of the persons who raised this general question during the war was a person at the very bottom of the list of those people considered qualified by Gastonians for political moralizing. He was Fred Beal, jailed leader of the Loray Strike, reformed Communist, now paroled from prison by the governor of North Carolina. Writing from New York City in 1943, he reflected on the irony that many Americans who hated his own association with Moscow in 1929 were now ready to embrace Russia as a wartime ally because it suited American interests to do so.

So now it turns out that the Fred E. Beal of 1929, who followed Stalin, almost to the point of landing in the hot seat, now is the enemy of all that Stalin holds dear, while my antagonists of 1929 are now groveling at his feet. Justice, where art thou![7]

Where, indeed? If his reformed worldview had permitted him to do so, Beal might have answered in the terms some Gastonians found themselves resorting to, as injustices and other assorted evils of war came home to the local imagination: the terms of religion. Unfortunately for his dialogue with the locals, he was apparently unable to speak at length about the danger that a nationalistic "idolatry" would take hold of that imagination.[8] In any event, the relation of religious faith to war and assorted symbols of patriotism was a disputed relation in wartime Gastonia. The dispute came down to the question of what degree of compatibility, if any, could attend the cause of war and the cause of the Christian religion. Several contrasting degrees of such compatibility can be detected in the spectrum of public statements on this issue that emerged in the war years. An initial picture of the form and content of religion and ideology in Gastonia can readily be painted from a survey of this spectrum.

Three Formal Modes of Relation Between Religion and Ideology

1. *Contradiction.* A sense of the possible contradiction between religion and international warfare haunted the minds of some local citizens most heavily in the early war years. If the western democracies of this period were slow to be stirred "morally" to corporate effort of war, religious antagonism may have accounted for some of the slowness.[9] So it seemed in Gastonia at least. A year before Pearl Harbor, the Managing Editor of the Gastonia newspaper, himself a member of the Main Street Methodist Church, reflected in his regular column on the horrible blessing which the Christian churches have sometimes illegitimately given to warfare. He quoted a "long forgotten" German soldier from World War I who winced at the spectacle of a priest's offering his benediction to a company of soldiers on their way into battle.[10] "I realize," commented the editor "that any voice against war is a lone voice in the wilderness, but so long as I have one breath left in my body, I will raise it against organized slaughter." And early in 1941, he justified his revulsion against war in explicitly religious terms, to the derogation of all political values whatsoever:

God Almighty cares nothing about the thing we call democracy . . .
He cares nothing about dictators or kings.
He cares only about man.[11]

A similar sense of contradiction crept into some Gastonia pulpits during the war. In the nationally hardpressed summer of 1942, the rector of the uptown Episcopal Church preached on the forgiveness which Jesus commanded his disciples to extend to their enemies. Christians, said he, should show

charity of heart and humanity of spirit, even toward those who may be engulfed in political and military objectives which are implementing mass murder and world chaos . . . This is the Christian philosophy of life, and until press, radio, and all public pronouncements accept it and stop prodding our people on to war-time zeal through the pernicious and pagan propaganda of Vengeance, there can and will be no peace on the earth! . . . There is 'another side' to every problem and policy—a certain balance of truth which stands as the safety zone of ultimate good for all things and all people, tempering the judgment and testing the procedure of all who heed its challenge. These things are Christian![12]

Here was the "tonality" of religion *par excellence,* fitting exactly the Berger-Luckmann concept: an "ultimate good for all things and all people." The mode of its relation to the other values of the culture was alleged to be starkly antagonistic—an allegation that, if consistently urged, could have posed a formidable array of psychological and political problems for a national people asking themselves if these other values were worth dying for.[13] But, happily or unhappily for the nation and for Gastonia, this view of the relation of religion and ideology was an increasingly minor note as the American war effort gathered to a crescendo.

    2. *Identification.*   To the contrary, and with far greater documented frequency, Gastonia religion rallied to the cause of American victory in the war. The most clearcut form of the rallying was the identification of religious faith with the causes for which the United States and its allies were fighting. This identification even had a secular subform explicitly unrelated to traditional religious symbolism. Early in 1941, a group of twenty-two local industrial firms sponsored a newspaper advertisement that attributed to "Uncle Sam" most of the qualities that religionists attribute to their deity:

Believe only in Uncle Sam. Help him and rely upon him. That is the best of good business. Whatever helps Uncle Sam, helps everything you hold dear. . . . Protect him and you protect *all.*[14]

Such rhetoric represented an utter collapse of theoretical or practical distinction between religious faith, ideological values, and economic interests. "Uncle Sam" was the source from which all blessings flow. The meaning ascribed to American citizenship was ultimate, universal, and absolute. That World War II had as one of its political issues the deification of the state was not a thought that seems to have occurred to the Gastonia sponsors or the Indianapolis authors of the ad.[15]

    The commandeering of traditional biblical symbolism for purposes of strengthening patriotic morale became more common as war came closer. During the Dunkirk evacuation, the editor-in-chief of the *Gastonia Gazette* compared the war of Britain and France against Germany to the war of King Hezekiah against Assyria. During the Battle of Britain, he challenged "ministers, educators, and other special groups" to show their "willingness to fight" for their country if necessary. And at the same time one local Baptist minister joined in the religious chorus of calls for "a revival of active patriotism in this country."[16] The chorus mounted sharply after Pearl Harbor and continued unabated until Hiroshima. New Year's Day of 1942 found Gastonia ministers conducting prayer services for the nation in their churches and on the floors of local mills. Christian flags and American flags began to appear more frequently in the chancels of church sanctuaries; and in the same week that his Episcopal neighbor was making a radical distinction between "the Christian philosophy of life" and "wartime zeal," the uptown Baptist minister urged his congregation to lay aside their reservations about the compatibility of religion and "force":

America was discovered in answer to prayer. . . . If freedom and liberty were worth fighting for at Lexington and Valley Forge, they are worth fighting for today. . . . God used force, he was the victim of force. We must defend our freedom with force. Our cause is righteous.[17]

Slow to stir to war, democracies are apparently uniquely full of fury once the stirring gains momentum. Gastonia furnished much evidence for this generalization in the concluding months of this war. The churches contributed their share to national mobilization in the form of bandages rolled, USO Christmas packages mailed, and bereaved parents comforted for the loss of sons in battle. But their major, public, institutional participation in the war took place in the realm of belief and symbol. As the end approached, this form of mobilization was unmistakable. "Invasion prayers" appeared in the paper. One called American pilots "warriors of God" whose sacrifices resembled those of Jesus Christ. Others called down imprecations upon the "pagans who have defied Thy will and flouted Thy teachings," and blessings upon "our forces, who have vowed to save the world for its Kingdom destiny."[18] And when news of the war's end reached Gastonia in August 1945, the fusion of religious and patriotic celebration took public shape as church bells rang, mill whistles blew, and

many a citizen turned to enter the doors of his chosen church and spend a few quiet moments in meditation and prayers . . . for enduring peace, the world's last, best and brightest hope.[19]

It was as if the fabric of a sacred canopy had been mended, the roof of a livable world, restored.

3. *Tension.* A third mode of relation between religion and ideology appeared in glints and snatches during the war years. We may call it the mode of tension, expressed in such occurrences as:

—the expressed hope of some textile executives that no Sunday work would be required in the mills because "many of the workers in our mills have strict religious scruples against working on Sunday."[20]

—the assertion of an uptown Presbyterian minister in 1942 that winning the war was not the "only consideration now," because "the main consideration . . . is the following after righteousness, loyalty to God, loyalty to his principles. . . . Unless righteousness exalts us our air force will not be able to lift us into the presence of God."[21]

Such statements presuppose real but uneasy compatibility between the claims of religious and national institutions. In the case of Sunday work, for example, the "contradiction" mode of relation, invoked by many a radical pacifist during the war, requires no work whatsoever in a war-production plant. The "identification" mode sanctions Sunday work as a religious necessity. The "tension" mode portends the possibility of institutional compromise, tradeoffs, and negotiation—a possibility realized on many occasions of church-state confrontations in American history. (A contemporary illustration was the decision of the U.S. Congress not to draft clergy into the armed forces of the war, at the primary insistence of the Roman Catholic church and with the ready assent of the major Protestant denominations.) This was the most subtle of the three positions, the most vulnerable to deterioration into one of the others, and the most subject to being judged muddled from the perspective of the others.

Gastonia ministers who had kept up with the debates of the thirties and forties over pacifism among leading theologians of the country would have associated the position readily with the name of Reinhold Niebuhr who indicated that it may be possible for a Christian to carry a gun, but he will carry it with a heavy heart.[22] But they were more likely to have listened to a version of the same view from a man who was on his way in the summer of 1943 to becoming the most famous politician to be produced by Gaston County in the twentieth century. His name was R. Gregg Cherry, a veteran of World War I who had been elected mayor of Gastonia in 1919 and who had gone on to become the North Carolina Democratic Party's nominee for governor in 1944.[23] Cherry's name will be important at other junctures in our narrative, but he is interesting here because both his speeches and his conduct in office bespeak a politician who perceived both differences and kinship between religion and ideology. An intriguing glimmer of this perception peeps out in a speech he made, during his campaign for governor, in Burlington, N.C. in July of 1943.[24] With eyes on two world wars, Cherry called his audience to demonstrate in this moment of history

that high pitch of whole-hearted enthusiasm and patriotism amounting almost to religious fervor which was achieved by America in 1917-18.[25]

What did soon-to-be Governor Cherry *mean* by his qualifier, "almost"? He died a decade before any author of this book thought to ask him; therefore, our answer must be somewhat speculative. We know that Cherry was an active member of the Main Street Methodist Church.[26] Did something of his experience in that church caution him against unqualified identification of the cause of

American victory in two wars with a cause that is worthy of "religious fervor"? Or as a politician was he aware that some people in his audience made such a distinction? Perhaps only sociologists and theologians would have their imaginations jostled by the question, but it is certain that in Cherry's mind the role of religion in human society had been given some thought beyond this little glimmer. We know this from a sermon he preached in the postwar year of 1948, the last year of his administration as Governor of his state. For the purpose of gaining a deeper look into the *content* of the religious and ideological motifs that dominate much of Gastonia's recent history, we must give some detailed attention to this remarkable sermon.

Gastonia Religion and Gastonia Ideology: Substantive Motifs

Gastonians shared so much of their fundamental orientation towards World War II with other Americans, that it would be easy to assume that, in the realm of generalized social value commitments, they are unexceptional participants in a single national culture. As Pope's readers know, there is truth and error in this generalization. Gastonians are more careful than many other Americans to state their major social commitments in religious terms, and in this they share the subculture of southern Protestantism. Moreover, as a community whose economic history has stemmed almost exclusively from the textile industry, social perceptions have been deeply colored by this history in ways expressed with extraordinary clarity in Governor Cherry's 1948 utterance from the pulpit of the Main Street Methodist Church.[27]

Addressing himself to "The Place of Religion in Our World," the Governor spoke to a full Sunday night congregation, and made three major claims:

Religion is the chief force for human progress.

"There's been no progress on this earth except the progress born of religious feeling, using the word religious as expressing man's duty to his fellow, especially to the weak and the poor, the wretched and the oppressed."

Religion is the guardian of personal freedom.

"Religious feeling is a power that lifts us above institutions and above governments. Communists who set themselves up as political idols know, like the Fascists, that they cannot compete . . . with free ideas and the souls of man."

Religion, through the church, is a power for harmony in society.

"Those who are acquainted with church history know that the Christian church stands for law and order, good government, and good morals. . . . Clear-sighted men and women and clear-sighted organizations realize that the words mutuality, oneness, and self-interest have and bear a very close relationship . . . no advantage that can be obtained by force or strategic circumstance will remain an advantage in the long run. In state and national affairs and in industrial affairs, no amount of force, economic pressure or bargaining can take the place of decent performance in line with the Golden Rule."[28]

The word of governors is but one word to which the ear of science must listen. For now, the important point is that a preeminent representative of power and success in this locale believed in the reality of these relationships between his religion and certain social values. Against the background of what we know about Gastonia from the Pope study, as well as others, we may begin to ask what the words "religion" and the triad of "Progress, Harmony, and Liberty" *meant to Cherry's audience*. In a preliminary exercise of historically educated interpretation, we may say that the words meant something like this:

Gastonians see the history of their community as primarily an ascent from poverty. Their grandfathers numbered themselves among "the weak and the poor, the wretched and the oppressed." Farmers almost every one, those pioneers of the early days—1880 and after—"had given up the struggle against tired and niggardly land, attracted by prospects of working in a cotton mill for 'cash money.' "[29] Progress thus meant industrialization; it also meant a sort of economic salvation that was tied profoundly, in the minds of some, to the Christian religion. Commemorating its own sixtieth anniversary as a publication in 1940, for example, the *Gazette* recollected, with mingled chagrin and optimism, that for many years prior to the solid establishment of the mills Gaston County was known as the "Banner Corn Likker Manufacturing County" of North Carolina.

At that time Gaston County was backward in government, education, religion, civic matters; in fact, it was short in almost every line that offered possibilities of progress. Then came a day when a small number of staunch and sturdy citizens, in the minority for generations, arose in the might of righteous indignation and drove liquor from the county. From that day on Gaston has grown steadily and has developed in all phases of its life.[30]

The spirit of a religious epic hangs about such descriptions, not only in Gastonia but among all those makers of the "New South" whose image of their own servitude was imbued with the post-Civil War devastation of their economy. In North Carolina during the forties, the connection of "progress" with religious symbolism could still be quite overt; opening the 1941 state fair in Raleigh, Josephus Daniels urged his fellow Tar Heels to gird themselves for war production "as well as textile products and cigarettes," and he went on to quote Moses: "speak to my people that they go forward!"[31]

A simple equivalence of economic prosperity and religious salvation has often been taken as the definition of the Yankee, not the southerner, in American cultural history; "their gain is their godliness" was an accusation hurled by the preachers of New England at their merchant congregations,[32] but not hurled often at anyone in the *post*-plantation South. In that devastated time, Southerners in general found themselves latecomers to a train of economic progress that had pulled out in the North and left them behind. As Gastonia participated in the great American myth of progress, therefore, it did so with the accent of the Henry Gradys of the South, not the Andrew Carnegies of the North. Furthermore it did so in 1948 with memories still troubled by a more modern trauma that had deposited a deeper sediment upon the local mindset than had the Civil War: concretely the Loray Strike was the most important *negative* event in Gaston County history.

"Progress," in short, was a codeword for much of this tangled history of economic crisis and renewal that had brought Gastonia safely out of the depths of hunger and despair in the eighties, the clutches of Communism and chaos in the twenties, and, so recently, the shadows of depression and totalitarianism. In all it was a powerful double "myth of whence and whither":[33] away from the Egyptian captivity of poverty, towards the Promised Land of abundance.

It was natural in this very context that to the theme of Progress, Gregg Cherry should join the twin theme of *Harmony*. In contrast to industrial growth, a compulsive concern for social harmony has long been a traditional feature of culture in the American South. Indeed, one could easily leap to the assumption that any Gastonian's acclamation for harmony is of a piece with "the southern way of life." That way of life was founded in its beginning upon chattel slavery and the nineteenth century insistence of the slave-owning classes of the South upon "law and order" functioned nicely to protect their interest in maintaining the legality of the slave system. In an economic order founded on such a system it made sense to accentuate harmony and nonviolence as social virtues because conflict and violence lay so close to the surface of the system itself.[34]

In fact, however, Gastonia's roots as a community largely postdated the Civil War; and above all, as part of the southern Piedmont, it shared in most of the economic losses but in few of the economic gains of the old South. Yeoman farms had always been the tradition in this region. The very mountain folk who came down to work in the early mills were the near descendants of immigrants who had been driven into the mountains in the first place by the system that awarded to black slaves the "privilege" of tilling the best farm land in the South. Not that Piedmont society was immune to participation in the racism inherent in the plantation system; for from the 1880s on, the cotton mills offered jobs to white people, not blacks.[35] But Gastonia's participation in that system

was at one economic remove from its center, so that—ideologically speaking—there was little nostalgia here for the good old days of the good old South.
There was even little leftover Confederate patriotism. This was a community
whose newspaper editor in 1949 could muse about the "bloody and useless war
of the '60s," and whose last surviving veteran of that war could be quoted in his
1943 obituary as being "glad that the North won the War Between the States
because it meant the preservation of our union"![36]

The unity that made the most difference to most Gastonians was a more
local, immediate unity than that of the United States. Pope's account of the
coming of great prosperity to the textile industry during World War I makes
very clear what kind of harmony textile management had to prize if the
two-class society of the nineteen twenties was to hold together: the harmony of
low-wage textile workers and increasingly rich textile owners. On the religious
side, Harmony meant the triumph of love, forgiveness, and forbearance in
human relationships—the spirit of "resignation" to the will of God in one's lot
in life,[37] and trust in God to right what was wrong with that lot. The ideological
substratum of this harmony was a preference for social order above any
conceivable social disorder, a rejection of violence as a tool for social change,
and indeed (in Cherry's own words) a like rejection of "force, economic
pressure or bargaining" as activities quite within the pale of "decency."

The most powerful recent compulsion behind the recommendation of this
virtue, of course, was the Loray Strike. Perhaps in earshot that night was
another member of the Main Street Methodist Church, a "pioneer textile
man," who this same year (1948) was to recall to the memory of the local
Rotary Club its 1919 origins. At that time, he said:

"Gastonia was split by factions which greatly retarded the progress and development of
the town. This club . . . and others more than justified their existence in that they
brought about the elimination of these factions and Gastonia has gone forward ever
since."[38]

Churches, said textile executives twenty years later, were useful to the community for much the same reason as civic clubs: they nurtured a "civic
consciousness," a concern for the whole of the community and not merely one
segment of it. Ironically enough, this tribute to the power of civic clubs to
"eliminate factions" completely omits the one event, ten years after 1919, that
most revealed the presence of factions in Gastonia. In its own way, however,
the pertinence of unfactional harmony, as a powerful ideological theme, is all
the more clearly silhouetted by the *absence* of any such reference in these 1948
speeches. Gastonians had to proclaim harmony the louder to drown out the

shrill and terrible clamor of 1929. Only the rank outsider needed his memory jogged anyway. Many another person in both the Main Street Methodist Church and the Rotary Club in 1948 could have testified that:

"The young men of my generation remembered it, and all of us have been anxious to see that that kind of situation was not repeated."[39]

Progress and Harmony are twin virtues in the local ideology. A third theme of Cherry's address is something of a half-sister to these other two: *Liberty*. Whether interpreted from an economic, a political, or a religious frame of reference, Liberty is a deeply rooted theme of southern Piedmont culture. Speaking of the early millowners and mill workers, a recent novelist declares: "They had this in common: the belief that, in the end, a man's honor and salvation depended upon himself alone, not on courts, laws, society or organizations."[40] They had such a belief in common with vast numbers of their fellows in the rural backwaters and the mountain coves of the South: an individualism and antiinstitutionalism that down through the years has been the frustration of officials as diverse as county agents, revenuers, and civil rights attorneys. But like other Americans, this breed of Southerner has gone to war believing that the value of "freedom" is the value most worth dying for. In the context of economic culture, he sees his "free labor" as a proud commodity. He is ready to work for, but not be enslaved to, any employer—a pride that asserted itself loudly in the stretch-out controversy which eventually provoked the Loray Strike.[41]

But truly sonorous resonance for the word "liberty" in this culture is reserved—as it is in the Cherry speech—for the religious context. "Religious feeling"—a weak and subjective thing by some definitions—"is a power"—a force to be reckoned with—"that lifts us above institutions and above governments"—those alleged monopolizers of "real" power. What else was the lesson of two great wars other than that the idols of the dictator must fall before the power of "free ideas and the souls of men"? The heritage of evangelical, individualistic Protestantism rings palpably in all this; and the line between the powerful Divinity who saves the soul and the power of that soul itself once saved is hard to draw.

Indeed, though Progress and Harmony as ideological themes seem compatible without being identical with the themes of Salvation and Love in Cherry's religion, the relation of political-economic freedom to religious freedom comes on here as virtually an identity. And Cherry was not alone, in these postwar years, alleging publicly such an intimate connection between the two freedoms. "A new understanding of the philosophy that the individual is more important than the state is long overdue," said the editor of the *Gazette* soon after the war. "This is the essence of Christianity. It is this and nothing else for which the people of the country are willing to stake their lives"—as real a test of real religion as any social scientist is likely to devise.[42] In 1952 a Lutheran minister brought on a standing ovation at the local Kiwanis Club by a speech extolling "rugged individualism, a faith in self that we could meet our needs by the sweat of our brawn and brain,"[43] a claim that matched the individualistic hardwork-ethic of the local scene, without raising the theological question of how, if at all, "faith in self" was to be distinguished from faith in God.

On the whole "the place of religion in the modern world" of Governor R. Gregg Cherry was a secure, established place; the warp of his religious worldview fitted rather closely with the woof of his ideology. But there are strain-and-stress points in his sacred canopy: even on a conceptual level, distinctions and possible tensions between religious claims and in-stitutionalized social interests peep out again in references to the peculiar concern of religion for the "weak and the poor" and the peculiar antagonism of the free religious soul to all overriding institutional claims whatsoever. Under certain circumstances, persons and groups who believed either of these propo-sitions could be dangerous to the claims of Progress and Harmony—especially a Progress serving chiefly the interests of the strong and rich, and a Harmony dependent upon quiet social neglect of somebody's self-interest. The dynamics of human relationships in the business corporation, schools, churches, and governor's offices, of course, are often concerned with just these strains and stresses. For all his celebration of these ideological and kindred religious virtues and for all his disclaimers about "force, economic pressure or bargain-ing" as ultimately advantageous in human affairs, Governor Cherry's daily life as a politician was full of these very kinds of negotiations. In church that night near the end of his term of office, he felt obliged to disparage the daily reality of politics, apparently because he believed that they were not all of the reality. But he left many a question of logic, social organization and social process hanging.

How then does it all relate in an understandable pattern? How, in the push and shove of concrete human relations do religion and ideology, religious institutions and other institutions, the interests of some persons and the interests of others, fit together? Not merely in the conceptual attractions and repulsions of celestial ideas. These may form the canopy of the society, but the demonstra-tion of what the canopy means socially is in structures and events under the tent. To those structures and events, down-to-earth every one, we may now turn.

NOTES

1. *The Gastonia Gazette,* January 8, 1940. Hereafter references to this newspaper will be made under the initials *GG.*

2. *Ibid.,* January 17, 1941.

3. Cf. above, Introduction, p. 45.

4. *GG,* January 6, 1941.

5. *GG,* December 19, 1941.

6. *GG,* December 30, 1944.

7. *GG,* June 7, 1943. Beal had been refused both parole and pardon by Clyde R. Hoey, a native of Shelby, N.C., twenty five miles west of Gastonia. However, Hoey did cut seven years off Beal's sentence, and his successor in the governor's chair, J. Melville Broughton of Raleigh, granted a parole. Efforts by some citizens to secure a pardon for Beal, in view of the irregularities of his trial in 1929, consistently failed. He died in 1954 at the age of 57. Cf. *MP,* pp. 305-306.

8. Cf. Fred E. Beal, *Proletarian Journey* (New York: Da Copo Press, 1971). Little in Beal's book suggests that he ever resorted to religious faith or rhetoric as conceptual-critical leverage over against ideology. His eventual rejection of Stalinism was sourced largely in his unrevised allegiance to a purer sort of communism whose primary values were "justice" and "truth"—two words that recur repeatedly in his book. But in its very end, its last sentence, he repairs to the religious concept of liberation from idolatry: the only path to a true communist society, he says, will be through "minds liberated from the worship of false gods and by spirits strong enough to face the truth in the quest for the truth." *Ibid.,* p. 352.

9. One team of historians has claimed that while the British people were both "morally and materially unready for war" in 1939, the French were "morally rather than materially unready." Frank P. Chambers, Christian Phelps Harris, and Charles C. Bayley, *This Age of Conflict* (New York: Harcourt, Brace and Company, 1950), p. 629.

10. *GG,* November 2, 1940.

11. *GG,* March 15, 1941.

12. *GG,* June 30, 1942. Coincidentally and by contrast, the *Gazette,* in this same day's editorial page, called for the execution of eight German saboteurs recently caught by the FBI. "They have taught a doctrine of hate and bloodshed. It is time for them to get a taste of their own medicine."

13. How common such pulpit sentiment was in Gastonia in 1941-45, we cannot judge with any accuracy. We know that this same Episcopal rector made his opinion on these matters known outside the church in a luncheon address to a local Civitan Club some two weeks later, comparing the universalistic cause of religion to the universalistic cause of science: "Science as well as religion proclaims a brotherhood of man which even the grim paradox of war cannot destroy. The wounded American soldier owes his life to the Japanese scientist who isolated the bacillus of tetanus. The German trooper is saved from typhoid by a Russian serum. The Britisher in the tropics is protected from malaria by the research of an Italian. . . . God made a sphere, not a hemisphere! God made a human race, not a collection of contending groups and classes and nations." *GG,* July 16, 1942.

14. *GG,* April 8, 1941.

15. A notation shows that the ad was nationally syndicated by a firm in the latter city.

16. *GG,* June 5, August 29, and September 2, 1940.

17. *GG,* June 22, 1942. In parallel rhetoric, the minister of a black Methodist church wrote a letter to his congregation's servicemen on Easter Sunday 1943, denying at length the idea that "Christianity and religion have no place and part in war. Christ Himself fought for us here on earth in order that we might be free. . . . Sin and Satan from time immemorial have waged war unsuccessfully against us. . . . That is why you are in the thick of battle."

18. *GG,* May 4, June 6, June 19, 1944.

19. *GG,* August 15, 1945.

20. *GG,* January 8, 1942. Outright opposition to war production on religious grounds led some American pacifists to refuse to work in such industries, while outright identification of religion with the war effort would have sanctioned war production on Sunday as well as any other day. This institutionalized segmentation of *time,* is a significant social-institutional recognition of the different claims of "God and Caesar." Here is some tension between the economic-political and religious interest, but no radical discontinuity.

21. *GG,* June 14, 1942.

22. Cf. Reinhold Niebuhr, *Moral Man and Immoral Society* (New York: Charles Scribners Sons, 1932).

23. *The Gaston County Historical Bulletin,* Vol. 7, No. 1 (March, 1961), p. 1.

24. A textile town 115 miles northeast of Gastonia.

25. *GG,* July 27, 1943.

26. Along with the owners and major editors of the *Gastonia Gazette,* the major stockholder and president of the town's largest locally-owned textile chain (Textiles, Inc.), and the president of its largest bank. The Main Street Methodist and the First Presbyterian could lay claim in this period to having the largest contingent of members at the apex of the local "power structure." Cf. below, Chapter Three, pp.110-112.

27. The validity of the assertion that this sermon is a salient summary of the ideological themes of the local society must be tested against much other material to be presented in this book. The circularity of the process behind social research is illustrated here: if we had not become well acquainted with a long segment of Gaston history extending into the late nineteen sixties, we would hardly have recognized in Cherry's sermon its apt summation of a key segment of local "thought-ways." But if we did not have this document, too, the case for the existence of such an ideology would be that much weakened. Cf. Appendix A, pp. 348-353.

28. *GG,* January 19, 1948.

29. *MP,* p. 213.

30. *GG,* June 24, 1940.

31. *GG,* October 14, 1941. The biblical quotation is Exodus 14:15, and concerns Israel's crossing of the Red Sea. For a similar, more extensive religious interpretation of southern industrialism as "God's way for the development of a forsaken people," cf. the sermon of a South Carolina minister quoted by Pope, *MP,* pp. 24-25.

32. Perry Miller, *The New England Mind: The Seventeenth Century* (Cambridge: Harvard University Press, 1954), p. 473. Cf. also James M. Dabbs, *Who Speaks for the South?* (New York: Funk & Wagnalls, Co., Inc., 1964), pp. 179-180.

33. The phrase is that of James Luther Adams in "Religion and the Ideologies," *Confluence,* Vol. 4, No. 1, (April 1955), p. 73. Overriding the sharp distinction between "ideology" and "utopia" made famous by Karl Mannheim, Adams argues that an ideological myth may take either of the two forms or both. Characteristically the architects of social movements need to motivate their followers with both the push of an evil from which they are fleeing and the pull of a good towards which they are striving.

34. Cf. James McBride Dabbs, *Who Speaks for the South?*, p. 216 and *The Southern Heritage* (New York: Alfred A. Knopf, 1958), p. 147. In the latter Dabbs says: "Southern violence . . . is . . . the base upon which we built our society. For we built it upon slavery, and slavery, however humanized by the grace of God, was established by violence and maintained by the threat of it. This was the smoldering volcano upon the slopes of which we built the Great Houses.

35. There were so few black employees in the mills in 1939, that Liston Pope methodically eliminated from his study any direct treatment of the black community, the black church, and race relations in general. Cf. *MP*, pp. 9-13.

36. *GG*, September 5, 1949; May 4, 1943.

37. Cf. *MP*, pp. 30-31. Though not totally comfortable with the word, a millowner quoted here by Pope says that he values the influence of religion upon the worker because "it makes him more complacent—no, that's not the word. It makes him more resigned—that's not the word either. . . . A churchman is more reasonable . . . more law-abiding."

38. *GG*, June, 1948. The year 1919 was the year of Cherry's own election as mayor of Gastonia, so his earliest political experience took place as the rumblings of the two-class system were just beginning to be heard in the town.

39. Above, Preface, p. 13. The unity of the local society was occasionally accorded explicitly religious value by a church leader during the early half of the period under study. "I wish members of our churches would catch the spirit of Rotary," said a minister nostalgically in a speech to the same club in 1954. "This would bring a unity of purpose." *GG*, May 27, 1954. "Real" religion, in this minister's own implicit theory here, sometimes resides outside officially religious institutions.

40. Ben Haas, *The Chandler Heritage* (New York: Simon and Schuster, 1971), p. 313. This is a recent novel about three generations of a textile-owner family in North Carolina. Haas is a native of Charlotte, N.C.

41. Cf. *MP*, pp. 228 ff. Pope concludes that the fundamental cause of the strike was not low wages, long hours, or poor living conditions in the mill villages, but the arbitrary imposition of work regulations upon the workers. The southern textile worker, says Pope, "has retained an individualism which leads him to resent encroachment upon his 'personal liberties' in his job . . . ." Other mills in the vicinity of the Loray effected a stretch-out of work during the late twenties, but only after consultation with workers. " . . .the impersonal and arbitrary methods of the superintendant appear to have been the most significant factors underlying the strike." *MP*, pp. 229-231.

42. *GG*, November 4, 1946. The editorial goes on to speak of "this Christian philosophy of the individual first" as "pervading every business enterprise big and little" and as being "the foundation of our government" and "worth more than life itself!"

43. *GG*, October 3, 1952.

Chapter Two

Progress:
Economic Growth in Gastonia from 1940 to 1975

During all the early decades of their local industrial revolution, Gastonians readily identified "economic growth" with "the growth of the textile industry." Progress was a one-industry thing, and the experience of the 1880-1920 era made that a natural belief for a citizen of Gaston County. But the experience of a later generation began to tell a different story and to evoke a more complex, if not a different, notion of "Progress." The slump of the early twenties, the bleak Depression of the thirties, and a too-brief postwar boom chastened the optimism of the sons of the textile pioneers, and afflicted their business-school-trained grandsons with a somewhat desperate spirit of innovation. In part therefore, the story of economic change in Gastonia in the past thirty years centers on the conflict between those industrial leaders who changed from the ways of their fathers with gusto, those who changed reluctantly, and those who changed not at all. Some of the changes, as we shall see, were thrust upon the local economy by homegrown persons and institutions; some, by forces as remote geographically as Hong Kong but as near economically as that city's textile mills. Whatever their origin, the tides of change in this thirty years brought complex patterns of profit and loss to the community and its increasingly assorted interest-groups. And in the midst of these tides—sometimes deep in the social current and sometimes on the surface—the debate over Progress went on. What is the difference between real and illusory Progress? Between the blessing of economic change and the curse? What combinations of changes must a community welcome or resist? These were questions of a far greater complexity than the grandfathers and the fathers had asked or had to answer. They were the burden of the post World War II generation.

Wartime Recovery and Postwar Boom

R. S. Dickson had been right:[1] the demand for textile goods in a nation at war would bring a great economic balm to the Depression-beset textile industry, and the postwar demand of a war-devastated world would bring on a period of wondrous prosperity. Indeed, if aggregate profits are a measure of beauty, the years 1947-1948 were the most beautiful years in recent Gastonia history. On the other hand, if sheer growth rather than profit was the measure, the wartime period itself was the great surge of renewed health for the community.

The statistics of growth in the war period point to the rapid expansion of the economy on all fronts. The following are exemplary:

—In the three-and-a-half-year period of the war, bank assets in Gastonia's two banks more than doubled.[2]

	1941	1945
Citizens National Bank	$5,315,688.72	$13,428,472.89
National Bank of Commerce	3,168,349.45	8,074,350.56

—When the Manville-Jenckes (Loray) mill was taken over by Firestone, Inc., in 1935[3] its monthly production of fiber goods was approximately 300,000 pounds; ten years later, as the war was about to end, its monthly production had increased to approximately 3,500,000 pounds.[4]

—Manufacturing employment in Gaston County increased from some 15,000 in 1940 to a 1944 average of 27,003.[5]

—Sabbatarians to the contrary, some mills throughout the county instituted seven-day work weeks, and in 1944 the War Manpower Commission ordered all mills to institute a 48-hour week.[6] By 1943 the War Manpower Commission declared most textile workers essential to the war effort,[7] and virtually to the end of the war, the War Production Board and the Army Quartermaster Department pressed textile firms for increased outputs.[8]

Wartime profits in the industry are hard to estimate, but Table 2:1 shows from several angles the growth-context in which profits accumulated during these years, both in North Carolina and in Gaston County. Though the number of textile firms remained relatively stable, employment in the yarn mills of North Carolina increased by 37%. Absolute dollars, wages and salaries, product value, and value-added were all approximately quadrupled; and per wage-earner dollar income was just short of having tripled.[9] During this same period, legal minimum wages for textile workers rose from 32.5¢ per hour in 1941 to 55¢ in 1945. Per worker annual earnings in Gastonia climbed somewhat higher than the North Carolina average to approximately $1,927.[10]

Table 2.1

COMPARATIVE STATISTICS FOR SELECTED INDUSTRIES
1939 and 1947

Industry	Year	
Cotton Broad-Weaving: North Carolina[1]	1939	1947
Number of establishments	128	113
Total employment, salaried and wage	72,985	71,017
Average number of wage-earners	70,115	68,394
Salaries and wages, total	$ 56,229,936	$146,111,000
Wages	$ 50,744,204	$135,371,000
Value of products shipped	$217,454,862	$632,821,000
Value added by manufacture	$117,829,021	$325,586,000
Cotton Yarn Industry: North Carolina[2]		
Number of establishments	198	207
Total employment, salaried and wage	39,792	54,409
Average number of wage-earners	38,455	52,480
Salaries and wages, total	$ 26,210,949	$100,457,000
Wages	$ 23,372,902	$ 92,623,000
Value of products shipped	$100,191,764	$448,485,000
Value added by manufacture	$ 45,009,885	$197,253,000
All Manufacturing: North Carolina[3]		
Number of establishments	3,158	5,322
Total employment, salaried and wage	293,258	381,480
Average number of wage-earners	269,238	350,207
Salaries and wages, total	$245,879,000	$ 758,895,000
Wages	$198,519,000	$ 641,966,000
Value added by manufacture	$544,181,000	$1,646,673,000
All Manufacturing: Gaston County[4]		
Number of establishments	(130)	179
Total employment, salaried and wage		28,879
Average number of wage-earners	(19,660)	27,589
Salaries and wages, total		$ 58, 112,000
Wages		$ 52, 894,000
Value added by manufacture	($ 25,567,000)	$120,617,000

[1]Figures for 1939: *Sixteenth Census of the United States: 1940, Manufactures: 1939,* Volume II, Part 1, Reports by Industries (Washington: U.S. Government Printing Office, 1942), p. 288.
Figures for 1947: *Census of Manufactures: 1947:* Volume II, Statistics by Industry, (Washington: U.S. Government Printing Office 1949), p. 156. (By 1947 all these statistics were rounded off by thousands of dollars.)

[2]Figures for 1939: *Manufactures, 1939,* Vol. II Part 1, p. 290.
Figures for 1947: *Census of Manufactures: 1947,* Vol. II, p. 156.

[3]Figures for 1939 and 1947: *Census of Manufactures: 1947,* Vol. II. p. 35, "General Statistics for Divisions, States, and Standard Metropolitan Areas: 1899-1947."

[4]Ibid., "General Statistics for Selected Counties," p. 45. The figures in *parentheses* are estimates secured from the American Textile Manufacturers Institute. No national census figures were compiled for Gaston County in 1939.

Profits undoubtedly saw some solid improvement during the war years,[11] but federal price control combined with federal taxes to keep wartime earnings modest. As Hoover and Ratchford summarize the matter:

The excess profits tax hit the industry especially hard because its earnings in the base period (1936-39) were low and because its invested capital is low in comparison with most manufacturing enterprises, partly because the turnover is comparatively high, especially in boom times. As a result, "including normal taxes, the industry paid out nearly 65% of its income to Federal tax collectors in 1942 and nearly 68% in 1943."[12]

And so, if the Second World War helped rescue the textile industry from the economic doldrums of the thirties, the rescue proved dramatic only in terms of preparation for the all-time profits of the immediate postwar years. With price controls off and wartime taxes eased, the industry geared to meet pent-up domestic demands plus the foreign demand generated by the Marshall Plan. For twenty years after 1948, a regular public complaint of the industry leaders would be that their production and profit levels lagged behind those of other major national industries.[13] That complaint was not made in the immediate postwar period. According to National Association of Manufacturers' figures for the period, after-tax income as percentage of dollar-sales was twice as high for textile mill products as for manufacturing as a whole. Federal Trade Commission and Securities and Exchange Commission (S.E.C.) reports do not show this dramatic a gain for textiles over other industries, but all reports suggest that textile stocks were excellent shortrange investments in these years, as a glance at both sales profit and stockholder equity gains in Table 2.2 will show.[14]

With textile exports booming and very few imports, Gaston County yarn-makers flourished as international free traders.[15] Exact financial figures for individual firms and the county as a whole have always been difficult to secure in this industry,[16] but available data on two companies during this period are an index to the contemporary prosperity of virtually all one hundred of Gaston County's textile mills: the first company owned a trio of mills in east Gastonia, employing a total of 625 workers. Its management typified the determination of the smaller companies to meet the competition of the new chain mills with equipment-modernization and production-specialization fitted to the capacities of the small corporation. Eighty percent of their profits of the late forties, reported the president of this company in 1950, had been plowed back into plant improvements. Production during this five-year period almost doubled, and net sales more than doubled from just over $2 million in 1944 to just over $5 million in 1949.[17]

Five times larger than this first company and the true bellwether of local business growth was a twelve-mill, locally-owned chain, Textiles, Inc. In

Table 2.2

PROFIT RATES ON TEXTILE MILL PRODUCTS, 1941-1974*

Year	Profit Rate on Sales After Taxes (Average Of Four Quarters)	Profit Rate on Stockholders' Equity After Taxes
1941	6.5	12.0
1942	4.6	10.3
1943	4.1	9.1
1944	4.1	8.4
1945	4.1	7.8
1946	5.6**	**
1947	8.2	23.9
1948	8.2	24.1
1949	4.1	7.6
1950	5.8	12.6
1951	3.3	8.3
1952	1.9	4.2
1953	2.2	4.6
1954	1.1	1.8
1955	2.6	5.7
1956	2.6	5.7
1957	1.9	4.2
1958	1.6	3.5
1959	3.0	7.4
1960	2.5	5.8
1961	2.1	5.0
1962	2.5	6.2
1963	2.3	6.1
1964	3.1	8.5
1965	3.8	10.8
1966	3.6	10.1
1967	2.9	7.6
1968	3.1	8.8
1969	2.9	7.9
1970	1.9	5.1
1971	2.4	6.6
1972	2.6	7.5
1973	2.9	9.6
1974 (1st Quarter)	3.1	10.1

*A composite of statistics quoted from Federal Trade Commission and Securities and Exchange Commission sources in the following issues of *Textile Hi-Lights* (Charlotte and Washington: American Textile Manufacturers Institute): October 1956; July 1958; July 1960; April 1961; February 1967; Fall 1970; September 1974.

**Figures for 1946 are not available from the above sources, and only National Association of Manufacture sales-profit figures for "Textile Products" are given instead. Cf., ATMI, September 1950.

Pope's period and ours, its board chairman easily qualified for the title, "Mr. Gastonia." His role in building the industrial, banking, and other financial institutions of the county was widely acknowledged in the community as indispensable and central. The companies and the bank which he founded were the dominant power in Gaston County economic affairs during the years 1930-60.

By the late forties the financial history of Textiles, Inc. was already acquiring heroic proportions in the minds of its owners and many of its employees. In 1952, for example, Charles D. Gray, Sr., a director of the corporation reported how the mill chain, purchased in 1931, was

born of desperation in the middle of this nation's worst panic, spent eight of its first ten years in receivership in which its barnacles were sluffed off, its body streamlined and its sail trimmed so that it emerged into another decade of successful and prosperous operations to become the nation's leading organization in the production of fine combed yarns in Gastonia, recognized as the country's capital of the fine combed yarn industry.[18]

The tones of the Progress-Epic reverberated here. The "barnacle-sluffing" included consolidation or elimination of mill units (down from 22 in 1931 to 12 in 1950), a reduction in number of spindles (from 275,000 to 160,000), a reduction in workers (from 4000 in 1931 to 3000 in 1951)—all resulting in a steady climb out of corporate indebtedness towards corporate profitability. "Progress" in this context was financial; no leader of the company is known to have suggested that shrinkage in jobs injected a note of ambiguity into the matter from the standpoint of some workers.

Surveying ten years of growth since their emergence from receivership, the Textiles, Inc. Board of Directors announced in 1952 that company earnings for the decade had been $32 million, of which $7,500,000 had been paid to stockholders in dividends, an average of "$1.145 per share per year on the $1.00 per value stock, the dividends ranging from 40¢ per share at the beginning up to $2.50 per share in some recent years. During this decade Textiles has paid $18 million to federal and state governments in income taxes and has paid $59 million to its 3,000 employees, probably the highest wage rates in the history of the industry. In addition it has spent $4,800,000 in completely modernizing eleven of its remaining twelve plants."[19]

Both the aggregate and the illustrative statistics are sufficient to make the point: the postwar years brought unprecedented prosperity to the Gaston textile industry. Whether it was a time of prosperity for everyone connected with the industry—workers for example—is a matter to be debated.[20] Not debatable is the fact that textile stockholders made a lot of money in these few years.

Consolidation

In spite of the above success story, the profitability of the small family-owned corporation, having suffered severely during the 1930s, continued to suffer after the abnormally good markets of the 1946-49 period. In the twenties it had been apparent to the most astute textile men that large *organization* and large *profits* would go together in the future of most production industries. As the Textiles, Inc. story illustrates, bankruptcies had hastened the consolidations of the thirties, but by the mid-forties even that locally-oriented chain was acquiring mills in South Carolina.[21]

That locally based mills were in a threatened competitive position was conclusively advertised in 1946 by the sale of Cramerton to Burlington Mills.[22] As the largest unincorporated mill-village community in the county, Cramerton had long been reputed to be a "showplace" of family-owned textile enterprise. It could boast one of the few "E" pennants awarded by the Army to Gaston County plants during the war. It employed 2,000 workers to run 60,000 spindles and 961 looms—making it the largest fiber-to-cloth operation in the county.[23]

The Cramerton sale was a genuine shock to many Gastonians. It was a form of Progress, perhaps, that great success should come to Mr. Spencer Love, president of Burlington and a native of Gastonia; but it was a blow to the personalistic, paternalistic ethos of the old order.[24] Though the *Gazette* editor—long accustomed to being the voice of local textile interests—could take comfort in the fact that Burlington had located its headquarters in nearby Greensboro rather than faraway New York, the lines of *control* over local industry were obviously shifting.[25]

True to its word[26] the new Burlington management continued a large number of the trappings of the paternalistic tradition in Cramerton. The community remained unincorporated until 1967. Its recreation facilities were expanded; and, though the mill village housing was soon sold to individual owners in line with a trend throughout the county, the old links between management, local business, and local churches remained intact. But the old localistic lines of economic organization and control were not intact anymore, and the most immediate impact of this upon the workforce at Cramerton was the sharp increase in standards of productivity.[27] Such "rationalization" meant intolerance of inefficiency; it also put other, smaller mills in the county on notice that the day of easy entry into the business and easy profit was fast fading. The whole textile industry was entering a bewildering new era in which production would climb while spindles and employment declined. Most ominously, profit would be increasingly skewed in favor of organizations that were large, heavily invested with new equipment, and ruthlessly unconcerned about their marginal competitors. Furthermore, successful battles with the unions over wage levels would increasingly be fought by companies with high relative investment in machinery and low investment in labor—a ratio that permitted them to raise wages at the cost of cuts in the labor force. Speaking from a 1957 perspective, *The Charlotte Observer* reported that the average textile worker was then producing 50% more than he did in 1947. "Most of the increase is due to better machinery and more efficient plants. . . . But it takes money to modernize. Mills which can't produce it are increasingly going out of business or merging with outfits with more capital."[28]

Then there were the small-company failures. In the four year period between 1952 and 1956, thirty-eight textile mills were liquidated in North Carolina.[29] Few of these were in Gaston County, but all the smaller mills of the county were now under pressure to "modernize or perish." Certain of the smaller firms in Gastonia did manage to modernize in the years following World War II; other, weaker firms would manage to survive the competition by benefit of the Korean and Vietnam wars, but the foundations of a new structure for competition were laid in the forties by the growing power of the new textile chain corporations. Upon the small family-owned textile mill was now written a doom already being read by the architects of the mergers. Two war-stimulated booms to the contrary, the president of Burlington Mills could say with satisfaction in 1956 that

"the decrease in productive machinery over the past twenty years has resulted in part from the dropping out of marginal producers due to intensive competition and a minimum of new plant construction because of poor return on investment."[30]

In sum, anyone with a few spinning frames and looms could make money in the textile trade in the golden years of 1946, 1947, and 1948. But those years flew by quickly. In textiles as in most other American industries in the latter half of the twentieth century, the people who made much money were the people who had or could organize sources of much money. If that was gain for some, it was unavoidable loss for others. Threatened with such loss, a group of young Gastonia businessmen as early as 1944 sent up a call wholly unorthodox in this textile-blessed community: "Industrial Diversification!"

Moves Towards Diversity

The economic argument for industrial diversity was obvious to anyone who took seriously the apparently regular "boom and bust" pattern of the textile business. Any one-industry town lives alongside a river subject to drying up. Wartime textile orders had swollen the river for Gastonia, but young men raised in the town were not anxious to repeat the insecurities of their own Depression childhoods. They were wise enough to attribute some of those insecurities to their town's overcommitment to textiles.

How heavily committed it was in 1945 is suggested by the following employment figures for Gaston County.

	1945	1960	1970
Total employed persons	37,946	54,895	67,420
Textile plant employment	25,691	26,760	27,890
	(67.7% of total)	(43.3% of total)	(41.4% of total)[31]

When one takes into account that the other 32.3% of employed people in 1945 included not only nonmanufacturing workers but also workers in industries that are wholly or partly supports for textiles (machine shops, transportation, construction), textile dominance of Gaston County was overwhelming.[32]

During the first two months of 1945 the Gastonia Junior Chamber of Commerce sponsored a series of 100 quarter-page newspaper advertisements for the cause of diversification. The ads walked a line between affirming and denying the blessedness of life in a textile town while advancing arguments for diversity taken from the future rather than the past. Eleven thousand young men and women, most of them draftees, would soon consider returning to this county, said the ads; but these veterans are not likely to want jobs that are (1) low-paying or (2) part of a paternalistic system. It was an accurate prophecy. Data from the first half of 1946 fed the suspicion that, after Paris and Tokyo, Gaston County's youth were not rushing in droves to get back to the spinning frames.[33]

Whether low pay or paternalism or something else about Gastonia turned some of its young men towards other places of employment is not certain. But the Jaycee authors of the early 1945 ads were breaking new ideological ground in Gaston by their open use of the word "paternalism" in public advertisements. No local individuals or families were named, but one ad in the '45 series asked, with mingled humor and contempt:

WHO'S AFRAID OF THE BIG BAD WOLF?

In his day, he really got away with running the town
    because in that day (a long time ago) every town
        had a "BIG BAD WOLF" who told all the little fellows
            just what to do and when to do it!

When Mr. "BIG BAD WOLF" said, "We don't want no other industry
    in here!" No one who had any sense at all would dream of getting up
        and saying, "Brother Wolf, you're talking through your
            Stetson hat."

But this is 1945. Education has changed the people. More of them can think than ever before—for themselves. The Paternalistic system having served so brilliantly in other days doesn't work so well for an educated and thinking people.[34]

In the wake of these spirited ads, no person in the public life of Gastonia stepped forward to claim the role of old-style paternalist. To the contrary: the man whom some might have nominated as the closest approximation to occupant of the role—the president of Textiles, Inc.—took pains to congratulate the Jaycees publicly on their recent work in a letter given wide publicity. He denied that local textile interests would oppose industrial diversification merely because it would "require higher skilled labor and would command higher wages" than the mills were now paying. No, the mill managers knew that

there has always been a difference in wages for various industries . . . and there always will be. I might incidentally mention, however, that during the last ten years the basic wage scale of textile operatives had increased 150 percent; therefore the wages paid in textile mills are equal in some respects to those paid in other industries.

But the murmur of a potential conflict of interests stirred at one point in this published letter:

. . . if your efforts will bring in new industries, particularly those of a different character, such as knitting mills, finishing plants, machine shops, etc., unquestionably it would rebound to the benefit of the whole community.[35]

Would *really* new industry be welcome in Gaston County? Industry that was integrated little or not at all with some phase of the textile business? In particular, what new (1) wage scales and (2) labor relations patterns would render a new industry decidedly unwelcome?

These were questions that would receive vigorous private and veiled public discussion over the next ten years. The public part of the story went as follows: At the initiative of a coalition of a Junior-Senior Chamber of Commerce leaders, the Gaston delegation to the 1945 state legislature secured the establishment of the Gastonia Industrial Diversification Commission (G.I.D.C.). By special local referendum, the city of Gastonia voted a tax-levy to support the body, the first such in the state. Hereafter the G.I.D.C. would advertise itself as "the only public-supported organization that creates wealth."[36] The new Commission soon bought property in east Gastonia, built warehouses there, and began its nationwide search for new industrial residents for the town. Success in the search came slowly. In the seven years from 1945 to 1952 the G.I.D.C. claimed direct credit for the recruitment of three new industries with an annual combined payroll of $445,000, acted to keep "a sizable Gastonia industry" from moving away, and (by 1957) was claiming indirect credit for the coming of new plants making business forms, paper boxes, plastic products, neon signs, and chain saws.[37]

From the beginning of this effort, the installation of textile-company managers as members of the Commission assured control of its affairs by those who had the interests of the textile industry at heart.[38] For some local leaders, the control was not sure enough; and in the tortuous political year of 1950[39] the very existence of the G.I.D.C. came under public attack. W. B. Garrison, a Gastonia candidate for re-election to the County Commission unsuccessfully requested his fellow commissioners to nullify the local town law permitting tax funds to support industrial development. His opposition, said Garrison, was shared by a majority of the members of the Gastonia Chamber of Commerce. (Not so, replied the president of the Chamber; we see eye to eye with the G.I.D.C.) Garrison's opponent in the upcoming election, Paul J. McArver, then sought to undo him by telling the public why, in McArver's opinion, Garrison opposed the G.I.D.C.: he was the tool of conservative textile interests. Gastonia and Belmont are both run by a minority of political-industrial "bosses," he said. They oppose the G.I.D.C. "because they do not want the wage scale disturbed. . ."[40]

Garrison beat McArver at the polls 6,433 to 3,580.[41] But for a challenger-candidate to pull that many votes against an incumbent claiming to represent the uptown business establishment was, in Gaston County, an achievement. The local tradition had been one of much lower voter turnout, especially among textile workers, who apparently went to the polls in unprecedented numbers in the spring of 1950.[42]

The evidence that textile employers actively resisted any dramatic break in the pattern of low-wage industry is elusive and mixed. On the one hand, diversification of one kind or another was coming to Gastonia through economic forces operating inexorably in the American economy at large. The proportion of textile workers in county employment declined from 53% in 1950 to 42% in 1960 to 41% in 1970. (Local manufacturing jobs as a whole, however, declined much more slowly in the same 20 years: from 58% to 53%.) As employment statistics from recent years in Table 2.3 suggest, relative concentration of the local economy in textiles is gradually declining. On the other hand, the greatest expansion of wage employment in this thirty-year period was in the non-industrial sector—a trend strictly parallel to the national picture.[43] Such a change could hardly be called "industrial diversification." Indeed, a profile of the achievements of the G.I.D.C. over the first 26 years of its work in the county, alongside the present profile of manufacturing firms in 1973, goes far to substantiate this generalization: the major share of manufacturing diversification has occurred *inside* the textile industry. Old Gastonia had

Table 2.3

PATTERNS OF EMPLOYMENT IN GASTON COUNTY, FOR YEARS 1962-1972, IN NUMBER OF EMPLOYEES

	1962	1963	1964	1965	1966	1967	1968	1969	1970	1971	1972
MANUFACTURING (TOTAL)	30,000	30,220	31,540	33,940	37,160	37,610	38,420	39,070	38,400	38,570	41,250
Food	560	580	550	580	590	610	550	520	560	610	610
Textiles	23,920	23,730	24,460	25,700	27,670	27,640	28,600	28,450	27,890	28,060	29,690
Apparel	970	1,080	1,400	1,730	1,880	1,960	2,040	2,160	2,060	2,110	2,030
Non-electrical machinery	2,360	3,390	3,600	4,260	5,140	5,240	5,010	5,260	5,220	5,230	5,970
All other manuf.	2,820	1,440	1,530	1,670	1,880	2,160	2,220	2,680	2,670	2,560	2,590
NON-MANUFACTURING (TOTAL)	15,040	15,070	15,660	17,670	18,570	19,110	20,040	20,930	22,600	23,310	24,230
Construction	1,170	1,260	1,330	1,510	1,540	1,540	1,440	1,540	1,720	1,640	2,420
Trans., Comm., Utilities	2,980	2,590	2,500	2,620	2,880	3,040	3,120	3,370	3,560	3,580	3,580
Trade	4,490	4,740	4,980	6,080	6,320	6,280	6,570	6,900	7,580	7,700	8,170
Fin., Ins. and Real Estate	710	760	770	780	800	850	910	990	1,120	1,120	1,160
Service	2,480	2,500	2,770	3,300	3,480	3,490	3,620	3,750	4,000	4,160	4,080
Government	3,180	3,180	3,270	3,310	3,510	3,860	4,340	4,340	4,580	5,070	4,750
Other non-manuf.	30	40	40	70	40	50	40	40	40	40	70
ALL OTHER NONAG. EMPLOYM.	5,390	5,370	5,890	6,190	6,220	5,950	5,860	5,860	5,750	5,860	6,030
AGRICUL. EMPLOYM.	1,080	1,150	1,050	900	860	800	720	690	670	660	640
EMPLOYMENT, TOTAL	51,510	51,810	54,140	58,700	62,810	63,470	65,040	66,550	67,420	68,400	72,150
UNEMPLOYMENT, TOTAL	3,190	3,130	2,670	1,890	1,480	2,120	1,490	1,380	1,900	1,800	1,230
RATE OF UNEMPLOYMENT	5.8	5.7	4.7	3.1	2.3	3.2	2.2	2.0	2.7	2.6	1.7

SOURCE: N.C. Employment Security Commission

Table 2.4

PERCENT EMPLOYED BY OCCUPATIONAL CATEGORIES—TOTAL POPULATION, GASTON COUNTY AND GASTONIA, CITY FROM CENSUS 1940, 1950, 1960, 1970

Occupational Category	Gaston County				Gastonia, City			
	1940	1950	1960	1970	1940	1950	1960	1970
Professional, Technical, and Kindred Workers	3.9	4.2	5.8	7.8	5.0	6.2	7.1	10.4
Farmers and Farm Managers	4.9	3.0	.9	.4	(4)	.1	.1	(4)
Proprietors, Managers, Officials	4.3	5.7	5.5	6.1	6.0	8.6	7.7	8.8
Clerical and Kindred Workers	7.3	5.2	8.3	11.7	12.1	8.1	9.7	12.0
Sales Workers		5.1	5.5	4.7		7.0	7.4	6.7
Craftsmen, Foremen, and Kindred Workers	7.6	11.1	13.3	16.0	7.9	10.0	11.3	12.7
Operatives and Kindred (including transport equipment operatives)	51.4	49.3	40.7	39.3	42.7	39.9	35.1	34.2
Domestic Service (Private household)	6.8	3.8	3.9	1.4	12.1	6.7	5.6	2.5
Service Workers, Except Domestic or Private Household	4.6	5.3	6.0	7.5	6.8	7.4	6.8	8.6
Farm Laborers and Farm Foremen	1.6	.8	.5	.3	.1	(4)	.2	.1
Farm Laborers (unpaid family)	2.0	.6	–	–	(1)	–	–	–
Laborers (except farm and mine)	5.1	5.0	4.4	4.7	6.9	5.4	3.8	3.9
Occupation Not Reported	.5	.9	5.1	–	.4	.6	5.2	–
	100.0	100.0	99.9	99.9	100.0	100.0	100.0	99.9

Source: 1970: U.S. Bureau of the Census, Census of Population: 1970 GENERAL SOCIAL AND ECONOMIC CHARACTERISTICS Final Report PC (1)-C 35 North Carolina. U.S. Government Printing Office, Washington, D.C. 1972. 1960, 1950, 1940: U.S. Bureau of Census, Census of Population for appropriate years.

Table 2.5

PERCENT EMPLOYED BY OCCUPATIONAL CATEGORIES–NONWHITE
GASTON COUNTY AND GASTONIA, CITY FROM CENSUS 1940, 1950, 1960, 1970

Occupational Category	Gaston County				Gastonia, City			
	1940	1950	1960	1970	1940	1950	1960	1970
Professional, Technical, and Kindred Workers	3.0	3.2	3.5	3.6	3.1	3.6	3.6	4.6
Farmers and Farm Managers	7.5	5.2	.7	.1	(1)	–	.1	–
Proprietors, Managers, Officials	.6	1.1	.6	.9	.9	1.6	.8	1.1
Clerical and Kindred Workers	.7	.9	1.3	5.5	.9	1.0	1.2	5.5
Sales Workers		.6	.8	1.3		.8	1.3	1.7
Craftsmen, Foremen, and Kindred Workers	2.3	5.2	6.4	5.2	2.9	5.0	6.6	5.1
Operatives and Kindred (including transport equipment operatives)	10.9	20.2	20.1	40.3	12.7	23.6	16.8	35.6
Domestic Service (Private household)	38.5	26.0	27.0	11.0	46.6	28.9	26.0	14.2
Service Workers, Except Domestic or Private Household	9.2	14.3	18.3	20.6	12.9	18.1	18.5	23.7
Farm Laborers and Farm Foremen	5.9	2.8	1.2	1.3	.3	(1)	.5	.3
Farm Laborers (unpaid family)	3.1	1.7	.3	–	–	–	.1	–
Laborers (except farm and mine)	17.6	17.5	13.3	10.1	19.3	16.5	16.3	8.1
Occupation Not Reported	.5	1.3	6.5	–	.4	.7	8.2	–
	99.9	100.0	100.0	99.9	100.0	99.8	100.0	99.9

Source: 1970: U.S. Bureau of the Census, Census of Population: 1970 GENERAL SOCIAL AND ECONOMIC CHARACTERISTICS Final Report PC (1)-C 35 North Carolina. U.S. Government Printing Office, Washington, D.C. 1972.
1960, 1950, 1940: U.S. Bureau of Census, Census of Population for appropriate years.

been "the combed yarn capital of the world," its economy overwhelmingly devoted to the production of some 80% of the entire American output of that item, which is widely used to make men's undershirts. As the director of the G.I.D.C. wrote in early 1975: "Now the textile industry includes garment manufacturing, industrial sewing threads, carpet yarns, a wide variety of synthetic yarns, and knitting . . . So we are no longer dependent upon one product."[44] The Commission participated in the coming of just such diversification: some twenty-four out of the fifty-three new firms which it helped usher into Gastonia in the 1947-73 period were textile-related firms.[45] The degree of intra-textile diversity may be judged from Table 2.6, drawn up from a listing of all county manufacturing firms by the Gaston County Chamber of Commerce. Though detailed knowledge of what each firm makes and to whom it sells its products would give a more accurate picture of the matter, a cursory sketch of this local economy is enough to demonstrate its continued overwhelming investment in the textile industry as such. Among all the communities in the county, the city of Gastonia itself has the best reason to think of itself as industrially diversified; but even in Gastonia, as goes textiles, so goes the community. The recession of 1975 was sober proof of that.

One other fact to be noted is that industries paying a textile *wage,* while making non-textile *products,* had their technical share in the diversification of the era, but this was hardly the diversity that the young promoters of the movement had in mind in 1945.[46] And most disconcerting of all—to them —were some hard-to-document occasions when an industry promising high wages was actively discouraged by local elites from locating in Gaston County. One such company in the early fifties was a national manufacturer of manmade fiber requiring a location alongside large amounts of fresh water such as that available in the South Fork of the Catawba River on the eastern side of Gaston County near the "model" mill villages of McAdenville and Belmont. Countywide rumor in the mid-fifties said that the county's textile leaders actively resisted the coming of the huge new plant, and in 1971 a prominent Belmont politician gave his opinion that "everything pointed" to the truth of that rumor.[47] The plant was eventually located a few miles away in a South Carolina county adjoining Gaston County.

"Revolution" by Personnel Relations

The large new textile firms of the forties introduced several new elements to the structuring of competition in all the Gaston Counties of the land: research facilities; capital resources for modernization of equipment; superior ability, as multi-mill organizations, for production changeover in response to changing markets; flexibility for the transfer and promotion of management; and—what will concern us most here—sophistication in certain new arts of "personnel relations." On all of these counts, managers of firms like Firestone and Burlington must have had no small task of maintaining complete rapport with their peers in the Gastonia business community of this period. Localistic, traditional social bonds were now under criticism by a new managerial ethos that measured progress in terms of technical research, efficiency curves, and other impersonal criteria applied by decisionmakers in offices far from Gastonia.[48] Moreover, behind the public display of relief that Cramerton was under the control of a new textile empire headquartered in nearby Greensboro,

Table 2.6
248 MANUFACTURING FIRMS IN GASTON COUNTY 1972:
DISTRIBUTION BY MAJOR CATEGORIES

Textile or Textile-related

Apparel Manufacturing	14	*Machinery:* General	22
Brushes	2		
Chemicals	6	*Metal Products*	14
Fasteners	1		
Aprons	3	*Plastics*	9
Card clothing	2		
Gears	8	*Food Products*	21
Reneedling	7		
Machinery: textile	56	*Printers and Publishers*	22
Sheet metal	11		
Ornaments: textile	1	*Building Materials and*	
Rugs	1	*Products*	15
Dyeing & Finishing	6		
Knit & Woven Products	21	*Electric Products*	10
Sewing thread	3		
Tire cord	1	*Other Manufacturers*	26
Blankets	1		
Yarn	60		139
Yarn finishing	2		
Miscellaneous textile products	3		
	209		

Source: Gaston County Chamber of Commerce, *Industrial Directory* (n.d., *circa* 1972.) The above chart involves some collapsing of categories and omission of others (under "other manufacturing") in this publication. Some judgments have been made by the authors, on the basis of the listing of products manufactured, as to whether the firm is more or less "textile related." This is a listing of firms, which means that the number of manufacturing units exceeds the totals, especially under the "yarn" category.

were some well grounded economic fears of this new "managerialism." Firestone and Burlington had the capacity in this period to pay high wages by textile standards. Ordinarily they took the initiative in any round of textile wage increases. Their jobs textile workers coveted most; especially as workers started buying homes outside the textile village, competition for the best workers in the "pool" was heightened for almost every company.

Less easily identified as new competition was the new context in which the job of the industrial manager was now defined by national textile chains. Distinctions between "owners" and "managers" had been uncommon in the locally organized textile companies; and "management," before the war, had not acquired connotations of a college-educated professional. But postwar industry saw at least three professionals introduced into the role structure of plant after plant in Gastonia: the engineer, responsible for progress in mechanical productivity; the plant manager, responsible to his home office for making sure that his unit was a "profit center"; and the personnel supervisor, responsible for attending to the needs of people as carefully as his engineering colleague attended to the requirements of machinery.

The aspect of the new look in textile management policies that encountered the least local antagonism was personnel relations. The larger companies were publicly vocal in their acclaim of the new "human" perspective on labor-management relations. Speaking to the Gastonia Rotary Club in the spring of 1944, the personnel director of Firestone Cotton Mills quoted a recent *Readers Digest* survey as showing that American production workers "feel that although their efforts form 68% of production factors they get only about 10% of the attention. . . . Workers in industry want to be treated as human beings and not as numbers on a payroll." He went on to assert that "they want to be led, not driven" to implement managerial decisions; and, as part of being treated humanly, they need to be aware of company policy affecting their interests; they want to know their chances for promotion in the organization; and overall they want in their jobs "a reasonable degree of happiness."[49]

It was a fair summary of an approach to the human side of industrial enterprise which gathered momentum among American businesses in the postwar era: treat the workers as individuals, not cogs, make them feel a part of the organization, take account of their off-the-job problems that may affect their on-the-job performance, take time to talk with them, and make clear to them the mutual benefit for worker and management in this or that policy change.

The new approach was widely hailed in Gastonia as based on the ultimate harmony of interests between workers and managers in the mills,—"there is no basic schism between labor and management."[50] On the other hand, the flurry of managerialism coincided exactly with the postwar revival of the labor union on the local scene. Would the human relations approach to the problems of intra-industrial conflict prove to be a middle-way between paternalism and unionism? By its new human-relations procedures, management in the forties and fifties delivered a vigorous, hopeful yes to the question. (In what ways the unions simultaneously delivered their dubious no will be the subject of much detailed narrative later in this book.[51]) Foremen and other supervisors were enrolled in training courses on such interrelated matters as the proper way of handling complaints and reducing waste. Boxes for complaints and suggestions for increasing productive efficiency began to appear in the mills alongside time clocks and workcard racks. An "open door" policy, permitting an employee to carry a complaint up the managerial ladder to the office of the president, was formally instigated—e.g., in Cramerton. Workers were informed regularly about reasons for the work changes which followed the rapid technological change of the next two decades. And personnel directors gravitated towards wider responsibilities in the area of public relations. In the larger companies they organized formal programs for acquainting various professional groups in the community with the operating policies of the mills. It was in these years —the mid-fifties—that faster machinery and increased workloads for individual tenders of the machinery were introduced into many mills, yielding the charge of a "stretch-out" by many workers and labor union organizers. To counteract this claim, clergymen and news reporters were asked by tour guides in at least one local plant in 1958 to observe carefully any signs of overwork in the employees on duty.[52]

According to its most avid promoters, the shift to the new psychology for industrial relations amounted to a revolution. To skeptical critics, it was the old paternalism in new clothing. And to deeply cynical critics, human relations in industry was a facade put up to ward off the plague of unionism. No *Readers Digest* or other surveys are in hand for estimating how variously the new stance was received during the forties and fifties among a random sample of Gaston working people. But incidental comments on the matter are available from enough Gastonians to suggest that many were aware of some *ambiguity* in the intentions and benefits of the new programs. One such comment came in the mid-sixties from the pastor of a church in Cramerton:

"The 'open door' policy is there to be used by any worker who wants to make complaint over the head of his foreman; but that's not the way a worker gets popular with his foreman. And foremen are themselves promoted partly according to how well they keep down the number of complaints coming from their departments. And since he is the one who has to forward the complaints up the ladder, he does everything possible to keep those complaints to a minimum. So the open door policy is not used very much."[53]

A yet more sober estimate of the new style of management was offered to one of the writers one afternoon in 1957 by a textile worker of twenty years' experience in Gastonia mills. Said she, from her front porch rocking chair:

"It used to be that the super would tell you how many (spinning) sides you had to run, and that was it. Now he comes down the alley, talks with you about the new machine or the new cotton or something else—he uses psychology on you. And he leaves you convinced that you *can* work those ten extra sides, which you try to do, and then you end up wondering how he ever convinced you about that thing, because it's too many sides to work."[54]

Recent Industrial Growth and Decline

Gastonia's internal debate on the meaning of Progress continued into the 1960s and early seventies. It was a debate constantly redirected and troubled by the winds of economic change. How contrarily the winds could blow is only too clear from a summary of certain economic data from the last five years.

Like World War II and the Korean War, the Vietnam War was a boon to the textile industry, which experienced its peak-benefits of the decade in the year 1966. Nationally the industry showed a "relatively flat" record of little growth over the following several years.[55] The usual two-year upswing seemed to hit in late 1971, but this was followed swiftly by the downswing of 1973 that was unusual by all postwar standards. The end of that downswing, as this is written, is not yet. But the accumulating problems of the textile industry did not need the recession of 1973-75 to erupt into visibility. As national inflation gathered momentum in the years 1968-71, textile wage raises failed to keep pace with wage raises in other manufacturing industries; and by 1972 the textile wage scale was barely maintaining its position in relation to national industrial wage averages of the previous decade: in 1961 a textile worker made 70% of the wage of the average American industrial worker; in 1971 he was making 72% of that average, and in 1975, 70%.[56]

During these same recent years, the local economic picture in Gastonia was one of deepening contrast between companies whose leaders knew how to "make it" even in times of recession and those who did not.[57] It was a period of unprecedented numbers of mill-closings—the price of survival which the larger chains were increasingly ready to impose upon their own and other people's organizations. In the two years just prior to January 1971, twenty-two textile mills closed in North Carolina; and of these, nine—or 40%—were located in Gaston County. Four of the nine closings took place in three large, non-locally owned chains (Burlington, Klopman, and Uniroyal), and the other five were parts of small companies.[58] Though the overall economic significance of these shutdowns was easily exaggerated,[59] Gastonia's economic future had some rather clear portents here. Big absentee corporations can close down local units as quickly as they can buy them; and in a time when "diversification" was also the byword for big-corporate survival, diversification could mean the closing of many a local plant. The place of local initiative, for local progress, in short, was less obvious for Gastonia in the seventies than at any other time in its history.

In the meantime and as a part of this same picture, Gaston County was treated to the unaccustomed news that its position as one of North Carolina's leading industrial counties was slipping—at least in terms of the comparative income of its workers. Not only did nearby Mecklenburg County (Charlotte) have a far higher industrial wage level—an ordinary contrast in recent local history—but Gaston manufacturing workers in 1970 earned only $105.39 per week in comparison with a statewide average of $112.27. In spite of the city of Gastonia's new motto, it was Charlotte, not Gastonia, that was economically the "Pacemaker of the Piedmont."[60]

By the mid-seventies, however, three other troubles were high on the horizon of the textile industry: inflation, unemployment, and the problem of worker-recruitment. Inflation-discounted comparisons of textile wages during our whole 35-year period are found later in this book.[61] A basic contemporary index to the growing pocketbook-crisis of the textile worker is the fact that, in November of 1974, the average textile wage was $123.55 per week, a seven-fold increase in dollars over the 1940 average which, discounted for inflation, actually amounted only to a doubling of income over thirty-five years. And the wage increase from 1973 to 1974 was a mere 2.4% over against the huge 1974 inflation rate of 12%. As this is written, in effect, the real income of the average American textile worker is back at its *1965* level.

It is back at that level—if the worker has a job. During most of the period studied in this book, the old, massive surges of unemployment in textiles, known only too well in the industry in the 1920s and 1930s, have seldom occurred. Since World War II, in the South generally, industrial unemployment has seldom climbed to national levels. (In mid-1970, for example, with job-lessness at 5% nationally, only 1.4% of insured workers in Gaston County were receiving unemployment payments.)[62] But in America's bleak economic winter of early 1975, the shadow of the thirties was returning to Gastonia. In December of 1974 the official local unemployment rate was 6.8%, but by February 1975 even the official rate was 19%. The actual rate had to be higher yet.[63] (The rate was back to 6.1% in August 1975.)[64]

So drastic an increase in the number of idle textile workers will greatly decrease, at least temporarily, the third problem of the industry: how to get enough people to accept its job offers. The problem began to surface in the mid-sixties, and by the early seventies was the subject of dramatic remedies by some local plant managers. Consolidated Knitting Mills, just north of the Gaston County line near Lincolnton, announced that it would institute in 1971 a "guaranteed annual wage" for workers who had been with the company three years or more. Absenteeism, said the president of the company, was a major reason for this offer. "On Mondays we've had 20 percent of them staying out."[65] A month later, Gurney Mills, owner of the plants that had seen one of Gastonia's earliest union-building attempts,[66] offered a 10% bonus to its workers for coming to work regularly and on time.[67] For the first time in local history, personnel departments sponsored a series of newspaper ads aimed at attracting young people to work in the mills. These ads constituted a standing admission of what most Gastonians had known for a long time: for young native Gastonians a job in the mills was the job of last resort. The average age of the textile worker nationally in 1970 was thirty-five years; in Gaston County the average was forty. It was an image that personnel managers wanted to change, and their proposal for a new image was a sun-glassed young man standing beside his sports car. "This is the Look of Success . . . the look you get in knowing that you're a young man on the way up . . . a young man who had a real job that pays real money, the kind of job that lets you stop worrying if there'll be a paycheck next week and a chance for advancement. . . ."[68] But Gaston youth acted as though they knew better. A two-year textile course at Gaston College in the fall of 1970 was in danger of being cancelled because only three students had signed up for it;[69] and in the spring of 1971, with the help of government grants, which leaders of the textile industry had long disdained, two local companies began training programs for "the hard core poor" of the county, in the hope of solving a labor problem at one and the same time.[70] "Anyone who will work" was now needed in the "frightening" post-recession textile labor market.[71] Indeed, in the summer of 1972, in some parts of North Carolina prisoners in the work-release program of the state prison system were tending spinning frames.[72]

The hard times of 1975 will no doubt moderate the worker-recruitment problem of the textile industry. But the very return of high unemployment in this industrial sector will also deepen many a worker's reasons for wanting to get out of such work altogether. Surely no young Gastonian who has the downpayment for a sports car will hesitate to use it to drive to Charlotte for a better paying job than he can get in a Gaston mill. Though the director of extension education of the North Carolina State University School of Textiles could say truthfully in the fall of 1970 that there were professional positions in textiles "going begging" now,[73] the more pertinent truth was probably spoken by a sample of Gastonia mill personnel directors who at the same time candidly told a reporter:

The great bulk of employment in textiles is operative. There are not that many chances of promotion. Workers go in as spinners or weavers, and they retire as spinners or weavers.[74]

In sum, whether one looks at the current problems of Gastonia's textile mills from the standpoint of import threats,[75] the consistently low profitability of the industry, or its credibility as a promising place of employment for ambitious workers, one is driven to the prediction that in the next decade or so the City of Spindles is likely to find its economic glory steadily diminishing unless it becomes economically a city of something else. Indeed, the day may yet come when "textiles" comes to mean, in the popular local mind, the Progress of the past that became the liability of the future. To become detached from that past is not a viable ideological option among the majority of Gastonians just now, but the tremor of even that jolting ideological reconception could now be blowing in the economic wind.

NOTES

1. Cf. above, p. 57.

2. The figures are from the statements of banks' assets and liabilities published in the *Gastonia Gazette* simultaneously on October 2, 1941 and March 24, 1945, respectively. In 1934 the National Bank of Commerce had assets just over one million dollars and had declared much of its stock defunct.

3. Cf. *MP*, p. 310.

4. *GG*, March 31, 1945. The plant's principal product was cord-fabric for tires.

5. Latter figures from N. C. Employment Security Commission. The 15,000 figure is based on statistics published by the City of Gastonia for the county (*GG*, October 10, 1940) and on an estimate of some 65% of total county employment (23,000) as being in manufacturing.

6. *GG*, April 21, 1944.

7. *GG*, March 30, 1943.

8. *GG*, February 3, 1943, December 13, 1944.

9. On wages in the total 1940-74 period, cf. below, p. 188, Table 5.2.

10. Another significant index to the wage picture in this period was the average hourly wage of textile workers in the country at large:

	1937	1941	1945	1948
Entire textile industry	.47	.56	.77	1.11
Cotton industry	.38	.49	.70	1.07

U.S. Department of Labor statistic, as quoted in "Building a Textile Union" [New York: Textile Workers Union of America (TWUA-CIO), 1948], p. 24.

11. A small sign that it was difficult for textile owners to "profiteer" during the war is the decision, announced in late 1942 by the principal owners of three large textile firms in Gastonia, that they were joining their peers in other cities of North Carolina to set up the Textile Foundation at North Carolina State University. (*GG*, December 29, 1942). In this period frequent public complaints about high war taxes made by various textile executives, were balanced occasionally by public complaints that wartime profits were getting too high. The truth that lay in between these public pronouncements is apparently that the industry was building up resources of equipment, trained labor, and longterm market potentials that were to be the basis of the impressive profits of the immediate postwar years. Investment in the Textile Foundation at N.C. State was one way of predicting and preparing for the coming boom.

12. Calvin B. Hoover and B. U. Ratchford, *Economic Resources and Policies of the South* (New York: The Macmillan Company, 1951), p. 148. Their quotation is from Jules Backman and

M. R. Gainsbrugh, *Economics of the Cotton Textile Industry* (New York: National Industrial Conference Board, Inc., 1946), p. 142. This assessment was further confirmed by a sample of some forty textile producers by the National City Bank for the years 1942-1945 which "showed a rate of earnings on net assets between 7 and 10 percent." Hoover and Ratchford, p. 149.

13. A typical comment: "Profits per dollar of sales for the Textile Mill Products Industry averaged 2.58 cents after taxes during the calendar year 1955 which was a very meager profit compared with the 5.40 cents realized by All Manufacturing Industries. Of 23 major manufacturing industries, arranged in a profit magnitude from a high of 11.03 cents for Petroleum Refining to a low of 1.33 cents for Apparel and Finished Textiles, the Textile Mill Products Industry ranked fourth from the bottom in this array." *Textile Hi-Lights* (Charlotte: American Cotton Manufacturers Institute), July 1956, p. 2.

14. N.A.M. statistics for the decade were as follows:

Net Income After Taxes as a Percentage of Dollar Volume of Sales

Year	Textile Products	All Mfg. Corporations
1939	−.6%	5.0%
1940	3.9	5.9
1941	1.0	4.7
1942	3.2	3.8
1943	3.6	3.6
1944	3.3	3.9
1945	3.3	2.9
1946	5.6	2.6
1947	6.9	3.3
1948	7.8	4.7
1949	5.2	5.4

N.A.M. Research Department, Washington, D.C., September 1950, as quoted in *Textile Hi-Lights* (Charlotte: American Cotton Manufacturers Institute, Inc.), p. 35, May 1951. The name of this latter organization was changed in 1962 to American Textile Manufacturers Institute, Inc. Future references to issues of *Textile Hi-Lights* below will be simply to "ATMI," and the appropriate issue of this publication, which has been issued quarterly from 1938 to the present.

15. U.S. cotton cloth and cotton yarn exports for the year 1947 were four times as high as they had been in 1940. (U.S. Dept. of Commerce, as reported by ATMI, May 1951, p. 36.) The excess of textile exports over imports was so drastic that well into the fifties the graphs show alpine peaks of export totals towering over scarcely visible foothills of imports. Cf. ATMI, April 1953, p. 31. Talk about the danger of free trade did not mount among American textile manufacturers until the mid and late fifties.

16. The industry is divided among a very large number of variably-sized producing units, capital is sometimes concentrated in a few hands, and competition between units is notoriously fierce. All these conditions make for some very careful guarding of company financial profiles.

17. *GG,* October 17, 1950.

18. All these quotations and statistics are taken from *The Employment Security Commission Quarterly* (Raleigh: The ESC), Vol. 10, 3-4 (Summer-Fall, 1952), pp. 108-110. ("Data for this article supplied by Charles D. Gray, Sr., a director of Textiles, Inc.," p. 110.)

19. *Ibid.*

20. Cf. below, Chapter Five, pp. 186-189.

21. One says "even" because the idea of a far-flung empire of textile mills spreading over the South and into many a foreign country was an idea at odds with a certain principled localism in the

building of Textiles, Inc. and other textile concerns in such towns as Gastonia. As late as 1950 the owners of Textiles, Inc., were glad to have it said of them:

Unlike many large corporations in the yarn and cloth manufacturing business in the South, Textiles' main offices are not located in New York City or some large Northern center, but are conveniently located at the base of company operations here. The men who direct the affairs of this corporation—it has assets of over 11 million dollars—are well known local men with their interests strongly integrated with the business affairs of the city. *GG,* October 17, 1950.

22. Among the early acquisitions of this new soon-to-be multi-national corporation, were two Gaston County plants purchased in 1940-41. Three more were bought in 1946. Burlington reported spectacular per share earnings for this period, which rose from $1.32 in 1945 to $3.47 in 1946 to $5.01 in August of 1947. (*GG,* January 7 and August 14, 1947.)

23. *GG,* July 19, 1946. Very few weave-mills are to be found in Gaston County, which advertises itself rather as "the combed yarn capital of the world." Certain kinds of clothing—most notably men's undershirts—require a finely-combed yarn suitable for knitting; and the county has long laid claim to 80% of the country's total production of this particular commodity. Such production is eminently suitable to small plants, which dot the countryside. Cramerton was a uniquely huge operation, comparable only to the Firestone (Loray) Plant in west Gastonia.

24. In his year-end, final communication to his employees, Colonel Stuart Cramer made it clear that he too was troubled by the sale but that the capital and management needs of the already-big business demanded that it become part of a yet bigger business.

"I shall not go into a discourse upon the present tax laws except to say that they do not favor family-owned corporations unless they are very small. I shall not go into details as to how the present tax structure affected our majority stockholders beyond saying that they were placed in a very dangerous position. It was evident that the Cramer family could not in any case long retain control of the company. It therefore appeared wise to put their affairs in order so that they would be able to pay their death taxes . . . As servant of the stockholders my duty was to act in what I believed to be their best interests. . .

"Mr. Love has assured me verbally and in writing that he hoped they 'could develop the personnel and property here along lines that will fully carry on the fine traditions of the past. . . .' " (*GG,* December 12, 1946.)

25. *GG,* July 19, 1946. Spencer Love had begun his career as a textile chainbuilder in Gastonia in 1923. Six months after this 1946 editorial the *Gazette* carried an Associated Press article headlined, "Yanks Gobbling Dixie Textiles," and stating that 41.4% of the cotton textile industry in North and South Carolina was "controlled by . . . New York, Philadelphia and Boston financiers, either through outright buying of mills or stock transactions." Ten percent of all spindles in North Carolina and over 20% of spindles in South Carolina "passed to outside control" in the single year of 1946. *GG,* February 11, 1947.

26. Cf. above, note 21.

27. Cf. above, Preface, pp. 22-23.

28. Don Oberdorfer, *The Charlotte Observer,* August 14, 1957, as reprinted by the *GG,* August 15, 1957. Oberdorfer illustrated this development in a North Carolina textile firm that in 1953 "sank a big wad of money in new equipment" and was able to produce with thirty-five workers the quantity of cloth currently being produced by a competitor firm with seventy workers.

29. *Ibid.*

30. Herman D. Ruhm, Jr., President of Burlington Mills, by then renamed Burlington Industries, in a speech to the New York Security Analysts, reported in the *GG,* December 18, 1956. He went on to claim: "Thus our ability to overproduce—long a bugaboo of our industry—is about gone."

31. Figures from U.S. Employment Commission for 1945 and from North Carolina Employment Commission for 1960. Figures included estimates of all employed persons, including agricultural workers and domestics. Cf. also U.S. Department of Commerce Bureau of the Census. *County Business Patterns,* 1945, 1960, and 1970 and above, Tables 2.3, 2.4, and 2.5.

32. An industrial survey completed by the Gastonia Chamber of Commerce and released on the day after Hiroshima's destruction went far to substantiate this dominance, though, ironically, Chamber officials purported to be demonstrating in the new statistics the diversification already achieved in the county. The local textile industry, said the survey, was increasingly able to carry the apparel-manufacturing process beyond the stage of spinning into knitting and weaving. In all, of the 139 firms and corporations doing business in "Greater Gastonia," 61 are producers of textile goods; 48 are in the field of foundries, machinery manufacturers, and machine service and repair shops; and 30 are concerned with miscellaneous products. It was only these latter 30 that an outsider would ordinarily recognize as among Gastonia's "diversified" industries. Many of the machine shops serviced other-than-local plants, but the bulk of their business was tied to the textile industry. One significant clue to the pattern of future change in the county as a whole, however, lies in the fact that of the 44 countywide industries listed as "miscellaneous" in the Chamber survey, 30 were located in "Greater Gastonia." As the largest town in the county, Gastonia would continue to be the place where diversification, such as it was, would tend to concentrate in the years to come. The 1948 survey located almost half (61) of the county's 124 textile mills in "Greater Gastonia." *GG,* August 7, 1945.

33. *GG,* June 19, 1946. Among the more prominent mills and their proportion of once-severed-and-now-employed veterans were the following:

Mills	Workers entering armed service	Veterans employed, June '46
Textiles, Inc.	908	228
Burlington	225	159
Firestone	545	402
Gas. Combed Yarn	327	76
National Weaving	245	66
Smyre Mfg. Co.	82	29

Note the high proportion of evident returns to Burlington and Firestone, the low proportions to the other mills.

34. *GG,* January 20, 1945. Yet another subtlety in the argument was the rarely articulated comparison between Gastonia and nearby urbanizing Charlotte. "What Has Charlotte Got That We Haven't as Much Of? Not a Thing in the World Except the Will to Grow . . . We've Been Asleep, Too Long, This Side of the River." *GG,* January 22, 1946.

35. *GG,* January 27, 1945.

36. In a laudatory article, *The Manufacturers Record* of May 1952, termed the new G.I.D.C. "a tax-supported arm of the private-budget Gastonia Chamber of Commerce." Some 1200 Gastonia Township residents registered for this special election, or 2.7% of a population of approximately 44,000. The tax passed 801-384. (*GG,* June 20, 1945) The resulting annual budget of the G.I.D.C. was $11,000. The Commission itself was composed of seven members: two appointed by the Jaycees, two by the Senior Chamber of Commerce, and three at-large members appointed by the previous four.

37. The "sizable industry" was a subsidiary of Textiles, Inc.—Threads, Inc., whose management engaged in an extended controversy with the city government over the latter's insistence that the company remedy the pollution caused by effluents from the plant. It is very dubious that this company ever seriously considered moving away from Gastonia. Cf. *GG,* March 14, 1945.

38. Chairman of the Commission was Charles D. Gray, Sr., Chairman of the Board of Textiles, Inc. As an example of diversification, Gray hailed the organization (by a local spinning firm) of a cloth-knitting company. "Such developments as this are directly in line with the program of our diversification committee (*sic*), which is placing the emphasis on textiles-related diversification in the initial phase of our efforts." *GG,* May 1, 1945.

39. Cf. below, Chapter Five, pp. 194-199.

40. *GG,* May 26, 1950.

41. *GG,* May 29, 1950.

42. Cf. below, Chapter Five, p. 198.

43. For the statistics that substantiate this generalization, cf. Tables 2.3, 2.4, and 2.5. Table 2.4 shows a steady climb in the proportion of persons in the county and the city who in the 1940-70 period were employed in the categories of: Professional-Technical, Proprietors, Clerical, Craftsmen, and Service Workers; and a steady decline in the percentage of persons employed as: Farmers, Operatives, Domestic Service, Farm Laborers, and other Laborers.

44. Correspondence with authors, January, 1975.

45. *Ibid.*

46. One such industry assembled electrical circuits and was known to Shriver through a member of his congregation who worked there in the late fifties. Its equipment was moved from a plant site in New Jersey to an abandoned mill in west Gastonia. It employed 500 people in semi-skilled work that involved pay, supervision, and high temperatures that were the subjects of widespread complaint among workers. Within several years, the company closed its Gastonia operation.

47. Interview, March 31, 1971. "The same thing happened to another plant—Talon Zipper," said our informant. "They actually came to Belmont and located there in the basement of one of the cotton houses. But, you see, Belmont is peculiar in that it does not own its own water works, its own water filtering system. It too is owned by the mills and in this manner they pretty well control who comes in and who doesn't." This is a characterization of the paternalistic ethos that obtains on this eastern side of the county in much the same way as it did in Pope's generation. The city of Gastonia, by some contrast, increasingly shows the marks of differentiation of economic-political control structures. Belmont would be an outstanding example of a part of Gaston County whose leaders "changed reluctantly or not at all" in face of external economic pressures during this period. (Above, p. 72).

48. The writers know from personal conversations with executives in both the local and the national-chain mills that the two groups of managers perceive each other with feelings that are rather predictable between persons representing organizations with great differences in power. The chain-manager who sojourns in Gastonia on his way up the corporate ladder is often perceived by local leaders as not really belonging to the community; and, on his side, the chain manager is likely to feel some scorn for the technical and managerial antiquation of the local mills.

49. *GG,* May 26, 1944.

50. Typical of speeches made to the Gaston County Personnel Association (organized in 1947), this particular statement was made by the personnel director of the state's then largest bank. In the same speech he suggested that one should not talk of labor-management "peace," because the word "peace" implied "opposed viewpoints." One should rather talk of "labor-management understanding." *GG,* January 10, 1947.

51. Chapter Seven.

52. Personal observation by Shriver.

53. Interview, July 22, 1965.

54. Personal conversation with Shriver, Spring 1957.

55. So characterized by industry spokesmen in *Textile Hi-Lights* (ATMI), Spring, 1971, p. 1. According to this same publication (June 1972, p. 13), net after taxes profits on textile mill products declined nationally from a high of $702 million in 1966 to a low of $413 million in 1970. National textile employment declined by 4.1% between 1969 and 1971, manufacturing employment in general by 7.7%. (ATMI, June 1972, p. 22). Profit-per-dollar of sales continued to be a little over half of the profit for manufacturing as a whole, but profit on stockholders' equity was about two-thirds of the all-manufacturing average. (*Ibid.*, p. 13.)

56. The all manufacturing average wage rose from $3.01 in 1968 to $3.57 in 1971, an increase of 18%; textile wages, from $2.21 in 1968 to $2.57 in 1971, an increase of 16%. (U.S. Department of Labor Statistics, quoted by ATMI, June 1975.) In May 1975 the comparable figures were $4.73 (32% over 1971) and $3.33 (26% over 1971).

57. For example, in the "bad" year of 1970, Burlington Industries added a thousand employees to its worldwide workforce of over 87,000. The mammoth company could boast a 3% increase in its sales and the continuation from 1969 of its stock dividends for $1.40 per share. In this same year, Textiles, Inc., still the dominant locally owned group of mills in Gaston County, kept its dividends steady. The latter's total business had doubled from 1960 to 1970; it sales rose from $67 to $85 million in the year 1971 alone, and its net earnings some 44%. (*GG,* January 20, January 27, and November 10, 1971.)

58. *GG,* January 27, 1971.

59. At least' one of the small mills subsequently reopened, a phenomenon that moved the Raleigh-based *News and Observer* to remark that under a cover of "closing" a number of mills were in fact retooling for product diversification, while helping the propaganda campaign of the industry against the growing competitive threat of foreign imports.

60. During the fifties and sixties the city motto had been: "The City of Growing Beauty." On the comparative economic statistics, cf. *GG,* January 14, 1971. The contrast between Gaston and Mecklenburg counties was calculated for all ESC-insured workers as $134.43 for Mecklenburg against $107.71 for Gaston. Construction workers in Gaston averaged only $113.11 per week in contrast to the statewide average of $123.57. Only in the category of transportation, utility, and communication workers did the county wage structure top the statewide average—$157.98 to $138.86.

61. Cf. below, Chapter Five, Table 5.2, p. 188

62. *GG,* August 8, 1970.

63. This was the opinion of a labor market analyst of the Charlotte office of the North Carolina Employment Security Commission in an interview, February 25, 1975. She pointed out that the actual rate of unemployment was undoubtedly higher than 19% in Gaston County, because the official rate includes only those who are insured under the ESC. Unemployment was considerably lower in Charlotte and Mecklenburg County, she suggested, because of higher industrial diversification in this neighboring county. Furthermore, as a UPI news article of late February pointed out, the unemployment statistic does not cover the equally grim reality of *under*employment in the textile and other plants of the community. "Many of the 77,000 persons (in Gaston County) considered employed are working less than three days a week." The article summarizes the rapid shift in local economic circumstance: "The industry that provided the community with one of the lowest unemployment rates in the nation a year ago now sends its workers to the unemployment lines in record numbers." (*Winston-Salem Journal,* February 21, 1975.) The economic reporter of the *GG,* Mr. Lyle Edwards, estimated in January 1975 that 4,000 textile workers in the county had been "laid off permanently and another 4,000 or 5,000 are on short time." (Letter to authors, January 17, 1975). From December 1973 through January 1975, national textile workers dropped from 908,000 to 756,000, or by 17%. Layoff and short-time work-patterns reduced the man-hours of production workers by 27%, according to TWUA Research Director George Perkel (*Textile*

Labor, Vol. 36, No. 6 June 1975), pp. 17, 18. Textile unemployment nationally (in January 1975) and in Gaston County were exactly matched at 19% (*Ibid.*).

64. *GG,* August 11, 1975.

65. *GG,* December 9, 1970.

66. Cf. below, Chapter Five, pp. 178 ff.

67. *GG,* January 20, 1971. A 20% absenteeism rate was reported for these mills also.

68. *GG,* April 2, 1970.

69. *GG,* September 17, 1970. But the school graduated sixty-six people in June 1974, at which time the school director stressed that offers of salary to graduates averaged about $10,000 per year, and the top offer of the class ($15,000) had gone to a much-sought-after black supervisor. (*GG,* June 21, 1974)

70. *GG,* June 17, 1971. One of the grants totaling $178,000 was from the U.S. Labor Department to a subsidiary of Textiles, Inc. for on-the-job training.

71. The first phrase was used in a news article on the labor shortage in the *GG,* May 6, 1971; the second by a national textile leader in a speech in January 1970.

72. Interview with North Carolina textile mill manager (not from Gaston County) August 12, 1972. By 1974 the labor shortage in some North Carolina communities—such as Hickory—was so severe that the local business people had adopted a temporary "no more industry" policy for their locales. (Interview with Mr. Scott Hoyman, Southern Director of the Textile Workers Union of America, April 24, 1975.)

73. The evidence on this prediction is mixed. The personnel manager of one plant in the Textiles, Inc. chain, in early 1975, complained that many unemployed textile workers were taking their full allowance of unemployment insurance in preference to available jobs, and that his company was finding it difficult to recruit workers.

74. *GG,* September 17, 1970.

75. As this is written, on the other hand, a series of bilateral agreements with far-eastern countries, passed under the Nixon Administration, plus two devaluations of the dollar on the international market, were easing the threat of overseas competition to the American textile industry. According to Scott Hoyman, Regional Director of the Textile Workers Union of America, cries against "foreign imports" have considerably diminished among industry and labor leaders alike. Rising labor costs in both Europe and Japan, furthermore, have made it profitable for industrialists in those regions to set up manufacturing operations, some textile-related, in the American South. The world's largest zipper factory, for example, is Japanese-owned and located in Macon, Georgia. (Hoyman interview, April 24, 1975.) TWUA officials have consistently been strong public supporters of the view that "any reduction in tariffs would have a particularly devastating effect on the textile industry." (A statement made by Research Director George Perkel before the U.S. International Trade Commission in early 1975, according to the union paper, *Textile Labor,* June 1975, Vol. 36, No. 6.), pp. 17, 18.

Chapter Three

Progress:
An Overview of the Churches, 1940-1975

The ethos of capitalism has a handy index to entrepreneurial progress: the black-or-red reading of the "bottom line." This straightforward financial test has vast prestige inside most business communities, verging occasionally towards an "ultimate concern." Whether in terms of everyday business enthusiasm,[1] or elaborated into a quasi-religious philosophical system,[2] the financial *description* is widely alleged to tell "the real story" of business enterprise. The very fact that statistics on the profits and losses of individual textile companies are hard to get from a corporate office itself demonstrates how value-saturated is the financial profile of a company in the minds of its managers.

We know from many studies of the meaning of work, money, and work-status among Americans, however, that no financial description in fact captures the full story of either the individual or the institutional reality of human life in an insurance company, an auto assembly plant, or a cotton mill. The personnel relations movement assumed as much; and, more dramatically, the American war effort of the forties. The daily activities of mill workers and mill managers assume the same, though the full reading on those activities is even harder to make than the reading on wages and profits.

Industrial spokesmen themselves fuel their own preferred image as hard-nosed moneymakers by stoutly denying, on occasion, that anything else but money motivates them in their work. One of the writers encountered a clear illustration of this in conversation with the group of Gastonia textile executives already quoted above.[3] Early in the conversation the executive of a successful locally owned mill pointed to other members of the group and said with pride, "You know, my biggest objective is to put these other men out of business. We are all competing for the same dollar." An hour later in the discussion, the question of how to manage the problem of aging, obsolescent employees came up. The same executive offered an example of such an employee, fifty-five years old, unable to keep pace with the new high-speed textile machinery.

"How long have you had this problem with him?"

"Oh, about five years," replied the executive.

"He is losing you money?"

"Yes indeed."

"So if moneymaking is what you're about, and efficient competition, why haven't you fired him long ago?"

He paused. "Well, I guess we just haven't had the heart to fire him."

If we took Gregg Cherry at his word and linked the cause of religion to "the weak and the poor"[4] and accepted too his designation of this emphasis as the religious dimension of "Progress," we must say by definition that something religious was preventing this executive from applying the standard of economic profitability wholeheartedly to this obsolescent employee. Or we could recollect the paternalistic ideology of Progress, and say that this is a holdover from managerial *noblesse oblige*. However defined, this inconsistency between the proclaimed philosophy of the executive and his self-reported conduct needs an explanation. One general explanation is that this industrial man does not live by profits alone; he lives by a complex of other values as well.

Just what complex of concerns, some ultimate, such persons live by, is one class of data we value as students of the sociology of religion in Gastonia. In Pope's generation—in a local ethos that embraced mill-supported churches and worship services on the factory floor—that data was ostensibly available in abundance. Yet even then, like other industrial employees in America, few persons in the textile industry gave much socially organized energy to articulating the religious meaning of their work during their time at work. As members of a differentiated society, they expected religious symbols to surface publicly in churches; economic symbols to dominate the surface of their workplaces. But to penetrate the surface of *either* institution, our model of society strongly suggests, is to detect kindred realities in both. Just as industry has its ideological and religious dimensions, churches have their economic and political dimensions. One must describe as best one can the totality of dimensions on both sides, if one is accurately to describe the industries and the churches of any community.[5]

As we launch our probe into the religious institutions of Gastonia over the past generation, therefore, we have to be concerned with at least three classes of data: (1) The statistics of membership and financial growth, formally parallel to our interest in the financial and work-force profiles of the industrial history. (2) Data on the distribution of the population between church-attenders and non-attenders; patterns of denominational loyalties; and patterns of congregational membership related to social class. Such an interest is analogous to an inquiry into the changing structure of the local economy in terms of industrial diversification, income levels, and job-status changes, all of which are themselves significant contributors to the reality and the dynamics of class divisions in any community. (3) Data on the culture, or symbol-system, which is intimately related to what the churches claim as their major "product"—the religious person and the religious community. Here we can be systematic about the churches in an area where, for the economic order, we have to be impressionistic. What is implicit about human existence in a cotton mill—its ultimate meaning—becomes apparently explicit in the churches, whose stock-in-trade, so to speak, is the public display of the symbols of religious faith. The pre-eminent occasion for that display, from the standpoint of the churches themselves, is public worship. So this first overview of the churches concludes with some general descriptions of the varieties of "symbolic lifestyles" that can be detected among the churches as a whole.

Church Expansion:
Thirty Years of Institutional Growth

Evidence on the growth of religious institutions in Gastonia over the past generation is available from many sources, though few data are as dramatic as those concerning the number of church organizations. In 1939, there were approximately 150 religious groups in the county, providing one congregation for every 580 residents—men, women, and children. By 1969, the number of congregations had increased to over 300, lowering the ratio to one for each 495 people, despite an increase of 70% in the population of the county. This congregation-population ratio becomes even more impressive when membership is considered, since the six largest congregations in the county claim a total of over 7,500 members and combined membership of the twenty largest congregations is 17,000.[6] Removing these persons from the population reduces the ratio even more, to a congregation for every 475 persons, or an average of 100 fewer persons per congregation than in 1939. By contrast, the national ratio is approximately one congregation for every 620 people.[7]

The data on denominations indicate that Baptists and sect groups have experienced considerable expansion, with relatively slight growth in other major denominations. Baptist churches numbered 40 in 1939 and 90 in 1969, comprising 25 and 30% of all local congregations respectively in those years. The number of sect groups increased from about 40 in 1939, or about 25% of all religious organizations, to perhaps 120 congregations and about 40% of the total in 1969. By contrast, Episcopal, Lutheran, Methodist, Presbyterian, and Roman Catholic congregations comprised half of the religious groups in 1939, but only one-fourth of the total in 1969.[8]

While figures such as these concerning church organizations are important in determining organizational trends, they are somewhat deceptive. Religious groups, particularly those of sectarian origin and character, are easily formed and just as easily dissolved. A group created through the work of a visiting evangelist or through the efforts of a local resident who receives a "call" to preach may soon come to grief *vis à vis* the social realities of the community. There is little doubt that sectarian groups in Gastonia experience serious challenges to their continuity and persistence: nearly half of the 84 identifiable sectarian organizations that were begun between 1940 and 1965 had been dissolved by 1969.[9] Those that have persisted in one location have frequently altered their names to coincide with a new insight or a new loyalty. In addition, many of the sect groups in the community are small, and it is difficult to assess the degree to which organizational visibility actually indicates a viable religious group. Only three of twenty sectarian-type meetings visited during field research had more than 100 people in attendance; and for half of the services, fewer than 50 persons were present. One can only conclude that the continued existence of a sect group in Gastonia is tenuous, and is often made even more problematic by the zeal of other religious groups in seeking converts from any source, including from other sects.

For those denominations which gather data from local churches,[10] information concerning the number of churches, number of members, and per capita contributions of all congregations in Gaston County for the 1939-1969 period are presented in Table 3.1. While all of the groups included in the comparisons had some growth during this period, the increases are concentrated in certain groups. Baptists more than doubled in terms of number of churches and members; and Wesleyan Methodists, Episcopalians, and Roman Catholics, though much smaller bodies, also experienced considerable expansion. While the number of United Methodist churches doubled, their total membership has remained relatively stable since 1949. Lutheran and Presbyterian groups have grown at about the same rate as the population of the county generally, and relatively few new churches of these denominations have been established. Two Presbyterian churches in Gastonia were dissolved and merged with other local churches during 1969, and two long-struggling Presbyterian churches in old mill-village areas were dissolved in this same period—symbols of the difficulty which this and other upper middle class denominations encounter in their attempt to build stable church organizations in communities composed mostly of industrial workers.

A comparison of the average contribution per member indicates that an increase in economic level among Gaston County residents in the last 30 years is reflected in the giving of members in every group. (See Table 3.2.) The average per member contribution in 1969 was at least six times that of 1939,

Table 3.1

PATERNS OF WHITE CHURCH MEMBERSHIP AND CONTRIBUTIONS IN GASTON
COUNTY FOR YEARS 1939, 1949, 1959, AND 1969, BY DENOMINATION

Denomination	Number of Churches	Number of Members	Average Size of Churches	Average Contribution per Member[1]
Baptist				
1939	38	13,725	361	$ 11.93
1949	56	20,350	363	45.69
1959	79	30,801	380	60.87
1969	90	36,435	405	95.53
Percent Increase[2]	137	165	12	701
Episcopal				
1939	3	340	113	$ 11.66
1949	3	421	140	170.33
1959	5	673	135	79.20
1969	5	749	150	150.69
Percent Increase[2]	67	120	33	1278
Lutheran				
1939	10	2,904	290	$ 10.71
1949	11	3,242	295	48.09
1959	12	4,578	382	117.24
1969	14	5,319	380	115.58
Percent Increase[2]	40	83	31	989
Methodist				
1939	17	7,923	466	$ 12.47
1949	21	10,368	494	30.77
1959	27	10,297	381	61.33
1969	32	10,192	318	90.67
Percent Increase[2]	90	27	-32	605
Presbyterian: US				
1939	17	3,399	200	$ 25.88
1949	25	4,340	174	77.39
1959	25	6,161	246	134.50
1969	23	6,170	268	150.90
Percent Increase[2]	35	81	34	483
Presbyterian: AR				
1939	5	1,053	211	NA
1949	5	1,388	278	$108.85
1959	5	1,400	280	83.65
1969	5	1,515	303	164.16
Percent Increase[2]	—	44	43	—
Roman Catholic				
1939	2	451	226	NA
1949	2	606	303	NA
1959	3	1,194	398	NA
1969	3	1,594	533	$ 50.20
Percent Increase[2]	50	253	136	—
Wesleyan (Methodist)				
1939	5	307	61	$ 45.48
1949	5	591	118	224.56
1959	7	777	111	142.92
1969	8	971	121	364.90
Percent Increase[2]	60	223	100	702

[1] Source: Official reports made by churches to denominational offices.
Building funds are included in the total, thereby inflating the average
giving, especially in smaller groups.

[2] 1939-1969   NA = Not Available

Table 3.2

COMPARATIVE DATA RERGARDING SIZE, CONTRIBUTIONS PER MEMBER, AND VALUE OF CHURCH PROPERTY FOR FOUR CHURCH TYPES, 1939, 1949, AND 1969

	Type of Church*			
	Uptown	Transitional	Middle Class	Black
Average Size of Congregation**				
1939	786 (6)	435 (13)	217 (6)	NA
1949	977 (6)	431 (18)	217 (10)	NA
1959	1,166 (6)	509 (20)	255 (15)	NA
1969	1,175 (6)	420 (22)	324 (18)	235 (5)
Average Contribution per Member				
1939	$ 22.66	$ 12.27	$ 14.34	NA
1949	78.48	60.13	50.42	NA
1959	115.90	63.79	88.16	NA
1969	129.68	112.96	149.03	$63.04
Average Value of Church Property**				
1939	$106,900 (6)	$ 20,600 (2)	$ 47,000 (2)	NA
1949	221,646 (6)	29,046 (3)	42,250 (2)	NA
1959	553,000 (6)	194,650 (4)	173,742 (3)	NA
1969	874,700 (6)	333,325 (4)	238,287 (5)	$100,000 (4)

*Data for sect type congregations not available.

**Number in parentheses refers to the number of units used to compute the average.

though if these figures are computed so as to take inflation into account the 1969 giving is approximately three times that of 1939.[11] Further, consistent with data from other studies, the reported per capita giving of the Wesleyan Methodist congregations is over twice that of any other denomination, and nearly $275 more per person than for the United Methodists. Unfortunately there are no data by which comparisons can be made with sect-type groups such as the Church of God or the Assembly of God.[12]

These data provide unmistakable evidence of the institutional vitality of the churches in Gastonia. Given these data, one is not surprised to learn from a random sample of Gastonians that the great majority of them tend to be active church participants. As seen in Table 3.3, half of the white residents and over 60% of the blacks attend church weekly. On the relationship of social class and church attendance, however, when comparisons are made among the class groups in our sample, no easy conclusions are possible: Gastonians in our

Table 3.3

PROPORTION ATTENDING CHURCH WEEKLY, BY SOCIAL CHARACTERISTICS

Social Characteristics	Race and Sex							
	Black				White			
	Male Percent	N	Female Percent	N	Male Percent	N	Female Percent	N
Total	65.0	60	61.1	72	48.4	180	55.5	92
Income								
Less than $4,000	66.7	21	69.2	26	50.0	18	44.8	29
$4,000-$6,999[a]	53.3	15	(71.4)	(7)	47.8	67	53.3	15
$7,000-$9,999[b]	—	—	—	—	72.2	18	44.4	18
$10,000 and over	—	—	—	—	47.3	55	—	—
Occupation								
High white collar[c]	—	—	—	(3)	59.3	59	(71.4)	(7)
Low white collar	—	—	—	—	40.9	22	77.8	27
High blue collar[d]	59.6	47	60.0	50	47.4	19	41.9	31
Low blue collar	—	—	—	—	40.0	65	—	—
Education								
8 years or less	67.6	37	66.7	39	49.0	51	47.4	38
9-11 years	64.3	14	56.3	16	36.6	41	55.6	18
High school grad[e]	(55.6)	(9)	64.3	14	56.8	37	60.0	15
Some college or more	—	—	—	—	50.0	50	65.0	20
Age								
39 or less	54.5	11	55.6	18	44.4	54	45.5	33
40-49	57.9	19	68.4	19	53.1	49	60.9	23
50-59	46.7	15	61.4	13	45.7	46	57.9	19
60 and over	0.0	13	58.3	12	53.8	26	62.5	16
Length of Residence								
Less than 20 years	(71.4)	(7)	(68.7)	(8)	17.0	53	36.4	22
20 years or more	62.3	53	60.0	60	49.6	123	66.2	65

a. For blacks, $4,000 and over
b. For white females, $7,000 and over
c. For blacks, white collar respondents are combined
d. For blacks and white females, blue collar respondents are combined
e. For blacks, high school grad or more

sample professed a remarkably uniform degree of attendance at church weekly. With one or two exceptions, all white groups attended weekly in proportions between 40 and 55%. The most important of all exceptions are high and low white collar employed women and men in the income-category group of $7,000-$9,999: almost three-fourths of these groups record weekly church attendance. Significantly, the longtime residents of Gastonia—twenty years or more—are three times as likely to attend church this frequently as are residents of less than twenty years. This is statistical confirmation of the assertion that religion is "one of the prevailing winds in Gastonia."[13] The long-term residents apparently perceive church-going as "one of the things people do" in the community; it is a major current in the culture, attracting most of those persons who intend to live in the mainstream.

Religious Institutions:
Their Social Composition

Over the past generation, perhaps the single most important sociological change in the signs that *identify* the "class" of an individual in the popular mind in Gastonia has been the decline of the mill village. In the ten years following 1945, the houses in virtually every mill village in the town of Gastonia were sold to individual owners, although this trend was slow to take hold in some of the outlying towns.[14] The old amoeba-cluster pattern of urban organization might still have been apparent from the airplane-view of the county in 1970, but the equation "mill house=mill worker" no longer matched social reality. Even by 1950, families with two members (typically a husband and a wife) in unskilled or semi-skilled jobs could accumulate the downpayment on a modest suburban house. The addition of a second-hand car to family assets then provided mobility, expanded job-access, and—correlatively—expanded church-access. A glance at the pattern of colored pins on the city map that hangs on the wall of many a minister's study in Gastonia speaks volumes about the change from the old days of the "mill church": residentially, the church's members have exploded outward from the local community; now they live all over town.

It is within this new social context that the composition of religious groups becomes important in understanding the role of churches in the community. As in Pope's generation, the churches continue to reflect the social divisions of the larger community. Most notably, in 1970, few blacks attended or participated in predominantly white churches; and few, if any, whites were involved in the programs or activities of churches in the black community, despite the attention that has been focused upon segregation in the church. Similarly, occupational and economic levels continued to be important factors in shaping the style of institutional church life, as will be illustrated below.

The large uptown churches remain in a position of prominence, but they no longer dominate the religious activities of the community as in the past. Rural churches, in several instances, have become city churches by the expansion of the city; and, in other cases, they have become similar to city churches in program due to the impact of the urban area upon their memberships. Former mill village churches, faced with the problems of continuity that affect sectarian groups generally, have evolved toward more traditional forms or have ceased to exist. Among mill workers and poorer residents, especially those in the older mill village areas, newly established sect groups continue to emerge and replace the earlier mill churches which are now in a transition from earlier years.[15] Churches in new suburban neighborhoods, founded in response to the growth of population, reflect the educational level and sophistication of the middle-class constituency to which they direct their appeal. This feature sets them apart, since in the Gastonia of the '70s, when two members of a family working in a mill together earn $10,000 or more, "mill worker" and "middle class" are no longer strictly antithetical. In addition, as we shall see, black churches (given no attention at all by Pope) have become increasingly active and visible in the larger community through their support for the civil rights movement.

It seems appropriate in contemporary Gastonia therefore to identify in rough fashion, five sociologically-defined categories of religious groups —*uptown*,[16] *transitional, middle-class, sect*,[17] and *black*.[18] These types reflect the social divisions of the community and generally encompass the social diversity of churches in the city.

To obtain a social-class profile of the five types, we have analyzed the membership lists of several churches in each of the five categories, classifying the occupations of the heads of the families into general occupational groups. Professional, managerial, clerical, sales, craftsmen or foremen, operatives, service workers, and common labor comprised the eight basic categories. Persons in military service, farming, and unemployed persons, together constituting fewer than one percent of the total in every church, were eliminated from the analysis.

Data for each type of religious group are presented in Table 3.4, illustrating the occupational profile of the membership among the various religious institutions in Gastonia. Among the membership of uptown churches, fewer than one in five families is in a blue-collar occupation, while over 80% of families in sectarian groups are headed by persons in blue-collar jobs. This relationship between class and religious institutions is further elaborated in Table 3.5, in which a different classification is used. The membership list of each church in the various categories was divided into a four-fold grouping of upper white-collar (professional and managerial), lower white-collar (clerical and sales), upper blue-collar (foreman and craftsmen) and lower blue-collar (operatives, service workers, and laborers). Employing a formula comparable to that used by Pope,[19] a minority membership was defined as at least 15% of the entire sample in any of the occupational categories. The conclusions are clear: no uptown church had a minority of either upper or lower white-collar members;

Table 3.4

OCCUPATIONAL DISTRIBUTION OF MEMBERSHIP BY
TYPE OF CHURCH, IN PERCENT

Occupational Category	Type of Church				
	Uptown	Transitional	Middle-Class	Sect	Black
Professional, Technical, and Kindred	16.6%	3.6%	7.5%	0.7%	14.8%
Managers, Officials, and Proprietors	32.7	13.5	21.0	6.4	3.5
Clerical and Kindred	15.5	13.5	11.3	8.5	2.3
Sales	16.0	9.2	11.0	2.1	3.5
Craftsmen, Foremen, and Kindred	11.2	24.4	20.4	18.4	9.6
Operatives and Kindred	3.0	17.7	11.6	44.7	8.1
Service: All Types	3.0	6.6	6.8	7.1	34.8
Laborers	2.0	11.5	10.4	12.1	23.5
TOTAL	100.0	100.0	100.0	100.0	100.1
Number					
Units*	1790	1057	663	141	345
Churches	6	6	10	2	3

*Number of occupational units (usually family units) upon which the percentage in each category is based.

the three black churches have a minority of upper white-collar and lower blue-collar members but none in the intermediate categories; and transitional and middle-class churches are the most diverse congregations in terms of occupational levels.

Five Styles of Church Life: Programmatic and Symbolic Accents

Few church leaders in Gastonia would divide the congregations of the city into five such groups, and few would describe their own congregations with just the accents evident below. Likewise, few will have had the opportunity of the social investigator who visits Sunday morning or Wednesday evening church

Table 3.5

MINORITY MEMBERSHIP IN CHURCHES OF VARIOUS TYPES, BASED
ON CONGREGATIONAL OCCUPATIONAL LEVEL

| | Number of Churches [1] | | Occupational Level | | | |
| | | | Upper White | Lower White | Upper Blue | Lower Blue |
Type of Church	Total	Sample	Collar	Collar	Collar	Collar
Uptown	6	6	6	6	0	0
Transitional	30	6	3	5	6	6
Middle-Class	25	10	9	8	8	9
Sect	38	2	0	1	2	2
Black	18	3	3	0	0	3

[1]Total churches is the number of churches in the city of Gastonia in this classification. Sample is the number included in the data in the table.

services, interviews church members, and looks at congregational records with the purpose of constructing an overview of the varieties of religious organization in the community as a whole. Every typification below borrows data from more than one congregation in the respective category and, in doing so, does some injustice to particulars. Such composite descriptions are the necessary and inadequate formulations to which both history and sociology must resort. For lack of "types," we would have the impossible task of describing all 300 organized religious groups in Gaston County. As far as the observing eye and listening ear can determine, however, these groups do share certain common characteristics, which we seek to portray in the word pictures below.[20]

1. *The uptown church.*   The uptown church has a long history and tradition, dating back nearly to the founding of the city in the 1880s. Early growth of both the church and the city was slow, and organizational expansion began only with the establishment of the mills in the area. By the turn of the century, the uptown Gastonia church was the leading church of its denomination in the entire county, both in size and prominence of members. Membership has continued to expand, typically to over 1,000 members, drawn from residential areas throughout the city and including many civic leaders. With one exception, all of the uptown churches are located within a two-block area of downtown Gastonia. (The exception is the First Presbyterian Church, recently moved to the eastern side of the city and into a large new structure costing $1,500,000.)

The uptown building includes a sanctuary large enough to seat several hundred people and complete educational facilities. In one church, over seventy classes meet each Sunday, though most have fewer such groups. The program of the church is highly organized and includes adult, youth, and children's choirs; youth activities; and men's and women's groups as well as the traditional Sunday worship services. Numerous committees—over thirty in one uptown church—are required to direct this program in addition to the professional staff, a fact which emphasizes the dominance of religious education over revivalism as the primary means of adding members to the uptown church.

The staff is comprised of two or three full-time pastors and several other workers, supported by the contributions of the members that may total over $200,000 annually. The minister is viewed as a scholarly person, a leader in the community, and a man whose basic responsibility includes the confirmation and interpretation of past traditions. Tenure of pastors typically is long—one uptown church has had only five different pastors in seventy years.

Upper and upper-middle-class families dominate the church. Family heads tend to be in professional, managerial, or proprietary occupations; and nearly all of the officers of the church are in such occupational categories. Further, a large proportion of the congregation is college-educated, a fact that is reflected in the nature of the religious services.

On Sunday morning a visitor to an uptown church walks up concrete stairs flanked by neatly sculptured shrubbery. He or she is greeted at the door by an usher and escorted to a seat. The sanctuary has stained glass windows, carpeted floor, padded pews, and elaborately decorated pulpit furniture. About 500 people, most of whom are middle-aged or older, all well attired, are present for the prelude, written by a classical composer and skillfully played on a pipe organ. The printed bulletin indicates the order of service, but also lists a large number of board meetings and interest groups scheduled for the coming week. During a processional hymn, the robed choir enters, followed by the ministers. The service follows the printed program without introduction and is conducted with quiet dignity and formality. The atmosphere of the service is suffused with a sense of stability, permanence, and devotion to time-honored truth.

Some idea of the focus of sermons in uptown churches can be derived from an examination of titles of sermons preached at various times during the period under consideration. While any list is likely to be inadequate to cover the entire range of topics, the following titles[21] are illustrative of the concerns of pastors in uptown congregations.

"It's Easy to Be Discouraged" (March, 1947)
"The Blessing of Labor" (Labor Day Sunday, 1949)
"Is There to Be Another War?" (July, 1950)
"The Dignity of Duty" (Labor Day Sunday, 1951)
"On Being Lazy" (February, 1953)

"The Church and Labor" (Labor Day Sunday, 1953)
"Tell Them of Jesus" (February, 1954)
"Freedom" (July 4 Weekend, 1955)
"Work Is Necessary and Worthwhile" (Labor Day Sunday, 1958)
"How Much Is a Friend Worth?" (February, 1957)
"Prayer Brings Serenity" (February, 1958)
"The Virtue of Meekness" (February, 1960)
"How Christian Should We Try to Be?" (February, 1961)
"Thanks for Freedom" (July 4 Weekend, 1961)
"Learning from Judas" (February, 1964)
"By Grace I Am What I Am" (Labor Day Sunday, 1965)
"How Essential Is Religion?" (February, 1967)[22]

The uptown church is clearly the leading congregation of its denomination in Gastonia. It is largest in size, has a larger number of community leaders, and exerts more influence than other churches in the community. In relation to economic and political affairs, the uptown church has made peace with the dominant order, though the minister and some members may pursue activities which seek to modify the status quo. That the uptown church reflects the dominant culture of the community is not surprising because (1) so large a number of the dominant people of the community are among its members and (2) the uptown church itself has been among the shapers of the culture from the earliest years of the community.

2. *The transitional church.*   The transitional church began in a mill village during the 1920s or 1930s and has continued without interruption to the present time. A great majority of these congregations are Baptist or Methodist in affiliation, though other groups and denominations are also represented.

The typical transitional church has grown to about 500 members, comprised of persons and families who are heavily upper-blue-collar, with varied income and educational levels. About two-thirds of the members under the age of thirty are high school graduates, more than twice the percentage of older members who have high school educations. No longer do members' homes cluster around the church building. Many of the regular participants drive several miles, usually past other churches of the same denomination, to attend services at the transitional church. Leadership roles are primarily filled by these persons from outlying areas. Members who live nearby are mostly mill workers who do not provide the leadership that the minister believes to be necessary in a large congregation.

Once the mills made some sizeable financial contributions to these churches but no longer. Despite this lack of outside support, buildings tend to be new, well kept, smaller-scale versions of the uptown churches. Educational facilities used on Sunday may be available for a day care center or a community recreational program during the week.

The full-time staff typically includes one or two pastors and a secretary, plus numerous volunteer workers. The giving of the congregation may total $100,000 annually, though contributions in most churches are considerably below that amount. The pastor is not viewed as a scholar but as a spiritual guide and leader, whose role involves the cultivation and maintenance of loyal members. Tenure of pastors varies widely, from one to over ten years.

The congregation of the transitional church is composed primarily of mill workers or former mill workers who have since moved to middle-class suburban areas. This combination of mill and white-collar families is reflected in the character of the religious services.

The visitor approaches the building from a paved parking lot, is greeted by several people at the door, and is directed to a seat by an usher. The decor of the sanctuary indicates the moderate prosperity of the congregation. In addition to an organ, there is carpeting, a divided chancel, unpretentious but attractive stained glass windows, overhead medieval-style lights, and modern, simple, pulpit furniture. Present are about 250 well-dressed persons, mostly in their 30s and 40s. The mimeographed bulletin describes a rather formal structure for the service, with written and pastoral prayers, public affirmation of faith and scripture reading. In spite of the formal character of the order of service, it is frequently interrupted for announcements or other concerns. The sermon is well prepared and delivered with enthusiasm by the pastor.

Sermon titles from the 1940-1970 era illustrate the theological focus of transitional churches.

"A Workman That Needeth Not to Be Ashamed" (Labor Day Sunday, 1949)
"Heroic Faith in War Days" (July, 1950)
"Condemning and Forgiving" (Labor Day Sunday, 1953)
"Hath Not One God Created Us" (February, 1954)
"God and the Workingman" (Labor Day Sunday, 1955)
"A Respect for Life" (February, 1956)
"The Bible Has the Answer" (Labor Day Sunday, 1956)
"Lukewarm Christians not Wanted" (February, 1957)
"The Work of Our Hands" (Labor Day Sunday, 1960)
"A Place for Prayer" (February, 1962)
"Who Stole My God?" (Labor Day Sunday, 1965)

Sermons are directed toward problems that confront the members of the congregation individually and collectively, usually with a heavy emphasis upon biblical solutions to the problems. Authoritative statements by the minister are usually preceded by: "The Bible says . . . ."

The behavioral priorities often urged in the sermon include respect for the Sabbath, attendance at church, the need for a well-developed prayer life and greater concern for the lives of one's fellow workers. One sermon in the mid-sixties explored the religious dimensions of the decision some members were facing: to stay or to move when a black family moves into the neighborhood. The same sermon expressed concern for the sickness of a church member, and all present knelt to pray for his recovery.

The transitional church is neither a mill nor an uptown congregation, though it incorporates elements of each. The loyalty of the people appears to derive from a sense of need for a religious experience, typical of that found among sectarian groups; yet, the church does not emphasize the emotional aspects of conversion, nor does it have the financial insecurity and tenuous future that characterize the sect. Rather it mixes the old traditional religious emphases of the mill church with the more formal religious patterns supported by the better educated, upwardly mobile members, typical of uptown congregations.

3. *The middle class church.* The middle-class church is relatively new, emerging in the suburban areas that developed with the industrial expansion following World War II. Typically such a church was founded during the 1940s or 1950s and has experienced considerable growth during the past two decades. All of the middle-class churches are affiliated with one of the major denominations, and most were sponsored by one of the older, established congregations in "Greater Gastonia." The church which Shriver served in the 1950s belongs in this category.[23]

The congregation embraces the occupational diversity of its own neighborhood. In contrast to both the uptown and the transitional churches, the middle-class church has a preponderance of neither white-collar nor blue-collar families. The typical church has about 325 members; for those in existence for over ten years, the average is 350.

Almost every church has a newly-constructed building, though the facilities are not adequate if the older churches of the community are used for comparison. The members of middle-class churches tend to be both better educated and younger than those in transitional churches, but they are also much more mobile and less likely to be long-term residents of the city.

The staff of the church includes a pastor and perhaps a part-time student assistant. The budget may total $50,000, small enough to limit the church program but large enough to require the minister to encourage a high level of church loyalty. Much attention is directed toward participation and fellowship. The tenure of the pastor is relatively short, averaging less than five years. Often such a church is the one that a pastor will serve early in his career.

The congregation tends to live in the neighborhood near the church, with a minority driving from other areas. The recent origin of the organization precludes long-standing traditions of form or practice. As a result, social fellowship and participation in relatively informal church programs become the dominant factors in the middle-class church as its leaders seek to relate varied social levels to each other.

A visitor to a middle-class church service finds it akin to the uptown church, but on a much more informal level. The sanctuary is pleasantly if modestly decorated, with some carpet and modern furnishings. The bulletin indicates a formal order of worship reflecting the high educational level of the pastor and the congregation. The 200 people in attendance tend to be young—mostly in their 30s and 40s, well dressed, and attentive.

An examination of titles of sermons preached in middle-class churches provides some evidence of the concerns of both clergy and laymen in these congregations.

> "Work, a Mighty Anchor" (Labor Day Sunday, 1950)
> "A Beatitude for the Nation" (July 4 Weekend, 1951)
> "The Call to Decision" (February, 1954)
> "Author of Freedom" (July 4 Weekend, 1955)
> "Carpenters of the Kingdom" (Labor Day Sunday, 1957)
> "The Love That Passes and the Love That Lasts" (February, 1958)
> "This Nation Under God" (July 4 Weekend, 1959)
> "Let Me Work with Thee" (Labor Day Sunday, 1961)
> "The Mind of Christ" (February, 1963)

The middle-class church is distinctive in that it emerged as a religious group without a transition from a sectarian beginning. Its program resembles that of the uptown churches more than that of transitional churches. However, the presence of blue-collar and white-collar workers in equal numbers clearly distinguishes it from the uptown church and largely precludes the development of an institution which could be classified merely as a supporter of the established order. At the same time there is also little likelihood that a concerted, organized challenge to the dominant order will emerge from these congregations, largely because in terms of social class they are the most diverse, inclusive, and heterogeneous of the churches—perhaps of all organized groups—in the community.

4. *The sect.* Sectarian groups have been a prominent part of Gastonia's religious life since its earliest days. Mill churches, regardless of denomination, were frequently sectarian in character, and sect-type groups have continued to emerge especially among the poor and socially marginal of the city.

Geographically, sect groups have been centered in or near old mill villages, in inexpensive housing. Participants in sectarian services are predominantly local residents who attend because of the proximity of the church building to their homes. Most sectarian groups are dominated by mill workers or unskilled workers in mill-related industries. The building is often of concrete block construction, though some meet in old churches that have been abandoned or sold by groups with newer facilities. The building includes an auditorium, perhaps with washrooms for men and women, but no educational facilities. Services are frequent, long, and led by any one of several people. The preacher has an elementary school education and may have taken some correspondence courses from a Bible Institute. He remains with the group as long as he feels that he is being supported by the people, or until he receives a "call" to another work. There is little formal organization and no public accounting of the meager finances of the group. Contributions are often small, forcing the preacher to obtain employment in secular work in order to support himself and his family.

A visitor to a sectarian service climbs three wooden or cinderblock steps to enter a small, bare room which has old, unmatched pews seating 150 people. On one Thursday night in the middle of a week-long revival, about 60 people—including 10 children—are present at the time the service is scheduled to begin. Drums, a guitar, a piano, and an electronic organ are being played, the songs having pronounced rhythms which involve the audience almost involuntarily in clapping of hands, tapping of feet, or movement of the body. The mood of those in attendance is informal. A dozen teenagers sit together and talk, while the older people move freely about the room to talk to others.

A crudely constructed pulpit and a speaker's pew are on the platform at the front. Hanging on the wall to the right of the pulpit is a bulletin board announcing:

Offering Today	14.38
Attendance Today	74
Attendance Last Sunday	61
Offering Last Sunday	14.36
Monthly Offering	74.35

Opposite on the left is a sign with large letters,

JESUS SAVES. WHERE WILL YOU SPEND ETERNITY,
HEAVEN OR HELL?

The preacher and his two associates move to the platform from the audience where they have been talking and shaking hands, and the service begins. After announcing the song, one of the men moves about, all the time singing into the microphone which he holds close to his face. The beat of the music is pronounced, and the people present respond with a rhythmic clapping. A prayer follows, accompanied by shouts of "Hallelujah," "Praise God," "Yes, Jesus," "Glory," and is followed by another hymn, and then another, again with rhythmic participation by the audience. The mood of emotional excitement builds; and a young woman, about thirty-five, begins to moan and utter "hallelujah." Several persons move into the aisles, arms waving in the air, eyes closed, heads jerking. A man skips around the room, while several women stagger into walls and pews as if intoxicated, in an apparent state of ecstasy.

Songs follow in quick succession, each a seeming jumble of noise and confusion. As a prayer is begun, the people kneel and pray aloud, each oblivious to the words of the pastor, whose voice only occasionally can be heard above those of the congregation. During the rising and waning of the prayers, one little girl puts her fingers to her ears. Four or five teenagers join in. Suddenly, the prayer stops. Those present rise as if by signal and take seats in the pews. Testimonies follow, with people exhorted to "tell about what Jesus has done." Brother Charles tells of his hospitalization for tests, ending with the statement that the doctors "spent all this time and they scratched their heads and can't find anything for certain—but Jesus is certain and I'll rely on him." Others offer testimonies that are barely audible above the frequent shouts of "Amen," "Praise God," "Thank you, Jesus." Another song, a prayer, and the Scripture reading follow, punctuated by shouts of the audience. Yet another song is sung while an offering is being taken, following an appeal for enough money to take care of a special need known by the pastor. The contributions are counted, and another appeal is made for additional funds while the song continues through innumerable verses and choruses, finally ending with shouts of "Glory," "Hallelujah," "Praise God."

The sermon begins with the preacher describing the "foolishness of most people in the world" and their careless disdain of the "fact that Jesus died for them, to deliver them from hell." Certain themes appear repeatedly in his sermon: "salvation," "punishment of the evil in these last days," "the danger of giving in to the world," "God will see you through," "open your heart to Jesus." The faithful of God are pictured as being free from the bonds of religious doctrine and tradition, and willing to "let God go" by shouting, clapping, dancing, and singing.

An emotional pitch is reached at the end of the sermon. The preacher exhorts all who have not been saved to come forward. Though almost drowned out by the singing and clapping, his fervor increases, and before the hymn is over tears are streaming down his cheeks as he pleads: "I've done all I can now. I've told you. When your time to die comes, don't say that I didn't tell you. Don't say I didn't tell you. Don't say I didn't do what I could."

One young man steps out of a back pew and comes down the aisle to the altar and kneels. Soon he is followed by a few more young people, one girl about eight years old and others ranging up to eighteen, though most are about fifteen. As they come forward, the preacher continues his exhortation. They gather around the altar and various adults come to "back them up" in their struggles. Amid weeping, moaning, and praying, those who have come are prayed over and "prayed through." Until well past 11:00 P.M., the shouting continues.

The sect meeting is a dramatic contrast to the uptown church service. The object of the sectarian meeting is not to communicate a message, but rather to induce a religious experience. The attender is to experience the euphoria of "feeling at liberty" and "being free," without regard to church form or structure or traditions. On the one hand, the activities of many sectarian groups appear faintly contrived, a form of "patterned spontaneity," in which the people respond to cues and appeals in a consistent way. On the other, the sect offers a religious outlet for those who seek an experience, providing for them a sense of community, participation, and euphoria not present in the more formal services. Despite this communality of spirit there is no evidence to suggest that these groups represent a challenge to the established order. They are poorly organized; they lack resources; and their understanding of social reality is privatistic, nearly synonymous to that of their uptown counterparts.

5. *The black church.*   The black church has achieved greater community prominence in the last two decades than it enjoyed in 1939, due largely to the role these groups played during the civil rights struggles of the 1960s. However, civil rights activities were not supported by all black churches; indeed, as much diversity exists in the black religious institutions as among those in the white community. Unfortunately, the number of black churches in Gastonia is so small that classification into separate categories is impossible, as might be expected from the fact that these churches serve some 13% of the local population. However, it should be recognized that they virtually span the sociological categories used for white churches and could be distributed among them.

Large stable black congregations with several hundred members are found in Gastonia, as are small sect-type groups with a few faithful participants. Those local congregations that are affiliated with major denominations—AME Zion, Methodist, Baptist, Presbyterian—are highly organized. At the other extreme are those groups whose continuity is dependent upon the energy and charisma of their leaders. These groups differ in organization, theological and social perspective, training of clergymen, and the program within the church itself.

Clergymen in the black "uptown" churches all have college and seminary degrees. Pastors of sectarian groups typically are poorly educated, with at least one of them unable to recall a single day spent in school. The staff of the black church includes only the pastor, often assisted by a volunteer secretary and other workers. Contributions vary by type of congregation, from a few hundred dollars per year to thirty thousand dollars. Most of the ministers in the smaller congregations find it necessary to supplement their salaries through outside work or employment by their wives.

Lay leaders in the uptown black churches tend to be professionals and white-collar workers who comprise an important part of such congregations. These churches have as large a proportion of professionals among their members as the white uptown churches, but also have over two-thirds of their membership in lower blue-collar categories. Such social diversity is not found among any of Gastonia's white churches, nor among the black sect groups; and it has considerable significance for the type of activities that are supported by these church groups. Given such differences, agreement within these congregations regarding social or political postures is unlikely.

A visitor to a black uptown service enters the building and is seated by an usher. The sanctuary is large, old, and in need of repairs. At the front is a large choir loft and a pulpit, with a piano on the side being played by a young woman. The entrance of the choir and the minister signals the start of the service, which follows a regular pattern of hymns, prayers, special music, offering, and Scripture reading. The service is similar to that in non-sectarian white churches but is conducted with greater vocal participation by the congregation. Shouts of "Amen," "Yes, Lord," and "Yes, Jesus" punctuate the minister's prayers. In the sermon, as well as in the prayers, emphasis is placed upon the ability of the people to endure in spite of the pressures and threats under which they must live. The entire service gravitates around the capacity of the individual, with God's help, to resist evil and to overcome personal problems.

That the church continues to be an important factor in shaping the feelings and activities of blacks in Gastonia is quite apparent. Given the churches' heavy emphasis on personal religion, however, the inadvertent consequence of much church participation may be to maintain life as it currently exists for most. The civil rights struggle of 1963 was an outstanding exception to this generalization—a story to be told in Part II of this study.

NOTES

1. For example, Shriver became acquainted, in the mid-sixties, with the vice-president of a major national company who supervised plant managers in several parts of the world. This man routinely ended many of his long-distance telephone calls with the admonition, "Make money!"

2. The outstanding contemporary example of such a philosophy is that of Ayn Rand, who ends her novel *Atlas Shrugged* with the hero's sacred-canopy-creating gesture of raising his hand "over the desolate earth" and tracing "in space the sign of the dollar." (New York: The New American Library, Signet Books, 1957), p. 1084.

3. Cf. Preface, p. 13. The anecdote here was part of a series of some seven meetings over a nine months' period in 1966-67 between Shriver, eight textile executives from Gastonia, and two local ministers. The meetings were both an element of this research and part of a series of professional-ethics dialogues which Shriver was conducting with businessmen, politicians, and scientists during this period. The most direct and extended account of the conversation in this textile group can be found in a published case-study centered around the question of just and unjust modes of competition in the industry: Donald W. Shriver, Jr. and Ralph S. Robinson, Jr., "The Case of the Constant Customers," *Harvard Business Review,* Vol. 46, No. 4, pp. 150-158 (July-August 1968). Cf. also Shriver, "Business Ethics and Religious Ethics," *Religion in Life* Vol. 37, No. 3 (Autumn 1968), pp. 346-363.

4. Cf. above, Chapter One, p. 63.

5. For an outstanding study of the church from these multiple perspectives—political, economic, social, and religious-symbolic, cf. James Gustafson, *Treasure in Earthen Vessels: The Church as a Human Community* (New York: Harper and Brothers, 1961).

6. Data are taken from official denominational statistics for these years. The one Jewish temple in Gastonia is omitted from these data since it is the only non-Christian group and contains a large proportion of northern born and educated executives whose cultural heritage is typically non-Gastonian and non-southern.

7. Computed from data in *Yearbook of American Churches,* 1969 (New York: Council Press, 1969), p. 182.

8. These figures are based upon a variety of sources, including the *City Directory,* the *Gastonia Gazette,* official denominational reports, and personal interviews.

9. Sectarian organizations were identified in several ways—by names, reputation, or visits to services. It is recognized that such techniques have serious limitations; unfortunately, no adequate measure of sectarianism is available. Cf. footnote 17 below.

10. Given the conditions under which sects emerge and develop, it is obvious that precise data are not available concerning their size and growth. Unlike the major denominational bodies which gather statistics from member congregations, most sect groups either do not keep such records, or they guard them carefully from outsiders. As a result, data which would permit comparisons to other groups are largely lacking.

11. Based on changes in the consumer price index: 1967= 100; 1939= 41.6; 1969= 109.8.

12. *GG,* April 23, 1967, claimed that the Church of God was the fourth largest body in Gaston County, with 3,000 members. In 1974, twenty-one congregations were being listed for the county as a whole in a weekly newspaper advertisement which lent a decided "denominational" image to these churches. Their impoverished, individualistic predecessor-congregations of a previous generation would not have sponsored such an ad. *GG,* August 10, 1974.

13. Cf. above, Preface, p. 17.

14. The persistence of the village-system in the smaller county towns (such as Belmont and McAdenville) is an accurate index to the continuing reality of the paternalistic system as a whole in these locales. In populous, modestly urbanized Gastonia, only one mill village remained intact by the late 1960s; and the manager of that mill (the man quoted above at the beginning of this chapter) explained that "we keep these houses at a loss to us financially, but we find that it is an aid in the recruitment of workers, especially those coming down from the mountains who are worried about where they will live." (Interview, May 1967.) Both managers, workers, and union leaders broadly agree that the selling of the mill houses in the forties and fifties was a financially rational decision for the mills. Cheaply constructed in the early part of this century, most of the houses were becoming very expensive to maintain; and, with the coming of new moderate levels of affluence and mobility to the mill worker, the houses were increasingly difficult to fill with tenants. Liston Pope perceived the coming of these changes with suberb accuracy: cf. *MP,* pp. 191-194.

15. Evidence for this statement comes from interviews with several ministers of local sectarian congregations, all of which were founded after 1950.

16. "Uptown" in this study is used to identify only six Protestant churches in Gastonia, in contrast to that term's application by Pope, cf. *MP*, pp. 91-95. The Jewish Temple is omitted from the "uptown" category because of its uniqueness, though it appears to have a membership with occupational, educational, and income levels similar to the memberships of these six churches. Our middle class and transitional categories include the remaining uptown churches of Pope.

17. The term "sect" is used here to describe congregations comparable to the mill church of Pope, cf. *MP*, pp. 84-91. The literature concerning sects is too extensive for a review here. The reader is referred to the following studies for additional commentary and research: Erich Goode, "Some Critical Observations on the Church-Sect Dimension," *Journal for the Scientific Study of Religion*, 6 (Spring 1967) 69-77. Ernst Troeltsch, *The Social Teaching of the Christian Churches*, Volumes I and II, (New York: Harper Torchbook, 1960), translated by Olive Wyon. See especially Volume I, pp. 328-349. Allan W. Eister, "Toward a Radical Critique of Church-Sect Typologizing: Comment on 'Some Critical Observations on the Church-Sect Dimension,' " *Journal for the Scientific Study of Religion*, 6 (Spring 1967) 85-90. Russell R. Dynes, "Church-Sect Typology and Socio-Economic Status," *American Sociological Review*, 20 (October 1955) 555-560. Russell R. Dynes, "The Consequences of Sectarianism for Social Participation," *Social Forces*, 35 (May 1957) 331-334. John Scanzoni, "A Note on Method for the Church-Sect Typology," *Sociological Analysis*, 26 (Winter 1965) 189-202; Nicholas J. Demerath, "Social Stratification and Church Involvement: The Church-Sect Distinction Applied to Individual Participation," *Review of Religious Research*, 2 (Spring 1961) 146-154. John A. Coleman, "Church-Sect Typology and Organizational Precariousness," *Sociological Analysis*, 29 (Summer 1968) 50-68. Paul Gustafson, "UO-US-PS-PO: A Restatement of Troeltsch's Church-Sect Typology," *Journal for the Scientific Study of Religion*, 6 (Spring 1967) 64-68. Werner Stark, *The Sociology of Religion: A Study of Christendom:* Volume II: *Sectarian Religion,* (New York: Fordham University Press, 1967). Peter Berger, "Sectarianism and Religious Sociation," *American Journal of Sociology*, 64 (July 1958) 41-44; Luther Gerlach and Virginia H. Hine, "Five Factors Crucial to the Growth and Spread of a Modern Religious Movement," *Journal for the Scientific Study of Religion* (Spring 1968) 23-40; Benton Johnson, "On Church and Sect," *American Sociological Review*, 28 (August 1963) 539-549; Benton Johnson, "A Critical Appraisal of the Church-Sect Typology," *American Sociological Review*, 22 (February 1957) 88-92; David Martin, "The Denomination," *British Journal of Sociology*, 13 (March 1962) 1-14. Benton Johnson, "Do Holiness Sects Socialize in Dominant Values?" *Social Forces*, 39 (May 1961) 309-316.

18. Black churches were not included in Pope's study because of the relative insignificance of black participation in Gastonia affairs at large in the 1930s. Cf. *MP*, p. 50, note 2.

19. Pope's comparisons were among three categories—rural, mill, uptown—and a minority was defined as 20% of the total. In our fourfold classification, 15% is used as the definition of a minority because it is approximately the same proportion of each possible category as in the methods used by Pope.

20. These descriptions are a form of "participant observation" which played only a small part of Pope's book. The nearest parallel would be Pope's descriptions of sectarian church services (found in Chapter Seven, pp. 130-133 of *MP*). In collections of essays on the sociology of religion, this is the chapter of Pope's book which is most frequently reprinted. One reason for its popularity, we believe, is this vivid, four-page "composite and impressionistic picture," which Pope set apart by a different size of type.

21. In an effort to control for seasonal factors, February titles were examined for the various years. In addition sermons recognizing special events relevant to our concerns, e.g., Labor Day

and Independence Day, were also considered. These and other following lists of sermon titles lack any entries from the early 1970s, largely because the local newspaper ceased publishing such titles from that time to the present. Incidental data from recent years, however, suggest little change from the content of these titles from the 1947-68 period.

22. We have little precise information regarding the content of these sermons. Some undoubtedly were general discourses about the social issues of the day or about theological issues, while others concerned the personal problems of members. There is, however, little evidence that the issues of labor relations, housing, or race relations were primary concerns of ministers in uptown churches during the '50s and '60s. On the treatment by Gastonia ministers of the 1974 Watergate Crisis, cf. Chapter Seven below.

23. Cf. Preface above.

Chapter *Four*

Harmony:
The Role of the Church and Its Leaders

In the Introduction of our study, we adopted the axiom that a society changes *significantly* when a part or a whole of its *value*-canopy is redefined in relation to the *organization* of its various corporate interests.[1] By this axiom, we are bound to be curious about the social values and organization of Gaston society as these have changed or remained constant from 1940 until the present. The analysis of this whole will occupy us, in terms of several crucial issues of change, in the second part of the book; but, as preparation for understanding the contribution of the church to that change, a closer look at another dimension of "organized religion" is in order. That dimension is institutional leadership, and most concretely this means the role of the minister.

Logically we are bound to take that role rather seriously. If.social change is fundamentally the changing relationship of legitimation and organization, the minister in American society should be a person with power to contribute something to social change and/or social stasis; for, in a way almost unique among other professionals, the minister is both an organizer and a legitimizer. Unlike most doctors and lawyers, he deals with people primarily in groups —ordinarily a group appoints, calls, or employs him. Unlike corporation managers and research scientists, he is charged by his employer with responsibility for dealing regularly and explicitly with religion, the highest level of symbolic legitimacy for human behavior. Unlike many artists, writers, university teachers, and other custodians of symbolic culture, he rarely expects to nurture his devotion to the reality of that culture apart from its meaning to the members of the voluntary organization that employs him. These distinctions between the minister and other professionals can be overdrawn; but, as material in this chapter will demonstrate, the range of group-building and meaning-interpretation skills which the minister is expected to combine, in communities like Gastonia, is very wide. This width of social expectation is sociologically intriguing, related as it is to the pluralistic, fragmented, voluntaristic, and politically "disestablished" nature of formal religious organizations in this country.

In this chapter we want to explore Gastonia ministers' and laypersons' understanding of the role of the minister. We shall be interested in the views which ministers have of their own role, the views they have of each other, and the views which members of their churches have of that role. We shall attempt in particular to understand *what ministers are expected to do to foster, inhibit, or avoid change* in the wider Gastonia community, in the awareness that this is only one particular angle of vision upon a role with other elements in it.

The data included in this chapter are chiefly drawn from interviews with some 400 members of the general population of Gastonia and from 66 of the 150 ministers who were resident in Gastonia and its principal satellite towns in the mid-nineteen sixties. The second section of the chapter will deal with aggregates of this data and general role-prescriptions preferred by this sample of Gastonians. Both "lay" and "professional" interviews are required for the construction of a coherent picture of any role, for a role by definition is a set of expectations for individual behavior shared by a given social group and the individuals who enact the role. This makes the very concept of role a useful bridge between the psychological and the sociological sciences. Roles link individuals and institutions; one might almost say that a role is an institutional presence in an individual and an individual presence in an institution. It is thereby a key concept for inquiring about the impact of the one upon the other.

Priorities for the Role of the Minister:
A Biographical Inquiry

We begin with a sketch of the professional life-story of ten Gaston County ministers.

For some methodological traditions in sociology, this is an uncomfortable way to begin, because those traditions thrive on aggregates rather than on examples. But another tradition—thriving on "everyday experience"[2] —resonates with one of the subjective impacts of our own field work in Gastonia: as the three of us interviewed those sixty-six Gastonia ministers, we often acknowledged to ourselves that it is no small thing to be permitted to share any professional's understanding of his or her work. In talking about that work, one is not only an "interviewee" but also a person wrestling with the meaning and importance of life. At the end of an interview one minister put this into words when he volunteered the comment, "This interview really makes you think of things you don't ordinarily think of. It is something of a 'counseling experience,' isn't it?" Some of our sixty-six ministers found it so, but it is more to the scientific point to observe that personal interviews logically have a place in sociology if the sociologist presupposes *the rootage of the social and the personal in each other*. It would be a travesty on the concept of role, in short, as well as an affront to the richness of individuality, if at some point we did not try to introduce the reader to the ministerial role in Gastonia by introducing at least some of the *ministers* of Gastonia.[3]

Robert Marsh

Marsh is a link between the world of church and community studied by Liston Pope and that of the subsequent generation. He is the only minister here whose career and memory concretely connect him to both worlds. His family moved to a Gastonia mill village when he was four years old to get jobs. He was sixteen at the time of the Loray Strike, during which he was asked to serve as a police guard at one of the small mills in town. "But we didn't have any trouble over there. That was the time our police chief was killed, and I guess that was when I first decided that if I ever had any troubles I would keep them to myself, and not worry other people with them."

During his life he has worked as a millhand, a bricklayer, a policeman, and a small businessman. "I tell my boys that if they don't become preachers, then they should become businessmen, because if a man does right in Gastonia, he can get into business and retire at the age of fifty. It's all right here to be made." Having "made it" in a respectable but not a big way, at the age of fifty Marsh felt a call to establish an independent revivalist chapel. At a time of sickness he asked God to "let me live, and I would become a preacher . . . Now I'm working every minute I can for the Lord. I got out of politics and police work altogether." But he continued to make his living as a businessman.

Marsh's ministry is directed almost totally towards mill workers, whom he sees as neglected by the conventional churches. He has .taken over a small chapel in the northern, most run-down residential section of town. Here he runs a Sunday school whose attendance ranges from twenty to thirty, holds three preaching services with sixty sometimes in attendance, counsels people in trouble, and seeks to support the radio broadcasts of his preaching whenever he can secure the money to do so. (The rate for such radio work at one local station in 1965 was $7.50 for fifteen minutes. Local business acquaintances support him for this ministry, but not regularly.)

What sort of minister do his people want him to be? "A good old-time revival minister. Someone fired up with the Lord, to make them feel good." Does the church help to make people better *workers* in industry? "Yes, if a man has got salvation in his soul, he'll work for eight hours. The church is the foundation of all of it. The church gives people a broader knowledge of how to cope with their troubles." But with the coming of some higher wages in the mills, says he, the troubles of people are apparently on the decrease. "People are less religious than they used to be. More money leads to more going off to the mountains and the beach in a car. I know some boys with whom I used to go to church in the mill village, when we didn't have a car to go anywhere else, but now they head off in a car on weekends, especially in the summer." The effect on independent revivalist chapel attendance, he implies, is very negative. "When poor boys like us get money," he admits wryly, "we stand on our own feet. Give a man money, and he heads for the beach on weekends, but when he's starving he'll come to church!"

As for the general role of the minister in community affairs, he sees himself as involved in all such affairs automatically through the lives of converted individuals. "You can't separate the church and economic things." But calculated or organized involvement is something else. "There are two ways, the way of heaven and the way of hell. And the individual must make up his mind which way to take. The Lord works on the conscience of every man, I believe." If a mill worker came to him with a problem related to his work, he says, "I would go into the prayer room with him and wait on the Lord to straighten it out. I'm not the type to tell another man how to run his business." Nor does he believe that anything good can be accomplished by any sort of "banding together," such as occurs in civil rights demonstrations and in labor unions. As for the rights of blacks, "He should let things happen as they come. If he did so, he would work himself into the best jobs in town. I wouldn't hurt any of them. The only thing is these marches—I think they should be stopped by any means. I would completely forbid banding together. The government should be big enough to stop those marches," presumably because it has power and organization to do so. As for the labor union, "I've been the type who if I were dissatisfied with my work, I just left it, and I didn't put my burdens on anyone else." His acquaintances feel much the same way, he suspects, but consistently enough he hesitates to speak for them. The same money that gives them occasion to be more independent of the *church*, he suggests, makes them likewise independent of the *union*. "We don't like anyone to tell us what to do. As long as we can eat and live, we're happy." It is an individualism that can fit the mill worker and the business entrepreneur equally. Marsh has done both jobs, and evidently he experiences no ideological strain in having moved from the one to the other.

He summarizes the matter of the minister's relation to the community succinctly: "The Bible is enough. If you preach it, you don't have time for politics." From beginning to end, his views of the ministerial profession, the well-being of the church, and the well-being of the local society are redolent with echoes of old Gastonia as described in books that he has not read.

"Gastonia boys have always cooperated with each other. We have done all we could to make everybody happy. All our lawyers have been among the best: they feared the Lord and sponsored all the church work they could." Spiritual progress in salvation, individualistic striving, and social harmony are the major themes in his understanding of a good church and a good community.

Marsh was summarizing a self-preferred version of his own biography when he said, "The Lord saved me, and I forgot about politics." That biography is an exquisite combination of all the major occupational elements that outsiders have come to associate with a Gastonia that used to be: mill worker, policeman, businessman, preacher. He is a mirror image of much of the local society; and, in a strangely haunting way, he lives at its center and on its fringe at one and the same time.

Thomas Dixon

He is the thirty-eight-year-old pastor of an Assembly of God church, founded about 1945, a few blocks to the north of Marsh's little chapel. Though the church claims a formal membership of only seventy-five, its constituency numbers about 300, almost all of them related to the textile industry. By most of the classical standards, the Assembly of God is a sect: salvation-experience is required for membership; speaking with tongues is a major part of the normative worship service; and no adherent is expected to indulge in worldliness such as alcohol, tobacco, movies, and dancing. Dixon has served one other working-class neighborhood in the South, but this is the first time he has worked in a textile community.

A long conversation with Dixon is enough to banish anyone's superficial generalizations about Pentecostalists. He immediately and unselfconsciously impresses the outsider with his religious integrity and his sensitivity to the problems of people.

The textile worker is very extreme in his religion, while the wealthy are more liberal and fit into the older denominations. Our church tries to steer a middle course between liberal churches and this extreme fanaticism. We are Pentecostal, and I believe the Holy Spirit is real, that the power of God in a man's life leads to change and a witness for life. Unfortunately, many believe in shouting and hollering and 'getting a blessing,' but they never go out and do anything for Christ. And there are some Pentecostal churches where there is speaking with tongues but no interpretation. We believe that God has a purpose for everything; Paul said an interpreter should be present, otherwise we should keep silent. . . . Though extremism is a risk when you have this freedom of expression, we must deal with it through teaching and patience.

Dixon moves conceptually, with hardly a blink, from the language of the spirit to the language of psychology and social analysis.

The spiritual problems of people in this part of Gastonia can be traced a lot to their working conditions. They seem to work hard, their wages are small, and expenses are so high. Both man and wife must work, and they don't have much family life. There is a high rate of marital problems here—much separation, divorce, and children five and six years old walking around at 11:00 P. M.   In the Assembly of God, we find it hard to work in North Carolina, and the best reason I know is that it is a textile area, where there are two extremes of people, the rich and the poor. One group is attracted to other denominations, and the other is just not very stable in his religion.

He goes on to speak of the psychological functions he believes Pentecostalism serves for many of these poor people:

Even in the psychological sense, this free sort of worship is a way of relieving them of their burdens and problems. People here have a very high rate of nervousness, especially among the women who work in the mills. While the mills do a lot of good things for people, their workers are underpaid and overworked.

In this context Dixon sees a need for the organization of textile unions.

We need some mediator between the worker and management. Unions now are mostly corrupt at the top, but they could certainly help the textile worker. When unions become too powerful, their members simply switch from serving the employer to serving the union. But I don't mention unions much to workers I talk with. It's really out of my realm. Occasionally I'll mention it to a textile worker who has got out of it. I do believe that most would favor unions if they were not afraid of losing their jobs. I don't see much difference between the mill village and the old plantation slaves.

In these and other perspectives, Dixon demonstrates his skepticism about the benefits of living in Gastonia. He is Alabama-born and Florida-educated, but he nourishes deep suspicions about the virtue of men who run the textile industry. "It was of some advantage to the worker that the mills offered the village houses for sale. But the mills got the best of it, really —the houses were bad and in poor repair. I doubt that the sale of the villages has changed very much the worker's degree of dependence upon the company."

Most of Dixon's readings of Gastonia come directly and exclusively through his dealing with people in his immediate congregation. He has only a rudimentary awareness of the leaders and the affairs of the town as a whole; but he knows that considerable change had recently come in race relations, and he knows that businessmen had a lot to do with that change. "Possibly they voluntarily did it because they saw it coming," he speculates. As for the appropriateness of public pressure exerted by blacks for their rights, he accepts the need for this "to a certain extent. It should be brought to the attention of the public." He has in fact brought the desegregation question to the attention of his official governing board. "I told the Board that if Negroes came to our worship services we should seat them with as little resentment as possible. The Board approved this, and soon I will be informing the congregation. In the early life of this church, I believe, there were some Negroes who attended."

As for his own ministerial role, he sees himself called to be "a good shepherd, a man concerned for the spiritual conditions of the community, and one interested in social problems," in that order of priority. One could easily—and incorrectly—identify his view of the church and social problems with the individualism of his neighbor Marsh up the street: "Jesus didn't have a slum clearance; he cleared the slums out of the hearts of people. All our problems are basically spiritual problems." But there is some very ordinary human flesh in his understanding of "spirit," if the total context of his theology and his ministry is any indication. He encourages his congregation to go to the polls; he helps them get jobs by writing employment recommendations for them; and he thinks it appropriate on occasion to inform a congregation about which side of the fence a given political candidate may be on. But the basic service he feels called to render people is that of a pastor, a man who will "understand their problems, live with their problems, visit their homes, to be one with them by living among them." So genuinely does he seem to carry on just such a ministry, and so clearly does he see the need for such in the social conditions of the mill community, that he somehow succeeds in filling the term "spiritual" with some very pragmatic meaning.

Arthur Bridges

The opinions and the lifestyle of some ministers in Gastonia have about them a certain predictability. Not so, the opinions and lifestyle of seventy-three year-old Arthur Bridges. He is one of those persons who make the sociological investigator stand in awe—at the end of the day—before the complexities of human nature.

Bridges is a Nazarene minister who was first ordained in 1923 in the Church of God Holiness. An evangelist all of his life, he migrated to Gastonia in the early forties from his native midwest, and for over a decade he was assistant pastor of the other Nazarene church in town. His church is located beside his house, which in turn is located in a section of Gastonia as close to primitive as any other section in town. He is the only minister among sixty-six interviewed for this study who would state that a sizable proportion of his (fifty-member) congregation were subsisting on welfare or disability checks. The shingled house and church are located at the edge of the railroad across the street from one of the early Gastonia mills. The church has an improvised steeple. Cracked boards, piles of pop bottles, and two television sets in ill repair meet the eye of the inside-visitor to the house, but the *signs* on his lawn and on his front porch are the real eye-catchers. Biblical quotations abound in the signs, and invitations to "counseling" that is available within. "I believe in signs," says Bridges. "People today pass by the clergyman and go to the psychiatrist, the lawyer, and the doctor. They don't care for the advice from the preacher, for he is inclined to stick to the Bible, and they don't want that!" Recently, he says, he advised a young girl, on biblical grounds, against marrying a man who was not a Christian. It is plain from his narrative that he is a very direct counselor. He tells people what to do.

The variety and range of his views on his own and other ministers' work in Gastonia amounts to a kaleidoscopic-mixture of what ordinarily passes for ideological liberalism and conservatism. A collage from his wide-angled lens of a mind, would read as follows:

There are too many Southern Baptist churches here in Gastonia, and Churches of God that believe in the tongues. They act as if theirs is the only church in the world. Too much copying of Charlotte, too. I hate for Gastonia to copy Charlotte, or New York City, where it's dangerous to walk on the streets at night. . . . The biggest recent improvement in the town has been the new community college. The person most responsible for this was ex-governor Sanford, who was probably the best governor we have ever had. . . . No, I don't favor a minimum wage law. Some people have greater abilities than others, and all employment should be a matter between the two persons involved. And I just can't see the need for the union. Some say that the rich will squeeze perspiration from people until the blood comes, but I don't think so. . . . No, the recent changes in civil rights for the Negro would not have come without some pressure on his part. He had earnestly to contend for it, or it never would have come about. There is a bully-nature in all people, a bully-disposition, which likes to crack the whip over other people; and against this you have to exert pressure: peaceable marching, demonstrations, but not violence. . . . As a body of ministers, in the Ministerial Association, we are for integration, and integration of the churches, too. The schools should integrate as well, and there should be equal wages. Things are getting better now: stores, hospitals, and I like this. Several years ago we had an evangelist from Georgia, and I told him—half in fun—to take a message from me to the governor of Georgia: "Ask him if it wasn't all right for Moses to have a colored woman for his wife!" In fact, I would prefer having an assistant pastor here from the North, because a southerner might be prejudiced against the Negro. I know that integration will mean more intermarriage, but that doesn't worry me. I think that marriage is the personal decision of any person. I have no bad feeling on intermarriage. Moses was one of the smartest men who ever lived! I tell my congregation that in the Old Testament intermarriage was forbidden only because of the wickedness of other peoples, not their race. The congregation reacted well to this. They saw that I had proved my point. On the race question, the church should teach the whole Bible—how Jesus integrated with other people, how Paul went to the Gentiles, and Peter finally went to the Gentiles after he had that vision. . . . It's fine for the minister to be active in civic clubs and the PTA, but not in political organizations. Politics are almost too tangled, too nasty for women to engage in, and the church should not meddle much in it, either. We shouldn't mention politics from the pulpit, either, unless a moral issue is involved, like the A.B.C. stores.[4] Certainly we shouldn't mention the labor union item. The preacher might stir up a hornet's nest of discontent: and the workers would start saying, "I'm moving north," and it would tear up the community. . . . But we've got to bring to our people's attention some of the issues of the day. The preacher needs to widen-out, to educate the people. For example, television. The minister must teach them when to turn the TV knob on, when to turn it off: not to throw away their TV sets but to turn it off when the devil is on! Television, like autos, is a dangerous thing when not controlled. The devil must not have all the autos, just because he uses some of them! And let me add one more: the space age. We should tell our people about this, how ignorant we are of this universe, how beyond our minds it all is. . . .

If Robert Lane were to subject Arthur Bridges' "political ideology" to analysis, he would probably dub Bridges a "morselist." He chews his values in small chunks that are ostensibly not of one piece. Yet within those chunks, he can be a consistent "ideologue." Pattern in his views comes in glints and snatches: he shares traditional southern culture in his attitude towards unions, breaks sharply with it on race. He is an economic individualist like Marsh, but totally rejects Marsh's view of public demonstrations as a means for achieving justice for the black man. Yet such action on the management-labor front he deems inappropriate. He believes in education, but the wealth which comes with education he sees as detrimental to the interests of religion. He has a sectarian, anti-worldly orientation towards going to the beach and even visiting relatives on Sunday; but he believes in an active church ministry in relation to the race question, the liquor question, the uses of television, and the importance of space travel. He superintends a scarcely-surviving sectarian church enterprise that—like the segment of society he serves—is clambering on the rim of disintegration; but he sees himself as an ecumenical Christian, and he identifies solidly and professionally with the Greater Gastonia Ministerial Association, even if he cannot, like Marsh, identify in his mind with the economic and political elite of the town.

In his yellow shirt, worn tie, and green suspenders, sitting on his porch behind all of his yard signs, he would make good copy for people who write comedy and parody about southerners. But he happens to be a transplanted midwesterner, and like Hamlet he has "that within which passeth show."

In all, he is a strange mixture, like his adopted town.

William McLean

Robert Marsh would be a bad case in point for any Marxist who wanted to illustrate the possibility of *resentment* coming to personal consciousness in a man brought up in a southern textile industry environment. But William McLean would be a good case, violating the Marxist system chiefly at the point

of his own claim that religion and the church are generators of that consciousness in himself and others.

McLean is only twenty-seven years old, and his small (membership:
sixty-four) mill-village church on the east side of the county is his first
pastorate. He was born in Charlotte and brought up since the age of eight in
Gastonia, where his father worked in one of the chain mills. He went to high
school in Gastonia, to college and to seminary in South Carolina at institutions
sponsored by the Associate Reformed Presbyterian church. Now he is a
minister of the Presbyterian Church in the United States, or Southern Presbyterian church.

Only a minority of persons in his congregation are workers in the mill. Most
of the membership is salaried, a fact that militates against congregational
support for his idea that the church should challenge paternalistic politics and
paternalistic economics in all of their guises. And on this side of the county,
where mill villages and mill-village traditions survive vigorously, paternalism
does not wear much disguise.

Little in his formal education would lead one to predict that McLean would
become a member of the activist "new breed" of clergymen; but that is what he
is. The forty-five years separating him and Arthur Bridges is silhouetted in
terms of theology and social ethics in McLean's statement: "A minister must
get involved in politics whenever there is a moral question,"—thus far a
conventional southern protestant view—"but right now I'm at a loss to know
how to separate the moral and the non-moral aspects of politics"—a subtlety
that is decidedly untraditional. He believes that the pulpit is not a place where
particular political causes should be regularly urged; it is the place for preaching
the gospel. "But when I step down from the pulpit, I become involved in
politics. Sermons are directed to me as well as to others, and we *all* go out to be
involved in the social realm."

These are hardly idle words with McLean. Over the past year he has been
involved in the politics of the two nearby family-dominated mill towns, in ways
that were unprecedented for any minister heretofore in the area. His coming as
pastor of the church coincided with a remarkable political revolt in the town of
Belmont, led by a thirty-four-year-old insurance debit-collector who had been
born in the mill village and who became his town's first effective challenge to
the ancient political tenure of the two major mill families. At the time of the
1963 local election, in which this man was running for a second term as mayor
of Belmont, McLean was the newly elected president of the local ministerial
association. The latter was a gateway to the "social realm" in McLean's mind,
a place wherein to engage in politics. So in the meetings of the Association and
in letters to the newspaper,

I said that we needed to take a stand on the problems of this community by helping to get the control of the City Council in new hands. What I wanted to do was to get the Association involved as a *group*. Organized, the ministers could do something. Though organized power can be misused, it is not being used at all in this town now.

It was a breaking of the image of the ministerial role that few people in Belmont found tolerable. Immediately after his public statements about the need for "new hands" on the City Council,

I got phone calls all day long. Some threatened me—mostly the threats were from influential people. I got letters from some of the ministers supporting me. On the other hand, some prominent ministers of Belmont said that I had misused my place as president of the Ministerial Association. One lady told me (she was a friend of one of the town's two leading families) that a member of that family went to the minister of the Presbyterian church and said that the new sanctuary of that church would not be built if I continued in my present course.

Pressure from people inside and outside his own congregation did in fact force him to alter that course. Backed by the ministers of "uptown" churches, the majority of the Ministerial Association officially repudiated his leadership. Then he was "encouraged" by leaders of his congregation to find another pastorate, which he did less than a year after this 1965 interview. His political wings clipped and a lot of personal hurt to the contrary, he had managed to stick it out for two years after the 1963 fracas. His longtime experience of Gaston County's economic structure fortified him to continue believing that the targets of his political activism were humanly as well as theologically worthy of attack.

I believe that the church has an obligation to every aspect of life. Getting $38.00 a week is more than a matter of "mere politics"; it's a moral issue. . . . It robs people of their dignity for all the control of their affairs to be lodged in a few people. Mr. _____ who owns all the mills in _____ has been mayor of that town for a long time, and when he became a county commissioner his cousin was elected mayor to take his place. He owns the town, and I don't think that you can own a human life. . . . Most laborers here are filled with a great deal of fear, even if this is the twentieth century. It's fear all up and down the line, from the worker to the section hand to the overseer to the boss to the owner—the workers even fear each other, as _____ said openly in his campaign for mayor of Belmont. Some workers have no bath facilities in their houses. And some people said during the election, "They don't deserve more than this." Why, people are even ordered to run for office around here. An elderly member of the city council wanted to retire from politics, but the mill owner told him that he would have to run. Also before the 1965 election voter-registration blanks were taken out to the mills to get the workers to register. It was virtually coercive registration, and the implication was there that they would vote for the "bossmen" who were running. The ruling families here also control what industries do or do not locate here. Two large national companies were going to locate here recently, but the family interests prevented that, through their control of the local water supply.

As for unions: I've worked in both union and non-union shops. I don't know. Unions are good and bad. The South has benefitted from the union movement—from the fear of unions coming in. In some cases, especially around Belmont, unions could help. I don't like strife and everything which goes along with unions. I won't ever push for unions, as _____, pastor of one of our smaller Baptist churches, says he would. He'd quit and work for the union, he says, if they ever started coming. The union *can* have a moral issue, you know. One man in Belmont made over one million dollars, I am told, when one-price cotton came. Who else shared in that million dollars? The workers got 5¢ an hour raise! We have jobs in Belmont paying $38.00 a week which, over in Gastonia, pay $100. There is a great difference between Gastonia and Belmont in textiles.

Like Thomas Dixon, McLean discerns the impact of economic conditions upon the religious experience of some of his parishioners:

A man making $38.00 a week does not have too much response to God. Few making those wages belong to the church. They have the feeling of not being cared for. "If people don't care for me," they think, "does God care?" Also, they can't clothe themselves and their families well enough to go to church, and they can't support the church financially. Recently, by the way, the Ministerial Association of Belmont set up some meetings with various supervisors and workers to discuss industrial problems. People had been complaining to the preachers about working conditions, and the bosses said that they were "unable to meet." They didn't even want to talk about it. It was upsetting the applecart of labor-management relations.

One of McLean's denominational peers remarked to the researchers on a certain instability that seemed apparent in him. "He needs seasoning in the ministry." One could say as much about any twenty-seven-year-old professional, perhaps. Even so, McLean is a rarity. He is one of a handful of Gaston County ministers who understands the power of economics and the economics of power, in ways called for by Liston Pope at the end of *Millhands and Preachers*. Not many of his neighbors in the eastern part of the county have gone on record as mourning his departure from their midst. But his brief career among them was an awkward meteor-flash they will not easily forget.

Stuart Henderson

Asked how one might explain the tendency among some ministers now to "bring social issues into sermons," Stuart Henderson replied with a self-characterization:

Many of us nowadays see ourselves as having been called, while *in* the world, *to* the world. We may be ministers now, but we do not come from a strict church background. We are not beholding to the past as some may be. We were called to the ministry late in life, after we had pursued other vocations for a while. We are mavericks, really.

Born in Indiana, Henderson graduated from college in High Point, North Carolina, where he worked for several years as a knitter in a hosiery mill. He served for seven years in the U.S. Army of Occupation in Japan after World War II. He was thirty-six years old at the time of our interviews with him, and was currently finishing up his work on a seminary degree. As part of his recent seminary studies, he did a term paper on the topic, "Socio-Economic Patterns of Protestantism in Gaston County," based primarily on the writing of Liston Pope and Ernst Troeltsch. He is one of six ministers interviewed who had read the Pope book in its entirety.

Henderson is a pastor of a Methodist church established as a chapel in 1920 in a west Gastonia mill village. The congregation now has some 300 members, 70% of whom live within one and one-half miles of the church. Their occupations encompass most sectors of the textile industry, plus various non-professional work categories which he has identified with the help of U.S. Department of Labor classifications. The church is located within throwing distance of the main offices of Textiles, Inc.; and, since he first came to the church in 1962, Henderson has sought consistently to establish rapport with the managers of this firm.

These fellows have really opened their doors to me. I have visited them in their offices, and in the hospital. The first year I was here, I said to them and to everybody in the congregation: "I may not like or dislike whom you like or dislike, but I accept you as you are, as I expect you to accept me."

He notes that the management of the chain mill now routinely gives $100 a year to every church in the city which has employees as members, "with no strings attached . . . These managers do not want to *use* any of us ministers so much as they want to know why the church now takes positions on social questions when the church is supposed to stand for separation of church and state." The issue that has most recently agitated his manager friends is the public opposition of the National Council of Churches to section 14-b of the Taft-Hartley Law. Henderson himself, as a former union member, supports 14-b. It is a necessary discipline upon union leaders, he says. He tries to walk a line between a simple pro-union and an equally simple anti-union position as he talks to both the workers and the managers of his neighborhood. He says that some managers who are members of uptown churches have turned to him to discuss the issue of labor unionism, evidently because the downtown ministers have shown little openness to communicating with them on this subject.

Twice in the past two years the TWUA has sought to organize the plant across the street. They lost the second time by only a few votes. Most supporters of the union cause were not fighting the company but certain work conditions, especially the mixup in the piecework and hourly pay scales. During the campaign I brought up the pending election in my pastoral calling. I tried to get their feelings about the question, and I was pleased to find that many of the workers were no longer applying the old '29 thing to the present situation. I discovered that the near-success of the 1964 election was due to the non-threatening manner in which the union supporters went about their campaign. And these persons did not lose their jobs later on. I think that unions will eventually come here, too. I have let it be known that I am just as proud to have a card-carrying member in this church as anyone else.

Henderson's sober view of unionism springs in part from a negative experience with unionizing tactics while working in a knitting mill in High Point.

They wanted me to be their spokesman; but then some toughies came in, started damaging property, and abusing people. I'm willing to sit down and talk with anyone, but violence is out of the question. But I am still sympathetic with unions in spite of High Point, especially after talking with John Ramsey, a deacon in the Presbyterian Church employed to relate religious and labor matters for the U.S. Steelworkers. He said that at one point the president of Bethlehem Steel said to him that he should give up his ordination as a deacon in the church! Collective bargaining I favor. Men on the job are under some terrible pressures. I know this from all the counseling I do. Of all thirty-six North Carolina counties in the district served by Broughton (Mental) Hospital in Morganton, Gaston tops them all in rate of admissions.

Does he make any distinction between a pastoral concern and a social concern in his ministry? "Not much!" he replies, and it is clear that he is constantly on the lookout for weaving together these two sorts of concerns in specific negotiations with his parishioners:

I don't like to see a fellow with all the answers, with whom you just can't talk. . . . Methodists officially subscribe to a "Social Creed," but few in this local church would agree with the creed. So that means we must do a lot of study and informing of the people, meanwhile using the church's influence on various social issues. The churches here used their influence a lot on the A.B.C. issue recently.

Why not do so, he implies, on many another issue?

Henderson is an active, registered Republican. He appears on campaign platforms with local Gaston County Republican candidates and is something of a party chaplain for these events. He was one of two white Methodist ministers in attendance at the October 13, 1963 civil rights protest meeting that preceded the theater demonstrations. (He was the only white local pastor.) He thinks that the theater demonstration did little actual good, but that unless blacks do exert pressure for their rights, "not much will be done." He is self-consciously a "contextualist" in his ethical theory on these matters. "The gospel does not have 'the answer' on all these social questions. We must use biblical reason and human reason together as best we can. Perhaps I am a disciple of Paul Tillich on this."

No easy answers, no easy harmony, and no easy definitions of the ministerial role: this is the tone Henderson sets in his thinking about the ministry. He too is one of the "new breed," but with considerable skill he blends his maverick interests with some of the traditional themes of the ministry in Gastonia. "Many people in our community still want a minister who preaches hellfire and damnation, visits like a trojan, offends no one, and stays out of politics. . . . That is, someone who doesn't do most of the things I do!" But unlike Bill McLean, he probably overstates the community's perception of him as a maverick. He does preach biblical sermons; he visits often in homes and work-places; he disagrees with opinions apparently without offending people; and he has effectively ruled out the possibility that his church should be an outpost of the Republican Party. "Over time, they'll come to accept a broader concept of ministry," he muses. Much of his own effort is directed toward that end.

Owen Palmer

Palmer is pastor of a Lutheran church founded in the open country in 1830, before there was a Gaston County. The church has no distinctive identification with the textile industry. Urbanizing Gastonia has simply grown up around it. Most of the current membership of 525 are employed as skilled workers, professionals, and middle-level managers in the mills, or independent small businesspersons. He was born in Kannapolis, North Carolina, and as a child knew first-hand the face of paternalism. (In 1974 Kannapolis remained the civic subsidy of Cannon Mills, Inc., and has been known to advertise itself as "the largest unincorporated town in the world.") In many respects he resembles Stuart Henderson, four years older than he. Asked what were the formative influences on his keen sense of the social mission of the church, he listed three:

(1) My education at Lenoir-Rhyne College, where I majored in sociology; (2) my close friends in the ministry, who are about my age; and (3) my observations of management's community leadership in Kannapolis, an experience that gave me some ideas about some different kinds of leadership needed in an industrial community.

At seminary in Columbia, South Carolina, he too read *Millhands and Preachers*.

Palmer sees a decided split between older and younger Gastonians in their expectations of the minister.

The older people want a ministry like the one they knew thirty years ago, when the congregation was small and the minister made long visits to their homes. The young people want a lot more; they want the minister to be a leader in teaching them how to get involved in the life of this community. In every congregation in Gastonia we have both of these groups, which makes for many a restless night for the pastor!

The leadership of his own congregation leans rather definitely, he believes, towards the more "involved" style of churchmanship; and he breathes an implicit sigh of relief that he has a set of young Lutheran laypeople urging him in this direction rather than the set of older fundamentalists with whom many of his fellow ministers must regularly contend.

The younger group, he says, "sees the church as too tied to old patterns that are no longer relevant. Once the church was the leader of the community, now it is not, and they want to see it become so again—to give *perspective* to all community activities. For example, the church might be a place where we could come to a perspective on the subject of public welfare. What is it to help another person? What is really helpful service? How can the cycle of poverty be broken? In order to answer such questions, one has to have some real knowledge of what is going on in a community. Many ministers have shown themselves ignorant of what is really going on. In the hassle over A.B.C. stores, you would have thought that some ministers didn't know about bootleggers in the county! And the recent effort of ministers in town to ban obscene literature from newsstands achieved very little. A long, carefully designed sex education program for our public schools is what we need to combat the obscenity problem. There are no quick, simple solutions."

Out of his instinctive distrust of much of the "social action" of ministers as a group in Gastonia, Palmer pins his hopes for a sociall relevant church upon lay members like many of his own congregation. (It was Palmer who, in the fall of 1963, challenged the Gastonia Ministerial Association to give its support to the civil rights demonstrations in front of the local theater. "The ministerial association here is not a real contribution to the community. We are Johnny-come-latelies on every issue, never on top of anything.") Says he, "A lot of church reform has come from the laity. In the civic clubs I talk to, the members are eager to talk about these issues. Maybe laymen in the churches *want* the church to become more involved with the community"—a view that seems to be confirmed by survey data. In order to liberate them and himself to become involved, Palmer is seeking a great increase in two-way communication between himself and various people in the church and the community. He is wary of taking anybody's monologues on a social problem, including his own, at face value.

Burlington Mills takes all of the local ministers on a tour once a year. One year I asked, "What will be the effect of automation on the workers?" And the reply was: "We don't plan to automate." Which was an out-and-out lie—they'll have to automate in order to compete. But over such an issue there needs to be two-way communication between industry and clergy, not just clergy "telling" industrialists or vice versa. . . . We must let the experience of other men *shape* our ministry.

In the summer and fall of 1965, Palmer was trying to do just that in a series of "congregational conversations," chaired by two experienced discussion leaders and focused on such local community issues as the hospital bond referendum, local elections, the alcohol problem, and the like. In all of this, he believes, the church must see itself as already "scattered" out in the community, as itself an agency for undertaking concrete services to the community, and as an organization always subject to reform. "We must be flexible enough to find new forms of ministry. Twenty years from now, the patterns may have to change. We cannot afford to baptize all the old forms with holy water." He thinks church facilities, for example, should be open to the local anti-poverty program for use in job training for the poor.

Palmer is one of a new breed of socially-oriented young ministers who sees his provocation for being so in a new breed of church members. In his opinion the people *most opposed* to the socially relevant ministry are those who are *least involved* in the activities of the church. "They are the ones who want the church to be wholly 'spiritual.' " In his view, the experience of being involved in an attempt to define and to carry out a ministry in society will so invigorate members of his congregation that they themselves will become the heart of a "church renewal" that is coterminous with "social renewal." Between the lines he suggests that the problem of the split between the "involved" and the "spiritual" members of the congregation has not really been solved in his ministry; but unlike some of the other ten ministers sketched here, he is happy to have a base of support for his ideas in a sizable segment of his church. He does not say so, but his theology on the matter represents a decided break with classical Lutheran social ethics. He is glad not to be a Baptist, but he is not an advocate of the "two kingdom" theory that was once the Lutheran version of the spirituality of the church.

James Patterson

Like Molière's M. Jourdain, who late in life discovered that he was speaking prose, James Patterson says that he never encountered "integration" until he arrived, at the age of forty-six, in Gastonia in 1964. He was so integrated in Oklahoma, his birthplace, and later on in Chicago, that he never knew himself to be so. He perceives the local society now as an open door of opportunity for all residents of the black community who have the motivation to work hard. "The Negro should now prepare himself to be accepted in society," he said in the summer of 1966. "There is not much to be done on the white side of the fence now. The Negro's major problem now is learning to live with his own people."

Patterson is pastor of the largest congregation of the National Baptist Church in Gastonia (1966 membership: 530). The church draws members from all parts of the local black community, and some from as far away as Shelby and Charlotte in adjacent counties. It is a congregation largely dominated by black middle-class leaders. Patterson identifies readily with the national denomination, and he hopes that he can make the Gastonia church much more conscious of its status as part of a national church. "Before I came," he says, "they didn't know that we had a publishing house, or that we owned a resort at Hot Springs, Arkansas." He sees his task in Gastonia primarily in terms of motivating his parishioners to shake themselves loose from hindrances to their own progress, especially economic progress. During a large part of his career, he has combined work as a pastor with work as a student and as a pipe-inspector in a sheet-and-tube company near Chicago. He was the first black man to hold an inspector's job with the company, and he is proud to relate how in six years only one carload of pipe was ever returned to him. In many ways he seems to affirm a protestant ethic of work—and it makes him appear right at home in Greater Gastonia: "There is so much opportunity here that the men and women north of the tracks have yet to take advantage of. Too many Negro young people don't want to work."

He has little doubt that strong ministerial leadership is vital to the progress of the black community. He sees two noteworthy improvements in the life of the community in the two and a half years of his pastorate: the opening up of a middle-class housing section for black occupancy, and the coming of "some young ministers to town who seem to be lifting the morale of the people. They live in town, not out of town as so many of the local ministers once did." These ministers have "started telling people about how to live, not just about how to die."

For most practical purposes "in town" means "in the black community" for Patterson. In two and a half years he has gotten a sure feel for the leaders of the black community, but is very little acquainted with the leaders of the white community. The one exception to this is his joking relationship with the Chairman of the Board of Gastonia's largest bank. When he goes to the bank the elderly board chairman calls out to him through the office door, "Are you making any money?'' "I tell him, 'How can I, when you've got it all!' " One senses that Patterson is the sort of black minister with whom the white community in Gastonia finds it easy to work. He is a very competent person, and his program for change focuses 90% on changes that need to take place within the black community, rather than on changes that may need to take place in the structure of its relations with the white community.

This particular congregation was not a major supporter of the civil rights movement of the early sixties in Gastonia. The major leaders of that movement were the ministers and members of AME Zion, Methodist, and Presbyterian churches in the black community. Patterson thoroughly supports the goals of the civil rights movement but he sees those goals as largely achieved now, and he understands the church's contribution to the progress of black people now not in terms of group demonstrations that get the "public eye" but in terms of individual Christian living. Like Robert Marsh and Arthur Bridges, he believes that the church and local industry engage in a mutual exchange of services when the one helps to make men good workers and the other provides workers the money that enables them to support the church financially.

The fact that his interviewer was a white man raises the conventional suspicion that some of his opinions he states in forms he believes to be most palatable to whites. Yet one of his responses bespeaks anything but intimidation: he is unambiguously pro-union:

No, I do *not* favor the right-to-work law (14-b). If an individual wants to work, he should do so according to the plans of the union, which can set a living wage for him. I believe in unions, and this law is anti-union. Unions are the best things that ever happened to the working man. If I am to enjoy the benefits of unions, I should support them.

Nobody among the white clergy of Gastonia—not even McLean and Henderson—could be counted on to endorse unionism so forthrightly as could Patterson. On this point he is so thoroughly converted by his experience in Chicago ("I was paid $30.00 a day") that no amount of inconsistency with the strain of individualism in him is likely to keep him from recommending the union to those members of his church who are beginning to get jobs in the textile mills.

But the burden of his ministerial concern remains with the problems of the black community over which he believes black people themselves have real control: bad housing, crime, a high rate of illegitimacy. A gospel of individual salvation yielding a life of "doing good" is the one which he will preach from his Sunday pulpit. And in this he will be joined by many of his white ministerial brethren on the other side of the tracks.

Fred Mitchem

He found it a "hard question" to be asked what he liked about the town of Gastonia. But the answer he offered reflected something about his career in the town over the past eight years: "Here you get to know everybody in both the white and the black communities, and especially in the business world."

But it was not always so for the black minister; obviously it is not so yet for some of his colleagues in the black community, and his own ministry in the town is one reason why it *is* so for him. Time was when no black man in Gastonia got to "know everybody in the business world."

He was one of the "seven ministers" whose part in the civil rights movement of 1963 has been detailed elsewhere in this book. He came to Gastonia in 1957 at the age of twenty-six to serve his first post-seminary pastorate in this church—an African Methodist Episcopal Zion church that some would judge to be the black community's most influential single congregation. Founded in 1885 during a decade that saw the mills arise rapidly in Gaston County, the church now has only 300 members; but among these members are some of the major leaders and constituents of the political gains which Gastonia blacks have been achieving since 1953.

In his zest for being an acknowledged leader of the black community and in being considered so by the white community, Mitchem exudes an exhilaration that is emblematic of the "new black minister" who found himself vocationally partly through the civil rights movement. "Ministers are caught up in the stream of things now," he says confidently. "A man's personality is related to his whole environment. The old preacher wasn't concerned about this. Now we have discovered our involvement in our city's happiness. It works both ways." Mitchem openly credits the civil rights struggle of 1963 as the turning point of his involvement in "our city's happiness." In a sermon preached to his congregation in the spring of 1967, he reflected:

In 1963 in October I think there was a great battle in the city of Gastonia. When demonstrations were so prevalent all over the country, it seemed like a new thing had broken through our time in Louisville and Chicago. But back in 1963 I was sorta lukewarm on the civil rights movement. So I prayed directly to God about it, and I heard his voice come loud and clear, saying: "We must show people their error. We must say to them and to all the South that men are possessed with the spirit of God." . . . and ever since that time I could reach out as part of the forward movement of the City of Growing Beauty. I think that we pricked the conscience of those who wanted to help progress, and I think that the Christian movement must do the same . . . Now God said to me, "There are dangers involved in this thing"—and I knew it. We read everywhere then about homes being bombed. But by faith God takes care of his own. I said that many times during the demonstrations, and I received many threatening calls and a lot of remarks that were not so good. But on the other hand, there were those who would come every day and would say, "Thank God for leadership." And my reply to them was that this is the thing that God had laid on my heart, and I never moved. I feel today that it was essential.

One of Mitchem's leading church members is the man who won the Ward 4 vote for city council in the spring of 1963 while losing out to the black "establishment" candidate in the citywide vote. He says of this man that he is a "good friend of mine who stood by me in 1963 and who is a pusher, too." He is one of the few ministers in Gastonia who is glad to characterize himself and his friends as "pushers." Since the autumn of 1963 his repertory of "push" tactics has expanded chiefly into the area of job placement. He is one of several black ministers whom white industrial leaders have used as mediators between job openings in industry and job applicants in the black community. Mitchem knows the power structure of the white community more astutely than the majority of white ministers in town, for he has been dealing with that structure with some regularity for the past two years.

He believes that demonstrations and crises are not the optimum path to better race relations in Gastonia. The town is in great need, he thinks, of "a more honest pipeline between the white and black communities in the church. We need to share ideas with each other, see what can be done with problems, have roundtable forums, and the like." Why have the white churches not been very open to participating in such an "honest pipeline"?

They are fearful of the results—they might lose members or have an upsurge. But for myself, I think that the church has to be interested in all community issues. Whatever hurts a man's relationship to the church is of concern to the church. If he is suffering at home, he can't be happy in the church. That sounds like the social gospel! I'm sold on it. I believe in feeding a man before preaching to him about Jesus.

In almost everything that he says about his role in the congregation, the black community, and Gastonia as a whole, Mitchem shows his relish in being a minister. It is as though he were saying: "It's a great time to be a minister, and a black one at that!" His empathetic understanding of what it is like to be a minister in one of the white, uptown churches suggests as much:

The business leader prefers his minister to be a preacher and pastor, but not much of a leader in the church or the community. The executive is going to run the church. He will dictate policy. The minister is meddling if he oversteps the pulpit and the pastoral part of his ministry. White ministers are not as active in community leadership as we Negro ministers are. They are too busy preparing sermons and visiting.

But in a like show of empathy for another class of white persons in Gastonia, he adds: "The mill worker puts more store than the executive in the minister as a community leader. He wants his pastor to be more of a community leader because he has no other leader to go to." He does not add, does not need to add: "In that, the mill worker is exactly like us blacks."

What kinds of community leadership, then, does he feel to be appropriate for a minister to undertake? He smiles. The very question implies a white man's segmented view of a minister's role in a specialized society. The answer for Mitchem is as existentially simple as it is morally comprehensive: "Whatever comes up. Wherever my services are needed."

Fletcher Monroe

Silence has hurt the ability of the church to help labor and race relations in Gastonia. As Fletcher Monroe said in a sermon recently, "People need to pay better wages, then we wouldn't need a government poverty program." He said he got some sour reaction to this, especially from _____, one of the leading executives in his church. Monroe is pretty rare—he is just bold enough to make that kind of statement. Stuart Henderson, too.

Such tribute from a Fred Mitchem is difficult to earn if one is a white minister in Gastonia. That Fletcher Monroe earned it after two years of being pastor of a large uptown church is all the more remarkable, for in Gastonia it is the custom for the minister of a large church to take his time "getting to know the people" before he makes statements from the pulpit on controversial subjects.

Monroe does not see himself as a controversialist. Quite otherwise: he sees himself as responsible for shifting his congregation's image of the minister from autocrat to facilitator.

There is a trend away from the old fundamentalism. None of the downtown ministers are fundamentalists, and twenty-five years ago all of them probably were. It strikes me that the traditional pattern of ministry in our city has been autocratic and dictatorial. I see myself as more pastoral. I want to win people's voluntary cooperation and lead the congregation into responsible decision making through democratic processes.

The church, with its 1900 members and large complement of major industrial leaders from the city, has a reputation for being an influence not only in Gastonia but in denominational circles throughout the state. Monroe was invited to fill this pulpit at the age of forty-one, a denominational tribute to his reputation as a preacher and a pastor. Most of his previous experience has been in middle-class congregations in the South, but in the late forties he served a small congregation in an impoverished mill community in Tennessee. Among other educational influences (like summer schools in Princeton and New York), he is one of that small group of local ministers who have read Liston

Pope. "I read *Millhands and Preachers* soon after I came here. Not many people here have read it. But some are aware of it." Perhaps the reading of the book has contributed to some of the generalizations which he is willing to make after two years of residence in Gastonia.

I have often described Gastonia as a young teenager flexing his muscles, trying to decide where it is going. There is a lot of energy here, optimism, and will to progress . . . I get the impression that the town is making a last ditch attempt to prove that free enterprise will work . . . But there is a certain "shiftless" class of people here who are the casualty of something—of a sociological process gone afoul, a paternalism which created a dependency feeling on the part of many people . . . I have never lived in a community with so much *personal* concern among so many people, e.g., projects for the mentally retarded, the Family Service Agency, the Mental Hygiene Clinic.

Monroe's view of the church's chief mode of social influence concurs with the view most widely shared in Gastonia: through the personal activities of its members in society, rather than through any corporate activity, the church makes its major impacts.

There are few leaders of Gastonia who are not churchmen. If the mayor does a certain thing, that is the church doing it, in my view . . . The church should send out into the community individuals whose creative insights can be implemented in community affairs. Something in me draws back from being a pressure group: the church is a leavening influence, the salt of society. But we are now at the point where some people think that unless the church puts out a resolution, it is not involved. The members of the church need to realize that *they* are the church in action. This idea needs selling more to the church itself than to society. Church members want to divorce the sacred from the secular.

His constituents, by implication, include few members demanding "involvement" in Owen Palmer's sense; but he is at one with Palmer in believing that the church should be the place where "we should expose ourselves to things on which we are in disagreement." To this end, the educational program of the church has recently sponsored dialogues with community leaders as ideologically far apart as the head of the local O.E.O. program who talked on poverty, a historian from the new community college who talked on world politics, and a conservative economics teacher from the high school who spoke on free enterprise. Monroe himself was a member of the local Human Relations Committee in the late sixties, and in the early seventies was appointed its chairman.

Quite in contrast to men like Bridges, Mitchem, and his own predecessor in this church, one of Monroe's dominant personal characteristics is a certain intellectual tentativity which comes across as principled rather than as the habit of a temporizer. He is a man who is willing to change his mind but is not likely to be pushed into doing so. In another North Carolina city where he was serving in 1960, he says, "I tried to clarify the church-state issue in the Kennedy-Nixon contest without focusing on either personality. Some people went out not knowing who I was going to vote for. I voted for Nixon, but during Kennedy's term I changed my mind, and I was planning to vote for him in 1964."

Many of his opinions about the social strategies and policies appropriate to the economic and political realm are imbued with this tentativity. He regularly acknowledges the social context of personal existence while somehow affirming that in the last analysis the personal is more vital than the social. On unions:

I lean towards a man's being able to choose whether or not he should join a union. I'm not ready to surrender that, for I believe in collective bargaining. But unions have as much moral responsibility as does industry. A struggle of power does go on, and perhaps there should be a balance of power. That is a part of the genius of the democratic and capitalist system.

On the use of group pressure for achieving racial integration: "The demonstration did not achieve much, but maybe little would have happened without the Civil Rights Law, either." And on Gastonia's housing problem:

Gastonia will make a last-ditch effort to improve housing through private enterprise. If they succeed, my hat will be off to them. If not, I would favor government housing. I prefer private enterprise to be daring enough to do the job, though the evidence is not promising in America that it can be done.

This careful balance between a preference for the personal strategy and an openness toward the corporate strategy runs straight across his conceptual profile. Asked to suggest strategies for response to hypothetical community events such as bond elections, industrial slumps, and traffic hazards, he consistently prefers a personally implemented strategy first, but still gives high secondary priority to "structured" social strategies. That he understands and is genuinely open to the latter betokens a shift in the option-agenda that has apparently taken place in the shift from his predecessor to himself. One is sure that Monroe is not likely ever to sacrifice his pastoral relationship to individuals in his congregation at the cost of the "boldness" that Mitchem credits him with in the pulpit and in the community; but neither is his congregation, so full of business executives, likely ever to be sure that he can be counted on to comfort the afflicted without also afflicting the comfortable. In that, he demonstrates a measure of independence of mind and role that does not match the freeswinging self-confidence of his admirer Mitchem but contrasts also to the uptown ministerial image that used to be.

Kenneth Barger

Barger's uptown church has among its members many key leaders of the local economy; his tenure as a minister in Gastonia (1952-1968) was so long and so nearly coincident with the years covered by this study; and his consciousness of his own and his parishioners' image of the ministry is so sharply honed, that he is inevitably a minister to be reckoned with in any assessment of the minister's contemporary role in Gastonia. Many of the forces that have begun to play upon Fletcher Monroe have played much longer upon Barger, and as pastor to many of the powerful people of the city he has had the opportunity to develop insight into some aspects of the community and its churches as have few other ministers. On his side of the tracks, he is the closest white approximation to Fred Mitchem.

As a symbol of his own image of the ministerial role and as a summary of what he believes to be the gist of his career in Gastonia, Barger volunteers the story of a theological liberal of a previous generation, Ernest Fremont Tittle, who had in his congregation a conservative businessman who disagreed sharply with Tittle's economic philosophy. The man's wife died; and that night he walked the streets of the city in grief, with Tittle walking at a distance behind him until dawn. Later on the man said: "There is no man with whom I disagree more on social issues than Dr. Tittle, and none whom I trust more as a friend." Such a minister is no small part of Kenneth Barger's professional ideal. "The longer I've been in Gastonia, the more I've had to think of the deep, personal, emotional problems of people in my congregation. That is where you have to plant your first emphasis. If you can help a man first here, you might influence him later in his social involvements."

Barger came to Gastonia from a background as pastor of two large churches in university communities in Missouri and Texas. He was Virginia-born, educated in a denominational college in North Carolina, and known as one of the leading ministers in the denomination. He came to Gastonia at the age of forty-three, left at the age of fifty-nine.

"I'm sort of a misfit," he says with a grin, "I'm here in a fundamentalist, conservative community which I'm trying to influence. There is need in this community for a less legalistic, more tolerant ministry than it has had. I can't say that I *like* the community in comparison with university communities I've lived in. Actually, I feel a certain amount of frustration in it, but I have enjoyed my ministry here."

The frustration is compounded partly of the continuing tension between his views of the church in relation to society and the views of many of his members. "The majority in my church have been brought up to believe that the church should not concern itself with political and economic affairs. They are always saying to me, 'I know you don't agree with me, but. . . .' " That they will still talk over their personal problems with him, in spite of their various disagreements with him, is a source of great satisfaction to him.

Less satisfying, and an additional element in his frustration, is his acknowledged inability to maintain contact with those leadership groups in the city with whom he does not have a direct relationship as a pastor.

When I came here in 1952, _____ (a key uptown leader) was very friendly to me. He used to invite me often to go fishing with him. After a while, this tapered off. Then in the late fifties, I went to see him to raise the question of doing something to meet the Negro situation here before it exploded. The suggestion left him cold. After that there were no more fishing invitations, and I got the feeling that he went out of his way not to see me. I also mentioned the issue to his pastor, _____. But I doubt that he ever went to see him.

The personal visit, the behind-the-scenes appeal, Barger regards as the chief instrument of influence open to a local minister. In this strategic preference he is at one with Fletcher Monroe and Owen Palmer. The "scattered church" of individual Christians is the agency for the church's service to society.

Denominations should take stands on social issues corporately, but these stands have to be implemented by laity who affirm these stands. At the same time, we do need strong councils of churches in local communities with strong lay representation. That seems impossible in Gastonia. We are overwhelmingly dominated by churches with a congregational form of government. That makes cooperation very difficult.

He would presumably be open, therefore, to Fred Mitchem's sense of the need for church structures that served as an "honest pipeline" for communication about local issues. But in his view only a minority of ministers in town are similarly open. The only public area in which such a pipeline has consistently operated over the years is that of Alcoholic Beverage Control, and Barger feels little affinity with the ministers who have chosen this as the only social issue worthy of their corporate attention.

This is yet another element in his sense of frustration about the church in Gastonia. The organization that ought to have the most ease in puncturing the barrier between the upper middle class and the rest of the town is as self-insulating as the economic structure.

Though it is not as bad as when I came here, there is a terrific caste-system in Gastonia, which limits me and other ministers in the people whom we see and serve. . . . I recognize that the fundamentalist churches and their emotional fervor meet a real need among the underprivileged people in town, but their sort of emphasis seems to make communication difficult. It contributes to a lack of unity among the ministers and between churches.

When he decided in 1952 that he would come to Gastonia, he read *Millhands and Preachers,* and from the beginning of his pastorate he has had a keen eye for political and economic reality in the city. As his choice of "the most important improvement in the community in recent years," he alone among sixty-six ministers reaches back to 1953 and nominates:

The political revolution under Harrelson Yancey, which broke the hold of the conservative elite in this community. But I'm worried now, with the very recent defeat of the hospital bond issue (1966), which is evidently rooted in the anger of poor people in this community over the raising of the property tax and their general resentment against the economic status quo represented by some men who favored the bond issue.

He is well aware of some of the justifications for anger and resentment on the part of some poor people in Gaston County. A leading Gastonia textile owner commented to him recently, during their visit together to Belmont, on how much Gastonia used to be like Belmont: company-dominated, controlled in almost every way by a few families. A relative of one of those families once informed Barger that one of its patriarchs believe that "God made him rich and poor people poor." "He's the dangerous, unbalanced sort of rich man," he comments, shaking his head. "One of our denomination's ministers in Belmont says that the ruling families don't know how much people in town are smouldering."

In contrast to Belmont, he observes,

The decrease in family-owned mills is slowly changing things in Gastonia, weakening the influence of Gastonia's old guard. It's slow, but we are gradually changing from a small town to a metropolitan area. Industrial diversification has brought in many new types of people. If it had not been for the defeat of the hospital bond, I would have said that the city is on the verge of taking itself seriously—becoming a real city.

Whether or not labor unions will come to Gastonia as it becomes a "real city" remains an empirical question for him. But he is far more positive about the value of the union movement than the large majority of his parishioners.

I see the American political system as a matter of constant struggle and balance between conflicting interests. So I believe in unions, though I wonder sometimes if unions have not gotten too much power. The Teamsters Union frightens me! I think that the worker should have freedom not to join a union, but if a majority of workers do vote for a union, I think each worker has responsibility for supporting the union because he benefits from it. So I don't know what to think about 14-b. I'm caught between two feelings here. But the principle and the need of unions is unquestionable.

Barger would be the first to admit that his "pipeline" to the workers' state of mind is very clogged, but it is clear from his communications with the Belmont situation above that he is more certain about the need of unions there than in Gastonia. "I'm pretty blocked off from these people," he says reluctantly.

Does the church perform any service in relation to the industrial structure of the community? Yes, it performs at least two services, and he is again alone among sixty-six Gaston County ministers in suggesting this particular pair of church contributions to economic affairs:

(1) Conscience has kept some of the older leaders from being as ruthless as they might have been, though they have tried to compensate in material ways, like Rockefeller, by setting up foundations. (2) The smaller churches have lifted the cultural-spiritual dignity of the less privileged people by giving them places of leadership and development.

And how do the mills serve the churches?

Anyone who has read Liston Pope, of course, would be looking for signs of some real *control* of the church by industry here. My impression from Pope is that the churches then really were tools of the mills. The control now has lessened. It is true, for example, that one of the mill foundations has given several thousand dollars to our new church building. But I have not seen evidence of "control" through these gifts. My guess is that if a minister actively urged his people in a mill village to unionize, there would be pressure on him; that the mills still give to churches partly to pave the way for people's resistance in opposing unions if and when they come.

The new church building was constructed during the latter years of Barger's pastorate, at a cost of about $1,500,000, paid in full by the congregation over a period of only four years. He is conscious of the moral questions which can be raised about an expenditure of that sum of money upon a new building whose physical and aesthetic proportions approach those of a cathedral, in a town where half the families subsist on no more than $5000 a year. How does he answer such questions? Chiefly in terms of his sense that rich Gastonians suffer from a kind of poverty that only their pastors get to know:

There are many "successful" people in this town who lack a truly satisfying home life. They make money and go to parties, but there is a void of meaning in their life. A void of culture and aesthetics, too. I know that only a minority of people in Gastonia, or anywhere else, are deeply and pervasively moved by religion. But the building of a beautiful new church sanctuary was an approach towards a new aesthetic experience, towards a new religious experience, for many of the people in this congregation. Some became active in the church for the first time in connection with this building. Now they bring outsiders to see the building as one of the few "sights" of the city.

As much as any other minister in an uptown church, Barger has made an effort to link his ministry to persons with an impact upon the social structure. But at almost every point he has had to deal with the inertias of the "uptown" ideology, with the power of leaders with whom personal relationships were not always possible, and with the power of his own commitment to pastoral care for individuals. Both the successes and the frustrations of his sixteen-year ministry in Gastonia are intimately connected with these three large "givens"—what in this study we have called the local particularities of ideology, interests, and religion.

Geographically, hardly a mile separates Marsh's chapel in the north of town from Barger's great new church on a piece of high ground in the east. Interstellar *social* distances separate the two men. But with the same three givens each has had his negotiations—in relation to ideology, interests, and religion, each has had to do some shaping of his notion of "minister." Indeed, however distant Marsh and Barger may be from each other in theology and professional style, what they have palpably in common is *Gastonia itself*.

The Structure of Role Priorities for Church Leaders: A Sociological Overview of the Ministerial Role

From a selective sample of ten interpretations of the ministerial role by ministers themselves, we turn to the opinions of some fifty more of their colleagues and some 400 of their parishioners in Gastonia. As we shall see, there is a remarkable parallelism in the distribution of opinions among all these strata.

1. *Orientations to change.*   Throughout this part of the inquiry, our interest focused on the prescribed *social* function of the minister. That is, we did not attempt to inquire in any depth into everything that ministers do or are supposed to do in Gastonia. Admittedly the line between a professional activity that is "society-related" and one that is not, is hard to draw; for, by definition, every professional relationship is social. But the context chosen here is largely institutional: the frontier between the internal workings of the churches and the social community (with its institutions) external to the churches. Should the minister be expected to cross that frontier? If so, for what purpose—to change the community in some way, or to keep it from changing? And what are the methods by which the minister should act as an agent of change or non-change? The latter inquiry—proper methods of social action—is an important supplement to the other questions. As the above description of Fletcher Monroe indicates, modern Gastonia ministers cannot be divided neatly between those who favor the changing of society's institutions and those who favor no change.

A sizable proportion of the ministers in the community favor certain changes but, like Monroe, believe that the highroad to social change is the changed (or converted) human individual. Ministers and their parishioners are inclined to see the ministerial role as more or less concerned with institutional change; they prefer more or less the "personal" versus the "social" approach to effecting institutional change.[5]

This pair of dichotomous variables our inquiry shared with a study from the early 1960s by Sister Marie Augusta Neal.[6] In her study of Roman Catholic clergy, she sought to determine (through respondents' positive and negative evaluation of short statements concerning the church, the clergy role, and general ideology) whether the persons in her sample saw the minister as an agent of "change" or "non-change," and whether or not they applied "universal" standards of judgment to ecclesiastical and social questions, or were "particularistic," i.e., inclined to see every situation as subject to its own rules and requirements. In one part of our inquiry into the preferances of ministers and laymen for the role of the minister, we adapted Neal's set of variables to the construction of a trio of short hypothetical case-studies related to the work of ministers in an urban-industrial milieu. We asked our respondents, lay and clerical, to say what a minister "ought to do" in each of these cases; and in the forced-choice set of answers we provided, each alternative action suggested a role-preference in one of the four combinations of analytical elements in the Neal study:

	Structural	Individual
Change	1	2
Non-Change	3	4

As linkage with terms familiar in the classic vocabulary of the Christian churches, we later ascribed four names to these four possible role-preferences: (1) Prophet, (2) Evangelist, (3) Priest and (4) Pastor. But our use of these terms in the following, it should be carefully noted, does *not* match with any precision the same terms in the theological and ecclesiological tradition. The deductive logic of this part of our inquiry required us to define the "prophet," "priest," "evangelist," and "pastor" more narrowly and abstractly than theologians would prefer. Each term is meant to represent a *stance* or orientation towards a general end (change—non-change) and a general means towards that end (person—social structure). Thus, in our context, (1) a prophetic minister is one who favors change in the structures of society at large and who brings general standards of judgment to bear upon those structures; (2) an evangelist is one who also favors change in the society but who believes that the changed individual is the source of social change; (3) the priest is one who affirms the social structure by bringing general standards to bear that celebrate and confirm the social status quo; and (4) the pastor is one who also seeks to conserve the society as it is, but does so chiefly by helping to bring some kind of restorative help to troubled individuals.

Recognizing that no one of these rather narrow role-elements would be likely even to approximate the social stance which any single respondent would attribute to a minister, we asked respondents merely to express relative agreement or relative disagreememt with four possible actions by ministers in the three cases; and as a further check on preference, we asked them to rank the four actions 1,2,3,4.

The three cases and suggested responses were as follows:

1. "A city election is approaching and the candidates disagree mostly on whether or not taxes should be raised to improve the local schools. If he believes the taxes should be raised, what should a minister of a local church do?"

[*Prophetic*]: He should feel free to speak out in a sermon for the school taxes, and he should get involved in a political organization supporting that side.

[*Priestly:*] The Sunday before the election, without mentioning schools, he should offer a prayer of thanksgiving for the privilege of voting.

[*Evangelist:*] He should present his views privately to people with whom he is acquainted.

[*Pastoral:*] He should give a talk at a church supper, presenting both sides of the question, seeking not to take a side himself.

2. "A local company has just announced its intention of closing down its plant because of business competition. This decision means a serious loss to the city. What should a local minister do?"

[*Prophetic:*] He should point out in a sermon that the free enterprise system does not always benefit everybody connected with it.

[*Priestly:*] He should remind the congregation and others that the company leaders are doing what they have to do, from a business point of view.

[*Evangelist:*] He should write a letter to the company president, asking him to reconsider. If the answer is "no" he should take no further action.

[Pastoral:] He should think about organizing food basket distribution and a clothing collection to help those who may soon be without work.

3. "A certain busy street corner near a church has no traffic light. One day a school child from a church family is killed by a car at this corner. In this situation, what should the minister do?"

[Prophetic:] He should investigate the need for a traffic light, should consult with the proper officials, and, if necessary, should lead a community action group for bringing pressure upon the officials.

[Priestly:] He should conduct the funeral service, remembering to ask forgiveness for everyone responsible for the death of the child.

[Evangelist:] He should appeal to his congregation and others to become safer drivers, and to school children to be more careful crossing streets.

[Pastoral:] He should visit with the family of the child and with the driver of the car to help them get over their grief and guilt.

Table 4.1 represents a partial record of the results of this test of our lay sample of some 400 Gastonians and some thirty ministers.[8] It is immediately evident that no clear consistencies mark these responses, and no simple conclusions about the "typical ministerial role" in relation to economic and political issues can be drawn for Gastonia on the basis of this part of the inquiry. On the first issue, the most obviously political of the three, black lay respondents were far more likely than whites to endorse the prophetic role; but even blacks were comparatively less enthusiastic for that mode of engagement with the issue than for the other three alternative actions. Our study of the black churches in the early sixties would lead one to expect that black parishioners are much more permissive about direct political involvement by their clergymen than are whites. But this predictable response to the three cases was confirmed in the first case far more clearly than in the others. In no other case is the pattern for black respondents strikingly different from that of whites. All four of the lay groups are surprisingly open to structural criticism of the "free enterprise system" by their minister in a sermon—an openness to which few sermons from Gastonia pulpits have historically made response.

The answers of white ministers are not notably different from those of white laity. One important exception to this convergence between lay and professional views, however, is the larger support which ministers gave to direct political involvement in the school-bond election. Even there, again, this was the least-preferred alternative of the four; and the overall pattern for ministers, as summarized in Tables 4.2 and 4.3, suggests a general relative downgrading of the "prophetic" stance. At the same time, especially if the focus of analysis

Table 4.1
PROPORTION OF RESPONDENTS APPROVING* OF VARIOUS MINISTERIAL ROLES IN SPECIFIC ISSUES, BY RACE, SEX, AND CLERICAL ROLE

	Race and Sex									Ministers	
	Black				White				White Only	
	Males		Females		Males		Females			
Issues and Ministerial Roles	Percent	N	Percent	N	Percent	N	Percent	N	Percent	N
Issue 1: School Tax Election										
Prophetic	42.6	61	60.0	71	17.9	163	18.9	90	38.2	34
Priestly	70.5	61	84.3	70	74.0	169	74.4	90	79.4	34
Evangelist	55.7	61	66.2	71	72.8	169	60.4	91	97.0	34
Pastoral	67.2	61	78.9	71	54.4	169	55.6	90	45.2	31
Issue 2: Closing of Company										
Prophetic	55.0	60	64.3	70	45.5	168	42.2	90	43.7	32
Priestly	66.7	60	64.3	69	68.5	168	66.7	90	53.1	32
Evangelist	45.0	60	50.7	69	54.8	167	45.6	90	66.7	33
Pastoral	86.7	60	78.2	70	67.7	167	67.9	90	78.1	32
Issue 3: Child Is Killed										
Prophetic	93.3	60	94.3	70	74.0	169	75.6	90	87.9	33
Priestly	73.3	60	70.4	70	70.4	169	71.4	90	78.8	33
Evangelist	100.0	60	97.1	71	88.8	169	84.4	91	94.1	34
Pastoral	100.0	60	97.1	70	91.7	169	90.0	90	100.0	34

*Approval = responses of "strongly agree" or "agree."

Table 4.2

**PROPORTION OF WHITE MINISTERS WHO CONSIDER
THE PROPHETIC ROLE LEAST DESIRABLE***

Issues	Percent	Number of Cases
Issue 1: School Tax Election	61.5	26
Issue 2: Closing of Company	58.3	24
Issue 3: Child Is Killed	17.4	23

*Based on a ranking of 4 (out of 4 alternatives). See footnote 7 for this chapter.

Table 4.3

**PROPORTION OF WHITE MINISTERS WHO PREFER
VARIOUS MINISTERIAL ROLES***

Issues	Pastoral	Priestly	Evangelist	Prophetic	N
Issue 1: School Tax Election	7.4	29.6	59.2	3.7	27
Issue 2: Closing of Company	24.0	28.0	44.0	4.0	25
Issue 3: Child Is Killed	61.5	11.5	7.7	19.2	26

*Based on a ranking of 1 (out of 4 alternatives)

is on cases No. 1 and No. 2, white laity show comparatively high regard for the "evangelist" stance, and white ministers show even higher comparative regard for the same—which suggests that both are change-oriented in their view of the relation of religion and society; but for them the individual tends to be the funnel through which religion must be poured in order to *reach* society.

Some interesting, broader interpretative possibilities emerge from the data related to case No. 3. The responses to this case are such as to destroy almost any theory constructed on the basis of the other two. Realizing that the death of a child was likely to touch the imagination and emotion of the respondent more directly than would a school bond election or even a textile mill closing, we phrased the "prophetic" response on the test in the strong language of "bringing pressure upon the officials." (We knew from our study of the labor union and race relations crises in recent Gaston history that the corporate bringing of "pressure" was negatively valued by most Gastonians.) But some social evils are apparently so great in the eyes of our respondents that they call—at least imaginatively—for a breaking of religious taboos on structured political action.

When so undisputable a value as the life of a child is to be served by political organization, politics becomes the religious order of the day. Here the prophetic response vies with the pastoral in the scores as a whole and even though the pastoral response is slightly favored, especially by ministers themselves, the prophetic ranks strongly in every statistical comparison.

Against the background of what we already know about lay and ministerial understanding of the church as custodian of "moral issues" in community life, we can see some consistency between the results from all three cases by underscoring the *singleness* of the child's life and the *indisputability* of the value of that life. It is psychological truism that people are more likely to become intellectually and emotionally aware of a social problem when the problem is embodied in a personalized event. That is all the more likely in a society that habitually encourages its members to understand and value the society in terms of personal experience. The highly personalized religious ethos of Gastonia churches is both contributor to, and a reflex of, such a society. Moreover, in contrast to public education and employment cycles in industry, the danger of bad traffic systems to the lives of children is incontrovertibly an issue about which "something" should be done. The temptation, especially in Gastonia, is for the ordinary citizen to define the other two issues as not quite "religious" enough to cancel the generalized cultural constraint against direct clerical incursions into local power politics. Alternatively, the tendency is to leave these economic and political issues to specialized experts.[9]

To generalize from this part of our inquiry: Gastonians believe that their ministers should be social-change minded, but action for social change should begin and largely end with the individual. Also, the minister should be strongly committed to the pastoral role, which (by our definition) is socially a non-change role-element concerned with helping the individual adapt to troubles for which society may be partly responsible. At the same time, Gastonians are not unequivocably ready for their ministers to carry on a mere "ambulance" ministry as implied by this narrow definition of "pastoral." White laity in the company-closing case strongly prefer both change-roles over both non-change roles, and the results are almost the same with black laity. To be sure, if the mild criticism of the free enterprise system implied in the "prophetic" response to case No. 2 had been changed to action involving a labor union or resort to government action, the responses might have been parallel to those in the school tax issue, where white laity and ministers consistently downgraded sermonic and organized political involvement. The test itself had severe limitations, of course; and its results compose only one piece of evidence of overall pattern in the norms of churchmanship prevailing in this community; but a minimal conclusion must be: *on all sides, the minister's social role is perceived as complex*. Gastonians have few expectations about the minister as an agent of structural social change but under some circumstances they are open to such agency. They prefer ministers to work at the business of helping individual persons to change *their* "ways," but some traditional professional tactics —sermons, personal persuasion, participation in citizen action groups—are perceived as relevant on occasion for remedying faults in the social structure. No simple "quietist" or "pietist" description of the normative ministerial role fits this evidence.

2. *Ministers' self-assessment of their role.*   These rather formal probes into role-prescriptions for ministers were supplemented in our study by a series of more informal open-ended interview questions of both minister and laity. Though these inquiries were more systematic than Pope's investigations in the 1930s, we were especially interested in discovering if Pope's general account of the normative cultural expectations of ministers would hold for the subsequent generation of Gastonians. Summarizing his impressions, Pope concluded:

Gastonia prefers ministers who . . . are "good talkers" in the pulpit, "good fellows" on the street, and sympathetic comforters in time of trouble . . . The role of the uptown minister . . . is not to transcend immediate cultural boundaries but to sympathize and sanction the rightness of things as they are.[10]

He also observed:

Most Gastonia residents expect that their minister shall remain strictly within the realm usually regarded as religious and resent any excursion into areas not associated with his profession.[11]

Answers to certain open-ended questions by our ministerial respondents in the 1960s indicate both continuity and change in these attitudes concerning the ministerial role. "What kind of minister do you think most people in the community like?" we asked. One *black* minister replied in terms that virtually replicated the views of *white* parishioners in the thirties as perceived by Pope:

. . . they want what he preaches to be rather old fashioned—sin, damnation, and sins of drinking, dancing, etc. One who will not become involved in social questions or if he does, not to get caught in a position of promoting a cause, such as integration, in a public manner, joining a demonstration, etc.

Signs of a preference for traditional (preaching and pastoral) activities were also in evidence in the response of a white Presbyterian minister to this same question:

A preacher for Sunday morning, a visitor when they are sick, a counselor when they have problems. This bothers me so much: people want attention—if they stub their toe. Sometimes I think they would be much happier if I forgot about the community, the new curriculum (Presbyterian, U.S.), the cancer society, and all the rest.

Generally ministers believe that lay people give a lower priority to the pastor's community-relations activities than to the traditional functions. A Lutheran minister seemed to agree:

(Question: "What kind of community leadership do you feel to be appropriate for a minister to take?") . . . study, visiting, looking after congregational affairs. The minister can't be a minister to his people and take a large amount of leadership in the community.

Despite such reservations and qualifications, our interviews indicate that various Gastonia ministers have been involved, to varying degrees, with community organizations, such as the PTA, United Fund, Family Service Agency, Human Relations Committee, and the Y.M.C.A. Significantly absent from such a list of "acceptable" community activities for the minister are *political* involvements. Presumably the above organizations are not controversial, and they are in this sense non-political. Qualified approval of civic participation does not extend, then, to unrestricted and unambiguously political involvement. Over half of the white clergymen made some reference to political involvement, and their preferences are shown in Table 4.4, but most of

Table 4.4

DEGREE OF POLITICAL INVOLVEMENT APPROVED BY WHITE MINISTERS, IN PERCENT

	Percent Endorsing
High (e.g., Can speak out on any candidate or issue, campaign for others, generally act as any citizen.)	5.7
Moderate or limited (e.g., Can speak out on "moral" issues, such as ABC—Alcoholic Beverage Control, can advocate voting, show an interest in campaigns and elections, etc.)	37.7
Noninvolvement	9.4
No answer (related specifically to politics)	47.2
Total number of cases	53

these men favor restricting political involvement, and several prefer complete noninvolvement.

As explanation of their caution here, ministers pointed to the dangers in being so "prophetic" that they risk alienating their members:

(Wesleyan) . . . I realize prophets spoke out on issues of the day, but a man has to be careful. (About what?) He may lose some people. He is out to win all men to the gospel.

At the same time, some ministers seem to disapprove of the timidity of their colleagues:

(Baptist) . . . The church is too interested in patting them on the back rather than in telling them the truth. A minister fears too much losing his pulpit, especially Baptist ministers.

Responses to another question suggested that some Gastonia ministers believe that in comparison with a previous generation of ministers they have gained more autonomy to speak out on social, political, and economic issues. Tolerance toward prophetic action, these men speculate, may have increased over the past thirty years.

(Question: "What do you see as the reasons for the tendency in some churches for the minister to bring social issues into his sermons?")

(Baptist) (He laughs.) The first reason is facetious but real: churches are easier to come by now! There is more demand for a minister. Second, people feel that preachers are entitled to their opinions even if they are wrong. Formerly they would run you out of the county, but not now—due to the rise in education, economic levels. Also it is a matter of timing: my fourth of July sermon if delivered at the actual election time would have led to their running me off. Then nothing said from the pulpit should be aimed at a particular party or candidate.

(The sermon to which he refers dealt with Federal government power and the threat to individual initiative.)

(Presbyterian pastor in a mill community) The changed social climate has meant a lot here: some ministers are less subject to feeling a danger of blowing the local situation up. He doesn't have to be as careful now about making his witness and departing.

(Salvation Army) He should play the prophetic role as did Isaiah and Jeremiah. The minister should have a free hand to speak out on any subject; to speak out against the evils of the day including strong drink, wages, deplorable housing.

The protection which a hierarchy may provide and the contrasting situations of priest and minister are illustrated by this quote from our sole Roman Catholic clergyman:

It would be foolish to discuss something that wasn't discussable! If anyone came to me to object, then I'd say, "You are a Catholic. If you can't see the truth of this, then that's too bad. It's a position of the church, and you are a part of the church."

In addition to the greater permissiveness of some congregations, other factors were mentioned which presumably have fostered the minister's freedom to speak to social issues: seminary training, the theological liberalism in such training, and the pressing nature of certain problems. One fourth of the white ministers (26.9%) expressed explicit regrets or reservations about the trend towards a "social gospel." Among the explanations given for the trend (by others favoring it) are the following:

(Baptist) Our seminaries have helped men to see that the gospel must be made relevant to the issues of society.

(Baptist) Better informed ministry, and people know the church is not secluded from society, that we must move the Christian idea out into the forces that make up society.

(Presbyterian) In my case I've learned a little more about what the gospel means! And there is a broadening of viewpoint going on among most people. They still might not agree (with the application of the gospel to social issues), but they cannot make much defense against it as Christians. They become silent, even if they are not yet converted on the matter.

Our interview responses from Gastonia ministers also provided more quantitative data which reinforce certain of the implications developed in the preceding analysis. As indicated above, our sample of clergy were asked this open-ended question: "What kind of minister do you think most people in the community like?" Since no responses were provided, the frequency with which a particular function was mentioned is an indication of its salience for the respondents.[12]

According to Table 4.5, the pastoral role (the understanding, sympathetic counselor) is most salient in the clergy's perceptions of lay preferences, and this finding is consistent with the conclusions of Samuel Blizzard.[13] Thirty-eight of fifty-three respondents mentioned pastoral activities.

Less than half refer to preaching, though this activity is also relatively salient; and less than one fourth include prophetic characteristics, e.g., "telling people the truth." Moreover, the third-ranked element of "prophet" is negatively evaluated by seven out of the twelve ministers who happen to mention it. Consistent with the Glock and Stark findings on parishioners' attitudes toward "office work" is the deemphasis of administrative activities, being mentioned by about one fifth of the respondents.[14]

The frustrations of time allocation elaborated by Blizzard are also revealed first, by a Presbyterian and second, an official of the Salvation Army:

Table 4.5

WHITE MINISTERIAL PERCEPTIONS OF LAYMEN'S ROLE PREFERENCES
IN ORDER OF SALIENCE*

Ministerial Role	Number of Ministers Mentioning the Role
Pastor	38
Preacher	21
Prophet	12**
Administrator	11
Community servant	10
Moral example	9
Educator	8
Moral traditionalist	6
Charismatic	5
Ritualist	5
Total white ministers	53

*Salience is defined here as the frequency of being mentioned as a possible role element, without respondent being probed by the interviewer.

**58% of the respondents who mentioned this role component indicated a negative evaluation of it.

The program of the church keeps a man so tied up with church activities that he can't study (for preaching), and so that he can't know his community well enough. Church members want the minister to take care of the clerical duties, the pastoral responsibilities, carry on a program, evangelize the unsaved. They keep me busy enough all right, but not with the things I feel I ought to be doing.

He should be a true pastor more than an executive, a true shepherd who gets down to their level, is in and out of their homes, their lives. The minister has psychological problems because of cross pressures between administrative demand and his need to be a pastor.

The obligation to be a moral example (someone to "look up to," "above reproach") was salient for approximately one of every six ministers questioned. The following response, not necessarily representative, indicates one man's perceptions and frustrations:

(Presbyterian) They want an honest man, even a god! Someone who doesn't make mistakes. You have to convince them that the minister is human. They want him educated, but not too educated. Sermons that are honest, but which hit someone else. A minister who is a church builder, but who will let them rest.

A majority of laity interviewed in our sample of Gastonians disclaimed this "exemplar" expectation of the minister, however. When asked, "Do you think a minister should be different from other Christian people in town?" over half (54%) replied no. Approximately one third (31%) answered yes, and specified their answer in terms of the absence of personal vices or the obligation of the minister to set moral examples and to provide "moral leadership."

3. *Conclusion.* What it may mean—conceptually and practically—for the minister to provide "moral leadership" in the social community, is no minor concern of church people in Gaston County. It is a major disputable question, among both ministers and laity. And this, if nothing more, constitutes a difference between the ministerial role as recorded in Pope's research and that described here. In Pope's Gastonia, consensus on the minister's role was relatively placid and unbroken; now there is dispute over the matter, as in many other parts of the United States. Though changes in the ecclesiastical weather seem to arrive in Gaston County on a tardier schedule than obtains in more urbanized parts of the nation, the signs of a "gathering storm in the churches" are beginning to appear too. On the other hand, there is apparently some difference between the storm now gathering in this southern Piedmont community and the one recorded in Hadden's well known study. Laity and clergy in Gastonia are apparently not so diametrically *divided* as they are in Hadden's national samples.[15] There is division enough among both clergy and laity over social activism as a component of the ministerial role. But polarities on the issue characterize *both* groups, and neither group has large numbers of radically "pro-involvement" or radically "anti-involvement" members.

The possible explanations for this "moderate disharmony" in Gastonia's image of the minister are many. In spite of much industrial diversification, Gaston County has been largely a one-industry economy. An urban ethos based in such an economy will not be associated with the variety of life-styles and ideological orientation that can be found in large cities everywhere, even in the American South. Small-town consensus still exists in Gastonia, enabling us with reason to speak of a "local ideology." That ideology pervades many sectors of community life, and certain sectors—notably economic and church institutions—in turn have molded and sustained the ideology. Further, like smaller towns everywhere, Gastonia competes with larger urban centers for its share of change-minded leaders. Innovative professionals, including innovative ministers, are likely to gravitate to these other cities. There the *scope* of conflict over major social-institutional issues is likely to be broader and more severe.

From another angle, it may be said that in this middle-sized urban county the "segmentation of radicals" is much more difficult than it is in large urban communities, where assorted ideologues can live insulated in their own respective institutions.[16] Both the size and the cultural traditions of Gaston County hinder the development of such insulated institutions. As in many another small town, people and their institutions have to learn to live together; they sense each other's presences in too many concrete, elbow-rubbing ways to tolerate an ethos of mere avoidance and "agreement to disagree." Gastonians' avoidance of talk and action leading to social conflict is profoundly related to this sense, which is also reflected in their consensus on the proper social role of the church and its leaders.

It is an increasingly wobbly consensus, as we have seen. But that very fact poses normative concerns for large numbers of Gastonians, particularly as they reflect on the need of their society for some consensus about social values. Many seem to expect the minister to personify at least the hope for such a consensus. Few are ready to speak of the minister as a one-talent professional. Even the more traditional among our informants suggest that the church and its leaders must (1) take both individuals and institutions seriously, (2) boldly speak the truth about social evil while modulating the speech so that the truth will not be drowned in a counterwave of hostility, (3) walk a line between identifying every social conflict as a "moral issue" and identifying few if any as such. Many imponderables, as hard for sociologists to measure as for the majority of their respondents to articulate, are present in all this. Certainly the beginnings of a very large storm in Gastonia churches, tpyified by the conflict over the minister's role, are all present in the community. But a commitment to resisting the potential viciousness of the storm underlies many of the communications quoted here. For reasons abundantly clear in Pope's study and ours, Gastonians have a deep, generalized fear of any social event that threatens to "tear this town apart." As the study of primitive religion has taught us, the fear of social disturbance that attacks the very roots of people's ability to live together is a generically religious fear, just as the hope for a "good" community is a generically religious hope.[17]

A large number of Gastonia residents entertain such fear and such hope; and, in dealing with the humdrum issue of role-priorities for a church leader, Gastonians are also dealing with the broad issue of how a society of many parts can keep these parts humanly related. *The threatening side of social structural differentiation looms here: who and what are to hold the structures together?* Almost inarticulately, many Gastonians seem to be answering the question in their contradictory prescriptions for the role of the minister: "Religion and its leaders must hold us together; what else can overcome the contradictions of society itself?"

On this hypothesis, the matter of the role-prescriptions for "the preacher" becomes a momentous issue for anyone who professes to a religious outlook upon society. The issue is not primarily professional. *The issue is finding a conceptual and institutional synthesis for social values whose unity a highly differentiated society inevitably threatens.* Looked at in the context of contemporary prescriptions for other professional roles, the terms used in both theology and sociology to analyze the minister's role presuppose a truly amazing combination of desirable talents: what other professional in American society is likely to have his role analyzed in so many broad, disparate, often fuzzy, emotionally-laden terms as "pastor, priest, evangelist, prophet"? Humanly speaking, it is no wonder that while other professionals are increasingly drawn towards specialized role-definitions, ministers should be drawn in the same direction, with many of them settling for one or another of these four "specialties." But the question that simmers in an unspoken way beneath much of the soul-searching of ministers and parishioners in Gastonia is whether or not, in personal and institutional ways, it is possible for an organizational leader to be both a friend-in-need and a critic-of-evil, both an afflicter of the comfortable and a comforter of the afflicted, both a guardian of good social order and an enemy of bad social order. This is a very high expectation for any person's effort in any society. The mind of the specialist sees it as impossibly high. But to the mind of many a Gastonian layperson and minister, it is analogous to the expectation of a society for its total life. For better or for worse, something about total social integration Gastonians see at stake in the question of the integration of the ministerial role. No wonder that, along the local ideological spectrum of Progress, Harmony, and Liberty, the affinities of the religious institution for Harmony should be especially strong in the local mind.

A final theoretical-pragmatic note: Gastonia and other ministers will condemn themselves to lives of mounting frustration if they fail to distinguish between the integrity of society and the integrity of a single human role, or fail to distinguish between the symbols (religion and ideology) that help to unify complex societies and the institutions—churches, governments, corporate entities galore—that share the task of sustaining, changing, and heeding those symbols. What should be the role of the explicitly religious organization in a society which seems to parcel out and conceal its religious-ideological commitments among an array of other institutions? The question cannot be answered without driving toward answers that are far more normative-theological than empirical-sociological. But the human struggle after role definitions recorded here, a sociological description, poses just such a question. In the next, concluding section of this book, we shall see how churches of Gastonia, over the last generation, have answered the question in relation to two salient issues of social change.

NOTES

1. Cf. above, p. 51.
2. Cf. above, p. 40.
3. Though they are examples and not a random-sample, the ten ministers were chosen for

inclusion here by criteria basic to this study as a whole: (1) We are broadly interested in both the continuity and the change of relations between the church and this local society over a thirty-year period; so we describe the careers and outlooks of a cluster of men who together embody both continuities and shifts in ministerial role prescriptions detectable in this period. (2) We are seeking to make meaningful generalizations about the churches and the community of Gastonia as a sociological whole, so this selection of ministers represents the four major social-class divisions that governed our sampling procedure for the population at large. The first four men largely serve wageworkers in the textile industry. The next man serves a church that once was identified with a mill village but now is "middle middle class." The next is pastor of what long ago was a country church and now also is middle class and urban in constituency. The next two serve churches wholly identified with the black community. The final pair serve large "uptown" churches. (3) The ecclesiastical coverage of the selection is broad without being rigorously inclusive: three sect groups and six denominations; congregational memberships from 20 to over 2000; budgets from several thousand dollars to two hundred thousand a year. The formal education of the ten men ranges from six to twenty years. (4) Most important among the criteria for selection, however, is the set of clues which these men offer us for answering a single basic question: *How has the ministerial role changed or remained the same in terms of the minister's own felt obligation to be an agent of change in the community at large?* A broad age-span was thus a further criterion for choosing the ten. The youngest man here is twenty-seven; the oldest, seventy-three. Two are in their fifties, two in their forties, and four in their thirties. (All but three have left Gastonia since being interviewed by us in the 1965-67 period. The names here are fictitious, and various details are omitted to protect anonymity.)

For a recent treatment of differing clergy orientations to social change and the church's relationship to social change, see J. Alan Winter, "The Attitudes of Societally Oriented and Parish-Oriented Clergy: An Empirical Comparison," *Journal for the Scientific Study of Religion,* Vol. 9, No. 1 (Spring 1970), 59-66. Winter concludes that "societally oriented" clergy become involved "in attempts to bring about social change. The 'new breed' reputedly stress the prophetic aspects of ministry more than the roles of priest, preacher, pastor, and parish administrator; the focus is more on the society and its ills than on the parish and its needs." Moreover, they regard power and conflict as necessary ingredients in any effective movement for social change. We found that certain of the men described in the following case studies could not be neatly categorized as "societally oriented" or "parish-oriented." Examples of combined patterns are Stuart Henderson, Fletcher Monroe, Thomas Dixon, and Kenneth Barger. One of the central issues of the subsequent discussion of this chapter concerns the struggle to resolve the tension between the minister's own role concept (a theologically-defined sense of vocation) and parishioner preferences. Some clergy exemplify a process which Jeffrey Hadden has called "resocialization" and defines as the changing of a professional's goals in the face of the "realities" of his experience *vis à vis* his constituency. The clearest implicit example of resocialization, perhaps, is the case of Kenneth Barger; the clearest explicit example, that of Shriver in his Preface, above. Cf. Jeffrey K. Hadden, *The Gathering Storm in the Churches* (Garden City, New York: Doubleday and Company, 1969), p. 220.

4. Alcoholic Beverage Control stores were voted into being in traditionally prohibitionist Gaston County in 1967.

5. In contrast to prevailing Gastonia preferences, Winter's "societally oriented" clergy stressed "the role of social structures in the etiology and alleviation of social problems." Cf. Alan Winter, *op. cit.,* 59-66.

6. Sister Marie Augusta Neal, *Values and Interests in Social Change* (Englewood Cliffs, New Jersey: Prentice-Hall, Inc., 1965.)

7. Since our sample included a relatively small number of black ministers (nine), we did not consider percentages based on this small total to be reliable. On the other hand, we felt that in view of some important differences in orientation and point of view—with regard to matters such as ministerial roles—combining black and white ministers would likewise be inadvisable.

8. Tables 1-3 show a relatively small number of ministerial cases since this test was not administered in some of our earliest interviews with clergy.

9. On the basis of Case No. 3 alone, one might predict that when bad traffic safety conditions lead to deaths in Gastonia, there would be readiness among church members and ministers to make this an occasion for political action. However, only one minister among those interviewed by us was conscious of traffic safety as an important "moral issue" in Gastonia, and he lamented that the town generally showed scandalous tolerance for one particularly outstanding traffic hazard: the series of railroad crossings that are strung through the middle of the city of Gastonia. There are some fifteen street-crossings of the local railroad line within the city limits, only two of which are traversed by tunnels or overpasses. Hardly a year passes, said our respondent, without some Gastonian—or a whole family—being killed in a rail-crossing accident within the city limits. "The slaughter goes on," said our minister-respondent ruefully, "and nobody seems concerned enough to do something about it." For many years, he said, the railroad company and the local government had discussed the question of who should pay for the installation of gates at some of the open crossings where lives have been lost. By 1974 a number of the crossings had been fitted out with flashing red warning-lights, but bells and gates were still conspicuous in their absence.

10. *MP*, p. 95.

11. *Ibid.*, p. 182.

12. The question, "What kind of minister do you think most people in the community like?" was open-ended. Responses were coded according to the categories shown in Table 4.5 with particular roles being mentioned positively, mentioned negatively or not mentioned at all. Some of the "typical comments" corresponding to particular roles might be helpful in illustrating the content of that role as expressed by the respondents and conceptualized by the investigators. (1) pastor: "able to meet all sorts of people," "one of them," "sympathetic"; (2) preacher: "presents a well-constructed message," "preaches to reach the sinner"; (3) prophet: "will tell them the truth," "not afraid to make people uncomfortable"; (4) charismatic: "dedicated," "man who has an influence"; (5) moral example: "above reproach," "they want to look up to him"; (6) moral traditionalist: "old fashioned morality"; (7) ritualist: "able to pray"; (8) administrator: "ability to lead," "money raiser"; (9) community servant: "involved in the community"; (10) educator: "a man of intellect," "one who studies." More details on the coding of this item may be found in Appendix.

13. Samuel Blizzard, "The Minister's Dilemma," *The Christian Century* Vol. LXXIII, No. 17 (April 25, 1956), pp. 508-510.

14. Charles Y. Glock and Rodney Stark, *Religion and Society in Tension* (Chicago: Rand McNally & Co., 1965). See Chapter Seven.

15. Among the six major denominational groups in Hadden's study—Methodist, Episcopalian, (United) Presbyterian, American Baptist, American Lutheran, and Missouri Synod Lutheran—there is lacking any of the provincial southern denominations (most notably the Southern Baptists) that dominate Gastonia. Cf. Hadden, *op. cit.*, p. 42.

16. Concerning the career patterns of some clergy with more radical or prophetic tendencies see Phillip E. Hammond and Robert E. Mitchell, "Segmentation of Radicalism—the Case of the Protestant Campus Minister," *American Journal of Sociology*, 71 (September 1965), 133-43.

17. On this theme, cf. further below, Chapter Seven, pp. 307-312.

PART **II**

LIBERTY AND JUSTICE FOR ALL:
The Church and Community Issues

Chapter Five

The Church as Opponent of Change:
The Labor Union Movement

Introduction

Among other questions asked Gastonians in 1966-67, as part of this study, was this: "In recent years, have local churches or church leaders had influence on any of the following? (1) elections, (2) housing, (3) labor-management relations, (4) alcohol, and (5) race relations?" Table 5.1 shows the weight of such influence which five sub-groups of 400 people in the sample ascribed to the churches. The meaning of this data is silhouetted if we look at the relative rankings of the five issues by these groups:

White Males	*White Females*	*Black Males*	*Black Females*	*Students*
Alcohol	Alcohol	Race Relations	Race Relations	Race Relations
Race Relations	Race Relations	Elections	Elections	Alcohol
Elections	Elections	Alcohol	Housing	Elections
Housing	Housing	Housing	Alcohol	Housing
Labor Relations	Labor Relations	Labor Relations	Labor Relations	Labor Relations

Two striking consistencies are immediately evident here: all groups see the churches as having relatively great influence in race relations, and all see the least churchly influence in labor relations.

Such findings pose some intriguing problems of method for the sociological investigator: shall the agenda of research into this community take its clues concerning what social issues to investigate from such a list? should the race relations issue be focal and the labor union issue peripheral? because a large proportion of interviewees see the alcohol issue as comparatively important for the churches, shall that issue claim attention too? on the other hand, does the solid bottom-rank of labor relations itself cry out for explanation?

171

Table 5.1

PROPORTION OF RESPONDENTS WHO BELIEVE THAT LOCAL CHURCHES OR
CHURCH LEADERS HAVE HAD INFLUENCE ON COMMUNITY ISSUES
BY RACE AND SEX

| Race and Sex | Community Issues* | | | | | | | | | |
| | Elections | | Housing | | Labor Relations | | Alcohol | | Race Relations | |
	Percent	N	Percent	N	Percent	N	Percent	N	Percent	N
White										
Males	25.4	142	11.3	150	9.4	149	80.6	160	53.6	151
Females	22.1	77	14.5	76	5.3	75	73.3	86	42.5	80
Black										
Males	53.7	41	28.9	38	13.5	37	35.7	42	64.3	42
Females	39.1	46	28.2	39	19.4	36	27.9	43	41.5	41
College Students	51.9	21	25.0	20	15.8	19	77.2	22	77.2	22

*Question was: In recent years have local churches or church leaders had any influence on any
of the following? . . . elections? . . . housing? . . . labor-management relations? . . . alcohol?
. . . race relations?

One can only answer such questions under the pressure of other inputs of
knowledge and assumption about a community and its investigation. Indeed,
one must make some choices partly on the basis of the investigators' own
interests. On the face of it, any student of Gastonia, following in the trail of
Liston Pope, has to be curious about the labor union issue in Gastonia, because
the Pope study centered on a union-related crisis. Then empircally, the labor
union movement, virtually invisible on the Gastonia scene for 15 years after the
Loray Strike, was to make a large renewed attempt at a comeback in Gastonia
after World War II: much human energy was spent in those postwar years
promoting and opposing unions in Gastonia.

As we shall see, not many unions got organized: so that to tell the story of
unionism after 1940 is to dwell often on things that did not happen. Would such
knowledge be reason enough to give short shrift to unionism as an issue around
which to organize any part of another book on Gastonia? The authors think not.
What some persons intend to make happen and others keep from happening, is
no small part of human history. Historians themselves might well pay more
attention to such prevented-events. Certainly the sociologist might more regularly collaborate with the historian to ask the question: from this array of
possibilities, why did these human intentions succeed, and these fail?

Our other strong, presupposed interest in the labor union question stems
from the definition of "social change" adopted early in this book: "A society

changes significantly when a part or whole of its value-canopy is re-defined in relation to the organization of its various corporate interests."[1] In these terms, the labor union raised a major issue of change in Gaston County in the 1940-75 period: who was to have the right and power to say what is legitimate in the organization of labor-management relations? During the past three decades, no organization has sought more regularly to change the community's traditional answer to this question; and the local churches, we have reason to believe, played a role in the community's apparent refusal to make such a change. We have been led, in effect, to doubt the judgment of our respondents that the churches have not been "influential" in the community's behavior around this issue.

Other data causes us to agree with them, however, on the relation of the churches to change in local race relations. Together these two issues are emblematic of two boundaries appropriate to any study of religion and social change: what religion may do to maintain the fabric of organization and legitimacies that compose a community, over against what it may do to change this same fabric. As it happens, a rich fund of data was available to us concerning both issues in both dimensions.

Having said this, however, we are the first to admit that other issues could as consistently have been chosen for the focus of what follows. Traditionally the churches of Gaston County have had a reputation for exerting great influence on political-legislative policy regarding alcoholic beverage consumption. Here, if in no other area of social concern, the Protestant churches of the South have demonstrated that they do have a "social gospel." One might have chosen alcohol, then, as focus for a study of religion and social change in Gastonia; and one would then be especially curious to explain why, after fifty years of successful prohibitionist lobbying by large numbers of local church people, the Gaston County electorate voted in 1967 for the establishment of A.B.C. stores. Was this a test of church power in community affairs?[2]

Again, from the other end of our respondents' ranking of apparent church influence on social issues, we might have inquired if the churches have been influential or not in the field of housing. Along the way, our inquiry into the 1940-75 era stumbled again and again into a massive unconcern, in the churches, in the government and in the community at large, for the problem of the county's deteriorating stock of housing. As early as 1940, former mayor Gregg Cherry campaigned with the Gastonia City Council for a federally-funded housing project, but such a project was not to arrive in Gastonia until the early 1970s.[3] Partly because, and partly in spite of the sale of mill-village houses by the mills in the forties and fifties, an intangible hopelessness seems to have pervaded the very discussion of bad housing in Gaston County. The proportion of county houses officially considered "delapidated" went from one fourth in 1940 to one fifth in 1950 back to over one fourth in 1960, while the comparable proportion for the city of Gastonia remained slightly under one fifth throughout the period.[4] The political, economic, ideological, and religious reasons for this low level of community attention to one of its easily identified human problems could well have become a major focus of our inquiry.

Yet again, issues not listed in our 1967 survey inquiry might have been our focus. In 1974, for example, the problem of crime had attained much publicity in Gastonia and was even the object of citizen organization and protest-marching, and one supposes that many people-on-the-street of the county would nominate this issue as one that churches should or do give attention to.

Our interests, however, have clustered finally around unionism and race relations for a complex of reasons already stated or implied: the rich combination of both ideological and organizational data available to us in the history of both issues in the community; the stark contrast between publicly perceived church involvement in the one issue and perceived non-involvement in the other; and—finally—our judgment that around these two questions the churches of Gastonia have most vividly identified how they are, and are not, forces for change in this local society.

One further introductory word to what follows: though separable as issues of social change, the unionism and race questions in Gastonia are formally one in their mutual relation to questions of *power* and *ideology*. Since these two themes will weave in and out of all that follows, a summary is in order—recapitulating the gist of Part I and forecasting the gist of Part II in just these terms.

1. *The power issue.* It will be clear from Chapter Two above that, in the aftermath of the Loray Strike, the dominant members of Gastonia's "community power structure"[5] were all associated with the management of the textile industry. The relatively simple economic organization of the county made such dominance almost inevitable: few local residents were uninvolved, directly or indirectly, in textiles; and sociologically the county and its towns were divided roughly into the two categories of "operatives" an "owners." Most mill communities were small and isolated from each other, making unlikely much contact among workers on a county-wide scale. The effort to achieve such contact largely failed in the 1929 strike, and whatever post-'29 complaints workers may have had against managers, the traditional individualistic style of personnel relations remained strong right through World War II.

By the end of the war, however, locally owned mills were faced with the new competition of the large national corporation; and the latter's purchase of some local plants brought new potentials for national and international interests to influence local government, business, and industry. From this standpoint, Gastonia's struggle over industrial diversification in the forties and fifties was a contest between old-line and newly-arriving industrial elites. Significantly, the year 1953 was the watershed year for the partial breakup of two exclusions in the traditional power structure: the exclusion of the nontextile business person from local political office, and the exclusion of blacks. The significance of each break was subject to very different evaluations over the ensuing twenty years: some observers would claim that, especially in Gastonia City, the presence of many different kinds of industries increasingly moved the community towards a really pluralistic structure of influence and power; others would claim that the officers of national corporations had so little material interest in most local political policies, that their influence at most was episodic. Furthermore, the economic policies of the old order—especially the relatively low wages of the textile industry—fitted the interests of the more affluent new industries by making their somewhat higher wages not so high as they might have been. And the formal power now claimed by Gastonia blacks was subject to even more diverse evaluation: was Gaston County's "progress" towards the achievement of political office by blacks a tokenistic inhibition of real power or, compared to other southern communities of its size, a remarkable interracial advance?

In terms of formal shifts in the locus of power, the renewal of national labor union activity in Gaston County after the war paralleled the coming of the big national corporation. But the interests at stake were radically different: some of the new corporations came South to avoid unionism, and they came equipped with formidable union-fighting weapons such as improved wage scales, professional personnel-relation skills, and new federal-state legislation epitomized in the Taft-Hartley Law. From 1940 to 1975, unions were to chalk up a checkered record of success and failure: considerable advance in the late forties, followed by recession of power in the fifties and new advances—especially in nontextile industries—in the sixties. But by the mid-seventies Gaston County was still by national standards an underunionized county in the least unionized of the fifty United States.

In short, if uniform domination of county affairs by a textile elite was gradually eroded during these decades, the erosion consisted chiefly of a differentiation of influence and power within the business community. The politics of the sixties, however, were increasingly complicated by incursions of power from three other sources: the federal government, the black community, and several political candidates who successfully mobilized and spoke to the interest of non-elite constituencies. First in the civil rights movement, then in the war on poverty, and finally in assorted programs of housing, environmental regulation, and highway planning, the federal presence grew steadily. Local "black power" grew, too. Most remarkably, perhaps, the late sixties saw the successful attempts of a few new political leaders to build broad support for themselves among the less affluent majorities of white and black Gastonians.

Crucial to this success was a level of public participation in elections that was very untraditional in Gaston County history. This, too, was the sign of growing distance between modern Gastonia and its mill-village past: easy control of all segments of life by the single hand of a mill owner was progressively more difficult now. Like the rest of urbanizing America, Gastonia by the early seventies was more than ever a place where the power of a person or an institution in one segment of society could not be *automatically* translated into power in all the other segments. In this sense, the master-issue of power during the whole three decades was: how, in a society of increasing differentiation, can the different segments achieve and maintain enough power over the other segments for the protection of self-interest?

2. *The ideological issue.*   In an ethos that widely acclaimed the virtues of a free-enterprise economy, the freedom of individual investors and corporations to manage their own affairs was axiomatic for most Gastonians. But the freedom of wageworkers to pursue their self-interest through the organization of a union was far from axiomatic in a community still living in the remembered shadow of the Loray Strike. Are individuals and groups at liberty to *organize* for the pursuit of any self-interest which they perceive themselves to have? When interests of equally "free" groups of people clash, whose liberty is to be given most scope for expression, whose should be restricted? When the social struggle comes down to the question of who will get the power to say what is legitimate or illegitimate liberty, by what ultimate criterion is the question to be answered? An appeal to bare coercion, an appeal to law, majority vote, profit and Progress, peace and Harmony, equality and Justice, or—in some connection with all this—the purpose and will of God?

Participants in public deliberations over labor and race relations in 1940-75 in Gaston County made appeal to these and other criteria as they moved or failed to move towards new structures of power and influence in the community at large. The next two chapters are devoted to a detailed description of these deliberations. We begin with descriptions of union-organizing campaigns of the period—on a methodological principle akin to Pope's organization of his study around the Loray Strike. As in that period, so in ours: union organizing times are sociologically revealing times in Gaston County history. As Donald F. Roy puts it, describing the occasion in other southern communities:

During the course of an organizing campaign the web of influences linked to union growth may become manifest. The campaign, as a sort of processual gateway, where facilitating and inhibiting forces converge and interact, thus bears watching. It is in the campaign that merchants, professionals, churches newspapers, the unemployed, Negroes, police, and other groupings or segments of the population show most clearly the thrust of their impact on union fortunes. It is in the campaign that the lure of competing and/or conflicting affiliation possibilities for the mill hand is made evident: urgings to join the white race, the South, Christianity, and the United States of America.[6]

In other words, union campaigns provoke the realities of interest, power, and ideology into public identification and visibility. By them our sociological curiosity is thereby aroused.

The National Union Context

In a country as large and complex as the United States, national and local histories are difficult to connect. No easy predictions can be made by extrapolating from the one level to the other in either direction. Gastonia's wrestle with the labor union question in the past thirty years cannot be abstracted from nor identified with dynamics of unionism in the rest of the country. Yet the national dynamic touched upon the local at many points. A sketch of the larger context is therefore an appropriate introduction to the local story.[7]

Ten years after the Loray Strike, approximately one fourth of the one million textile workers in the United States had joined a union which did not exist in 1929: the Textile Workers Union of America, formed in 1936 as a member of the Congress of Industrial Organizations. The formation of the TWUA was partly a response to the sagging fortune and reputation of the AFL-affiliated United Textile Workers, whose union had struck the Loray Plant. For the next twenty years the two organizations were to be rivals for the loyalty of both union and non-union textile workers throughout the country. It was a large, undecided constituency. By the end of the war, the CIO had some 400,000 members in the South,[8] but of these only 10,000 were in the TWUA. UTW membership in the South was 13,000 in 1946 out of a total national dues-paying membership of 60,331.[9]

Unionizing in the southern textile industry has always confronted a formidable array of structural inhibition: characteristically small production units; dispersion of ownership among hundreds of individuals, families, and corporations of various sizes; the tradition of purposeful migration of the industry from New England southward in flight from unions; the perpetual oversupply of potential textile workers in the agricultural labor pool of the South; the doleful instability of the textile market that threatened investments and jobs; and —added to all the other inhibitors—an ideological individualism which apparently rendered the southern white textile worker immune to the lures of organization. The same structural problems did not afflict unionization drives in other economic sectors of the South, so that during World War II the movement made giant strides in some southern states—e.g., Texas. But the same wartime factors that aided the organization of other southern industries were of dubious help to the union sympathizer in textile communities.

A tight labor market ordinarily is a help to unionization, but ironically, the tight wartime market probably helped deprive nascent textile unions of some of their leaders. Potential leaders of textile unions were the very workers most attracted to higher paying non-textile war industries in other parts of the country. Moreover, the same power which a labor-sympathetic federal government often exerted to keep wages controlled during the war was mostly exerted to raise wages in the textile industry. Some textile owners welcomed these raises as assurances to workers that they could secure economic gains without the aid of unions.[10] The 55¢-minimum wage in 1945 was powerful reassurance to workers who four years before had been getting 32¢.[11]

At the end of the war the proportion of the southern textile workers in labor unions stood at 20%, as over against 70% of their northern colleagues.[12] By 1946 a drive to better this percentage was high on the agenda of both sides of the nationally divided labor movement. Especially in the textile sector, the two were to fight each other as vigorously as they fought employers. (F. Ray Marshall calculates that in the postwar years the AFL and the CIO as a whole engaged in jurisdictional disputes involving some 385,000 workers.[13] " 'In these tugs of war AFL unions won 40,000 members from the CIO and the CIO won 44,000 from the AFL. In other words, the two federations spent millions of dollars for the net exchange of approximately 4,000 members.' ")[14]

Viewed in a national perspective, in short, few other southern work forces outside of agriculture posed so severe a test to the organizing skills and resources of the burgeoning American labor movement as did the textile workers. That these very workers were the key to the triumph of unionism generally in the South, however, was acutely understood by national labor leaders, who at the end of World War II, set their sights on a great organizing campaign throughout the South—"Operation Dixie." Said Van Bittner, the leader of that campaign, " 'When you organize the textile industry of the South, you have not only the textile industry of America organized, but you have practically all industries in the South under the banner of the CIO.' "[15]

Union-building in Gaston County: 1943-1960

1. *Early organization: the mid-forties.* As Liston Pope completed his book in 1941, no Gaston County textile mill had a functioning union; and no local NLRB election had ever been conducted under the Wagner Act of 1935.[16] The first break in this even pattern of worker disorganization came in the spring of 1943 when the employees of Gastonia Weaving Company, a small

label-weaving mill, voted 40-4 to accept a UTW union as their bargaining agent. In a quiet little news article, the *Gazette* noted:

Held under the jurisdiction of the National Labor Relations Board, yesterday's election established a precedent in marking organized labor's first victory at the voting box in Gastonia's history.[17]

Other small breaks in precedent followed shortly. In two months the local leadership of the new UTW union joined with others "in the vicinity" to set up the Gaston Textile Council. The officers included two chaplains. At its first meeting the Council was addressed by a local attorney who congratulated the organization on its prospects for "securing contracts and better working conditions with . . . employers." It was, he said, "an opportunity which has been so long denied them."[18] A second NLRB election victory came to the UTW in September of the same year at the Flint Manufacturing Company, a spinning mill. Workers voted 320-112 for unionization. That the Flint mill was one of the twelve mills comprising Textiles, Inc., made the victory seem especially auspicious to union leaders. So far, they said, "Results are more than encouraging in every mill."[19]

Numerical encouragement came the next summer with an election victory in a three-mill spinning complex known locally as the Clara-Dunn-Armstrong mills, which employed 1200 persons. This particular UTW union—Local No. 12—was to prove to be the most enduring yet most problem-beset textile union in the county. The crises it experienced over the next ten years make a case study in the unhappy course of union-formation in Gaston County.

Though the union was hardly favored with a birth announcement after the August 1944 election,[20] its contract signed with the company in the spring of 1945 was well publicized. In an "amicably-concluded" agreement, the company consented to rules governing seniority, vacations, overtime wages, work load control procedures, and even company maintenance of the employee's union membership.[21] This early promise for collective bargaining in the CDA mills did not endure for long. Though labor strikes were flooding the country in the fall of 1945, the national turmoil was complemented in Gastonia by a deafening quiet. Daily outcries against the usurpations of John L. Lewis and the chicanery of the NLRB filled the *Gazette*, but in the midst of labor storm elsewhere, Gaston County was calm. A break in the calm came with a strike by UTW's Local No. 12 in early 1946. Unfortunately for the cause of unionbuilding in Gastonia, this strike was precipitated initially by a local intra-union squabble which would sap the energies of many a party to the subsequent conflict. In January the officers of the Washington-based UTW international union had decided to suspend Local No. 12 for the local leaders' "refusal to submit a cash report on local union status" and for their unauthorized use of funds for publishing a local labor newspaper.[22] The local had apparently laid claim to more autonomy in its financial affairs than the international wanted to grant—a clear, perhaps very southern instance of demand for "liberty."[23] A month after the suspension of the local, the CDA management announced a wage raise, and, when the local inquired about a date for new contract negotiations, management replied that the local was not now authorized to bargain. International UTW headquarters in Washington was then treated to the spectacle of a CDA vice-president's calling by phone to advise the union that "management desired to raise wages" but did not yet know to what union agency, if any, it was to communicate this desire officially! "Amicability"[24] to the contrary, management now saw an opportunity to get the union to destroy itself from the inside.

On February 28, 1946, Local No. 12 went on strike. Management immediately produced correspondence from UTW Washington headquarters ordering the company not to bargain with Local No. 12 nor to turn over checked-off union dues to any other agent but international officials.[25] Parenthetically management let it be known that only 586 employees participated in the checkoff system, that the union statistics of 85% union membership in the 1,264-employee firm was inflated. The vice president speaking for the company also "called attention to a no-strike clause in the (current) contract," a detail which management was later to use to buttress its claim that Local No. 12 "no longer existed."

By telegram UTW international officials ordered the striking members of Local No. 12 back to work. A mass meeting of the local union members voted to disregard the order,[26] and the strike entered its seventh day unresolved. Now tempers arose on picket lines, deadly weapons appeared (allegedly an "iron weight" in the hands of the company personnel director and a knife in the hand of a worker), and twelve arrests were made by local police. At this, Governor R. Gregg Cherry in Raleigh ordered ten state highway patrolmen to be diverted to Gastonia, and the Raleigh *News and Observer* editorialized under the ominous question "Gastonia Again?"

Many who observed the effect of the use of force in Gastonia in 1929 and who have observed it elsewhere are convinced that such methods usually provoke more violence than they prevent.[27]

The local editor spoke of another mistake to be avoided in the brewing crisis:

We do not believe there has been any difference between the management and the strikers that could not have been handled by arbitration.[28]

To these writers' knowledge, this is the first time that any local leader of Gastonia opinion had suggested publicly that arbitration procedures were the solution to a local labor-management dispute.[29]

International UTW representatives finally arrived in Gastonia when the strike was a week old, and the next day Local No. 12 called off the strike. Simultaneously the CDA management announced that it was raising wages 10¢ an hour with a 65¢ per hour minimum wage, quickly noting that the raise was voluntary and not the result of contract negotiations. Local No. 12's business agent took this occasion to announce that the international officials were "irresponsible racketeers." The international president replied from nearby Salisbury that Local No. 12 was guilty of "flagrant violations" of the international union's constitution.[30] But the *Gazette*, on behalf of the entire community, merely breathed a sigh of relief:

Let us be thankful that this strike has ended so quickly and so peaceably. There were signs that we might have some trouble reminiscent of the days of 1929 and the notorious Manville-Jenckes strike. . . . We were just about on the verge of suffering again from bad publicity in connection with a cotton mill strike.[31]

In fact the struggle over bargaining rights and responsibilities had just begun in the CDA community. By June the local and international unions had patched up their differences, but in the meantime management declared the local "nonexistent." An international organizer now appeared in Gastonia to legitimize the existence of Local No. 12. But this show of workingmen solidarity was too late to stave off the plague of legal obstructionism. One year passed before the union, the company, and the NLRB agreed to resolve their conflicts by the medium of a recertification election. By 1947 the local TWUA campaign was accelerating, and its local organizers made sure that its union also appeared on the ballot at CDA. This insertion of inter-union rivalry into a situation already made sticky by intra-union conflict precipitated a runoff. The first election showed:

UTW	330
"no union"	338
TWUA	134

Such a division among the voting workers showed only one third of the work force as inclined to rehabilitate the UTW union. Management was prompt to claim that 378 of its employees did not vote in the election and that some union votes were cast by persons not now employed by the company. Local No. 12 officials replied that these persons were fired for union activity, and that their cases would soon be before the NLRB.

Almost two years after the suspension of its hapless local, the United Textile Workers finally recouped their position at CDA by winning 490 ("UTW") to 342 ("no union") in December of 1947.[32] It was by many measures a Pyrrhic victory. For the next decade, the strength of Local No. 12 would be perennially in doubt among managers, workers, and many members of the Gastonia public. So Gastonia's most visible postwar experiment with textile unionism was—in a phrase to be used by TWUA's Emil Rieve of Operation Dixie itself—"something of a flop."[33]

What gains textile unionism did count in Gastonia in the forties, however, came chiefly between 1945 and 1947. A new openness to unionization seemed about to take hold of the community in these few short years. One such sign was an editorial comment in the *Gazette* interpreting the meaning of the owner-ship-change from Textiles, Inc., to Burlington Mills at Flint Manufacturing Company in early 1946. If Burlington was willing to pay $1,750,000 for this plant, said the editor, there must be big money in the postwar market. But in addition the ownership transfer demonstrated two important changes in patterns of labor-management relations in the South:[34]

That the new owners bought the mills with knowledge that the day of unions and collective bargaining has come to stay and expect to operate under agreements with the workers.

That the archaic appeal to outsiders to bring their mills South "to get cheap labor" no longer attracts. Mill workers of equal skill and making like products are entitled to and should receive the same pay that prevails in New England.[35]

Again, to these writers' knowledge, this is the first time in Gaston County history that a *Gazette* editor publicly suggested that local industry was now prepared to live with labor unions. Events of the next fifteen years proved this suggestion quite mistaken. But it is a sign of the power that the unions seemed about to achieve in the county that such statements should have been made at all, these seventeen years after the Loray Strike. It was, as if, fresh from their wartime participation in national affairs, some Gastonians had decided to join the mainstream of American labor-management relations.

The most remarkable verbal testimony to this possibility came in this same period (one week before the CDA strike) from the pen of Ben E. Atkins, the man who in 1940 had condemned Christians for putting their moral support behind any party to a war.[36] Son of the owner of the *Gazette,* Atkins was the most articulate of exception-takers to certain themes in the Gastonia ideology ever to speak regularly in a local medium.[37] Not often in any public meetings of this period, at any rate, was anyone credited with an analysis of unionism as many-sided as the following:

During a strike, the striker suffers far more than anybody else. He draws a pittance from the union to keep body and soul together. He wants to work and to make a living wage. But he knows that unless he sticks by his union and strikes when the union gives the word he has hardly a chance. It's a period of pure suffering for him.

Often the labor unions have been in the wrong. Today, many of us believe that the unions are demanding more than they need and more than they should have.

But that is a relative question, and no man who hasn't worked with his hands and been a part of a union can answer it with any intelligence. . . .

Up until 30 years ago, management definitely had the upper hand. The worker got what management pleased to pay him. He took it, whether he liked it or not. Management chuckled up its sleeve, passed out an occasional bonus, and piled the profits as high as they would go. . . .

The tradition of special privilege has a lengthy and ignominious record in American history.

The wealthy and the powerful have always believed—and apparently believed in all honesty—that they were entitled to hold other less fortunate people in servitude.

From the early days of slavery in the South—and through all the decades and even centuries in which the helpless have been held in servitude—that peculiar and selfish notion has persisted.

Today, in some respects, the idea of special privilege is just as strong as it was a hundred years ago.

But special privilege, no matter how strong the belief and no matter how far back go the roots, is a thing of the past.[38]

To advocate the abolition of "special privilege" and the "evening up" of power-relations in the industrial system was not far from saying that *the interests of one group in the community must be protected against the overexercise of the liberties of another*. It was not far from saying that liberty must be infused with justice: a relatively new, scarce ideological point in Gastonia.

Workers at several other textile mills in the county were organized between 1946 and 1948.[39] The earliest-organized UTW union (Local No. 2640) at Gastonia Weaving Company successfully carried off a strike for higher wages,[40] but this very strike demonstrated that textile management was beginning to master a strategy for union-prevention: the announcement of wage hikes, with the rhythm and regularity of a musical canon, in prompt response to announced union wage goals or even in advance.[41] Now, not only did the number of elections decline, but the voting margins got tighter.[42] In one instance in early 1945 an apparently strong local AFL machinist union went on strike, then endured a U.S. Army shop seizure, and finally lost out to "no union" in a recertification election in 1947.[43] The peak of postwar unionizing in Gastonia was already passing, as it was in textile communities across the South.

The most important signal of trying times ahead for unions in Gastonia was the 1946-47 attempt by the TWUA to organize Firestone Textiles, for twelve years the owner of the famous Loray Mill. Economically and ideologically, the Firestone plant was important for turning the ripple of local unionism into a wave. As in 1929, this company was still the largest one-plant employer in the county. Its workers in 1946 numbered some 2,100; its weekly payroll was the highest in the county. Unlike nearby Cramerton, it had long ago been taken over by a national corporation some of whose plants were highly unionized —and this was an asset that few textile mills could offer to union organizers in the 1940s. Firestone's public relations material spoke proudly of the plant as one of the largest in America. "It covers two square city blocks, is six stories high, and has more than fourteen acres of manufacturing floor space. Its warehouse area embraces more than four acres."[45] More proudly yet, the company management took pains to cultivate longevity of employment among its workers. Among its 2000 employees at the end of the war, 252 had been given ten-year pins, another sign of the "cooperation and cordiality" and "minimum of labor trouble" since 1934.[46]

TWUA leaders must have been aware of cogent symbolic reasons for their attempt to organize Firestone. If *this* plant could be organized seventeen years after the trauma of 1929 without a strike and without violence, the distinction between unionism and Communism might at last penetrate the public mind in Gastonia.[47]

In the spring of 1946, TWUA leaders announced from Charlotte that Cannon Mills in Kannapolis, Hanes Mills in Winston-Salem, and the Firestone Mill in Gastonia were the three principal targets of the new organizing drive.[48] Five organizers came to Gaston County. Their job of contacting Firestone workers was immediately rendered difficult by several circumstances: the growing dispersion of worker residences around the county;[49] the scarcity of meeting halls for union purposes; the virulent anti-CIO propaganda that rained out of the public media during the next few months;[50] and finally, a local ordinance "Prohibiting Unnecessary Noises Within the City of Gastonia," whose fourteenth section banned the use of sound trucks inside the city except by special permission of the city council. This latter ordinance TWUA leaders decided to subject to a legal test.[51]

The details of this test are important for understanding the interrelation of political, economic, and ideological structures in the postwar decades in Gastonia: little in the incident suggested that local government was any less controlled by textile-interests than it was in Pope's period. But equally interesting is the assiduous attempt which the TWUA made during the next six months to bend legal-governmental structures to the service of their interests. This was to be law-abiding and law-using unionism at work: the organizers subjected themselves calculatedly to arrest at least four times. The community was thus given a chance to consider if at stake in the case were not "the rights of free speech for which a war has just been fought."[52] Official victory in the matter eventually went to the TWUA. Its patience with law was rewarded by the North Carolina district court in Kannapolis, which decided that a sound-truck law on the books of that city was unconstitutional. Accepting this decision as a probable precedent, Gastonia solicitor Basil Whitener nolprossed the local case.[50]

TWUA leaders now confidently announced that a CIO affiliated union was in the process of being organized at the Firestone mill. At a meeting attended by seventy-five "union members," officers were elected and speeches were made by a regional TWUA leader who assured his listeners that the CIO does not resort "to the organizing techniques used in the past here by other unions," and did not expect to conduct a strike.[54] The strategic implication was clear: Gastonia can tolerate strikes in other places, but not at the Loray Mill!

But a TWUA union was far from being organized at Firestone. The soft-sell campaign approach proved to be no match for the combination of forces that discouraged the Firestone workers from responding in large numbers to the appeals of the union leaders. The campaign was never consummated in an election. A major drive to organize this mill would not be attempted again by TWUA until 1955 when the election-stage would actually be reached. Some account of this and other campaigns in the fifties and sixties we reserve until later in this chapter. In the meantime some attention is due to a train of factors that accounted in part for the slowdown of union success in Gaston County from the late forties on: the defensive strategies adopted by textile and other managers of industry during this period.

2. *Strategies of managerial defense: 1945-55.* So defensive were the *minds* of some Firestone managers about the 1947 TWUA campaign that one assistant personnel director of the company, interviewed twenty-five years later, said to an interviewer: "The question never came up. It's the first time I have ever thought about it, really. My guess is that there was probably not much support for it among the workers, for the memories of '29 were still fresh, and the union image was still bad. It was never a serious factor during the four years (1943-47) I was there. I don't know of anything the company did to discourage unions. Management then was not the type that would unduly exploit labor. If there had been much of a union-organizing attempt, we would have known about it in Personnel."[55]

Surely Personnel *did* know about it at the time; but its focus of attention, just as surely, was on more objective, less psychological ways to "discourage unions." For the industry as a whole, the ways were primarily three: wage raises, fringe benefits, and political-legislative action. On all three fronts, industry response to the union challenge, over the five years, was dramatic.

a. *The wage hike initiative.*   In their canonical variations on the wage theme, unions and management in the late forties found themselves confronted with the opportunities and the problems of prosperity, which gave the worker economic justification to ask for higher wages and management extra leeway to accede to the request. From the standpoint of intra-union politics, however, it is important to leave any bargaining table with some concessions ostensibly forced from managemet. Even if management is "good hearted" and wants to concede, the building of union loyalties among union members requires at least the appearance of a power struggle. The classic rituals of bargaining are all played out here. Thus the issue of defining the "best procedure" for resolving such conflict is partly ideological: that the relationship should be defined in terms of power and its balances, as over against voluntariness and uncoerced good will, would have amounted to a significant conceptual shift on the part of many an industrial worker in Gastonia in the post-1940 era. As one TWUA leader, reflecting on this period, put it:

. . . white southern textile workers tended passively to accept their surroundings as they found them and looked at themselves as people to whom things happen rather than who could join together and exercise control over their own destinies through union organization. I think the contrasting attitude of blacks in the late 60's arises out of their own self-realization that joint action by black people could win civil rights battles and could force changes for the better in southern situations.[56]

Little in the religious or ideological thought structures of the Gastonia community prepared workers for such a shift: neither Progress, Harmony, nor Liberty seemed to call for corporately structured balances of power. And on the side of religion, neither the transcendent justice of God nor the universality of human brotherhood had been characteristically interpreted in Gastonia in ways that would yield the political realism of the democratic concept that every power needs its counterpower.

The contest between the managers and the unions of the textile industry over who should get the credit for rising wages in the industry is a good example, therefore, of the mixture of Weber's "ideal" and "material" interests in the concepts that people entertain about how social institutions work. The unions had a vested interest in believing that management only yields wage raises under pressure; management had a similar interest in offering a wage raise as a voluntary gift to workers. It had a like interest in picturing wage decisions as dependent upon "the market," rather than upon the pressures of organized political power-relations. As their actual behavior demonstrated, the postwar boom put textile managers in a position to raise wages at an unprecedented rate. That owners never raised wages to the extent that they could have been raised would be the regular claim of the unions; that management raised wages as fast as the market and "good management" practice allowed would be the equally regular counterclaim. At stake in a worker's *interpretation* of the pertinence of each claim was the question of how institutions work or fail to work to benefit their members. It was a matter of practical sociology, politics, and ethics: who in the industrial world can be trusted to make decisions relating to the welfare of employees?

The Gastonia textile worker's answer to that question in the postwar years was relatively clear: management. He was apparently little moved by the union's claim that it was the real catalyst in the upward spiraling of textile wages. There was strong evidence to support the claim. Hardly had the TWUA announced in July of 1946, for example, that it was demanding a raise in the minimum textile wage from 65¢ to 77¢, when Burlington Mills (two days later) announced a raise to 73¢.[57] The dialogue between the unions and the company wage-setters did not always occur on such a prompt schedule, but the seesaw dynamic was highly visible. The morally logical lesson for textile workers may well have been that they should "join unions because the unions are a factor in the rising levels of wages."[58] But the practical lesson could be just the opposite: if the mere threat of unionism is as effective in motivating managerial generosity as unionism itself, what better arrangement could be imagined? As Marshall puts it, "If they joined the union the workers would lose the value that this threat gives them."[59] Right up to 1974, the threat was apparently helping to raise wages in the textile industry.[60]

Table 5.2 shows the upward climb of wages in the American textile industry from 1940 to 1974. In dollar-terms, the climb is dramatic—a 700% increase. But corrections for the inflated dollar reduce the increase from 1940 to 1974 to 200%. In the late sixties a twenty-dollar increase in weekly wages barely enabled the textile worker to hold his purchasing power level, and in late 1974 his income actually dipped back to the 1965 standard. During all these past fifteen years, in the absence of some careful figuring, many workers must have been only vaguely aware of how little their relative economic position was improving. The union, in turn, was busy making members and non-members aware of such relativities.[61]

During the fifties and sixties, the textile unions also sought regularly to make workers aware of one other dimension of their economic position: their place in the national wage picture. That textile wages lagged behind those of

Table 5.2

HOURLY AND WEEKLY AVERAGE EARNINGS OF PRODUCTION WORKERS
IN UNITED STATES TEXTILE MILL PRODUCTS INDUSTRIES, 1940-1974

Year	Average Hourly Earnings	Average Weekly Earnings	"Real" Weekly Earnings in terms of rising consumer price index (1967=$1.00)
1940	.505	17.45	41.55
1941	.516	19.39	43.19
1942	.596	23.23	46.54
1943	.658	27.39	51.80
1944	.690	28.88	52.17
1945	.733	31.07	57.63
1946	.858	34.68	58.30
1947	1.035	40.99	61.28
1948	1.155	45.28	62.80
1949	1.181	44.41	62.22
1950	1.228	48.63	67.45
1951	1.32	51.22	65.82
1952	1.34	52.39	65.91
1953	1.36	53.18	66.37
1954	1.36	52.09	64.70
1955	1.38	55.34	69.01
1956	1.44	57.17	70.26
1957	1.49	57.96	68.74
1958	1.49	57.51	66.42
1959	1.56	63.02	72.16
1960	1.61	63.60	71.68
1961	1.63	65.04	72.58
1962	1.68	68.21	75.30
1963	1.71	69.43	75.75
1964	1.79	73.39	78.97
1965	1.87	78.17	82.70
1966	1.96	82.12	84.50
1967	2.06	84.25	84.25
1968	2.21	91.05	87.41
1969	2.34	95.47	86.97
1970	2.45	97.76	84.07
1971	2.57	104.34	85.98
1972	2.73	113.44	90.64
1973	2.95	120.66	90.74
1974	3.26	123.55 (Nov.)	80.31

Sources for hourly and weekly earnings, 1947-72, *Handbook of Labor Statistics 1973*, U.S. Department of Labor; for 1972-74, *Monthly Labor Review*, U.S. Department of Labor, January 1975; for 1940-1946, *Monthly Labor Review*, for those years, using the March statistic for each year. (These latter statistics are figured on a base of data not exactly comparable to that of the post-1946 data, but for purposes of the comparisons of this chart, the possible variations are not significant.) Averages here include overtime. Calculations of "real" income, discounted for the rise in Consumer Price Index over the 35-year period, were made using table no. 656, p. 404, of the 1974 edition of *Statistical Abstract of the United States*, "Purchasing Power of the Dollar: 1940-1973." (U.S. Department of Commerce, Bureau of Labor Statistics.) The latter table of the Abstract omits a c.p.i. for the years 1941-44 and 1946, so comparable figures were derived from the c.p.i. for these years as recorded in *Historical Statistics of the United States: Colonial Times to 1957* (U.S. Department of Commerce), using a base of 1949 dollars.

many more sophisticated industries was well known in Gastonia; it was one condition that shaped the postwar industrial diversification campaign.[62] Among the initiatives seized by textile management in the post-World War period, however, was its attempt to narrow the long famous wage-differential between northern and southern textile workers. The great movement of textile mills from northern to southern locations during the twenties and thirties had yielded in the forties a textile industry 80% located in the South. At the same time, the reverse ratio obtained in the proportion of textile union members in the two regions: 80% of textile union members were located in the North, and the drive of southern industrialists to close the wage gap between themselves and the northerner, ironically enough, put the textile unions nationally in an ambiguous position. Wage increases bargained for in the North pushed the northern textile *owner* to argue for a closing of the differential in the South to protect his own market position, and the same increases moved the southern owner to consider wagematching as a continued protection against unionization. In the debate it was obvious that unions actually benefitted politically from the differential, which demonstrated to southerners their economic need for unions.[63]

The visible point still left to the unions was the very considerable wage differential between the textile industry and average wages paid in American manufacturing as a whole. All during the period being surveyed here, the U.S. textile industry, second-largest manufacturing employer in the nation, hovered at about nineteenth in wage levels.[64] In 1970, for example, the average manufacturing hourly wage of $3.40 was $1.00 above the average textile wage.

Having largely closed the differential within its own national shop and having adjusted to an upward spiral of wage levels, therefore, industry leaders could give every appearance of heaping benefits upon textile workers without recourse to collective bargaining. As a strategy of defense against unionization, it was eloquent and effective.

b. *Fringe benefits and personnel relations.*   Some account of the "managerial revolution" in Gastonia textile circles has already been given. Additional perspective on this development can be gained by looking at it in the context of union-organizing efforts of the 1950s. Five months after the second failure (May 1955) of TWUA to organize the Firestone Mill, for example, the Gaston Medical Society heard an Asheville physician recommend management-sponsored company health programs as a way to avoid losing control of these programs to unions. Local doctors should advise local managers of these political facts, said the visiting practitioner and should urge them to adopt health programs with their accompanying benefits to employee morale and productivity.[65] An Industrial Health Committee was being concurrently organized by the local Society to push for both "preventive" and "constructive" industrial health programs. During the next several years some type of on-the-job medical program was established in most of the larger mills in the county.[66] (So far as reported public discussion indicates, there was little interest among Gastonia doctors in systematic study of actual health problems associated with the textile industry. The absence of such interest was to be silhouetted a decade later when a federally sponsored team of medical researchers uncovered the facts of byssinosis—so-called "brown lung"—associated with high concentrations of lint in the air of the mills.[67])

New medical insurance and treatment plans were only one example of a series of benefit-programs that multiplied throughout the fifties in most of the textile plants of the county. Industry took pains to distinguish the new programs from old-style paternalism—a defense ideologically vital to the managerial revolution. One such account from 1953 stated:

A few years ago the word "paternalism" was often heard in connection with the early efforts of textile management to offer better living opportunities to workers. Today, the public begins to realize paternalism is the wrong word. People who live in better communities make better citizens. Better citizens make better business.[68]

As an example of "better communities" the account points to the sale of the mill village and to the fact that in North Carolina (in 1952) some 50% of the state's textile workers lived outside of a village. Some 25% owned their homes, either former mill-village houses or houses in other parts of the community. "Now, it's the worker's choice, not the mill's necessity, which populates the mill villages."[69]

Recreational programs were zealously developed by many mill managers during the fifties. Firestone Textiles established a summer camp complete with lake and cottages for family vacations; and its athletic program was diversified from the traditional Gastonia preoccupation with baseball to swimming, bowling, basketball, softball, and scouting. An "All-Sports Banquet," an occasion for winner-awards and addresses by nationally famous sports figures, was heralded as "the highlight of the recreation year" in the company.[70]

Of all the innovations in fringe-benefits, however, the most important in this era was the formal retirement-income plan. The lack of such plans had been a strong point in union indictment of the textile industry during the thirties. In Gaston County a dramatic local illustration of this lack was publicized and inadvertently symbolized in 1946 in a news story about David A. Kelly, eighty-five-year-old textile worker who had gone to work in a mill at the age of ten: he was still working at his job after *seventy-five* years and *one* day of absence![71] Mr. Kelly was a folk-hero of the era of which Pope wrote. He personified the ethic of hard work. But behind such heroism, for many other less hardy souls who worked in the textile industry, there loomed the constraint that, social security to the contrary, a textile worker saw himself as virtually forced to work to death. The retirement plans that began to be common locally in the forties and fifties promised some alleviation from this specter.

Not much diminished, amid all these new benefits, were the paternalistic activities from the old days: Burlington and Textiles, Inc. continued their lavish Christmas parties for all employees; in 1950, the fiftieth anniversary of the founding of the parent corporation, Firestone Textiles sent 9000 workers and family members to the circus in Charlotte;[72] and, indeed, such emblems of the "old days" would persist, among some textile companies, right into the nineteen seventies.[73]

As the tide of labor union organization increased in some parts of the South in the mid-fifties, some management spokesmen in Gastonia were frank to interpret the new fringe-benefits as an argument against unions. An instance of this tactic was the communication that went from the Firestone management to its workers on the eve of the TWUA's next major organizing attempt in May 1955. In a long letter sent to all 1900 employees eligible to vote in the forthcoming NLRB election, the general manager stressed themes well tested for their anti-union appeal in Gastonia: the danger of outside interference in the liberties of the worker; the exploitative desire of union leaders for dues; the danger of a recurrence in this very place of the "violence, bloodshed, and death" of 1929; the importance of the employee's right "to come in and settle with us personally any problems you might have"—the "Open Door Policy" of the new managerialism. And among the reasons for thinking that more benefits would come to the worker voluntarily from management than could ever be coerced by a union, was this:

When it comes to such things as vacations and vacation pay, and pensions and retirement pay, and insurance, including life, hospital, surgical, sickness and accident coverage, paid for except as to dependents, entirely by the Company, and good conditions of work and recreational facilities, and other similar benefits—all these you have without paying any Union dues to obtain them.[74]

Management urged all Firestone workers to cast ballots on the union question. Almost to a person, the workers obeyed, with the result:

| For the union | 509 |
| Against | 1,374 |

Viewing these results with satisfaction, the general manager publicly suggested two reasons for the company victory: steady employment for workers over the past twenty years and "Firestone's fringe benefits which amount to 23 cents an hour" out of an average hourly wage of $1.25.[75] In its congratulatory editorial on the event, the *Gazette* noted that the vote was a challenge to the company to keep its wages high, to maintain the "open door" policy, and to keep its good working conditions, including its exemplary fringe benefits.[76]

c. *Legislation and politics.*   As is well known, American management's reaction to the Wagner Act of 1935 built to a climax in the immediate postwar years and found a powerful countervailing legal expression in the passage of the Taft-Hartley Act in 1947. Having been subject for twelve years to a "relative deprivation"[77] of its power to influence the structure of labor-management relations, organized management groups became newly political during these years on a national level. Even in Gaston County, politics and government were to play increasingly open roles in this conflict.

Taft-Hartley put new tools in the hands of union-pressed managers. Now unions were as subject as management to legal prosecution for "unfair practices." Unions could no longer refuse to bargain collectively when it suited their interests not to do so. Management could exercise "free speech" to express non-coercive antiunion opinion during elections. Secondary boycotts were outlawed; and, in other ways, the benefit of doubt in labor-management disputes was shifted back to the management side. TWUA officials pointed out that in the five years prior to the Act the union had won 58% of its plant elections and had actually organized ¾ of the plants won. The comparable record in the five years after Taft-Hartley was 37% and less than one-half.[78]

Nothing was more salient about the Taft-Hartley Act in Gaston and kindred southern counties, however, than its virtual irrelevance there. The labor union had barely arrived in the South, not to speak of the textile south, which had little local occasion to "put an end to the abuse of union power." Yet in the field of union-curbing law during this period, legislative leaders of no section of the country exceeded the productivity of southerners. As one Sanford Cohen says, "The highly industrialized states of Illinois and Ohio enacted practically no legislation dealing with unions, while many of the agricultural states, where unionism was almost non-existent, pushed through some of the more severe anti-union measures. In the South especially, the quantity of labor union legislation that appeared was impressive. The areas where unions had only tenuous footholds were bracing themselves in anticipation of future organizational drives."[79]

Taft-Hartley had made the closed shop illegal but had permitted the union shop.[80] But in its subsequently famous Section 14-b, the Act allowed state legislatures to pass more stringent laws regulating union membership. Eleven state legislatures promptly passed so-called "right-to-work" laws. Six were southern states, and one was North Carolina.[81]

Meeting in the spring of 1947, the North Carolina General Assembly in

Raleigh passed the law in circumstances that left no doubt that North Carolina was and might continue to be the least unionized of the United States. The bill sent to both houses of the legislature was a virtual copy of the one passed by several other states,[82] and it had the remarkable fate, unique for bills with statewide impact, of surviving the entire legislative process without amendment.[83] The new measure outlawed the closed and the union shop, as well as the checkoff and union-membership-maintenance provisions in union-management contracts.[84] During the legislative debate one of the few speeches critical of the bill was delivered by Senator Lawrence Wallace of Johnston County, who pointed out that in 1946, a time of many labor strikes in the country as a whole, North Carolina strikers numbered three-tenths of one percent of the nation's work force. "The bill," said he, "would prohibit management and labor the rights they have exercised for more years than are within the memory of anyone in this room." And in a late appeal to free-enterprise doctrine, one senator from Durham, (the state's most unionized city) declared himself personally in favor of the bill's content but opposed to subjecting such matters to legal regulation. "I hold these questions to belong properly in the field of negotiations between management and labor."[85]

By voice vote the bill swept into law in what the Raleigh *News and Observer* editor termed "an exhibition of arrogance."[86] Little or no discussion of the law can be found in the media of Gaston County. One presumes that all of its senators and representatives in Raleigh voted for the bill. As they did so, union organizers in the county must have muttered to themselves some form of the irony that such organizers now "found themselves faced with a Taft-Hartley Act before they were in a position to take advantage of the Wagner Act."[87] It was the *weak* unions, in fact, who would be the real victims of Taft-Hartley.

The pressure which North Carolina industrialists brought upon the state legislature in this matter was almost certainly, therefore, a part of a general attempt to keep unions altogether out of the state. Large economic and ideological interests were beginning to battle publicly in this legislative incident, and this conflict was to escalate over the next several years in statewide politics. Indeed, in the two biennial elections of these years, the Tar Heel State was to come close to politically overt economic-class conflict.[88]

3. *The 1948 primary.* The presumed front-runner for Democratic nomination for governor in the spring of 1948 was Charles Johnson, state treasurer and latest candidate of the weakening "Shelby dynasty" that had sent a line of governors from O. Max Gardner to Gregg Cherry to Raleigh. Widely predicted as runner-up was R. Kerr Scott, Haw River dairy farmer whose following of "branchhead boys" had Populist kinsmen of fifty years before. Acknowledged on all sides as the probably sure loser was R. Mayne Albright, young

Raleigh attorney and war veteran. It was Albright's visit to Gastonia, one day before the primary election, that most stirred the specter of class politics in the minds of many local observers. He first encountered local resistance in the 1929 anti-loudspeaker law, still on the books. For months he had been criss-crossing the state in a car-and-trailer equipped with loudspeakers. Gastonia police required him to speak without amplification. He then encountered a second put-down from the *Gazette* editor, who commented that Albright was expected to get many votes tomorrow, "particularly among the working class. Albright has been endorsed by most of the groups from organized labor."[89] This was relatively unprecedented public rhetoric in Gastonia. There had been a large "working class" in Gaston County for many decades, especially in the eyes of those who saw industrial society through socialist spectacles; but it was remarkable that a Gastonia editor should use the term on election eve. It was, in effect, an ambiguous play on the "no-factions," Harmony-of-Interests theme in the local ideology. It was as if Albright were being accused of finding class conflict in a town where there was supposed to be none.

Johnson carried Gaston County with 4,468 votes; Scott trailed at 1,278; and Albright came last with 1,182 votes. On the same ballot, longtime Congress-man Bulwinkle was renominated, in spite of weak support in certain mill-village precincts—perhaps, theorized the *Gazette,* because Bulwinkle had voted for the Taft-Hartley Act.[90] Plainly, not all mill workers had voted either for Bulwinkle's Republican opponent or for pro-union Albright. In the company-owned village of McAdenville, Bulwinkle had won 107-15. Indeed, as the union organizers of the county were learning, much to their sorrow, in these very months, a politician who could prove that he was *against* unions could still convince many local workers that he was their friend. National and state legislation over the past year had assumed that workers as well as managers needed protecting from the ravages of unionism. By labeling him as a union candidate the day before the election, the local newspaper was banking on the likelihood that union support in Gaston County was still the kiss of death.

Many of Albright's supporters went over to Scott in the runoff, so that a month later Scott was the Democratic nominee for governor of North Carolina.[91] Since nominated Democrats in state politics in this era were virtually assured of election, the biennial political drama was closed in June; but a second edition of a class-conflict-tinged campaign, more vicious than any played out in '48, would occur a bare two years later.[92]

4. *The 1950 primary.*   Gubernatorial politics in North Carolina have been less subject to "machines" than have some other southern states, but the Shelby dynasty had enough of a machine-reputation to make many see Governor Kerr Scott as the new broom in Raleigh. Among the confirmations of this theory was

Scott's early appointment of Dr. Frank Porter Graham, for twenty years President of the University of North Carolina, to fill a seat in the United States Senate vacated in March 1949 by the death of J. Melville Broughton.[93] Under Graham's administration the name Chapel Hill had become a symbol of intellectual enlightenment and social change in the South. By the same token, "Frank Graham" and "Chapel Hill," inside the state, were names for political conjuring, especially among conservatives in search of liberal targets. Since the thirties, the quiet-mannered Graham had stirred up in the state a unique mix of friends and foes. Ambivalence towards him was visible in Gaston County as early as 1940. During a controversy over the appearance of a Communist speaker on the campus of the University, Ben E. Atkins hailed Graham as the only public official in North Carolina for whom he had unqualified admiration.[94] But nine days later, with the controversy over "freedom for the thought we hate" still simmering in Chapel Hill, the *Gazette* reprinted an editorial from the weekly Stanley township newspaper, calling for Graham's resignation and protesting against the use of North Carolina taxpayers' money to subsidize appearances of Communists in Chapel Hill.[95] In sum, the division of opinion over Graham ran right through the minds of some of his Tar Heel contemporaries, who entertained towards him a peculiar blend of pride, affection, and suspicion. People high and low in the state considered him a peculiar national treasure and at the same time a peculiar local burden. As he greeted Kerr Scott's appointment of Graham to the Senate in March of 1949, for example, the *Gazette* editor praised the statesmanship of the act while confessing that he could not always concur with "some of (Graham's) socialistic proposals."[96]

Graham had more than a year to serve in the Senate before having to stand in a primary election. He had been a member of President Truman's Civil Rights Committee in 1947, and in the 1949 Senate he took part in the debates over the constitutionality of a federal Fair Employment Practices Commission. The "moderately liberal" image that Graham promulgated in the upcoming primary was typified by his public statements on the FEPC. Summarizing his approach to the knotty problems of justice for the black man, he said in a 1950 campaign speech:

The solution to these problems should not be sought through outside compulsion but through the influence of religion and education. That is the North Carolina way.[97]

If Graham's opponent in the 1950 election—Raleigh attorney Willis Smith—had merely accused him of flirting with federal government intervention into "the North Carolina way" in race relations, he would have done nothing unusual in southern politics in 1950. But early in the primary campaign, the supporters of the two leading candidates moved to identify each with a respective economic class-interest; from then until June political rhetoric on this theme rose from a murmur to a shout. "Without knowing too much about the identity of Mr. Smith's. backers," wrote Ben E. Atkins in February, ". . . we feel sure that he represents what we usually designate as the 'conservative' element in the state, which includes of course the large corporate interests, and there is no secret about Senator Graham's being a liberal. We have dismissed, and will continue to dismiss, as pure balderdash all the rumors and asides to the effect that Graham is a Communist. . . ."[98] Atkins went on to express his support of Graham over Smith and his confidence that it would be "a clean, straightforward fight minus mud-slinging and personalities."

But that proved to be wishful predicting.

At every political level in Gastonia that spring there had been open appeal to economic-class interest. This was the campaign in which county-commission candidate Paul J. McArver accused the economic "bosses" of Gaston County of being opposed to industrial diversification.[99] Another challenger to local incumbent power was Kenneth E. Dellinger, owner of a small business, who in an election-eve advertisement proclaimed, "If you make less than $10,000 a year then cast your vote for 'Ken!' "[100] (Dellinger, running for the state Senate, lost 5329 to 3005.) In the midst of the buildup to the first primary, even the *Gazette* found itself agreeing with McArver and Dellinger that too much of the county's political business was in the hands of too few of its citizens. ". . . It would appear that about fifty Gaston County businessmen are handling the affairs of the 40,000 eligible voters."[101]

But local supporters of Graham and Smith rang the loudest changes on the class-antagonism issue. Their shrillest appeals were reserved for the weeks just prior to the runoff. Smith won the first primary in Gaston County, 6,705 votes to Graham's 6,071; but Graham led the statewide ticket, missing by only 5,600 votes a majority of the 618,000 votes cast.[102] The day before the first primary Graham forces in Gastonia described the difference between the two candidates as that between a lawyer who represented some thirty-six banks, insurance companies, and other big-money interests; and a man who was a friend of labor, an advocate of collective bargaining, and withal a "Roosevelt Democrat, Christian Statesman, and Fighting Marine."[103] But three weeks later a pre-runoff Graham ad reduced the matter to more direct terms:

Frank Graham is for higher wages for the working man. He is not a wealthy man. He has spent his life in public service to improve the well-being of all the people —not in piling up money. Frank Graham is probably the only member of the United States Congress who wears shoes that have been half-soled. He knows what low wages mean to the working man.

Willis Smith is a rich man. He gets his huge income from fat corporation fees and dividends on stocks and bonds, and he has the financial backing of the large corporations throughout the county and state.

During his 20 years as president of the University of North Carolina Frank Graham spent many of his own hard-earned dollars to aid struggling boys and girls to complete their education. Now you have an opportunity to come to his aid when the fortunes of the favored are pitted against him.[104]

On the Smith side, supporters made an equally explicit, opposite appeal to the voter to save America from the socialist menace. On the eve of the first primary they appraised Graham thus:

Apparently Frank Graham has for years believed in and worked with Leftist, Communistic Front organizations and fellow-travelers. No doubt, he is, and will remain, permeated with that atmosphere.[105]

Then, just prior to the runoff Smith people asked voters to consider if the preservation of the capitalistic system were not at stake in this election. A small boy with a baseball glove plaintively posed the questions:

When I'm a grown man with a family, will I be allowed to run my own life, or will I be just a social security number in a government file?

. . .

Will I get a chance to make my own way in competition with others? If I work a little harder, or better, or get lucky, will I be able to keep any more of what I earn than the other fellow who didn't work as hard or as well, or get lucky?

. . .

And that's just why I hope you'll remember just one thing about this country—just don't forget that the only reason Americans produce so much more and live so much better is that they have the whopping supply of tools of production in which people are willing to invest their savings.

. . .

How About Giving Me A Chance At America The Way You Found It When You First Came of Age?

A Vote for Willis Smith for U.S. Senator is a vote for a man who worked his own way through college, who has earned his own position in life, and who believes in and practices the American way of life. His friends have never had to explain or apologize for his membership in any un-American organization.[106]

It was as *exclusively* an ideological appeal to economic liberty over economic justice as had appeared publicly in many a year in North Carolina; it was also a clearcut instance of an alleged fusion of particular interests with society-wide interests which is the hallmark of radical ideology as defined earlier in this study.[107] In the Smith ad, the gain of the hardworking, saving, industrious individual *is* the gain of the whole society. Such excesses stamped both sides in the campaign, though at the height of the second-primary struggle Graham publicly disavowed certain exclusive claims to political virtue made on his behalf.[108]

The climax to this ideological warfare came on election-eve in a frenzied broadside against Graham from Smith headquarters in Raleigh:

Frank Graham poses as a friend of the common man and the working classes! So did the Fabians in England who wouldn't call themselves Socialists! BUT WHAT HAPPENED WHEN THEY GOT IN POWER? Today, the American working man with a wife and two children pays only $26 in taxes on $2,800 income. IN ENGLAND THE SAME WORKER PAYS $288 IN TAXES—ELEVEN TIMES AS MUCH! . . . FRANK GRAHAM WANTS TO KEEP ON TAXING AND SPENDING! DO YOU WANT HIS HAND IN YOUR POCKET?

There is only one REAL DEMOCRAT in this Senate race—WILLIS SMITH! Day after day FRANK GRAHAM is going around over North Carolina trying to explain how he got mired up with this, that, and the other COMMUNIST AND SOCIALIST organization. He says he just didn't know these organizations he joined were Communist-controlled! Well, after having joined so many of them, HE MUST EITHER BE STUPID OR HE CAN'T BE TELLING THE TRUTH! . . . THE ONLY PARTY WILLIS SMITH EVER JOINED WAS THE DEMOCRATIC PARTY! WHICH DO YOU PREFER? WILLIS SMITH AND THE NORTH CAROLINA DEMOCRATS—OR FRANK GRAHAM AND HIS BUDDIES —HENRY WALLACE, PAUL ROBESON, AND EARL BROWDER? REMEMBER—THIS WILL BE YOUR LAST OPPORTUNITY TO DEFEAT COMMUNISM AND OTHER FOREIGN ISMS IN NORTH CAROLINA—AND MAYBE IN THE UNITED STATES![109]

How such rhetoric influenced Gastonians the next day at the polls, we cannot be sure. The local public was deeply and hostilely divided on the matter: the sociological divisions of the vote demonstrated as much. The depth of division was also plain in the election-eve withdrawal of its endorsement of Graham by the *Gastonia Gazette*. "As to whom you vote for for U.S. Senator, . . . we are making no recommendations." For business or whatever reasons, even Ben E. Atkins wavered.[110]

Smith won the nomination from Graham by a statewide vote of 277,672 to 257,156—a margin of 20,516, or 53.8% of the votes cast. In Gaston County the margin was wider: 7,275 to 5,976, or a margin of 59.1%. In the interval between the two primaries, Graham lost a net of 95 of his local supporters, and Smith gained 570. The most revealing part of the county voting profile was visible to those analysts of the thirty-four precinct returns who took care to distinguish between precincts that could be generally assigned to "uptown" or "mill-village" categories respectively. In five towns in the county large enough to have multiple-numbered precincts, all but one of the "No. 1" precincts gave majorities of over two-thirds to Smith. By contrast, every one of the sixteen precincts going for Graham was located in a predominantly mill-village district, and these precincts voted for him in equally large majorities. Cramerton, High Shoals, Stanley, Lowell, Dallas —mill towns all—plus various mill districts of Gastonia, voted for Graham. Among the "little towns" outside of Gastonia, only Cherryville and McAdenville showed an impressively solid front of citizens unwilling to split politically along economic lines.[111]

The significance of the Graham-Smith fight in Gastonia was broader than its evocation of slumbering antagonism between labor and management; but it was one tangible expression of that antagonism, as well as of the influence which business-oriented politicians had over local citizens. By implication, because labor unions were an explicit issue in the campaign, this primary was a test of the relative power of pro-union and anti-union sentiment in the community. As such, the Graham-Smith conflict set the tone for union-organizing in the fifties in Gastonia, when union fortunes sank steadily.

One day after Graham's defeat at the polls in North Carolina, the Korean War erupted. How badly Graham might have been beaten if the war had started a day earlier, is a matter for speculation; but in all probability the Smith supporters had every provocation now to say, "We told you so." Nationally the McCarthy era was about to begin.

The Churches and the Labor Unions: The Cherryville Incident

Overt participation of Gaston County churches in the tortured history of labor unionization is hard to detect in the records on which this chapter has depended so far. This absence is telltale on two counts: on the one hand, it suggests a continuation of that latent support of existing economic relations which, in Pope's terms, rendered the churches one of industry's "modes of control" *vis à vis* the threat of social disintegration in 1929: but the churches are even more invisible in our narrative than in his at this point; and this suggests, on the other hand, that some new relationships were developing between industry, the unions, and the churches in the 1940-70 era. This latter hypothesis receives some confirmation and specification in an event which is the leading exception to the generalization that the churches are absent from the labor union story of these decades. We may call the event "The Cherryville Incident."

In 1950 the town of Cherryville, in the northwest corner of Gaston County, had a population of some 3500. Most of the town's residents were employed at mills owned by two leading families. At one of these—the Rhyne-Houser Manufacturing Company—the TWUA conducted an organizing campaign in early 1953. On February 10 an NLRB-supervised election was held. Ten days prior to the election, management sent out to its employees a six-page letter typical of letters sent to textile workers during the campaigns of the forties and fifties. The sum of the argument was as follows:[112]

1. The union aims chiefly to get its hands on the workers' money, in the form of dues. "What they ask is that you *vote for them* and *then start paying them!*"

2. Officials of this Union admit that over the past few years they have lost ground as an organization. They have spent millions of dollars in a fruitless attempt to get new members; and "all the money that they have spent, *they got from the pockets and paychecks of working people.*"

3. The Union cannot increase your wages because "your pay is already on the top level of our competitors in the combed yarn industry in this entire area."

4. All the fringe benefits that you now have you will continue to have without a union.

5. The company is constantly at work improving working conditions: it doesn't require a union to keep on "providing these things for you."

6. This Union has recently had a big internal political fight, and your dues would only go to finance more such "rows and wrangles."

7. "Do you think you will do better with us whom you know, who operate these mills, furnish the jobs and meet the payroll, or with these Union agents who are here today and gone tomorrow?"

8. The Union has "no magic power" to serve your interests. Usually it tries to exercise power "*by pulling you out on strike.* Now, without intending to seem abrupt, we hope you will realize and understand in advance that this Company has no intention to yielding to any such pressure as that."

9. Strikes are probable where there are unions. "Everybody knows that! And everybody knows that strikes mean trouble and dissension, strife and misery, lost work and lost pay. From time to time you have heard and read of trouble that has come with the Union at other places —trouble that often winds up in cutting and shooting and bloody violence. A Union often costs people more than just the dues it collects from them!"

10. No one has ever to belong to a union to keep his job with this company.

11. "A Union often furnishes an easy opportunity for persons who have a hankering for small-time politics. A few such people usually stir around

in the Union, pull strings and get themselves set up as shop stewards and committeemen so that they can handle everybody's affairs and 'lord it' over all their fellow employees. Look around you and see who are active in pushing this Union. Are they persons whom you consider to be capable of handling your problems and into whose hands you are now ready to trust your business and your affairs?"

The letter closed with vigorous encouragement to all employees to vote and with the summary argument:

" As matters now stand you have a steady job at good wages, an up-to-date mill to work in and a good community here to live in. We all hope to make things even better. There is certainly no good reason to bring this outside Union in here, pay dues to it, and at the same time run the risk of tearing apart everything that you now have."

Soon after the distribution of this letter, apparently at the initiative of one of them, the seven ministers of the seven major churches in Cherryville "met for three or more hours in discussion and prayer on the matter and decided that it was our Christian Duty" to send a letter of their own to the employees of the Rhyne-Houser mills.[113] "When the letter was written by the group," recollected the leader of the seven, "I took it to Mr. Houser, and then he made the request that we not send it out." Just why Houser made this request he did not publicly explain, but this minister's reason for not honoring the request, he reported, was his own sense of conscience: "I believed it was my Christian duty to my community . . . I think there is a time that a pastor has to take a stand and let his voice be heard as an individual on certain matters."[114]

Mimeographed in a church office, the letter was sent by mail to the 330 employees of the mill. It read as follows:

Cherryville, N.C.
February 7, 1953

Dear Friends,

We feel that a situation threatens to arise that will disturb the good spirit and fellowship of our Community. We want you to know we are deeply concerned about your welfare. Recently we have had it called to our attention that a CIO Labor Union election is to be held in your mill Tuesday February 10. We realize that this decision rests entirely with you.

However, we feel that we would like to let you know our feelings in this matter. We are thoroughly convinced that it would be greatly to your disadvantage to have the Union to represent you. Many of the benefits and special favors which you have had would no longer be yours under the Union.

Let us urge you to get out and Vote and Vote your Conviction. We suggest that you consider this matter prayerfully before voting, and May God Guide you in your decision.

Yours in Christ's service,
(signed by Seven Ministers)[115]

On February 10, Rhyne-Houser workers voted against the TWUA, 234-93. Hardly any eligible worker could have been deaf to management's plea that each employee go to the ballot box; in its letter, management had mentioned "330" as the potential number of voters.

How much influence had been exercised on workers by a letter from seven Cherryville pastors? No one could be sure; but Emil Rieve, newly elected national president of the TWUA, announced from New York that the ministers' letter would be the occasion of an unfair-labor-practices charge against the company. In the meantime, Rieve wrote his own three-page letter to the chairman of the Cherryville Seven, suggesting thereby that he thought of the ministry as having considerable influence on labor-management relations. His letter entered into sharp historical, political, and ethical debate with the content of the ministers' letter:

Do you doubt the ability of your parishioners to govern themselves? I must conclude that this is so; because a union is merely a step in the direction of economic self-government, yet you view it as a threat to "good spirit and fellowship." I suppose there is great "good spirit and fellowship" in all totalitarian societies, since the right to dissent is effectively smothered. I thought most of us in this country agreed that the merits of self-government outweighed the advantages of autocratic unanimity. . . .

Autonomy—Liberty—was at issue here, Rieve implied. Did the Cherryville ministry believe in Liberty for owners only? Then on the question of how mill workers acquired "the benefits and special favors" they now enjoy, Rieve went on to make a theoretical connection between Liberty and Justice and to connect the achievement of both with social-political organization:

Have you studied the history of the textile industry? Are you familiar with the long struggle of the workers for a living wage? Do you realize that this struggle was fruitless until the formation of our union? Do you know that wages in unorganized mills have risen only as a result of gains won by the union? Are you aware that wages and working conditions in Cherryville—including those "benefits and special favors" you refer to—are far inferior to wages and working conditions in unionized mills?

In all charity I must conclude that the answer in each case is in the negative. Otherwise you could not, as a man of the cloth, advise your parishioners or any other Christians to vote against their own best interests merely to safeguard the profits of the Pharisees.

On the relation of union goals to those of the church, Rieve said:

Our movement, like yours, is devoted to the improvement of mankind. You seek to exorcize spiritual degradation, and to salvage man's immortal soul. We seek to exorcize physical degradation, and to make man's life on earth richer, freer, more rewarding, or at the very least, more endurable. . . . We should not be enemies, but allies. Surely you do not want a nation of Jobs, infinitely patient in the face of infinite trouble.

And he concluded by expressing his disappointed hope that the churches of the land had begun to abandon industrial paternalism for industrial democracy:

I thought the time was long since past when the mill-owner dictated policy to the clergy in his domain. I was encouraged to think so by the many declarations of policy adopted by central bodies of almost every denomination.[116]

Taken side by side, the three letters quoted here compose a critically important collage of conflicts over fact, perspective on history, ideology, and religious-ethical judgment. The Cherryville affair, as it thus began to unfold, contained in cameo many of the principal issues that simmered below the surface of labor-management-church relations in Gaston County in this and other periods of the local history. Who had been the promoters of the violence that Gastonians had come to associate with unionism of the 1929 strike? What grounds for a reputation for violence or peacefulness had the unions established in their *recent* activities in the county? Would wages and working conditions in Cherryville be at their present levels without the remote but real presence of a union movement? Who is the best representative of the interests of workers? Can a union be counted on to "lord it" over workers in ways more absolute than are at the disposal of a management unimpeded by a union? What are the benefits that workers are likely to lose from the presence of a union, over against the benefits likely to be won? Whose power in the industrial setting is in fact the most humane and trustworthy? And what is the proper relation between structures of power, justice, and "the good spirit and fellowship" of a community?[117] What, in short, is the proper way to organize an industry and a local society for the pursuit of Progress, Harmony, Liberty, and Justice for all?

There is little evidence that the Cherryville ministers were raising or discussing such issues with their parishioners. If they had taken the details of the pre-election company letter and put these up beside the details of the Rieve letter, some long and sobering discussions might well have taken place in the meeting of elders, deacons, stewards, Sunday School classes, and other groups of churchpersons in the town. (They might have calculated, for example, that a raise in hourly pay of four or five cents was enough to pay a textile worker's union dues for the rest of his or her life.)[118] But the ability to carry on such discussion, especially in the glare of publicity that began to descend upon them, was not much to be noted in the contemporary or the subsequent public behavior of the seven ministers. When Emil Rieve made his letter public, the ministers replied through a spokesman that their letter was their own doing and not that of the mill management.

We are innocent of the charge made by Mr. Rieve. We are letting silence be our answer to the charge.[119]

When pressed immediately by a nearby Charlotte-based official of the TWUA to admit that stationery, postage, and the mailing list for the pastors' letter came from the mill, a second spokesman for the seven conceded that the mailing list had indeed come from the mill at the request of the pastors; but they had furnished all the other necessary supplies.[120] This was the final public statement on the incident offered by any of the Cherryville ministers.

In the meantime, the TWUA filed an official complaint about the incident (against the company) with the NLRB. The union thus set a new precedent, putting the churches on notice that easygoing collusion between churches and mills was now subject to legal discipline. That a national union should openly attack the credibility of ministers in Gaston County was a new thing. Remarkably enough, to this one criticism from outside the locale was added a second: two national church denominational bodies now entered the Cherryville affair. In early March, Dr. C. Franklin Koch, executive head of the United Lutheran Church Social Missions Board, shared with the press his letter to the Cherryville Lutheran pastor in which he said:

While every man has the right to exercise his own judgment in these matters, I am of the opinion that your recent action was not in harmony with the official action of the United Lutheran Church in regard to labor unions.

That official action had included the statement: "It is the right of every man to organize with his fellow workers for collective bargaining through representatives of his own free choice." Koch went on to assure reporters that since this was a social rather than a theological issue, "there is no likelihood of disciplinary action by the synod" of the Cherryville Lutheran minister. Simultaneously, in a statement directed at the local Methodist ministers, an unidentified spokesman for New York headquarters called attention to the fact that recent national Methodist conferences had adopted a policy statement "supporting the right of both employer and employee to organize for collective bargaining."[121]

Further reactions of the Cherryville ministers to these winds of criticism from afar go unrecorded. What is striking about the incident is the multiple ways in which is signaled *a meeting of old and new structural conditions* for churchly foray into labor-management affairs in Gaston County. The TWUA was unable to make good on its charge of unfair labor practices against the Cherryville company; but the very fact that it could call the company and the ministers to account for their alleged collusion was a new, discomforting social fact for the local churches. And when to this secular challenge was added a parallel challenge from national denominational sources, the ministry of this mill town probably experienced some new dimensions of "cognitive dissonance." Seldom if ever before in Gaston County history had the quiet, implicit support of local churches for the interests of management been subjected so abruptly to the spotlight of specific national criticism from labor and church sources. None of the two or three extra-Gastonia denominational responses to the 1929 crisis, as quoted by Pope, had so pointedly criticized the churches for their role in that crisis.[122] The prompt, public, and national nature of these criticisms, must have shaken the traditionally comfortable relation between ministers and managers. And the object lesson to many other ministers in the county must have been: "It's not safe any more to go on record as opposing the union." Ideologically, the letter of the Cherryville ministers was strictly continuous with the paternalistic tradition; but the aftermath had in it an "unpleasant whiff of apprehension" about the future.[123]

In effect, the Cherryville minister was now colliding with a complex of new social facts. By the mid-forties, with the selling of the mill villages, structural church dependence upon the mills was on the decline, bringing a correlative decline of the direct economic pressures which mill management could bring upon ministers and churches. Further, both the new laws governing union organization and the new company defenses against unionism gave management reason to resist publicly-ideentifiable "help" from the churches. This trend was both revealed and reinforced by the Cherryville affair. Other evidence not forthcoming, one can believe that negotiations between the ministers and the management was substantially as reported: that the letter was the ministers' idea; that they asked for a mailing list from the company; that they paid for the postage and the typing; and that they were *re*paid chiefly in terms of the "mental income" of the economists, the "ideal interest" of the sociologist, or the intrinsic religious reward which the pastor acknowledged when he said: "I believe it was my Christian duty to my community." It is doubtful, in fact, that any Gaston mills, in 1953, were making large direct economic "payoffs" for anti-union support by ministers. Once the collaboration of the two may have been that gross, but the climate was changing even in Cherryville in 1953. The available data suggests that ministerial support for the company was utterly voluntary on their part. *If so, the gesture reflected ideological support for paternalism and opposition to unionism more profoundly than it reflected the*

gross economic interest of the churches. There was an old way of *thinking* at
work here, not chiefly an old way of getting paid. Or, to put it more relatively:
the ideological agreement of church leaders and industry leaders was the more
visible here because the economic dependency of the churches upon the mills
was the less direct. If the action of their ministers was the test, the churches
were no less the enemies of unionism in Cherryville in 1953 than they had
probably been in 1929. But the nature and context of the opposition had
undergone some changes.

Routinization of Labor-Management Relations:
The Fifties and Sixties

Over the next twenty years the history of labor-union organization attempts
in Gastonia were almost predictably monotonous: during the fifties, no textile
unions were organized; a few non-textile unions were organized, but union
defeats in the NLRB elections were more common than victories.
Management's strategies of defense against organization were as superbly
successful during the decade as they were routinely used: continued well-timed
wage hikes, astute changes in personnel relations policies, refinements in
fringe benefits, and increasingly skillful uses of law and lawyers. A flurry of
union activity, several hotly contested plant elections, and some NLRB
unfair-labor-practices cases all suggested that management enjoyed less than
the total confidence of Gaston workers; but the rising union tide, threatened so
soon after the war, seemed remote in 1959. When the tide did again rise a little
in the sixties, it met with plucky management confidence that it could be rolled
back yet again. Though the textile-union story was beginning·to be written in
terms of new success in some other parts of the South in 1975, TWUA
Southern Director Scott Hoyman was summarizing thirty years of union effort
in Gaston County when he said: "We don't have any presence there."[124]

Precisely because the story of the grinding-to-a-halt of unionism's Operation Dixie in the early fifties tended to be the story of much of the next two
decades of labor (non)organization in Gaston County, no lengthy account of
several incidents of heated union-management conflict need be entered upon
here. The incidents are worth brief accounts, however, for they are a summary
index to the validity of the generalization with which this chapter begins and
ends: as regards unionization, Gaston County remains an island of resistance,
most notably in its textile industries.

The 1958-61 period demonstrated that the resistance could be rough and
damaging to the image of the managerial revolution. A sharp rise in textile
unionizing activity had come in 1957 with what textile management called

"plant modernization" and many workers called a "stretch-out." If one judges by the public attention given the stretch-out controversy of the late fifties in Gastonia, the technical and human relations sides of managerialism were out of phase with the other. For example, in June and July of 1957 a remarkable debate went on in the local newspaper between an anonymous group of textile managers and an almost anonymous half dozen textile workers. In their concerted attempt to "allay rumors accusing some of the mills in the county of engaging in a 'stretch-out' of workloads," the managers issued a statement to the newspaper which said in part:

. . . Through the installation of more efficient machinery, it is now possible for an employee to take care of more spinning frames . . . than it was in the past.

But that does not mean that the employee is doing more work. The increased efficiency of the machines, plus better working conditions provided by the modernization program, have equalized the work loads. . . . If anything, ease of handling and better lighting have made the average job easier.

Going on to review the slight (1%) decline in spindles in North Carolina textile plants during the past decade, the modest rise in employment (3.1%), the sharp rise in wages (33%), and the problem of foreign competition and "two-price cotton," the statement concluded with comments of individual executives. Said one: "The loyalty of our employees in this county is the thing that makes our business possible. Certainly we would do nothing to endanger that relationship."[125]

Over the next four weeks a set of articulate contrary views from textile workers appeared, some with the suggestion that the writers did not expect their letters to be printed.[126] The letters were remarkable not only for the details which workers marshalled in criticism of technological "modernization" but also for the assorted hostilities which they expressed about other issues as well:

Autocracy in personnel management

They dismiss workers who have worked many years longer than those retained. Anyone who hunts with the overseer may get first shift jobs. The superintendent refuses to listen to complaints, justified or not.

There are no collective bargaining provisions at the plant where I am employed. The personnel representative was dismissed long ago. The authority of the overseer is final. The Cone Mills allow employees to register complaints, and bring other employees to aid in the presentation of the facts. Gaston County mills are afraid of the truth. They are forcing workers to migrate north, or seek union membership.[127]

Overemphasis on industrial engineering at the expense of human relations:

At this time the mills would rather employ two time-study men who try to break the worker's back, rather than allow us a personnel or complaint department. The cry of our injustice is unheard by them. The attitude of management is if you don't want the work load someone else does.[128]

Inequitable distribution of profit accruing from modernization:

Overseers (have recently gotten) from 30 to 40 percent increase (in pay), hour hands from 3 to 5 percent increase, section hands from 10 to 15 percent, and piece work hands were cut 8 percent.[129]

The ideological implications of economic inequality:

For years Americans have been told by the Communists that our laboring people are exploited by the capitalists (or management). Naturally we knew this was propaganda. However, from the way some local textile plants are doubling the work load of their employees, I am beginning to believe the Reds are right . . . management did not raise wages in proportion to the increase in work, and did not cut the price of their products. . . . They surely realize that this causes their employees to harbor resentment against them and to look favorably at labor unions and socialism. Such acts create more Communists than Stalin ever did.[130]

And a rare posing of a labor-relations issue in terms of religious conscience:

The modernization article (by the managers) was false. The reason many of those men did not want their names printed was because they are members of churches and know it is wrong to maltreat workers.[131]

Letters like these were weighing the fifteen-year development of the personnel relations movement and finding it wanting. They were also emblematic of the social-psychological impact of the changeover from founder-owner to professionalized management in the mills.

After years of attempting to gain a foothold in the major local chain of Textiles, Inc., on November 13, 1958 TWUA came within thirty-four votes of winning an election at Threads, Inc., one of the key plants of the parent corporation. The union followed up this narrow defeat by pressing charges of intimidation, blackmailing, blackballing, and other unfair labor practices against the local management. These charges were processed in a series of local NLRB hearings that stretched into the fall of 1959. The Board found Threads, Inc., guilty of at least one set of the charges, but a second election at the same plant in the fall of 1959 was less successful for TWUA than the first. The months between the two elections coincided closely with the disastrous textile strike in Henderson, N.C., 180 miles northeast of Gastonia. The pall that fell over the TWUA in that beleaguered city now cast its shadow on Gastonia—or so local spokesmen moved local workers to believe. While allowing that "it is a gross oversimplification to conclude that labor organizations are everywhere misguided and merit extinction," the *Gazette* had no trouble concluding on the basis of the current violence in Henderson,

that the textile unions have not been blessed with responsible leadership, but rather plagued with men who will resort to violence in order to accomplish their ends. . . . The greatest challenge to labor organizations is to rid themselves of men like Boyd Payton.

The labor bills now before Congress do not envision the destruction of labor unions. They are here to stay.

But the legislation is designed to create within the labor organization a system of checks and balances which characterize other democratic forums.[132]

Missing in this editorializing, of course, was the central issue in the Henderson strike: the ancient lack of checks and balances in the textile industry. Management in Henderson during these months was openly contradicting the proposition that local unions "are here to stay."[133] Governor Luther Hodges, himself a former textile executive, gave a candid summation of what the Henderson strike symbolized in the state. Having conferred six days with the parties to the strike in his Raleigh office, he said plainly: "It is not a question of misunderstanding: [President] Cooper and [TWUA Regional Director] Payton understand each other all too well. We're not union-organized much here in the South, but of course we don't go around bragging about that."[134]

Given the assumption that a union victory was a mark against any management record and a union defeat was a credit, the managers of many plants in Gastonia over the next several years had reason to congratulate each other. In 1975 not one of the county's 130 textile plants was organized, though a group of machinists at Textiles, Inc. did join a non-textile union in 1970.[135] Among five non-textile industries that had union elections in the 1959-61 period only two issued in union victories. One of these latter (a local box factory of a national company) was achieved on the fourth election attempt. The management of the other (a printing company) ultimately defeated the union after a costly strike and the successful introduction of new non-union workers to operate the plant.[136] In 1970, after years of effort, the United Auto Workers finally arrived on the Gastonia scene by winning an election at the new grease-seal plant by a close margin (154-133). About the same time the International Association of Firefighters attempted to organize the Gastonia firemen; but after three weeks of much public and private discussion of the matter, they did what so many other Gastonian workers have done for the past fifty years: they laid aside the union membership-application cards without signing them.[137]

That any scholar could follow the union-organization story so far beyond 1940 into the early 1970s and be so regularly subject to a sense of *déjà vu* is index enough to the profound "routinization" of this story in sociological terms.[138] As late as 1969, TWUA leaders like Scott Hoyman were presenting evidence to Congress to substantiate the textile worker's fear that if he so much as expressed a favorable opinion about unions he would be subject to economic reprisals in the form of company blacklisting. The evidence hardly suggested that textile managers considered textile unions "here to stay." Then there was the dinosaurial lethargy of NLRB trial-proceedings. "There is no area of law," said Hoyman to the House Committee on Labor, "in which it is more true that justice delayed is justice denied."[139]

"Justice" is the great ideological word of the labor union movement. We have seen that it was infrequently uttered on public occasions in Gastonia. But it was the right word for the ethical issue in the political and ideological debate that simmered during all these years: is countervailing, organized power essential to the achievement of social justice? was a concept of justice really missing from the constellation of virtues symbolized by Progress, Liberty, and Harmony; or did those terms sufficiently describe a just society? The debate goes on as this is written, but it is safe to conclude that a broad spectrum of Gastonians have already made up their minds and their organizational affiliations on this matter. Surely few of them found surprising a 1970 *Gazette* editorial headline which read:

"Unions Likely Will Continue to Find Tough Challenge in Gaston."
And surely few rose up to dub mistaken the historically-redolent, mellow editorializing that followed the headline. It could as easily have been written in 1940:

Perhaps not enough time has yet been put between the bloody strike of 1929 and the present. As a result of that strike, just the word "union" has been akin to a bad word.[140]

The Churches and Unionism:
An Attitudinal Profile of Gastonians

No reader of the above historical survey will be surprised, either, to learn that a sociological attitudinal study of Gastonians in the years 1965-67 colors and enriches the texture of that history without contradicting it. The sociological data is, with few exceptions, a confirmation of the historical.

Our survey utilized three related interview items concerning labor unions: (1) "North Carolina has a law which allows a man to work in a unionized plant without joining the union. Do you approve of this law?" (2) "How do you feel about labor unions in general?" (3) "Does Gastonia need labor unions?" These data are presented in Tables 5.3, 5.4, and 5.5, both by race and sex and by social characteristics.

Table 5.3

PROPORTION OF RESPONDENTS WHO APPROVE OF THE "RIGHT TO WORK" LAW,* BY RACE, SEX, AND SOCIAL CHARACTERISTICS

	Race and Sex							
	Black				White			
Social Characteristics	Male Percent	N	Female Percent	N	Male Percent	N	Female Percent	N
Income	62.5	56	73.2	56	84.5	174	91.5	82
Less than $4,000	60.0	20	65.0	20	88.2	17	91.7	24
$4,000-$6,999[a]	65.0	20	80.0	10	76.9	65	88.2	34
$7,000-$9,999[b]	—	—	—	—	77.3	18	(100.0)	(9)
$10,000 and over	—	—	—	—	96.4	55	—	—
Education								
8 years or less	73.5	34	84.4	32	72.3	47	84.4	32
9-11 years	53.9	13	36.3	11	80.0	40	93.8	16
High School grad[e]	(55.6)	(9)	84.6	13	83.8	37	92.9	14
Some college or more	—	—	—	—	93.0	49	100.0	20
Occupation								
High white collar[c]	(57.1)	(7)	(33.3)	(3)	98.3	58	85.7	7
Low white collar	—	—	—	—	86.4	22	100.0	24
High blue collar[d]	61.9	42	76.2	42	88.9	18	81.5	27
Low blue collar	—	—	—	—	72.1	61	—	—
Age								
College Students[f]	—	—	—	—	92.6	27	—	—
39 or less	72.7	11	68.8	16	88.5	52	93.1	29
40-49	71.1	18	68.4	19	83.3	48	95.5	22
50-59	53.8	13	(83.3)	(6)	86.7	45	88.9	18
60 and over	70.0	10	(85.8)	(7)	82.6	23	84.6	13
Length of Residence								
Less than 20 years	(66.7)	(8)	81.8	11	86.2	58	95.7	23
20 years or more	(66.0)	47	68.2	44	37.0	115	93.2	59
Ministers	(86.7)	(9)	—	—	72.9	48	—	—

*Question was: North Carolina has a law which allows a man to work in a unionized plant

a. For blacks, $4,000 and over.

b. For white females, $7,000 and over.

c. For blacks, white collar respondents are combined.

d. For blacks and white females, blue collar respondents are combined.

e. For blacks, high school grad or more.

f. There were too few college students in our sample to subdivide according to sex.
   Age categories which follow refer to adult.

Table 5.4

PROPORTION OF RESPONDENTS EXPRESSING FAVORABLE ATTITUDES TO-WARD* UNIONS IN GENERAL, BY RACE, SEX, AND SOCIAL CHARACTERISTICS

	Race and Sex							
	Black				White			
Social Characteristics	Male Percent	N	Female Percent	N	Male Percent	N	Female Percent	N
Income	69.0	49	60.9	46	44.8	165	36.2	80
Less than $4,000	77.8	18	52.9	17	46.7	15	31.8	22
$4,000-$6,999[a]	61.1	18	70.0	10	30.5	59	29.4	34
$7,000-$9,999[b]	—	—	—	—	38.9	18	(11.1)	(9)
$10,000 and over	—	—	—	—	5.5	55	—	—
Education								
8 years or less	71.4	28	55.6	27	36.3	44	25.8	31
9-11 years	80.0	10	(62.5)	(9)	27.8	36	50.0	14
High School grad[e]	(66.7)	(9)	54.5	11	26.5	34	26.7	15
Some college or more	—	—	—	—	48.9	45	10.0	20
Occupation								
High white collar[c]	71.4	(7)	—	—	10.9	55	(20.0)	(5)
Low white collar	—	—	—	—	40.0	15	28.0	25
High blue collar[d]	75.0	36	65.6	32	46.7	15	31.6	19
Low blue collar	—	—	—	—	36.7	49	—	—
Age								
College Students[f]	—	—	—	—	66.7	19	—	—
39 or less	(66.7)	(9)	81.8	11	23.8	42	32.0	25
40-49	85.7	14	57.1	14	22.7	44	25.0	16
50-59	76.9	13	(57.1)	(7)	25.7	35	50.0	14
60 and over	60.0	10	(50.0)	(4)	42.0	21	14.3	14
Length of Residence								
Less than 20 years	(85.7)	(7)	(83.3)	(6)	39.6	53	18.2	22
20 years or more	63.8	42	57.5	40	27.7	112	19.0	58
Ministers	(62.5)	(8)	—	—	59.6	52	—	—

*Question was: How do you feel about labor unions in general?

a. For blacks, $4,000 and over.

b. For white females, $7,000 and over.

c. For blacks, white collar respondents are combined.

d. For blacks and white females, blue collar respondents are combined.

e. For blacks, high school grad or more.

f. There were too few college students in our sample to subdivide according to sex.
  Age categories which follow refer to adult.

Table 5.5

PROPORTION OF RESPONDENTS EXPRESSING BELIEF THAT GASTONIA NEEDS UNIONS,* BY RACE, SEX, AND SOCIAL CHARACTERISTICS

	Race and Sex						
	Black				**White**		
Social Characteristics	Male Percent	N	Female Percent	N	Male Percent	N	Female Percent	N
Income	76.0	50	78.3	46	37.7	162	40.0	75
Less than $4,000	82.4	17	72.2	18	40.0	15	39.1	23
$4,000-$6,999[a]	72.2	18	(88.9)	(9)	57.3	61	32.3	31
$7,000-$9,999[b]	—	—	—	—	43.7	16	(62.5)	(8)
$10,000 and over	—	—	—	—	20.8	53	—	—
Education							
8 years or less	85.2	27	66.7	24	54.3	46	40.0	30
9-11 years	68.2	13	90.9	11	33.3	36	46.7	15
High School grad[e]	60.0	10	81.8	11	34.4	32	30.8	13
Some college or more	—	—	—	—	26.5	49	41.2	17
Occupation							
High white collar[c]	57.1	(7)	—	—	21.0	57	(16.7)	(6)
Low white collar	—	—	—	—	47.6	21	45.8	24
High blue collar[d]	80.0	40	72.2	36	35.3	17	52.4	21
Low blue collar	—	—	—	—	49.1	55	—	—
Age							
College Students[f]	—	—	—	—	60.9	23	—	—
39 or less	70.0	10	92.9	14	31.9	47	40.0	25
40-49	88.9	18	62.5	16	39.1	46	26.3	19
50-59	66.7	12	(77.8)	(9)	35.7	42	50.0	16
60 and over	70.0	10	(100.0)	(5)	41.7	24	35.7	14
Length of Residence							
Less than 20 years	85.7	(7)	(85.5)	(8)	34.0	53	50.0	18
20 years or more	74.4	43	76.9	39	87.8	49	36.8	57
Ministers	(100.0)	(7)	—	—	35.7	42	—	—

*Question was: Does Gastonia need unions?

a. For blacks, $4,000 and over.

b. For white females, $7,000 and over.

c. For blacks, white collar respondents are combined.

d. For blacks and white females, blue collar respondents are combined.

e. For blacks, high school grad or more.

f. There were too few college students in our sample to subdivide according to sex. Age categories which follow refer to adult.

Analysis of tables reveals that, by and large, union-related attitudes among white Gastonians—both the clergy and laity—are negative; but both race and socio-economic status affect those attitudes. Blacks tend to be more favorably disposed toward organized labor than whites. In all three questions, black men were the subgroup most in favor of unions, followed by black women, white men, and white women respectively. However, over 60% of the black men favored the so-called "right-to-work" law, while nearly 70% expressed positive attitudes towards unions in general and over three-fourths felt that Gastonia definitely needed unions. In contrast, more than 80% of the white men supported 14-b; less than one-half favored unions in general, and slightly more than one-third said that Gastonia needs unions.[141]

As for the effect of socio-economic status, blue-collar men and women were more favorable to unions than white-collar respondents; men whose annual family incomes were $10,000 or more were decidedly least favorable to unions.

Certain implications can be drawn from these findings. Though comparable figures are not available from Pope's study, it seems likely that (1) persons in the upper strata of the industrial hierarchy in Gastonia are as united as before in their opposition to unions, (2) tolerance for unions among the middle income white people may have increased since Pope's time, (3) the largest single potential for union growth rests with the new black employees of the mills, and (4) the lowest paid white workers remain an impediment to unionization, in spite of the conformity of their economic interests to that of the new black employees.[142]

What about a change in the attitudes of Gastonia ministers on this issue over the past thirty years? Concerning the attitudes of white clergy, Pope observed that "ministers in Gaston County have continued to oppose unions, often publicly, or else to qualify the principle so stringently as to nullify their endorsement of it. . . . Union organizers have consistently regarded ministers in Gaston County and in the South generally as among their worst enemies."[143]

When we compared the responses of our white ministers to those of lay respondents, their answers were strikingly like those of the middle-class white laypersons: more than seven in ten approved of 14-b, about 60% had positive attitudes toward unions in general, but only one-third said that Gastonia needs unions. Among those who did not feel the need for unions in Gastonia, several reasons were given, such as (1) the absence of abuses by management, (2) the apparent satisfaction of most mill workers, and (3) the fact that working conditions and/or wages and other benefits are already good.

In response to another interview item, several ministers indicated that labor-management relations had been hurt by the stretch-out or speed-up. A Presbyterian represents the group:

(Question: "Have industrial leaders done anything to help or to hurt labor-management relationships?") [Relations have been hurt by] increasing the work load of people in the mills. Most of the complaints on this come from men middle-aged and above. The conditions of work have improved over the years, but so have the requirements in both quantity and quality. [Have you talked to workers about these things?] Yes. [What do they say about, say, the rest periods?] They have decreased. Now you grab your sandwich and go to the bathroom on the run.

In response to this question, nearly half of the ministers (47.2%) accentuated the positive and eliminated the negative, citing only ways in which industrial leaders had improved their relations with workers.

Despite their pro-management tendencies, compared to the situation of the 1920s and 1930s, ministers' opposition to organized labor is apparently less uniform today. The following quotations illustrate three different positions toward various aspects of organized labor—opposition, ambivalence, and support.

Opposition. (Methodist, regarding 14-b): I think every man should have a chance to work where he wants without being forced into a union. I'm opposed to that kind of coercion. A number of us southern Methodist ministers feel that the National Council of Churches is out of line on this issue. We Methodists, who believe in personal freedom, object to selling ourselves to a large movement. . . . In the case of 14-b, you will find more vocal opposition to it coming from churchmen than anyone else. (Have you taken such an opposing position?) Yes, in.official board meetings though not from the pulpit.

Ambivalence. (Presbyterian): As for unions in Gastonia, I'm not as certain as I once was, for I don't hear much grumbling and outcry from the workers themselves.

Support. (Lutheran): Yes, Gastonia needs unions because a lot of people are getting rich at the expense of the . . . workers. Millhands are on a tight budget and get used to it, but I wouldn't live like that, waiting for one's master to pet him (give him a raise). I feel that the average millhand is being used.

Support. (Presbyterian): I'm prejudiced against the concentration of power wielded against the laboring man. I question the real sincerity behind the claims of "democracy" in _____ [a leading mill]. It may just be anti-unionism. It is a mighty convenient argument to say that "we must maintain the worker's freedom to work." On the other hand, some unions have abused their privileges and need more federal regulation, but I feel we need strong unions over against strong industry. I'm sympathetic to the fact that non-union labor rides on the coattails of gains won by unions elsewhere at considerable cost.

The instances of ambivalence were numerous. Frequently our minister respondents would say in effect: "While the principle underlying unionism is good, unions now have too much power." The comments of many were strikingly like those of Pope's day when they acknowledged the legitimacy of unions but added the qualification "if properly organized and conducted."[144] It was as though the record of unions in other parts of the country were now so tarnished that they had already rendered themselves illegitimate in Gastonia. At the same time, among some local residents, clergy, and laypersons there lingers a sense of illegitimacy in management tactics in resisting unionism. Some workers feel that their jobs will be endangered if they express pro-union sentiments. One minister reported that one of his parishioners had been blackballed in 1959 because of participation in union activities and therefore had to leave Gastonia to seek employment.

In short, numerous forces oppose the cause of unionism in Gaston County, and after one has accounted for the influence of churches as contributors to this antagonism, the list of other forces remains very long. William Spinrad was summarizing some of these restraints when in 1960 he sketched "a profile of the union activist" in the following terms: the typical "union activist" is skilled, enjoys high job status and pay, and is a member of an ethnic or racial minority; he and his co-workers form an "isolated mass," segregated from the rest of the community but closely integrated with one another; he has few personal contacts with supervisors, non-union or anti-union friends, or non-working class neighbors; he neither is alienated from his work nor aspires to a supervisory position, but he has satisfaction in his craft and identifies with the working class.[145]

The southern textile worker, by contrast with this picture, possesses relatively little skill or status, is not very well paid, is still typically a white Anglo-Saxon Protestant, presumably has many contacts with non-working-class consciousness.[146] Class consciousness had been overshadowed in the South by racial, ethnic, and religious differences. These "tend to crosscut and inhibit class consciousness and solidarity."[147] In addition, southern textile workers apparently have a low sense of self-confidence, plus a sense of impotence and parochialism, and they tend to be "suspicious of and even hostile toward outsiders."[148] At the heart of the matter, as a union leader put it, is "One of the hardest decisions the worker ever makes: to take a position in opposition to his boss, to shift from depending on a subordinate-superior relationship to depending upon his peers."[149]

In all, it is a formidable set of psycho-social obstacles to the labor union, a movement which has lacked support from almost every organization in the community including the churches. *Neither* in terms of "the abstract 'What?' " *nor* in terms of "the sociologically concrete 'Says who?' " does Gastonia society offer hospitality to unionism.

Church Membership and the Future of the Labor Union in Gastonia

Neither social science nor the local society's leaders can afford to believe that the future will be just like the past.

The question of the role of church membership and participation in the shaping of the Gastonians' attitudes towards labor unionism is complicated by the fact that a majority of the general sample of persons interviewed for this study were church members and frequent participants. Among the categories of membership and participation, there is no dramatic difference of opinion about unions nor is there a difference between the general population and the group of sixty-six ministers interviewed for the study. However, some ministers demonstrate a knowledge of unions and arguments for them that contrasts notably with the ministers interviewed by Pope: there was little or no evidence of a William McLean or a Stuart Henderson in that former era.[150] But the influence which these "liberal" ministers have on the attitudes of their parishioners on the union question is debatable. Some of these very ministers—"pro-union" in a general sense—are aware that their views on this subject do not get a very ready hearing in their congregations.[151] During the Cherryville incident, a news reporter, in a semi-editorial comment, observed that:

The letters may have had some influence on the outcome [of the union vote], although many Cherryville people doubt it.[152]

To be sure, the question of church influence in the cultivation of positive and negative union sentiments cannot be equated with the question of ministerial influence; but the more important summary point here is one that our opinion-distribution data support dramatically: *on the union issue, Gastonians share an ideology that overrides religious, class, and even racial differences.* On few other issues, in fact, is ideology so clearly apparent in the array of interview-data on this subject.

Tables 5.6 and 5.7 summarize these data comprehensively for our respondents who are classified into textile-related and non-textile-related occupations, by residence and race. The number of respondents in these tables is quite small and varies within the tables because on certain questions related to labor unions a sizable proportion of Gastonians either would not answer the question or said "I don't know"—approximately 20% of all respondents. Against the background of much that has happened in Gastonia on the union question from 1929 to 1966—when most of these interviews took place—this absence of expressed opinion is a very eloquent datum on local culture: unionism is still not

Table 5.6

RESPONSES OF GASTONIANS TO QUESTIONS ABOUT UNION ISSUES
BY RACE, RESIDENTIAL AREA, AND EMPLOYMENT, IN PERCENT

Union Issues	Race, Residential Area, and Employment					
	Textile Related Employment			Not in Textile Related Employment		
	Black	White		Black	White	
		Mill Village	Other		Mill Village	Other
Right to Work Laws						
Favor	69.6	81.4	85.4	69.4	89.2	93.7
Oppose	30.4	18.6	14.6	30.6	10.8	6.3
N	23	59	41	85	37	111
Labor Unions in General						
Positive	90.5	26.5	11.4	64.1	46.4	26.3
Ambivalent	4.8	22.4	34.3	23.4	28.6	35.9
Negative	4.8	51.0	54.3	12.5	25.0	37.8
N	21	49	35	64	28	92
Gastonia Needs Unions						
Yes	71.4	27.6	13.5	74.3	55.6	33.7
Uncertain	4.8	8.6	5.4	8.1	7.4	7.6
No	23.5	63.8	81.1	17.6	37.0	58.7
N	21	58	37	74	27	104

a *safe* subject to discuss with strangers. But Gastonians who discuss the subject show certain striking agreements among themselves. The data in these tables suggest that:

—a large majority of all white groups (except non-textile workers living in mill villages) believes that Gastonia does not need labor unions,

—an overwhelming majority of all groups favors the so-called, "right-to-work" law that outlaws the union shop,

—*negative* union sentiment is higher for white groups related directly to the textile industry than for others,

—among the reasons for joining a union, a majority of all groups sees "higher wages" as the most important reason,

—the argument from "the need for organizational power" ranks extremely low for all groups, and among those in the textile industry it is *not mentioned at all,*

—all groups see "job protection" as a major secondary reason for unions,

—all groups tend to agree that "fear of reprisal" and "strikes" are major reasons why Gastonia workers might be negative towards unions.

Table 5.7

RESPONSES OF GASTONIANS TO QUESTIONS ABOUT REASONS FOR JOINING OR REFUSING TO JOIN UNIONS BY RACE, RESIDENTIAL AREA, AND EMPLOYMENT, IN PERCENT

	Race, Residential Area, and Employment					
	Textile Related Employment			Not in Textile Related Employment		
	Black	White		Black	White	
		Mill Village	Other		Mill Village	Other
Reasons Given for Joining Union						
Fringe benefits	21.0	—	3.2	—	4.3	3.4
Shorter hours	5.3	—	—	—	—	1.1
Job protection	10.5	14.3	3.2	19.5	13.0	14.9
Non-discrimination	5.3	14.3	3.2	19.5	13.0	14.9
Power in organizing	—	—	—	—	8.7	4.6
Spokesman for labor	—	8.6	6.5	2.4	4.3	1.1
Higher wages	47.4	62.8	64.5	48.8	60.9	55.2
Improved working conditions	5.3	5.7	12.9	17.1	8.7	12.6
Smaller work load	5.3	8.6	9.7	—	—	6.9
N	19	35	31	41	23	87
Against Joining Union						
Apathy and ignorance	50.0	5.3	—	—	4.8	9.1
Benefits insufficient	—	13.2	19.4	4.3	—	12.5
Costs too great	7.1	—	19.4	8.7	9.5	14.8
Historic reference to 1929	—	5.3	8.3	—	4.8	4.5
Individualism	7.1	10.5	16.7	8.7	19.0	11.4
Distrust of organization	14.3	13.2	5.6	4.3	28.6	14.8
Fear of reprisal	14.3	26.3	8.3	47.8	23.8	15.9
Strikes	7.1	21.0	22.2	13.0	9.5	12.5
Other	—	5.3	—	13.0	—	4.5
N	14	38	36	23	21	88

To enumerate the agreements in this way is to distort some of the striking divergences; but on the whole signs of "ideological warfare" are exceedingly rare in these statistics. Such signs are to be seen chiefly in contrasts between the opinions of whites and the opinions of blacks. *But even Gastonia blacks share the community's general aversion to the union shop and are apparently oblivious to the argument for unionism in terms of organized power as a prerequisite to social justice.* Though blacks in the textile industry indicate that apathy and ignorance are the most important impediments to unions, they also share the community's general sense that the best reason for joining any organization is that it yields more money to its members. Management anti-union propaganda that focuses on the "union dues" argument, therefore, is obviously well targeted.

It is plain, on the other hand, that Gastonia blacks strongly favor labor unions, displaying little difference between those employed in the textile industry and those who are not. Their response to the union question is statistically opposite that of whites not in mill villages or a suburban high income group.[153] And, while Gastonia white ministers interviewed express pro-and-anti-union sentiments in proportions roughly similar to those of white collar rather than blue collar whites, black ministers are among the most forthright supporters of the union idea.

A *prima facie* conclusion is that Gastonia's non-mill-village whites continue to influence the community's presumptions about labor unions and that the white churches of Gastonia have done little to shake these presumptions. The opinions of ministers, the opinions of a majority of the interviewed white laity, and the scarcity of union-related issues in the educational activites of the churches all embody a mindset that in some respects pervades even the black community and that has not radically changed since Pope's day.

How then can an undeniable difference in attitude towards unions between blacks and whites be explained? One explanation is: Gastonia blacks have been excluded from participation in the general structure of the dominant textile industry during most of Gastonia's history. They have been therefore excluded from long, thorough conditioning by the anti-union stance of that industry and the Gaston community at large. They have been as free to identify imaginatively with the economic gains of unions in other parts of the country as they have been free to identify with the Democratic Party and its New Deal support of unionism. Prior to 1960, only a few Gastonia blacks could be threatened with the loss of a job in a mill, for the vast majority did not hold such jobs. Reverberations of horror over the Loray Strike were never as deep in the memories of blacks as it was for whites; for, after all, that strike did not happen *to* the black community. It was a crisis inside the white community. Next to ignorance, the most often-mentioned reason against joining a union for blacks was "fear of reprisal"—which suggests that they are already educated to believe that loss of jobs is a characteristic threat whereby Gaston industry seeks to protect itself against unions. Whether black textile workers will maintain pro-union sympathies against the possible reality of that threat in their new employment situation in the mills is a question for the future. Since their strongest reason for their sympathy with the union is higher wages and their weakest reason is the desire for the power of an organization (a pair of preferences parallel among fellow white workers), the mills' success in keeping out the unions will probably continue to hinge on the level of wages.

Summary

The role of the churches, white and black, in opening or closing the gates of the Gastonian's mind to labor unionism remains hard to document. But it seems fair to conclude that the white churches, like the white minister, continue to serve in a much vaguer way than in the old days as opponents of unionism. At the same time, they are no longer in a position to be either "among the worst enemies"[154] of the labor organizer nor among the best friends of management. The Cherryville affair demonstrated that. Little that ministers say and little that white churches do is exceedingly *relevant* to the issues of labor-management relations in their modern form, either in the personnel relations movement or in collective bargaining. In the former, the churches may be seeing a shift of some of their own former role to the industrial psychologist; and, though some themes in their own religious-ethical heritage might enable local church leaders to address the issue of justice in collective power negotiations, the devotion to individual religion and social harmony inside the church constricts inquiry into such questions.[155]

The case with the black churches would seem to be noticeably, but not radically, different. In the past the black church has been the major social organization in the black community outside of the family. Recently in the civil rights movement some black churches of Gastonia provided a base of opposition to uptown industrial powers, but in the aftermath of the movement black ministers worked diligently with industrialists to locate candidates for new job openings. Thus, ironically, the better and more numerous the jobs secured by members of the black community the more vulnerable they become to anti-union arguments. The more integrated they become with the mainline industrial structure of Gaston County, the less friendly they may be to church leaders who want them to demonstrate for economic justice by joining unions.

In sum: one may fairly predict that educated black ministers will continue to hold strong convictions about Gastonia's need for unions, but what about their parishioners? The latter's education on the subject will take place increasingly in Gastonia's traditional or newer industries, none of whose managers intends to offer any instruction on the advantages of the union. The large general sympathy for unionism among Gastonia black wage workers may thus become a background for some very painful choices by them in the future: unless their fellow white workers begin to support unions in proportions similar to their own support, the union cause in Gastonia could become identified with the interests of one race; and the old shadows of racism would return. Gastonia blacks, and especially Gastonia black church leaders, can be counted on to resist that development passionately. One suspects that they will draw back from wholehearted open support for unionism before they forfeit the gains of economic integration. A further tragic possibility from the black standpoint is that over the next decade or so the textile industry may become so marginal to the American economy that blacks again will find themselves "last hired and first fired"—this time in terms of a whole industrial structure. Textile unions would then be a poor substitute for a taste of the employment plums now enjoyed by middle class whites of the South.

The one possibility among the black churches that might contribute to the telling of another story would be that ministers and laity alike might turn the Gastonia discussion on unionism away from the hysterical context of violence towards the context of ordinary democratic politics. Theirs would be the pioneering task of exploring the broad interface between economic structures and the *organizational* meaning of "liberty and justice for all." Leaders of the dominant black churches have a head start on most of the white churches in understanding themselves as having a political role in the community at large, and one supposes that the discussion of unionism could be much more easily carried on in the black churches now than in the white. Indeed, recent evidence from other parts of the South indicates that black churches, in counties less compulsively afflicted than Gaston by memories of a Loray Strike, have already served the union cause in very direct ways. Reported one union official in 1975:

"In some of our campaigns black ministers will invite a union organizer to speak to his congregation in the Sunday worship service, and to use the church building as a union meeting place. Recently in the Oneida strike in Andrews and Lane, South Carolina, the black minister spoke at strike meetings, led in the demonstration march, and arranged to have his choir sing for the occasion! Nowadays white ministers know that they have people on both sides of the union-management argument, so they say that they are 'neutral' on the issue. But black ministers see no such contradiction between the interests of their members and the interests of the union. The experience of many black ministers and textile workers in the civil rights movement were a good preparation here: it taught them not to be afraid of trying to change society and its institutions."[136]

How just such an experience came to pass in Gastonia is the subject of the next chapter.

NOTES

1. Cf. Introduction, above p. 51.

2. Or was a more valid test the fact that, in 1973, 97 out of 100 North Carolina counties, including Gaston, voted 2–1 against legalizing liquor-by-the-drink? *GG*, August 11, 1974.

3. By 1974 the new Gastonia Housing Authority had 564 units of public housing under its jurisdiction, most of it located in the western side of the city. *GG*, June 27, 1974.

4. Source: U.S. Bureau of the Census, U.S. Census of Housing for 1940, 1950, 1960, and 1970; and *General Housing Characteristics, North Carolina*, HC (1) A 35, pp. 7 and 13.

5. No member of our research team is a master of the skills of political science, and in our study as a whole we did not attempt to mount what that discipline would term a formal "power study." The term "community power structure" was made famous twenty years ago by a book of that title by Floyd Hunter, reporting on his study of Atlanta, Georgia. (*Community Power Structure* [Garden City, N.Y.: Doubleday and Co., Anchor Books, 1963.]) Hunter's work inaugurated a series of inquiries into the subject of who-controls and who-is-controlled in the corporate affairs of civil communities, and a basic methodological issue emerged in this series of power-studies: how does one *discover* who has the "real power" in a given society? Two major answers were debated among political scientists. One answer was Hunter's own: one asks a variety of people in a community who they think has real power; then one asks the latter who they think has power; and thus one builds up a picture of the divergent *reputations* for power enjoyed by various people in a community. The other method of investigation, represented by the work of such scholars as Robert Dahl (cf. his *Who Governs?* New Haven: Hale University Press, 1961), and partly in reaction to Hunter, presupposed that reputation for power may be one thing and actual power to influence a given community *decision* may be quite another thing. One never really knows "who governs" until one observes and discovers who, in the press of actual political struggle, was able to get the decision to go his/her way. Though not totally at odds with each other, the two methods imply very different allocations of energy in field-investigation of a community: the one requires the investigator to scurry around to many conversations with a gradually decreasing number of people, and the end of the scurrying is usually the discovery of a powerful elite at the pyramid-tip of the community power structure. Dahl's method, on the other hand, impels the researcher to look at specific events in the history of the community and to try to discover who directed those events to their specific outcomes. Such an approach may take the researcher to see very different people in connection with different decisions made in the community; and, as it happens, decisional-studies of American urban communities have usually yielded a more pluralistic picture of multiple power-centers than the "power structure" approach usually yields. Like so many other conclusions of social science, the variation of discovery is related systematically to variation in the methods of investigation.

The following two chapters have traces in them of both approaches to the study of power and influence in Gaston County over the past thirty years. Interviews with a variety of persons reputed to be powerful were undertaken by the three of us in the 1965-70 period, but systematic interviewing of all the persons named in the interviews was not undertaken. More to our particular interest was an inquiry in our interviews of a sample of the Gastonia population at large concerning who the "man in the street" believed to be influential in Gastonia. (The results of this inquiry illuminate our discussion of the resolution of the civil rights issues towards the end of Chapter Six.) Then, by focusing upon the two cases of labor unionism and race relations so extensively, our attempt to understand the who and the what of decisions in this area took us into a great variety of interviews with persons known to have some connection with these decisions. Because Gastonia is a relatively small community, and because knowledge of a single "powerful person" soon accumulates from a variety of local sources, we often came to know that a given person was either a strong candidate for the local "power elite" or a very influential person in a given instance of local decisionmaking. To the resolution of the question of which theory is the more useful for investigating and interpreting power our study makes no definitive contribution. But we are prompt to say that our partial use of both methods has contributed to our understanding of social change in Gastonia what neither alone could contribute.

6. Donald F. Roy, "Change and Resistance to Change in the Southern Labor Movement," in John C. McKinney and Edgar T. Thompson, eds., *The South in Continuity and Change* (Durham: Duke University Press, 1965), pp. 234-235. Roy has been a participant-observer of many union campaigns, especially in North Carolina.

7. Overall union-growth statistics for the years 1939-1953 offer some basis for the generalization of Roy that "as the nation goes, so goes the South." (*Op. cit.*, p. 226). Drawing upon Leo Troy's "The Growth of Union Membership in the South, 1939-1953" *The Southern Economic Journal*, 24 (April 1958), pp. 407 ff. Roy states that union growth during these years was actually somewhat faster in the South in relative terms. While national members grew from 6,517,700 to 16,217,300, southern members grew from 591,500 to 1,700,500—a growth of 148.8% nationally vs. 187.5% in the South. (Troy, pp. 409-410.) We shall see that such statistics have little predictive or other value for the Gaston County scene, which, especially on the union question, displays unique historical characteristics.

8. F. Ray Marshall, *Labor in the South* (Cambridge: Harvard University Press, 1967), p. 227.

9. *Ibid.*, p. 235

10. *Ibid.*, p. 245.

11. For the wage picture over the total 1940-74 period, cf. above, p. 188.

12. Marshall, p. 246.

13. *Ibid.*, pp. 252, 264.

14. Marshall quoted from *Grogan*, John Riffe, p. 103.

15. Marshall, *ibid.*, p. 261. Quoted from TWUA, *Proceedings of Fifth Biennial Convention*, 1948, pp. 64-65.

16. *MP*, pp. 200-201.

17. *GG*, May 15, 1943.

18. *GG*, July 13, 1943.

19. *GG*, September 17, 1943.

20. The Gastonia newspaper is an exceedingly essential but untrustworthy source of labor union news in this and all the other years covered in this study. If news about the August 1944 NLRB election got into this newspaper, the notice was so obscure as to elude the microfilm-blearied eyes of the authors of this study. The point is important for underscoring the well-known connection between news that is "fit to print" and the ideological presuppositions of its editors. News of union *victories* in the *Gazette*, if they appear at all, are likely to be sequestered in the back pages.

21. A contract negotiation between the management of a local machine shop and the AFL Foundry Workers Union had come to grief on this last point during this same period, spring 1945. As the CDA contract was signed, in fact, the local machine shop was under seizure by the U.S. Army at the order of the War Labor Board.

22. *GG*, March 4, 1946. This was the local business agent's version of the reasons for the suspension.

23. In 1948, apparently in reaction to the events about to be described, a "Brotherhood of Textile Workers" was organized in Gaston County. It proved to be a short-lived local movement.

24. A term used to report the April 3, 1945 CDA-UTW contract by the *GG*, April 5, 1945.

25. *GG*, February 28, 1946.

26. *GG*, March 4, 1946.

27. Reprinted in *GG*, March 8, 1946.

28. *GG*, March 7, 1946.

29. This editorial even went on to quote the Christian Science Monitor on the point: "We shall not solve the problem of strike violence until management and unions learn greater wisdom and skill in labor relations, until governments provide more adequate mediation service, and until society as a whole provides machinery for the peaceful arbitration of deadlocked disputes—and insists that it be used." The absence of such a structure for resolving corporate conflict is precisely the vacuum that the union movement was seeking to fill, of course, however ineptly, in this unionless community.

30. *GG*, March 8, 1946.

31. *GG*, March 9, 1946.

32. *GG*, December 4, 1947.

33. *GG*, April 28, 1948. In the late fifties, the CDA union members became dissatisfied with the UTW and voted themselves into the TWUA, which renegotiated a contract with the CDA management. But in 1966 the national TWUA withdrew the local union's charter, because of poor local membership support. (Interview, April 24, 1975, with Scott Hoyman, Southern Director of TWUA.)

34. It is important to note that the editor responsible for the following opinion has been editor since 1919—i.e., during the 1929 crisis.

35. *GG*, February 23, 1946. This editor retired in 1947.

36. Cf. above, p. 191.

37. Atkins was a 1927 graduate of Duke University, and during part of World War II he served in the Office of War Information as night cables editor in New York City. His father, James W. Atkins, had been principal owner of the newspaper since 1906. Three other members of the family held major positions on the staff. The Atkins family had strong ties to the Gastonia establishment, e.g., one of the brothers was Gregg Cherry's campaign manager in 1944 and was editor of the *Southern Textile News*, an industry publication. Ben E. Atkins served the paper variously as book review editor, managing editor, and finally (in the fifties) editor. In 1942 he penned the review of *Millhands and Preachers* which Liston Pope later termed "one of the best reviews of the book" ever to appear. ("Postscript" to the new Introduction, by Richard A. Peterson and N. J. Demerath, III, Yale paperbound edition, 1965, p. xlix.) Atkins said in the review that he considered the work "an eminently fair book, both in its generalities and its treatment of the ill-begotten Gastonia strike of 1929. . . ." That he entertained no unqualified sympathies for the management side of the textile industry was implicit at one or two points in his review, especially in the language of his reference to Pope's treatment of preachers who "have licked the boots of the mighty money-bags that make the mills." (*GG*, May 16, 1942) In many things that he wrote Atkins maintained a sort of distance from the widely acclaimed values of this local culture. It is this aspect of his mind that gave it a religious quality, in the terms with which we have defined religion above, pp.

38. *GG*, February 16, 1946. Atkins could be critical enough of what he regarded as special privilege sought by union leaders, too—e.g., John L. Lewis' misuse of the right to strike, a right which Atkins reaffirmed repeatedly. (CF. *GG*, May 27, 1946.) An example of "critical distance" on the race problem appeared in his column a year later: "I love the South as much as anybody on the face of the earth. But I must admit, even though I don't like to, that the South, despite its remarkable progress in industry and economy, is still a hotbed of racial hatred and misunderstanding." (*GG*, April 5, 1947).

39. A hosiery mill in Gastonia (Wisteria), and a small cotton mill in Dallas (Morewebb) organized in early 1947. *GG*, January 14, 1947; May 7, 1947.

40. *GG*, December 21, 1946.

41. See above, p. 187.

42. E.g., the small Dallas mill voted for the UTW by 58 to 49 in early '47.

43. The Cocker Machine and Foundry Company. Vote tabulation was 73-63 for "no union." *GG*, November 3, 1947.

44. Cf. F. Ray Marshall, *op. cit.*, pp. 313-314, on the pressures which can be mobilized by union organizers who have support from unions in other branches of the corporate structure.

45. Material prepared for *Gastonia Gazette 70th Anniversary Edition*, October 17, 1950.

46. Editorial, *GG*, April 3, 1945.

47. TWUA leaders in other parts of the South took much pains to distinguish collective bargaining from strikes, violence, and communism—and with good political reason. In July of 1946 *The Charlotte Observer*, in an editorial reprinted in the *Gazette*, accused "the Communist leaders of the CIO" of forgetting the lesson of 1929, which was not the lesson of southern "hostility to organized labor, but a determination not to enlist southern labor in a Communist union." *GG*, July 5, 1946.

48. *GG*, May 27, 1946. The organization of Cannon Mills, as this is written in early 1975, is again the object of intensive TWUA campaigning—to date unsuccessful.

49. The selling of the Firestone mill village was underway at the beginning of World War II, but had been suspended until 1949-50, when all of the houses were finally sold. Jobs at this mill were highly prized among Gaston textile workers, and this further accounted for the wide dispersal of the work force.

50. An ancestor of the future Citizens Council movement in the Carolinas, perhaps a front for the Ku Klux Klan, the Farmers' States Rights Association, Inc., headquartered in nearby Rock Hill, S.C., bought many pages of local newspaper advertising in the summer and fall of 1946. These ads nailed the red star of Communism on the CIO and sought to educate the textile worker in particular to the CIO's "message of death." The same ads included a rash of references to the CIO's national support of Fair Employment Practice legislation. The most blatantly racist of these latter articles was a reprint from the *Southern Textile Bulletin* which accused the CIO of being both communist and racially equalitarian. An FEPC law, it said, would force a company on occasion to put "a Negro overseer . . . over white girls. . . . It is not a question of union or non-union. A man may still believe that a union is best for the employees of a mill, but can refuse to accept social equality with Negroes or to forget that he and his wife and his sons and daughters have Anglo-Saxon blood." *GG*, July 23, 1946.

51. *GG*, October 12, 1946. Passed during the 1929 crisis, the ordinance had been irregularly enforced. Other sound trucks had operated in the city recently, said the police chief in a city council hearing, but "licensing of these trucks must have been overlooked." One councilman said that "it appeared to him that the CIO was asking to be allowed to do what other people have already been doing," but this was as far as the council got to acceding to the organizers' formal request that the ordinance or its enforcement be officially suspended.

In the early 1970s this ordinance was still on the books, but policemen themselves were enough aware of the law to enforce it against themselves in an instance of their own plan for a community shopping center recreational event in east Gastonia. Not having the Council permit in time, they cancelled the event.

52. Letter by Clyde Jenkins, CIO Organizing Committee representative, to the City Council, *GG*, October 16, 1946.

53. *GG*, January 14, 1947.

54. *GG*, January 27, 1947.

55. Interview, January 6, 1972. Given all the newspaper-reported details on the 1946-47 organizing attempt, the lack of any memory of the event in the mind of this competent professional speaks volumes about the psychology and sociology of knowledge.

56. Scott Hoyman, Southern Director, TWUA, personal communication, August 30, 1972. On the dramatically different union attitudes of blacks in the mid-sixties, referred to by Hoyman, see below, Chapter Six.

57. *GG*, July 23, 1946; July 25, 1946.

58. Such an argument was used, for example, by TWUA organizer Lewis Conn when he spoke

to 400 Gaston textile workers in a meeting at the county courthouse in early 1951. "Non-union management has kept employees relatively happy by jumping on the bandwagon," he explained to his audience. *GG*, March 19, 1951.

59. Marshall, *op. cit.*, p. 336.

60. According to TWUA director Hoyman, wage-raises in the textile industry have ordinarily been awarded on 18-month cycles. In the early seventies, both a tight labor market and the fear of unions, he believes, telescoped this cycle dramatically. In the 18 months between December of 1972 and May of 1974, the average raises offered by the industry were successively 5½% (December 1972), 7½% (October 1973), and 10% (May 1974). Interview, April 24, 1975.

61. For example, TWUA leaders in 1971 were pointing out that in 1970 textile wages in the South rose 6% while prices climbed 9%. Associated Press, *The News and Observer* (Raleigh), June 28, 1971.

62. For example, cf. above, p. 79 ff.

63. Cf. statement by Mr. Seabury Stanton of Fall River-New Bedford Cotton Rayon Association before the Wage Stabilization Board in Washington, in mid-1951: half of his association was considering a move South if wage-equalization between the regions was not forthcoming. *GG*, June 18, 1951.

64. The U.S. Labor Department lists 21 "major industry" groups, of which "Textile Mill Products" and "Apparel and Other Textile Products" are two. Added together the two related industries are the largest employers in the country. In 1971 their average wages were $2.46 and $2.45 respectively, at the bottom of the list. Cf. *Handbook of Labor Statistics 1972* (Washington: U.S. Dept. of Labor, Bureau of Labor Statistics), Tables 39 and 100, pp. 90-91 and 224-225.

65. *GG*, October 14, 1955.

66. Ascertained by Shriver through visits to some of these mills, 1956-59.

67. The implications of byssinosis-research for occupational safety standards in the textile industry are still being argued by industry, union, and Federal government agencies as this book goes to press in 1975. The Senate Watergate Committee of 1973 had evidence presented to it that the director of the Occupational Safety and Health Administration (OSHA), as a gesture for the support of industry in the 1972 election of Richard Nixon, softened its enforcement of "controversial standards" regarding cotton dust. In the fall of 1974, byssinosis was still not one of the "compensable diseases" under the workman's compensation law. Cf. testimony by TWUA Research Director George Perkel before U.S. Senate Labor Committee, reported in *Textile Labor*, Vol. xxxv, No. 9 (September 1974). In 1975 the issue of byssinosis had become the subject of church action, however, in the form of a project called the Southern Institute for Occupational Health, headquartered in Columbia, South Carolina and supported by several local and national church bodies. Chief activity of the S.I.O.H. in May 1975 was the organization of disabled textile workers into "Brown Lung Associations" for the filing of compensation claims and legislative lobbying. As this is written, an attempt to organize such an association was going on in Gastonia, according to the Staff Director, Mike Szpak. (*S.I.O.H. Newsletter*, May 27, 1975.)

68. Mildred Barnwell Andrews, "Textile Industry Aids State's Sociological Development," *Employment Security Commission Quarterly*, Vol. 10, (Summer-Fall 1953), pp. 76-79, and pp. 119-120. An only slightly revised version of this same article was reprinted in this same state-government-based publication in the winter-spring issue of 1959.

69. *Ibid*.

70. *Economic Security Commission Quarterly*, Vol. 10, pp. 119-120. During this same decade other mills upgraded their playgrounds with new equipment, and Groves Thread Company in east Gastonia rebuilt a burned-out gymnasium at a cost of $102,000. The list of other "modern" programs instituted during this period was very long: summer vacations paid and scheduled according to length of employment with the company; group life and health insurance plans, college scholarship and loan funds, non-contributory retirement-pension plans; and even bonuses

to employees in the form of company stock. (An incidence of the latter moved the *Gastonia Gazette* in 1947 to commend the action as "unprecedented in these parts" and as embodying the sound notion "that labor troubles can be kept to a minimum by this show of friendship and good will." The national company in question distributed to 4000 of its wage workers a half million dollars worth of stock, according to the number of years that the employee had worked with the company—an average of $125 of stock per employee.)

71. *GG*, October 5, 1946. A 1974 account rang the changes on an identical theme: Mrs. Mozelle Watts in that year had completed sixty-one years of work in Gaston mills. She was now seventy-one years old, having first gone to work in the mills at the age of ten in 1913. Her superintendent at the J. P. Stevens plant in Stanley believed that in longevity she outranked any textile employee in the county. *GG*, June 16, 1974.

72. Cf. *GG*, December 20, 1948; December 23, 1948; October 24, 1950.

73. In mid-1974 the president of Groves Threads was given a national award for his work in employee-recreation programming, including "the Easter egg hunt for all employees' children, a week of July 4 events, Thanksgiving dinner for all company employees . . . an Old Timers' party . . . and a wide variety of Christmas week activities." For its celebration of July 4, 1974, Pharr Yarns, Inc., held its traditional barbecue for 10,000 persons in the McAdenville ball park—owned like the rest of the town—by that company. (*GG*, June 18, 1974; *GG*, June 17, 1974.) As this book is published McAdenville remains virtually as pure an example of an unincorporated, company town as any described by Liston Pope.

74. *GG*, May 13, 1955. These and similar quotations above are examples of what labor union organizers call company "sweet stuff"—according to Donald F. Roy, *op. cit.* (above, note 6). Roy sees the human-relations accent as "pseudo-paternalism," to be distinguished from the companion management strategy of "coercion." Pseudo-paternalism is an institutionalized pattern, in Roy's terminology; and managerial improvements invented especially for the occasion of a union campaign, he dubs "quickie sweet stuff." (Roy, p. 239.)

75. *GG*, May 19, 1955.

76. If *other* industries in the country set the example, fringe benefits in the southern textile industry were never exemplary in the 1950-75 period. Said a TWUA publication in mid-1975: "The average expenditure by southern textile employers for fringe benefits is still less than 20¢ an hour compared to the national factory average of 80¢." (*Textile Labor*, July/August 1975, pp. 2-3.)

77. This term is frequently used in social science to describe the lowered status *felt* by a social group which, without losing any power, sees other groups as gaining it. See Robert K. Merton and Alice S. Rossi, "Contributions to the Theory of Reference Group Behavior," in Robert K. Merton, *Social Theory and Social Structure*, Revised Edition, New York: Free Press, 1957, pp. 225-280.

78. These figures are quoted in Douglass Cater, "Labor's Long Trial in Henderson, N.C.," *The Reporter*, September 14, 1961, pp. 36-40.

79. Sanford Cohen, *Labor in the United States,* Second Ed. (Columbus, Ohio: Charles E. Merrill Books, Inc., 1966), p. 485. Used by permission.

80. In a closed shop, the employee must be a union member as a prior condition of employment; in the union shop, he must join the union after being employed. The former provision put somewhat more power in union hands than the latter. Taft-Hartley permitted members of a unionized work force to vote on whether or not they wanted a union shop, but the demand for a formal vote was removed from the law in 1951 because unionized workers so routinely proceeded to vote in the union shop.

81. Cohen, *op. cit.*, pp. 231-232. All but three of the nineteen state right-to-work laws in force in the mid-sixties were passed in the 1947-54 period. Until 1957, when Indiana, a major industrial state, passed its law, only southern and other predominantly agricultural states had such legislation. In 1965 the Indiana law was repealed. *Ibid.*

82. "The place of origin generally accepted," said the Raleigh *News and Observer* editorially, is the National Association of Manufacturers. Debate on the bill in the House indicates that its authors were aiming at strikes which have occurred in other states and not in North Carolina. The bill would not reduce strikes in North Carolina, which are already at virtually an irreducible minimum . . ." *The News and Observer*, March 6, 1947. Excerpts from *The News and Observer* used by permission.

83. *Ibid.*, March 14, 1947.

84. Both the content and the legislative procedures related to the bill were pointedly criticized by the leading Raleigh newspaper, which observed editorially in early March: "[The House Labor Committee] gave the bill only a superficial examination on its own account, not even bothering to consult the Attorney General or the Commissioner of Labor and brushing aside all amendments." (Editorial, *News and Observer*, March 11, 1947.) The final vote on the bill was preceded by an attempt of a tiny minority of the State Senate to compel its members to record their votes on the issue. Less than 20% of the senators would agree to a recorded vote, so the public at large never knew exactly who in the North Carolina General Assembly was willing to be counted as a friend of labor unions. "By far the largest crowd the Senate has drawn this year" overflowed the galleries of the Senate chamber, many of whom "had waited at the Capitol since shortly after dawn for the meeting which began at noon" and most of whom were workers and union members. (News article, *ibid.*, March 14, 1947.)

85. *Ibid.*

86. The allegation of "arrogance" had to do chiefly with the secrecy and anonymity that attended the passage of the law from the first to the last of the Legislature's dealings with it. No legislator would publicly admit to the origin of the text of the law; only four out of fifty senators would go on record as favoring a recorded vote (the number required to force a recorded vote was ten, and in committee meetings on the bill reporters were not permitted to record the individual votes of committee members. The latter motion in committee was made by a senator from Lincoln County, Gaston's neighbor to the north; the one Gaston County senator on the committee later opposed its amendment on the floor of the Senate. It was apparent from the tenor of the procedure that few North Carolina politicians felt that they could afford to treat the question of labor unionization as publicly discussable.

87. *Ibid.*

88. The flurry of labor-union activity in 1946 and 1947 in Gastonia had apparently heightened public perceptions of labor-management conflicts of interest. In the spring of 1947 some ten days after the passage of the right-to-work law in Raleigh, for example, a Gastonia man wrote a letter to the *Gazette* stating a string of opinions about religion, labor unions, and the current political scene. The letter was part of a printed interchange with a Gastonia woman who accused the man of favoring both "open Sundays and labor unions." Some sorts of recreation on the Sabbath, he confessed in reply, he did indeed favor. Furthermore: "Personally, I'm for them (unions) 100 percent. All Northern labor is organized and it fares a lot better than the Southern. At long last the Southern textile workers are making the same as the New England mills are paying, and it is due directly to the Southern mills that do have unions. The South would not be so far behind the North if it would copy them in a few things. We have far too much conservatism, Jeffersonian democracy, and old-fashioned hard-headedness to progress very fast. . . . We have too many Southern senators like Cotton Ed Smith, Doughton, Rankin and Bilbo to represent us. Now our great (?) state has banned the closed shop which is very fine for the employers. But it sure doesn't help the working man. Yet the average laborer will return to the polls next election and vote and vote for the same characters. That's what I like about the South. Oh brother!" (*GG*, April 4, 1947.)

89. *GG*, May 28, 1948.

90. *GG*, May 31, 1948.

91. The runoff in the county: Johnson, 4,343; Scott, 3,593. *GG*, June 28, 1948.

92. In the national election of November 1948, Gaston County gave some 8,964 of its votes to Harry S. Truman, 6,280 to Thomas E. Dewey, 3,757 to Strom Thurmond, 68 to Henry Wallace, and 2 write-in votes to Norman Thomas. A simple "class-war" theory of Gastonian politics in this period would have scant support in such statistics. It should be remembered, in this particular analysis, that we are merely pointing to the relative visibility of such antagonisms in the political life of the locale in these years. Except for baleful events like the '29 strike, these antagonisms had found little other public recognition in the modern history of this community. One of the plain lessons of these latter election statistics of 1948 was that a large number of local voters were beginning to vote Republican on the national level. In the next two decades, their willingness to vote Republican on the state and local level would steadily increase.

93. It was widely believed that Scott had been persuaded to make this appointment on the urging of Jonathan Daniels, Democratic National Committeeman from North Carolina, Editor of *The News and Observer*, confidant of the two latest Democratic presidents, and one of a cluster of men responsible for North Carolina's "liberal" image in the nation as a whole.

94. *GG*, June 8, 1940.

95. *GG*, June 17, 1940, from *The Stanley News Press*. Stanley, located in the northeast corner of Gaston County, was the next-to-smallest town in the county in 1940 (pop. 1,036).

96. *GG*, March 23, 1949.

97. *GG*, April 27, 1950.

98. *GG*, February 25, 1950.

99. Cf. above, p. 82.

100. *GG*, May 26, 1950.

101. *GG*, April 19, 1950.

102. *GG*, June 23, 1950, Associated Press. Graham led Smith 303,605 to 250,222 in the largest vote ever recorded in a North Carolina primary to that date.

103. Gaston County Graham Committee, *GG*, May 26, 1950, signed by a leading local Democrat.

104. GC Graham Committee, June 15, 1950.

105. Smith for Senate Headquarters, *GG*, May 26, 1950.

106. *GG*, June 20, 1950. The uses of the fact of Smith's wealth in contrasting ideological frameworks offers a striking example of the subtlety of the idea of "class" in American politics. To the Graham people, Smith's "piling up of money" is interpreted as an instance of a standing injustice but the Smith people can point to his wealth as a sign of his hard work and ambition. Each side seeks to appeal to an ideological theme embraced by more than one economic class in the society. The mere possession of wealth is not on either side self-interpretive. Graham, after all, is advertised as a "Roosevelt Democrat."

107. Cf. above, pp. 45 and 60.

108. Several days before the runoff some persons in Graham's organization put out handbills describing Smith as a "rich cotton mill owner" who would put the textile worker back to the pre-New Deal days of the seventy-two-hour week at "10, 15, and 20 cents an hour." Graham disavowed the handbill with a strong public expression of political realism: such a retrogression in the textile industry, he said, "cannot be brought back to the United States working man regardless of who is elected. Neither Mr. Smith nor anyone else can take away the protection the working man has today. I just don't want things like that in any campaign." (Associated Press article, June 19, 1950) Instead of applauding this disavowal, the Smith forces promptly took it, published it in advertisements, and advised the voters that they should take Graham's words as warning against the "baloney" of "wild wage statements" being put out by "some Graham supporters." (*GG*, June 23, 1950) It is not recorded that, prior to the election, Smith disavowed any of the literature that some of his followers fabricated, including a now-famous fake photograph of Graham in attendance at a controversial, racially integrated meeting.

109. Smith for Senate Headquarters, *GG*, June 23, 1950. Whether Graham's case in the voter's mind was hurt more by the Communist issue than by the race issue is hard to say. Publicly Smith's speeches bore down hardest on the racial liberalism of his opponent. He denied having injected the race issue into the campaign. It was Graham, rather, who injected it by being a member of President Truman's 1947 Committee on Civil Rights; and Graham's black supporters injected the issue by voting for him as "a practically solid bloc" in the first primary. Associated Press article, June 23, 1950; *GG*, same date. Graham stuck consistently in the campaign to a "no compulsion" view of racial change—he opposed the FEPC and also legal termination of public school segregation. Cf. *Ibid.*

110. *GG*, June 23, 1950. Atkins was editor-in-chief at this time.

111. The statistics were as follows:

		Smith	Graham
Gastonia Precinct No.	1	820	383
	2	344	204
	3	514	232
	4	140	304
	5	301	552
	6	199	268
	7	220	361
	8	490	354
	9	58	104
	10	60	29
	11	210	155
Bessemer City	1	321	229
	2	118	134
Bakers		48	62
Belmont	1	725	272
	2	333	318
	3	213	260
Lowell		164	199
Cramerton		146	173
South Point		47	25
McAdenville		198	74
Union		86	38
Cherryville	1	132	43
	2	222	53
	3	173	45
Kisers		46	36
Carpenters		29	49
Dallas		271	414
Alexis		24	12
High Shoals		55	134
Mt. Holly	1	233	109
	2	160	170
Lucia		38	42
Stanley		137	142
		7,275	5,976

112. This summary is taken from the text of the letter as made available to us by a minister serving in Cherryville at the time. Italics in the following are in the original. Where no quotation marks appear, we have summarized a longer paragraph.

113. Quotation from a communication received from one of the ministers, January 17, 1972. This respondent states that there was "no mill church as such" in Cherryville, and he never noticed any class distinctions in the churches. Pope enumerates seven churches in Cherryville, a number which had evidently not changed by 1953. In other words, the pastors of all the churches in the town were together in deciding to write and send a letter to the mill employees. Two of the churches were Baptist, one Presbyterian, one Methodist, one Lutheran, one the Church of God, and one Wesleyan Methodist.

114. Communication, January 17,1972.

115. Original copy from files of the above respondent. The *Gazette* published a repunctuated version of the letter in full on February 23 after the union leadership had decided to make a public issue of the matter.

116. Letter dated February 19, 1953, from files of the above Cherryville pastor. Briefer excerpts of the letter were published in the *GG*, February 23, 1953.

117. How was one to evaluate the fact, for example, that in this same February of 1953 the Rhyne-Houser Manufacturing Company joined a coalition of other smaller mills in Gaston County to fight one of the last economic measures of the Truman administration: upping the minimum wage for government-contract industries to $1.00? *GG*, February 25, 1953.

118. Based on current (1975) TWUA union dues scales of $1.75 per week. (Interview with TWUA Southern Director Scott Hoyman, April 24, 1975.)

119. *GG*, February 23, 1953.

120. *GG*, February 25, 1953.

121. *GG*, March 7, 1953.

122. Cf. *MP*, pp. 168-170.

123. W. H. Auden, "For the Time Being," *Religious Drama/1*, ed. Marvin Halverson (New York: Meridian Books, 1957), p. 67.

124. Interview, April 24, 1975.

125. *GG*, June 12, 1957.

126. A letter published June 6 ended with the statement: "I don't have any idea your paper will print this because you are a big business tool, and also anti-labor."

127. *GG*, July 1, 1957. Note the criticism of some mills as ready to modernize their machinery but not their personnel-relations program, and the implicit comparison of the chain mill (Cone) with the backwardness of the "Gaston County" (small locally owned) mill.

128. *Ibid*.

129. *GG*, June 17, 1957. Signed, "A Tired Worker."

130. *GG*, June 24, 1957. This is the one letter in the series that is personally signed.

131. *GG*, July 1, 1957. This letter was signed: "A Textile Worker."

132. *GG*, July 30, 1959. Concerning the interim between the 1958 election and the renewed organization attempt in 1960, one TWUA organizer reported another "strategy of managerial defense" as follows: "Before the next election they fired some (of our union sympathizers), promoted others, and got others to change their minds. We've made management some of its best supervisors, whom they've hired after we trained them to be shop stewards! . . . They tore our structure to pieces that way in 1960." (Interview with James R. Prestwood, August 13, 1965.)

133. At issue in Henderson was not the organization of a new textile union but the maintenance of an old one under contractual conditions that had already been in force for some years. Mill management wanted to repossess its right to veto arbitration procedures for grievances, to eliminate the checkoff, and to have the freedom of employing non-union labor during strikes without

picket-line interference. Mill president J.D. Cooper told an N.E.A. correspondent in April 1959: "If the union is so important to these people, let them collect their dues themselves. Let them strike if they want to. But don't let them tell me how to run my mills." (Ward Cannel, N.E.A. Staff Correspondent, in an article published in the *GG*, April 16, 1959.) Said Boyd Payton to this same reporter, "If they break this strike, they've broken this union. And if they can break this union, they can break any union in America." For years this strike would be used widely in Gastonia to disparage the TWUA. When Beaunit, Inc., of Lowell appeared at a NLRB hearing in 1962 to decide if a TWUA election should be held for 450 employees, R.C. Reinhardt, vice-president, said, "This is the same union that was involved in a long, bitter strike in Henderson. We don't want this union in the Lowell plant and we are urging our employees to keep it out." *GG*, October 12, 1962.

134. *GG*, April 16, 1957.

135. In 1974 the most promising recent TWUA victory was in the J.P. Stevens plant in Roanoke Rapids, N.C., but by April 1975 the company was refusing to sign a contract with the union. At issue were not wages, but dues-checkoff and automatic arbitration. (Interview with Scott Hoyman, April 24, 1975)

136. On this latter strike and the relation of some churchpersons to it, cf. Shriver, Preface pp. 24-26. In a news article on the union election pending in one of these five companies, the *Gazette* ended its account with a paragraph about the fate of workers who had unionized themselves at another of the five companies recently: "The last union election won in Gastonia was by the workers of _____. This resulted in a strike, however, in which many workers lost their jobs and had to leave the city to get employment." *GG*, January 12, 1960.

137. *GG*, April 6, 9, 16, and 24, 1969. Some half dozen active unions were in Gaston County in 1974. The main ones were: The International Association of Machinists; The Communications Workers of America; The United Paperworkers International Union; The Oil, Chemical, and Atomic Workers Union; The United Auto Workers; and The Teamsters Union. Ironically, the most successful unions in the county continue to be in plants where wages are already relatively high.

138. One more vivid example of how the campaign-process worked itself out with almost ritualized predictability can be found in the 1960-61 UAW attempt to organize a local oil filter plant, which had close economic relationships with Textiles, Inc. Successively in this campaign: the twenty-five-year-old local anti-handbill ordinance was invoked against a UAW literature-distributor; a personnel supervisor was bruised in a brief nighttime attack by an unknown assailant (*GG*, October 24, 1960); the *Gazette* followed immediately with an agitated reminiscence of "the foaming disorder of the Loray Strike," a solemn tribute to the greatness of Samuel Gompers, a dire warning about the "men of ill repute" now in charge of "the country's largest unions," and a clincher-reference to "the bad taste of Henderson" still in the mouth of North Carolinians (*GG*, October 26, 1960). Soon after, election day at the filter plant yielded a union defeat, followed by a sequel of unfair labor practice charges by the union. Some of the charges were ultimately confirmed by the NLRB over the appeals of the company. As the upshot of another long-drawn-out campaign in a Gastonia plant, a half dozen pro-union workers were reinstated at their jobs (cf. *GG*, March 17, 1961; March 22, 1961; August 21, 1961). Late in this campaign, the anti-union workers found a spokesman for their point of view in a local woman who explained why she did not read UAW literature offered her: "We at_____ feel that it would be a waste of valuable time to read this literature. . . . Our superiors are working to make this the kind of place the people want and need." (*GG*, September 4, 1961)

139. Associated Press, *Ibid.*, May 26, 1971. The facts about the alleged black-list are fugitive, of course. Certainly intercommunication of managers in the textile industry remains as close now as ever before. The local five-county organization of personnel professionals, Associated Industries,

is as active as ever in providing information exchange about a variety of personnel-policy matters, and information about a union sympathizer is easily transmitted in a variety of channels. Hoyman's comments on "justice delayed" through NLRB hearings had a grim exemplification in the hearings connected with the closing of Darlington Manufacturing Co. in Darlington, South Carolina in 1956. These proceedings were still dragging on into the spring of 1975, long after reinstatement of jobs or back wages had much meaning for workers in the case. (Interview with Hoyman, April 24, 1975)

140. *GG*, April 19, 1970. In this same month the U.S. Department of Labor announced that in its proportion of unionized non-farm workers, North Carolina had recently gone from forty-ninth to fiftieth among the states, with 7.5% unionization. Associated Press, April 3, 1970. It should be noted that the local news medium, principally the *Gazette*, still serves the ideological and economic interests of industrial management by minimizing news reporting of union activity in Gaston County. For example, twice in early 1969, small articles announcing the UAW campaign at the grease-seal plant appeared in the "one star" edition of the paper, only to be eliminated in the "two star" or final edition of the same evening. *GG*, January 23, February 6, 1969. The conclusions here tally very closely with those drawn by TWUA leaders themselves over the past several years. Interviewed in May, 1973, William Duchessi, national Secretary-Treasurer of TWUA, was asked by us, "In the South, what is the biggest obstacle to maintaining a textile union once it is organized?"

A: "Keeping the members from being afraid to continue their membership."

Q: "What do they fear?"

A: "Oh, the constant harassment. The foreman coming up all the time and saying, 'Say, what do you really get from paying those union dues? Nothing!' But when the workers are pushed to a recertification election—because the dues-paying membership is down to something like 200 out of 1500—we almost always win by a margin of about 1200 votes, especially when the number of blacks is high."

Q: "Why are the blacks not as afraid as the whites?"

A: "Oh, I don't know. The civil rights experience, maybe. And hating the union hasn't been taught them from the beginning of their lives."

In 1974, less than 20% of the 700,000 textile workers of eight southeastern states were unionized. TWUA had 57,000 members in the South out of a national membership of some 200,000, according to Harold McIver, TWUA's Director of Organization for the Carolinas, as reported by *U.S. News and World Report*, September 23, 1974 (Vol. LXXVII, No. 13, pp. 83-84). In what was termed by the Associated Press as TWUA's "first major victory in 11 years of attempts to unionize the nation's second largest textile firm," however, the union won elections in seven J.P. Stevens plants in the Roanoke Rapids, N.C. area in August of 1974. (*GG*, August 29, 1975). Wilbur Hobby, president of the North Carolina AFL-CIO, greeted this victory in tones reminiscent of Van Bittner in 1947: "J.P. first, the textile industry second, and then the whole South." (Cf. above, p. 8.)

141. In his 1958 Detroit study Lenski observed that Negro Protestants were the socio-religious group most likely to attend "all" or "most" union meetings and to report that they were strongly interested in their union. See Gerhard Lenski, *The Religious Factor* (Garden City, New York: Doubleday and Company, 1961), pp. 98-102.

142. For a discussion of the relationship between worker characteristics and labor union activism see William Spinrad, "Correlates of Trade Union Participation: A Summary of the Literature," *American Sociological Review*, 25 (April 1960), 237-44.

143. *MP*, p. 201.

144. *Ibid*.

145. Spinrad, *Loc. cit.*

146. See Robert Blauner, *Alienation and Freedom: The Factory Worker and His Industry* (Chicago, University of Chicago Press, 1964) for a related discussion. The alienation of the southern textile "operative" from his work is strongly indicated by evidence like that presented earlier in this book on the low status of textile work in the Gaston community at large. Cf. above, p. 16 and pp. 79-80.

147. Leonard Broom and Philip Selznick, *Sociology* (New York: Harper and Row, 1968), 191-92.

148. Richard A. Peterson and N. J. Demerath, "Introduction" to the paperbound edition of *Millhands and Preachers*, xlv-xlvi. One of our prominent informants from Belmont speaks to this point in contrasting his own political success with the failures of the union organizers:

". . . I think the prime difference was I was born and raised right there with them. They knew me—they knew what I would do and what I wouldn't do. Here's a union organizer from New Jersey. They don't know him from Adam's house cat and could care less. All they know is big daddy up in the front office don't like him and if daddy don't like him, I don't like him. I don't know what he'll do. I don't know how much it'll cost me. I don't know whether I'll lose my job over it or not."

149. Interview with TWUA Southern Director Scott Hoyman, April 24, 1975. Donald F. Roy, who, more than any other social scientist known to us, has participated as an observer in many unionizing attempts in southern communities, sees this isolation of the textile worker from peers as a crucial factor in the inhibition of union organization. Long accustomed to relate to each other in terms of management paternal largesse, southern textile workers often see themselves as individuals who can only deal with the manager in a one-to-one social mode. This individualization of labor-management relations is an essential dynamic, of course, in the "open-door" policy for complaint negotiation, and management understands its utility as such. Roy comments:

Such isolation is especially striking in industrial communities where management-worker relations are strongly coercive. In one observed campaign, management's firings were so numerous and so effective that workers were extremely reluctant to communicate union sentiments with each other, even in such small neighborhood groupings as car pools. Union talk could not be developed, and organizers had to communicate with these workers on an individual basis, by house calls. Of course, mass meetings were out of the question. Such paralysis of communication is quite understandably to management's advantage. The voting situation on election day is so "scary," claim the organizers, that unless the worker can receive his ballot under conditions of strongly felt cohesion, he is likely to be afraid to vote union. Technically speaking, the organization of a union follows victory at the polls; actually, to win such a victory, organization must precede the voting. (Roy, *op. cit.*, note 6 above, pp. 243-244.)

150. Pope's interviews and historical records indicated that support for the Loray Strike among ministers varied strictly according to the economic status of the churches to which the ministers were related (*MP*, pp. 274-278). Both McLean and Henderson, who are sketched above pp. 131-137, are pastors of "establishment" denomination churches in mill-related communities. Along with some of their peers in larger churches of the same denominations, they are informed about the pro's and con's of unions, and they show sympathies for unionism, which stand in some apparent contrast to Pope's ministers. Though he investigated the more specific question of sympathy and public support for a particular strike, our evidence suggests that support for unionism in general has gone up faster among the *younger* members of the established denominations than among sectarian ministers as a group.

151. Cf. above, pp. 22-23. (Shriver Preface)

152. *GG*, February 25, 1953.

153. An important qualification should be noted here from Table 5.2 above, where some income groups of whites are more nearly in agreement on "unions in general" with blacks than with whites in the over $10,000 income group.

154. *MP*, p. 201.

155. See below, Chapter Seven, for some concluding comments on this same theme.

156. Interview with TWUA Southern Director Scott Hoyman, April 24, 1975.

Chapter Six

The Church as Proponent of Change:
Race Relations

Observing that the Gaston County textile industry employed only a minute percentage of black millhands in 1940, Liston Pope gave no focal attention to race relations in *Millhands and Preachers*.[1] Social, economic, and ecclesiastical segregation has so largely prevailed between the races in Gastonia that as late as 1967 a county demographic survey team could remark that the 1960 census figures for blacks (13.1% of the county's population) was emblematic of the economic history of the community.

Gaston County has a lower percentage of non-white population than does much of the surrounding area and only about half that of North Carolina. This perhaps can be traced to the dominance of textiles in the employment total for the county. This has traditionally been a low non-white employer.[2]

Even as these latter words were written, however, Gastonia had undergone some major shifts in the discriminatory patterns of its institutions, including the textile industry. In this chapter, we shall describe these changes and the role of local churches in effecting them.

Segregation with Growing Social Consciousness: 1940-1954

White visitors to Gastonia from the deep South in the 1940s surely remarked to each other that a community with one-seventh black population could not really know "our problem," as it was sometimes called in the "black belt." Visitors from the North, on the other hand, must have looked at the shabby housing north of the railroad and remarked with equal certainty that Gastonia was a "typically southern town."

The general truth, even in the first half of the 1940-70 era, lay somewhere in between these two judgments. To describe community race relations in this period is to deal with at least several dimensions of community life. One dimension was ideological; another was the realm of social-service institutions; and yet another was politics. In all three of these areas, race relations in Gastonia were neither typically nor untypically "southern"; they were rather something Piedmontish and in-between.

1. Ideological strain. We know that the ideological theme of Harmony in Gastonia has never carried the same racial freight that it has often carried in the less industrialized South.[3] More interesting for students of the ideological components of social change, however, is the clash between discriminationist and equalitarian thinking slumbering in this industrial town's commitments to economic "progress" and individual "liberty." With increasing frequency in the 1940-70 era, Gastonians discovered that the dynamic of modern industrialism puts strain upon consistent racism. During World War II many of Gastonia's talented blacks secured jobs in the factories, armed forces, and government agencies of a nation at war. If employment of blacks in the wartime textile industry did not increase much, this was partly because a Depression-weary white work-force was not as ready to move to other regions as its children would be twenty years later in a more affluent society. By the 1960s, pressured by a tight labor market, the textile industry began to find that a rational, non-racist employment policy was good business. But the critical ideological point was that white Gastonians had seldom reserved the ideas of Progress and Liberty to themselves alone. For long they had naïvely assumed that all social groups wanted to better their economic lot, and that each individual person was at Liberty to do so. This was economic liberalism in the historic sense: considerable evidence can be found in the press, the private communications, and other utterances of local whites suggesting their belief that economic ambition could work for blacks as well as whites. Discriminatory employment policies in the mills and a variety of segregated public facilities proclaimed a huge gap between the idea and the actuality of Progress and Liberty for members of the black community; nevertheless there was more room in this ideology for the economic aspirations of blacks than had ever prevailed in the agricultural South.[4]

Some unprecedented effort to secure economic justice for blacks began to stir in Gastonia during the war years. In mid-1942, a group of black domestics demanded higher wages provoking a defensive resort to paternalism from the *Gazette*. Its editor recited the social services recently provided the black community: the new hospital, new playground, Boy Scout troop, and exchange of pulpits between white and black ministers.[5] The "mistake" the blacks were making was in pushing for justice in an *organized* rather than *individualized* fashion. As the war years went on, however, the indignity of old-style white paternalism seemed increasingly unacceptable to young blacks of Gastonia, and organized change was precisely their remedy for this indignity. The white world's personalized ethics are inadequate for the American Negro, said a young college instructor home from Kentucky in 1943. "What the black population needs," she said, "is some changes in legal rights brought about through concerted, not individual, action and court appeal. Once legal justice has been secured for the Negro, perhaps all talk about 'colored citizens' and 'good white people' will cease in towns like Gastonia." The Constitution "makes no such specifications of citizenry." And if these are words that disturb some Americans in wartime, she suggested, they should reflect on the principle that "any time is ripe for the meting out of justice."[6] Such public language in Gastonia was parallel to speeches about economic justice that were made in these same years by labor union leaders who targeted on industrial versions of paternalism. Common to these utterances was the theme that the *Progress* of economic growth should be mated with the *Justice* of economic opportunity, even if such progress put a strain on social *Harmony*.

The ideological gap had long been there; and, as the war years ended, there were signs in Gastonia's black community that its members had some new expectations about the filling of the gap. "This Is Our War, Too," proclaimed an advertisement for the first War Bond campaign to be sponsored by local black leaders in 1944.[7] The end of the war found many of these same leaders ready to undertake a domestic version of "our war." Wrote a local black minister in 1947:

During the war, I heard many teary voices talking to God. We were shocked by the barbarity of the Japanese . . . But Negroes were not so shocked. We have been the object of such action for more than eighty years . . . I can no longer tell my people to live so that they will go to heaven when they die and get a starry crown and a long, white robe, and have a mansion. They are awakened and not as dumb as they act by a long shot. They are beginning to realize that a man is better off dead in many instances. They no longer fear hell. They have been in it all their lives. They are thinking.[8]

In short, the war years were as much an ideological watershed for Gastonia's blacks as for large numbers of other black people in America. As Howard Odum, writing in 1943 from Chapel Hill, summarized it: "It was as if some universal message had come through to the great mass of Negroes, urging them to dream new dreams and to protest against the old order."[9]

2. *Separate, unequal institutional services.*   In 1950 Mrs. Daisie Hasson Adams, a resident of the black community, was asked by the local newspaper to contribute to its Seventieth Anniversary Edition a column recounting the growth of social services for Negroes in the town over the past few years. In a

succinct summary of facilities recently made available to her people, the writer spoke of a bookmobile, a bloodmobile, Boy and Girl Scout programs, the Gaston County Negro Hospital, the financial backing of Negro churches by some white citizens, and the very recent employment of five Negro men as members of the local police force. A due sense of ritual gratitude, native to the paternalistic interracial ethos, hovered about this letter. But Mrs. Adams went on to remark that such services "are monuments to our dead, who died dreaming of justice and love." As the motif of unrealized justice sounded clearly in Mrs. Adams' summary, so also was her description replete with the marks of Progress, Harmony, and Liberty. She went on to call upon local black people to "progress with the times . . . to educate ourselves . . . to do many things for ourselves," and to expect a "boost by our white comrades."[10] Twenty years later black Gastonians writing this way would be branded Tomish; instead of a "boost" from whites, local blacks would ask rather for justice; but when they asked for that in the context of some other social virtues in the forties and fifties, they were talking like the Gastonians—and the Americans—who they were.

.   Gastonia's struggle to turn the separate-equal doctrine into social policy was a cameo-version of the struggle in many another American community during these years. Certain events of the forties and fifties suggest that Gastonia deserved some prizes for achieving some increments of justice in advance of many another community of its size in the South. Between 1943 and 1955, for example, the black community could count gains like a branch of the county library,[11] a bond issue of $125,000 for a community center in a new black-middle-class residential section,[12] the desegregation of the municipal golf course,[13] a new swimming pool,[14] and a string of local editorial opinions *celebrating* causes that only a minority of southern newspaper editors celebrated in the summer of 1949: the decision of the Presbyterian Church in the U.S. not to withdraw from the Federal Council of Churches, a local slum clearance program using federal government funds, with or without the support of "landlords who are ready to shut their eyes to the sight of leaking shanties," the recent death of the Grand Imperial Wizard of the KKK, and the courage of freshman Senator Frank P. Graham in becoming the first southern senator to appoint a black youth to West Point, in spite of the amusement of most North Carolina politicians over the political ineptitude of Graham's action.[15] Such data suggest that this southern Piedmont community was making real, incremental steps towards racial justice in advance of many another textile-town, and in advance of the national watershed-decade of race relations still to come—1954-64. For some local residents, such data meant "progress"; for others, "tokenism." The difference in those evaluations was undoubtedly related to the difference in reference-criteria; compared to other southern communities, Gastonia had something of a record; weighted in the balance of its own ideology and the ideals of its churches, the record was one of repairs to a basically defective structure.

Other sorts of data, in fact, were beginning to spell the doom of the separate-but-equal doctrine in the Gastonias of America in these same pre-1954 years: chiefly data on the social costs of effecting the doctrine. A convincing illustration of this doom was the twenty-five-year struggle of white Gastonians to combine conscience, finance, and professionalism in the operation of Gaston County Negro Hospital. Founded in 1937 from contributions of Gaston County residents and a grant from the Duke Foundation, the local facility functioned to maintain the "white only" status of the two older Gastonia hospitals while eliminating the necessity for local black patients to travel to Charlotte.[16] For many years its Board of Trustees consisted of white members, and its superintendent, a woman, was white. Some ten years after its establishment, the hospital began operating in the red and in 1950 almost closed its doors from lack of county funds.[17] Apparently one reason for the budgetary resistance of county officials was the hospital's poor patronage by local blacks,[18] one of whom, interviewed in 1966, recollected why they had long preferred to be ill at home rather than in "their" hospital:

". . . patients were brought from the Negro hospital to Gaston Memorial Hospital to be operated on, and then brought back to the Negro hospital. We are not yet permitted to get beds in wards at Gaston Memorial, but only private rooms which are $5.00 more expensive."[19]

For the care of up to thirty-eight patients in the one-story building on North Marietta Street, some two black physicians were ordinarily available as late as 1961, along with two or three registered nurses. During all these years, the cost of quality medical care was steadily climbing in the United States; and the equipping of two county-supported hospitals in separate-but-equal style was an increasingly impossible objective for Gaston or any other county. The resources and the will for obtaining the objective began to show exhaustion in the early sixties, a time when segregationist vigor was flagging on many another front.[20]

The failure of the community to provide equal social services, the obviousness of that failure to any citizen who looked down the dirt streets north of the railroad, and the care which prominent citizens took on occasion to admit the failure, added up to a complex public fact by the mid-fifties: a widespread consciousness among many white and black people that separate facilities were not only inherently unequal; for Gaston County, they were institutionally impossible.

The indices to such a consciousness in the early fifties were nowhere more abundant than in the public schools. In June 1951, a white university student, home in Gastonia from Chapel Hill, wrote to the local paper describing in anguished tones how he had come upon a "small, wooden-constructed, rotted-out colored elementary school" on the western side of the town where a cluster of black families resided. He went on to plead that other schools in the community not be allocated funds before this school building got repaired.[21] "Let's really work at equality of facilities for these people," he urged. Two years later, a U.S. Supreme Court grand jury found virtually *all* of the county's black schools in unacceptable disrepair.[22] In response to this news the Gastonia Superintendent of Schools admitted publicly that providing truly equal faculty for a minority student population was financially impossible. "If we keep up this line of thinking," he exclaimed, "Negro schools will for all practical purposes become better than those for whites!"

In short, the Supreme Court that ruled against school desegregation in May of 1954 was addressing a fiscal as well as a moral problem, as Gastonians who had been reading their local newspaper knew very well.

The Beginning of Political Integration

As sequels to the tempest of the 1950 primary, the early 1950s saw two developments on the local political scene: a rise in black political activity, and several challenges among white voters to traditional "uptown" political control of Gastonia. Textile-leaders had long dominated the official boards and commissions of local government. The domination was so traditional that in 1950 the manager of the Gastonia Chamber of Commerce could say with satisfaction:

Fortunately those who govern the city are those who conduct successful business enterprises and who, therefore, are familiar and sympathetic with the business and manufacturing enterprises which have accounted for the community's growth.[23]

Local election records from the postwar period confirm this estimate. In a 1947 City Council primary, five uptown business leaders won over seven "independents" by a 2-1 margin. Several of the independents resided in mill-village areas, in whose precincts they polled a large vote; but this support was so weak on a citywide basis that four of seven losers in the primary, eligible for the runoff, withdrew their candidacy.[24]

The most clearcut evidence of continuous textile-industry control of local government during all these years was at the county level. County commissioners came from six districts, each with its share of mill villages. Persons elected to the office were routinely the owners, managers, or other close associates of textile companies. One dramatic emblem of this tradition in the fall of 1952 was the reelection of R.L. Stowe as County Commission Chairman at the age of eighty-six. Stowe, one of the "pioneer textile men" of Belmont, had been elected to the board in 1914 and its chairman in 1922.[25] He served in the position until 1955, retiring after forty-one years of membership on the board.[26] During these latter years, local residents remember, he was carried to board meetings in a wheel chair up the steps of the county courthouse.[27]

Gastonians had seldom voted in large numbers,[28] but in the postwar period they came out increasingly for elections whose candidates offered some non-traditional choices. The 1950 Graham-Smith contest drew approximately 12% of the city and county populace to the polls, a record previously topped only by the local beer-and-wine legalization vote of 1948.[29] Then in the '51 election, a thirty-one year old architectural designer, Harrelson Yancey, offered himself as an independent candidate for mayor. Teamed with two other newcomers to local politics, Yancey ran on a platform that included two-term limitation on council tenure, adoption of a ward system, and "independent city government" unconnected with "any clique."[30] Against the trio of independents was arrayed a "Progressive" ticket of five persons, by common knowledge representing traditional industrial interests. Gastonians, said a pre-election ad of this group, are the stockholders of the Gastonian corporation. Why not then elect some "proven directors" to govern the corporation?

A rash of 2,115 new voter-registrations preceded election day—encouraged in part by publicity given the antiquated state of local registration lists.[31] This more than doubled the probable voter turnout, since never in local history had more than 1,500 persons participated in a single election.[32] In the runoff stage, 4,444 ballots were cast, with Yancey leading the field with 2,742 votes, twice as many as any Gastonia councilman had ever received. Two members of the conservative "Progressives" survived the election, yielding an uneasy 3-2 majority of "independents" on the new Council.[33]

Among the defeated candidates in this 1951 election was one of the first members of the black community to run in a local election, a medical doctor who ran tenth in a field of ten, polling 1,040 votes. "Political observers estimated that not more than 300 Negroes bothered to go to the polls. If that is true, then Dr. Carter got more than half his votes from the white population."[34]

Judged in terms of professions of the elected councilmen, political offices still rested in the business community but not so clearly in the textile industry.[35] The shift in power must have generated considerable hostility inside the business community. Newly-installed Mayor Yancey had reason to pray at his swearing-in:

If there is any bitterness, may it be forgotten. May this City Council truly represent the citizen by working harmoniously for a still greater Gastonia. May all our acts be just in the eyes of God and in the interest of all the people.[36]

The major issue of the first Yancey administration was the institution of a ward system. Blacks had considerable stake in such a system, because it would give them power to elect a black member to the City Council.[37] The City Council, at loggerheads on the issue, decided to submit it to the voters in the 1953 election. The stage was set for the most active political springtime of recent Gastonia history.

An unprecedented number of blacks participated in the '53 election. Openly allying himself with leaders of the black community—chiefly ministers—Yancey asked for black support for himself and the ward system. He backed up his appeal by support for the candidacy of Nathaniel Barber, president of the highly successful Excelsior Credit Union, about which a black-owned newspaper in Durham had recently observed:

When Negroes in a county of only about 7,000 of their own race can build an organization of $300,000 in 10 years, we think its leadership deserves the highest praise.[38]

What better ticket to leadership can an industrial community demand of anyone than proven success in a business enterprise? It was a strong argument for electing any Gastonian, white or black.

The Yancey-led "People's Ticket" included Marshall Rauch, a young Jewish textile executive who in the sixties would become a state senator. Rauch symbolized the change and the continuity in power-relations about to take place in the community.[39] Since some of his business interests were textile-related, he had ties with the culture; but he was part of the industrial diversification movement. Overlaying, undercutting, and manipulating the interracial issue in this election, in short, was the intercultural and interindustrial issue of whether the old textile elite was to continue to exercise exclusive control of the town's formal political structure. It was high time, said Harrelson Yancey at the climax of the campaign, for city council members to come from all over town: three out of the five in recent years had lived in two uptown blocks. "If we did that nationally with our Congressmen," he chuckled, "the whole Congress could come from Chicago."[40]

It was the beginning of a change from small-town to urban-style politics. In the election, Gastonia voters adopted the ward system by a margin of eighty-seven votes, 2,045-1,958. Some 750 blacks cast votes in the election, over twice as many as voted in 1951. Hundreds of textile workers went to the polls in spite of rainy weather. Since the ward issue was so clearly identified with the two tickets, white textile workers and blacks voting together must have spelled the margin of victory for Yancey, (who won over his chief opponent 3,297 to 2,690), Rauch, and Barber. However, some members of the opposing ticket also won, and the ward system adopted was a compromise version that required candidates to come from different sections of the city while permitting all voters to vote on all candidates. Such a system put pressure upon a minority constituency to assure election of its representatives through coalition-building. *The Gastonia Gazette*, in a post-election commentary, congratulated the black community for the election of its first councilman in Gastonia history, and the editor reflected that the time for such representation was long overdue. Barber, in fact, was now the first black city councilman in North Carolina history.

The day of a permanently politicized citizenry in Gastonia, however, was still far away. The excitement generated in two successive elections and the mixed administrative success of Mayor Yancey frightened enough leaders and constituents on both sides to elect in 1955 a set of councilmen openly disenchanted with "reform."[41] But some reforms had come to stay. Among them was Yancey's message to his black supporters that the power of law stood behind their right to vote. Yancey had warned blacks not to believe anyone who told them

that their employers will know how they vote, that they may be evicted from their homes if they vote, or that their names may be "put on the tax books."[42]

How real or widespread may have been such threats from members of the white community is hard to determine. But for a white politician to be saying these things openly was a new thing in Gastonia politics.

Also new was a public role which the black church began to play in Gastonia for the first time in this election. The role of the black church in political affairs was well known inside the black community, but it was not a role with high public visibility. Just before election day, a group of black ministers decided to give it visibility. In a resolution adopted on election eve by the Gastonia Negro Ministers Association, they addressed all "the citizens of Gastonia." The resolution was printed in full in the newspaper, and it is worth reprinting in full here as one of the most significant social-political-religious statements to emerge from any social group in Gastonia in the 1950s:

Before this very heated political campaign comes to an end, we the Negro ministers of Gastonia feel that we should make our position clear relative to the stand we have taken in the campaign. We feel that as the spiritual leaders of our community that it is incumbent upon us to furnish our people what guidance we can.

It has been brought to our attention that we should stay out of politics because most of the white ministers refuse to participate in political affairs. But they are forgetting the fact that many of the white ministers do not need to take a position on political questions —because they have in their churches business men who are past masters at that job. But our people, unfortunately, have not engaged to a large extent in political affairs.

Many of those who are qualified to furnish the proper leadership refrain from that responsibility. Consequently the people look to the Negro ministers for counsel and leadership.

Two years ago Mr. Harrelson Yancey and a group of men asked to meet the ministers' association. They were permitted to do so. They made us several reasonable propositions that were very conducive to better living conditions, better streets, and better police protection. They further promised to keep the people informed as to what goes on in the city government. We feel that Mayor Yancey has attempted to carry out his promise, but was blocked by strong opposition. We especially were impressed with the idea of being informed of what takes place in the city government for educational values.

There were several things of which we were not aware, however. First, that unless the mayor comes from the business men's ticket that he can't be successful. Second, we didn't know that the business men hired Negroes as a special accommodation to our people. We thought it was a mutual advantage—that the business man needs help and the Negro needs to work.

It was a very generous act on the part of the city fathers to give us the hospital, to give us Erwin Memorial Park, and to give us whatever else they saw fit. However, we thought they approved these projects because they were worthy investments, and because the Negro citizens were worthy of these investments. We did not know that we would be reminded of that in every election campaign.

We have our own convictions and cannot afford to switch from one political camp to another. A vast majority of the Negro citizens have accepted us as their true leaders and we will under no circumstances deceive them.

Some of our people have become frustrated and even afraid . . . Afraid of losing their jobs, afraid of losing their homes, and even afraid of losing their old age pensions. They don't need to be afraid. The Constitution of the United States guarantees every citizen the right to vote, the right to a secret ballot, and our people don't have to be afraid to exercise their sacred rights. Therefore we appeal to the voting public to vote for Nathaniel Barber and the People's Ticket.

The greatest fear is fear itself. So win or lose, we are befriending our people.

Finally, we wish to say that there has been no other agency or person authorized to represent the Negro citizens of Gastonia.

Rev. J. A. White, President[43]

It was the language of a new day.

School Desegration: 1954-1956

In the early fifties, what they began at the ballot box, Gaston County blacks continued in the courtroom. In August 1951, in a case initiated by a black attorney from Charlotte, two white Gastonia city policemen were charged with "detaining" the attorney in the Gastonia bus station for attempting to violate the North Carolina Statute 6-136, which required racial segregation in public transportation.[44] Two years later, from the NAACP chapter in Stanley, one of the county's smaller towns, came a legal suit against the County School Board charging unequal opportunity in school facilities. It was the first such suit in North Carolina.[45] Over the next three years Stanley was to provide Gaston County an easy-to-understand local demonstration of what "Brown vs. Kansas City Board of Education" was all about on the national level.

At the beginning of their school protest, the Stanley black community was publicly at peace with the principle of segregation. According to the PTA of the black primary school, black community leaders had recently equipped their building with water lines and electricity—an eloquent demonstration of the previous lack of these amenities. Wood stoves heated the school, and recreation equipment on the playground was minimal.[46] But it *was* the black community's school. So when in September 1954, the school board quietly closed it down and ordered black children to ride the bus to nearby Dallas, seventy-five black students refused to go.

At the head of this rebellion was Rev. R. H. McDowell, a twenty-five-year-old black Methodist minister in Stanley.[47] Under his leadership over the next two years, in the name of the neighborhood school, the Stanley NAACP came experientially to agree with the Supreme Court of the United States: the only way to get equality-education *in Stanley* was to integrate its schools. In April of 1955, the Stanley NAACP so petitioned the County School Board; and McDowell filed notice that if the local white school were not open to blacks by September 1955, he would file suit within a week in the federal courts. This threat from a minister of the gospel drew a pair of letters to the *Gazette* editor that vividly portrayed the divided mind of local whites on school desegregation. Each of these letter-writers argued from theology: one ("a white citizen") expressed chargrin that a minister would become party to "any move or recommendation to create ill will and confusion where only peace and good will should exist in America. My Bible teaches me that Christ came . . . to bring peace." The letter went on to exhort McDowell to trust the county superintendent "within the boundary of his limitations" to "leave the Constitution of the United States alone"; to "be cooperative with each other instead of forceful"; "above all, not to impose on others' rights and privileges"; and, finally, "to render unto Caesar the things which are Caesar's and unto God the things that are God's. A preacher's calling is to be a Christian teacher and leader and not a part of any scheme to disrupt order."[48]

The second letter-writer, a resident of Stanley's neighbor-town of Belmont, reflected that if you are a white person in Gaston County you should "put yourself in the place of the colored people in Stanley" and should remember that the Constitution itself had to be fought for, as did Christianity. "Any man who thinks himself better than another had better examine the God he worships." This citizen signed his name.[49] Together the letters comprised two very different slants on Christian theology as it pertained to a public issue, two very different appropriations of the same sacred canopy.[50]

Early public reaction to the '54 Court decision in Gastonia was remarkably composed, even positive. The pastor of First (formerly Main Street) Methodist Church endorsed the decision in a sermon. Parts of this sermon were broadcast nationwide over CBS-Radio. Local reaction to the endorsement, according to a Wesleyan Methodist minister, was generally favorable.[51] No immediate change to a desegregated school system is likely, editorialized the *Gazette* editor in his first comment on the court's decision; the change is likely to "take two years or more."[52] During the same week Mayor Yancey turned down an invitation to step before the CBS television cameras to express his opinion about the recent court decision, on the grounds that he had "always stood for equal treatment for our citizens of all races" and did not care to risk the "sensationalism" of national publicity.[53] And one year later, in response to the June 1955 Court decision on school-desegregation "with all deliberate speed," the *Gazette* editor remarked matter-of-factly that the court's will would have to be obeyed "in the end, and all dodges are just dodges."[54] It added up to no enthusiastic acclaim for the United States Supreme Court, but it was a far cry from the shout beginning to go up from some southern politicians: "Never!"

North Carolina had its share of such politicians, and at this point they affected the Gastonia adjustment to school desegregation via legislation passed in Raleigh: the "Pearsall Plan" of 1956, which permitted local school districts by referendum to abolish the public schools and also permitted the State Department of Public Instruction to make tuition grants to any parents—white or black—who chose to send their children to a private school. Considered "moderate" in comparison to the "massive resistance" of Virginians to the north and Carolinians to the south, the Pearsall Plan was an artful dodge, designed by the state's political leaders to accommodate various degrees of rage at the Supreme Court among North Carolinians.[55] The evidence on Gastonia suggests that its *leaders* were prepared to accept desegregation on a much faster schedule than were their fellow Tar Heels to the east, but the Gaston County vote on the Pearsall Plan raised doubt that local white citizens were as reconciled to such a change. With little black participation in a record voter turnout,

Gaston voted for the Plan 7–1, the largest majority accorded the plan by any of the one hundred counties in the state. On the face of it, such a vote radically contradicts the suggestion above that a certain liberalism on racial questions characterized Gastonia in the fifties. Public survey data from the 1960s, reported later in this chapter, will shed some light on this apparent contradiction; but for now this observation about "liberalism" itself is in order: in reaching their compromise on the Pearsall Plan, the state's political leaders made much appeal to the *classic* liberalism of individual choice, local control, and toleration. They advertised the plan to voters as consistent with the moderate "North Carolina way in race relations." By making comparisons with other southern states they convinced many Americans outside the South that North Carolina was indeed "liberal." It was a form of liberalism that resonated deeply with the history of Gastonia. Progress through individual effort, the Liberty to decide one's own future, and Harmony between differences: the Pearsall Plan had all the "right" ideological tags, and some Gastonians must have voted for it under the impression that it would enable any ambitious white or black child to get an education. That it would result in massive dislocations of whites and blacks from any schooling whatsoever, was a certainty which black leaders in the state perceived with crystal clarity.[56] But not all blacks in Gastonia perceived that: half of those who voted at all voted for the plan. For them, ideology may have worked to obscure social fact and their own welfare. In this sense, the overwhelming support of the Pearsall Plan by Gaston County voters was of a piece with historic "Americanism," with its overstress upon institutionalized liberty at the expense of institutionalized equal opportunity. In 1956, it is just possible that the equivalent of the Pearsall Plan might have passed in a majority of American towns from Maine to California.[57]

The Calm Before the Storm: 1956-59

In tune with the mood of the Eisenhower era, the late fifties in Gastonia were times of superficial quiet in matters of racial change.[58] Singing that tune, Congressman Basil Whitener of Gastonia, said in June of 1957 to his fellow national legislators that in North Carolina generally and in Gaston County particularly there was little if any "civil rights issue."[59] No black citizen had applied for admission to a white school in the county; the Stanley case was in a state of suspension if not in a state of settlement; and shades of the Little Rock school crisis, just over the horizon of the coming September, seemed far removed from Gaston County.[60] In the meantime, the city of Gastonia could very possibly claim to be the only town of its size in the South that had on its city council one black and two Jews—one of them the mayor. The new plateau of interracial political unity paralleled the outward amity of labor-management relations in this same period.[61]

Nineteen-fifty-nine saw a break in both sorts of harmony. Dr. T. H. Williston became the first black to run for the Gastonia school board.[62] Hundreds of blacks registered for this election, along with hundreds of whites—evidence enough that the schools were the real center of local political controversy during these years. In spite of Williston's plea to white voters to "consider the harmony and good relationship which Gastonia has enjoyed over the past six years because you have elected a Negro to the Gastonia City Council," whites voted against him in large numbers, blacks voted solidly for him, and his opponent won 2,927-881.[63] What the election showed conclusively was the weakness of the claim that local blacks opposed school integration. However much public leaders liked to point to the record of black participation in political life in the fifties as "proof positive that Gastonia race relations are fine," the statistics of the 1959 school board election proved decisively otherwise.[64] A quick succession of events in the early sixties were to prove the very same thing on a much larger scale.

The Desegregation Crisis: 1960-63

By early 1960 the Montgomery bus boycott was a year in the past; the lunchcounter sit-in had begun in Greensboro, N.C.; and Gastonia blacks were showing signs of interest in the emerging civil rights movement. Wrote Mrs. M. F. Jones:

. . . It isn't the lunch counters or the schools alone but everything as a whole . . . [Negro] men fought in our armed forces defending our country the same as whites, so why can't they be treated the same in other ways? . . . is it right for the white man to sit and eat his lunch in comfort while the Negro pays the same price to go in the back doors of the restaurants, stand up and eat in the kitchen, or take it out when all the money goes in the same cash register?[65]

That the lunchcounter sit-in movement had begun in North Carolina must have been a discomforting fact for Gastonia city officials during this period. In September 1960, the threat of lunchcounter sit-ins in Gastonia moved the mayor to appoint an Inter-Racial Commission, composed of six black and six white leaders. "Here in Gastonia," the mayor said in announcing the new body, "we have had good relations between our white and Negro citizens. We want to keep relations on a good level." And we want to make sure that "Gastonia can avoid any possible incidents that would bring us bad publicity."[66] It was a long-familiar pair of themes—Harmony in the service of

Progress—which would dominate the ideological atmosphere over the next five years.

During all this period the politics of interracial change in Gastonia had as its background the politics of North Carolina. In a campaign that had raised some of the specters of racism that had haunted the 1950 Graham-Smith battle, the 1960 spring Democratic primary in North Carolina focused on the campaign for governor. The contest came down to Beverly Lake and Terry Sanford, and the issue that distinguished them in the public mind was whether North Carolina should close the public schools rather than desegregate them.[67] Sanford favored desegregated schools to no schools at all. He went up and down the state declaring that North Carolina would not follow Virginia's route: "What we need is massive intelligence, not massive resistance. . . . Let's not close our schools, let's improve them."[68] A majority of Democratic voters agreed with him, and Sanford went off to the Democratic convention marked as the only southern governor-nominee who had publicly implied that his state could live with a desegregated public school system.[69]

In November North Carolinians voted for Sanford by a 122,000-vote majority over his Republican opponent. They voted for Kennedy, too, but by a margin half as large. Gaston County joined the rest of the state on Sanford without joining it on Kennedy. The two largest Gastonia "uptown" precincts voted 13–8 for Richard Nixon, and gave Sanford's Republican opponent a small majority. Sanford and Kennedy polled a 2– 1 majority in the predominantly black precincts of the city, and everywhere in the county their respective votes were roughly parallel. Sanford's majority over his Republican opponent in the county as a whole was 21,417–19,469; and since in a single largely black city-precinct some 1,500 Gastonians had voted for him, the importance of the black vote for Sanford's Gaston County victory was easy to discern.[70]

Once in office, the Sanford administration in Raleigh began programmatically to link the theme of economic progress for North Carolina to the causes of education and civil rights for citizens black and white. In a 1962 speech to his fellow Methodists of the Gastonia District, for example, Sanford called attention to a sobering fact:

A major reason . . . for North Carolina's low per capita (income) standing (among the states) is that Negroes do not have adequate economic opportunities. If we counted the income of white citizens only, North Carolina would rank thirty-second in per capita income instead of forty-second.

He concluded with an appeal to Gaston Methodists out of the New Testament:

If we are true to our religious heritage in North Carolina and if we believe the lesson of the parable of the Good Samaritan, we should help those in need of help. It is as simple as that. But it is powerful in its capacity to achieve broader opportunities for everyone, the helped and the helpers alike.[71]

The Civil Rights Movement

After its appointment by the mayor in early 1960, the Gastonia "bi-racial committee" had reluctantly addressed the lunchcounter question.[72] It ultimately initiated interviews with owners of all the local lunchcounters. These negotiations yielded a decision to desegregate the counters as of January 2, 1961. After achieving this increment of new access to public facilities, the committee went into eclipse, meeting approximately once every three months over the next year and a half.[73]

All through the "hot summer" of 1963, Gastonia participated at a distance—as it had long participated in the labor union movement—in the national civil rights movement. Only occasionally did any local white person suggest that tension between the races over matters of civil and economic justice was as ready to boil up in Gastonia as anywhere else in America. But early in 1963 the Gastonia black community itself began to provide such suggestions. "There isn't a single (black) stenographer downtown in any office or in any of the department stores," wrote a black college student in February 1963. She went on to add that neither was there a single black salesclerk in so much as a ten-cent store. "A (white) high school girl . . . can get a job downtown clerking in a store when I can't and I'm a college student. This shouldn't prevail in the twentieth century."[74]

But the major straws in the racial wind that spring were political. In the city council election in May, there occurred the first major public division of the black community in ten years.[75] In the council election, black voters went overwhelmingly for a young dentist who represented a challenge to the "establishment" coalition of black and white businessmen. The coalition and its black member won by its margins in the white wards.

The time was one month after the Birmingham riots.[76] Among his first post-election acts, the newly reelected mayor of Gastonia (overseer at a plant of Textiles, Inc.) appointed a new enlarged Human Relations Committee, headed by Marshall A. Rauch. (Said Rauch himself two years after the event: "This community had to have it made, if they could elect a New York Jew to be chairman of such a committee."[77])

It was time, some local leaders now concluded, to raise the issue of industrial job opportunity for blacks. At its first meeting on June 3, 1963, the new HRC debated this agenda-shift in terms long familiar in the rhetoric of interest-group relations in Gaston County: one side, chiefly white businessmen hoped to "keep our town from going through things other North Carolina towns have gone through'' and to ''do nothing to tear down good relations of previous years.''[78] One business-member allowed that the committee's job was to take ''progressive steps . . . for all our citizens.'' One black professional then defined progress as the promotion of ''the social and economic well being of all Gastonia citizens by serving as a medium of communication among these people''—a definition of its duties that the committee adopted verbatim.[79] Further discussion at this first meeting centered on whether the committee should meet on a ninety-day or a thirty-day schedule. Apparently only one white member agreed with the black members that ''we may not have 90 days to study the problems that now confront the community.'' ''Young people are not satisfied and will not settle for what we ourselves have settled for,'' said one black, while a business member observed cautiously that ''we should not forget the progress we have made. God's calendar moves slowly.''[80]

1. The black churches. Theological differences on the chronology of change were about to become a community issue. ''Time'' does not change things automatically, Martin Luther King had written in mid-April from a Birmingham jail,[81] and five black ministers in Gastonia now declared their agreement with King in the matter. Seven—rather than thirty or ninety— days after its June 3 meeting, the Human Relations Committee was confronted by the five ministers, who announced their intent to join fifty of their parishioners in a ''prayer pilgrimage down South Street to . . . city hall.'' Object of the march was to demand the desegregation of public facilities and the opening up of job opportunities for black people in the city.[82] Urged by the committee, the ministers called off the demonstration, but Gastonia was now on notice that the black community had leaders capable of mounting demonstrations. On June 24 the black Ministerial Alliance presented the Human Relations Committee with a comprehensive list of seven local institutional sectors deemed appropriate for prompt desegregation. One or another of these sectors was to occupy the HRC's attention during almost every week of the next six months.[83]

Within the city limits of Gastonia were some thirty all-black churches. Of these, seven furnished the leadership for the pressure-tactics of 1963.[84] The ministers of these churches shared certain characteristics that made them difficult for knowledgeable white leaders in Gastonia to dismiss: (1) they were among the best educated black ministers in the city, (2) they were relatively young, (3) one had been a Greensboro campus-leader of the original sit-in movement, (4) all were pastors of middle-class black congregations attended by the moderate business-oriented black leaders of the fifties, (5) all were identified with the community as resident fulltime clergy, and (6) their initiatives had support both from other church members and from denominational church officials. It was a combination of characteristics which fitted these seven to exercise some formidable, unprecedented pressure for social change over the next few months in Gastonia.

2. *The white churches.*   In June 1963 one of the seven black ministers reminded the white public that Gastonia "was no exception to any other town" in its vulnerability now to demonstrations which "can dig deep scars and wounds that will hurt for many years."[85] But few longtime residents needed the reminder. For some whites the fear of such tension had a religious dimension which their own churches—ironically—now seemed too busy to notice.

I've almost made up my mind to quit going to church. . . . The only thing we ever talk about in our church is the budget . . . and the building fund . . . and the Fellowship Club . . . and the annual picnic. No stand is ever taken by the church on issues of importance.

"He was a white man," editorialized the *Gazette*, "and he had reference to Birmingham. . . ." The editor went on to reflect that there is less "shouting" in the churches now, less of the old-time pulpit-pounding; more pipe organs, colleges, and old folks homes. But for all these improvements:

the silence of the church on the issues of the day—the real, important issues—comes forth with such a thunder that it drowns everything else out. And there are people who grow weary of it. They think they just might quit going to church and stay home.[86]

A month later the editorial word to Gastonia's white churches was more explicit: Pope John XXIII, elected the day before, once "spoke of the church as the protector of the poor and the guardian of social justice."

This is the church as it should be. We wonder if it is as the church actually is. We wonder if the churches of Gastonia, for instance, can look into their past and their present and see if there is anything written in their deeds that would indicate that they are the protectors of the poor and the guardians of social justice.

. . . .

No, we didn't mean (in our editorial of a month ago) that the churches should come out flatly for integration. . . . Our churches simply are not taking stands on important questions. If they see the need for integration, let them stand up. If they see that this would be bad, then let them stand up.[87]

In the midst of a crisis which some felt to be as dangerous as that of 1929, he seemed to be saying: we need the social guidance of religion.[88]

White church participation in the desegregation crisis of the next six months took three overt, corporate forms: official public endorsement of the work of the Human Relations Committee by four of the five large uptown churches,[89] the announcement by the First Presbyterian Church that its deacons would seat any person of any race in any pew for services of worship,[90] and one or two integrated meetings in churches for discussion of the desegregation problem.[91] According to some leaders of the black community, however, the most direct contribution of the white churches to the civil rights cause this fall was that of the one white minister appointed to the new Human Relations Committee: Harry M. Moffett, minister of the First Presbyterian Church. "He was one of our best friends in the civil rights struggle," reflected one of the "seven" two years after the '63 incidents. "He was very impressed with Martin Luther King's Birmingham jail letter, and he distributed it to the Ministerial Association and to the Human Relations Committee."[92] "I'd put him at the top of the list," said another black leader. "He isn't always on a soapbox, but what he does in a quiet way is profound."[93] Moffett's behavior and that of his ministerial predecessor on the HRC[94] suggest that some white ministers in this era used their rapport with the local economic elite to expand the latter's social policy *agenda*. Unlike their colleagues in the "uptown" black community[95] they did not push the civil rights issue on to the agenda. But once the black community inside and outside Gastonia had raised the issue, some white ministers in town were able to hasten discussion and action on it. Significantly, the work of these ministers in the community at large was more remembered (by the black community at least) than their work of changing the policies of their own congregations.

Within a month of the HRC reorganization, a dozen or more public facilities had been desegregated, largely through the Committee's strategy of sending its leading business members to call on the owners of restaurants, motels, bowling alleys, and theaters. "We must do it together," the business leaders agreed, "in order that no one will lose business to another because of integration"[96]—the argument that would make the Civil Rights Bill of 1964 easy to accept among businessmen around the country. But such negotiations over public accommodations did not touch the heart of the black community's self-interest in social change: it was in the sphere of job opportunity that overriding questions of Justice and Progress for black Gastonians were now beginning to concentrate.

3. Job opportunity. By 1963 city garbage collectors, largely black, were being paid $1.05 per hour at a time when the federal minimum wage was officially $1.15. A two-hour strike on August 1 asked for a pay-raise to the federal minimum. Threatened on the spot with the loss of their jobs by the City Manager, the garbage collectors went back to work, but the community had again been served notice that its black citizenry was beginning to grasp some unprecedented political weapons. Garbage collectors no longer were safely in their economic place, not to speak of black college graduates who wanted to work in banks.[97]

New job openings for blacks were announced during the next few weeks, as the businessmen of the HRC visited their Gaston County peers. The very announcements were grim testimonies to the segregated-employment tradition of the community: front office work in a chain saw plant, an opening in the press room of the newspaper, positions for nurses in the largest local hospital, drivers for the city bus company, clerks for four department stores, and (one by one over the next twelve months) a steadily increasing number of nonsweeper jobs in textile mills.[98] Fortunately for the textile industry's relation to the Federal Government over the next several years, booming market conditions were beginning to make the employment of blacks an economically inviting innovation. As a conservative, knowledgeable leader of the black community put it, reflecting on the changes in employment and public accommodations for blacks in these months:

When the Gastonia power structure says they really want something, they get it. They use discretion, and they don't always move as fast as we wish. But we know they can move if they want to, since they have so many things moving for them. Moreover they have a serious desire to keep a peaceful community; and when the changes come, they are philosophical about it.[99]

The "philosophy" of the matter was spelled out repeatedly in mid-1963. For example, in an editorial responding to the announcement of the September desegration of Gastonia's schools, the *Gazette* intoned the themes of Progress, Harmony, and Liberty with ritualistic clarity. Now that our schools are to be integrated, said the editor:

Gastonia and Gaston County stands on the threshold of its greatest era. We are now laying the groundwork for an economy that will grow steadily and be much stronger in the years to come.

This is an economy that holds promise for everyone—Negro as well as white. But the promise will mature into satisfactory fruition only if the two races know and understand the problems of each other and continue to work in harmony in trying to solve these problems . . .

We are just as proud of our community as we can be. And because there have been no demonstrations here, and because integration is going ahead smoothly and steadily, we get the idea that this is the way the Lord would have it done.

We get the idea that there is a better feeling all the way around than Gastonia has known in a long time.[100]

On the very same day in its editorial columns, the *Charlotte Observer* quoted a letter from a Gastonia reader who asked if communism were infiltrating the civil rights movement as it had the 1929 Strike. Alluding to Liston Pope's work on the subject, the *Observer* observed that both the Loray Strike and the civil rights struggle illustrate "the need of dealing with grievances in such a way that solutions are produced without violence."[101]

Graded distinctions between "legal pressure," "demonstrations," and "violence" were rare in the minds of many editors and readers across the South in these months. Martin Luther King's insistence on the *non-violence* of the public demonstration as a *legal* means of protest against the constitutional and *moral* deficiences of a particular law entailed a train of interlocking concepts that few white ideologues apparently grasped. But a dramatic change to grasp just these subtleties was now at hand in Gastonia.

4. The demonstration. It was the closest approximation to a Loray Strike in the thirty-five years of local history recorded in this book. That it was objectively a *slim* approximation is all the more reason for paying detailed attention to the affair. For many Gastonians the demonstration-incident of 1963 re-evoked the memories of 1929 and put on display yet again evidence for the claim that local societies maintain continuity and effect change partly through the motivating power of a widely shared ideology.

On September 15, 1963, while local NAACP leaders were in the very process of considering a demonstration before the two downtown theaters, news of the bombing of the Sixteenth Street Baptist Church in Birmingham reached Gastonia, bringing ideology, local history, and local religion into painful focus: "It mustn't happen here—again," was the gist of local feeling about Birmingham. Gastonia can sympathize with that Alabama city, the *Gazette* editor reflected.

Have the scars left by the 1929 strike healed completely? Do we not, thirty-four years later, still hear of the terrible events surrounding that unfortunate incident, and it did not concern itself with racial problems?

We find it "hard to blame" younger Negroes in Gastonia who are impatient with the "wrongs" done them in the past, he conceded; but we can be thankful that in Gastonia "there have been thus far no demonstrations, no governmental pressure, and no chaotic interruptions of business and commerce." Instead, we have had for over ten years a steadily growing record of improvements in race relations: a city councilman, the county library, the golf course, the lunchcounters, a minimum standards housing ordinance, a hospital, a bowling alley, a Merchants Association resolution favoring the desegregation of public accommodations, the first desegregation of our schools, new job opportunities, and a host of other "fruits of the conference table" that are "just as sweet as those of the street." It is time for all Gastonians to commit themselves anew to harmonious, uncoerced progress.

The white citizenry must know that much of what is being asked is justified and should be granted. We cannot espouse brotherhood and have one brand for one color of citizens and another for the other. By the same token, the Negro citizens must realize that they are interrupting a successful building program if they turn themselves over to outside agitators, equally as bad as the white race-baiters.

If Gastonia becomes another Birmingham, or even High Point, Lexington, or Greensboro, the responsibility might well rest with either side.

We hope, may we pray, that it will not. We, in Gastonia, know that there is another way.

Where good will and love are practiced, can anger and prejudice prevail? Can hate predominate? By the grace of God and with the efforts of all of us, we think not.

"Thou shalt love thy neighbor as thyself." Matthew 19:19[102]

There was, in short, a large increment of establishment pride riding on the possibility that Gastonia could survive the civil rights movement without the active presence of the much-feared demonstrator. The pride was matched with fear, and both were undergirded by the terms of religion.

Gastonia's two downtown theaters belonged to one owner, who met the pleas of his Human Relations Committee visitors during the summer of 1963 with a firm no. He was not the only holdout in the area of public accommodations,[103] but he was one of the most aggravating holdouts in the opinion of many younger Gastonia blacks. Some years before, the Palace Theater north of the tracks had fallen into disrepair and disuse. There was now no indoor theater for a black citizen to attend. At a called meeting of the HRC with the theater manager, he offered to "fix up the Palace Theater," which he also owned; but he stated that he considered the desegregation experience of other North Carolina theater-owners economically unsatisfactory. Black members of the committee retorted flatly that "plans are now being made to demonstrate. . . . Negro young people of Gastonia are greatly influenced by what has happened in other places that have integrated their theaters. . . . They are impatient with waiting."[104] As some of the leaders admitted privately, young blacks were harboring an identity that few white people understood: "It was a cleansing of the soul for many to join with other Negroes from across the state."[105]

From a less psychological, more political point of view, demonstrating was part of a viable overall strategy for social change, and a large proportion of black leadership understood it as such. Later interviews with both the "old school" and "new school" political leaders of the black community[106] strongly suggested that, though the older men disagreed with the younger on the timing and the targeting of the theater demonstration, the political appropriateness of the strategem was accepted almost everywhere in the black community. At last the Loray Strike was to become relevant to the interests of that community!

An Activist Minister: "In our conferences with the power structure we told them: 'If you don't change, we see the chance of bloodshed, riot.' (It was a threat!) 'We see the chance of CORE or SNCC or others coming in here and tearing the town apart.' We even put it out a time or two that they were in town as a sort of scare. It had its effect. This community was afraid of any uprising. Some years ago they had a strike, and a few people were killed, a police chief, I believe; and it holds a memory in the minds of people. Also we were in the process of trying to get the All America City award. They wanted to be able to say, 'We've had no demonstrations.' "[107]

An Old School Political Leader: "It told the complacent that 'it' could really happen; that Gastonia was not immune to what other counties were experiencing. Certain parts of the power structure thought everyone was satisfied. . . . Some HRC members did say that it impeded progress, but I could never get them to pinpoint just how."[108]

A Young Demonstrator: "The demonstrations brought the problem to the attention of everybody. You identify the problem, then give everybody time to get around the negotiating table."[109]

A New School Political Leader: "You see, our ministers were trying to act as a catalyst to provide the representatives 'at the table' with evidence of backing in the Negro community. The Negro members of the HRC had said that there *will be* demonstrations unless improvements were made, and if we had not had the demonstrations, it would have hurt the prestige of the HRC members. Also, it burst the bubble of frustration and the seething unrest of the Negro community."[110]

From August through November, largely in the black churches and the local chapter of the NAACP, the threat of a theater demonstration was nurtured and finally activated. At least four of the black churches opened their facilities to meetings of the NAACP during these months, sometimes over the objections of prominent congregational officials. Early in the summer, said the local black Presbyterian minister:

"Our church was the only one in town in which people were permitted to meet to discuss the possibility of a demonstration. A member of our church protested about it 'in the name of common sense.' I told him and the congregation that we could take a stand on this matter partly because the General Assembly of the United Presbyterian Church had taken its stand."[111]

And another of "the seven" recollected:

"Some leaders in the Negro community said to the white power structure: 'We have them [the potential demonstrators] under control.' So the whites weren't worried. But once the demonstrators started meeting in our church, one of my prominent members objected both to me and the church being a part of the thing. White people were calling him and saying, 'You ought to be able to control your pastor.' "[112]

But potentials for "control" of a minister's behavior were different in the white and black communities. In the civil rights cause activist black ministers had an opportunity to arouse their parishioners to their own interest in social justice and also an opportunity to practice a style of leadership that required no prearrangements with uptown white leaders. They were almost the only professional group in the black community whose base of economic support was not directly tied to such arrangements, though they were well aware that the livelihood of people in their congregations was thus tied. One of the activist ministers described the opposition in his congregation largely in these financial-pressure terms:

" 'I work in Mrs. So-and-So's kitchen,' they would say to me, ' and they don't want trouble.' Or they would say, 'I once paid $1.00 regular [as a weekly church contribution], but I'm not going to do it anymore.' Or: 'Reverend, you should get out. The church might be bombed.' And: 'I don't care if you stay or go when Conference comes.' "[113]

These views were countered in the same constituency with a rage against tokenism, especially among younger blacks. Numerical estimates of the opinion-division are hard to make, but the very fact of a division gave the black minister room for maneuver. "We saw that our young people might *really* upset the community without any common sense or leadership at all, so we were pushed to make a move. We felt pressure, too," from a side of the black community that was larger than the white community preferred to consider real.[114]

The activist ministers now proceeded to invite Rev. B. Elton Cox, an official of the Congress of Racial Equality, to address a meeting of citizens at St. Peter's AME Zion Church on Sunday night, October 13. Cox had all the marks of the radicalism that Gastonia feared: he had spent time in jail for the civil rights cause; his base of operation, High Point, had been in an uproar over demonstrations during most of the summer, and that town (some ninety miles away) was already on Gastonia's least-to-be-imitated list. Cox evidently came to Gastonia on October 13 with the intention of initiating the demonstration that the ministers had already declared their willingness to lead—though not on that particular Sunday. In effect, he forced their hand. They could have thus blamed the demonstration on an "outside agitator," but they would have done so at the cost of losing their own leadership of the demonstration movement, and neither old school or new school leaders in the black community wanted Gastonia's first racial demonstration to be led by anyone else but ministers. "I think that ministers should have been in a position to lead such a demonstration," said one of the old school leaders, "especially to keep the emphasis on nonviolence. The minister's duties should take him beyond the pulpit."[115] It was this reasoning and this base of political support that accounted for the fact (as the police chief would understate it the next day to the HRC) that "the ministers did not fully cooperate" to keep the theater demonstration from occurring.[116]

At the St. Peter's AME church meeting, in a rousing speech that mixed the images of Christianity with the images of American democracy, Elton Cox declared that Gastonia theaters must be fully integrated by Christmas or else he would be in jail on that date. "Segregation is sin, and as a minister of the gospel I am fighting sin." He was also fighting injustice, he said. Communists like Krushchev and Castro could come to Gastonia and go to the movies, "yet I can't, although I'm an American citizen." In conclusion, instead of an altar call, he invited the congregation to come with him to the theater.

"I've got my walking shoes on. I've got the price of a ticket and I have bail money in my pocket. I feel like taking a walk down to the movie. Do you want to go with me?"

Approximately 160 people in the congregation answered yes with their feet.[117] The trek to the theater was one mile—down a street notable for institutions along its sidewalks long related to the weal and the woe of Gastonia's black community: the Highland School, for decades "the" grammar school for blacks, the black-owned funeral home, the Palace Theater with its cracked marquee glass and its assorted emblems of economic inviability; midway, the black business district: the credit union office, the drug store, the beauty parlor, the doctors' offices; down in the hollow: the row of "shot-gun" houses, prime example of slums north of the tracks; around the corner: the city water works, whose services had never been segregated, the downtown railroad tracks, still without benefit of a safety gate; then, all in glancing distance, the assorted monuments of "uptown": the major bank, the Confederate statue before the county courthouse, the Gregg Cherry Highway Marker, the marble-engraved version of the Ten Commandments in front of the City Hall, and finally, a half block more, the downtown theater.

All along their way the marchers were accompanied by one black member of the town police force, some twenty white town or county police, and a contingent of firemen. Arriving at 9:30 P.M. at the theater, they were met by the theater manager, the mayor, television cameras, and a closed box office—all suggesting that the Gastonia constabulary was anticipating the demonstration. One of the AME Zion ministers led the group in prayer "that discrimination would end and hate be cleansed from men's minds."[118] Soon after the demonstrators dispersed for the night. They would lift placards in front of the two theaters for the next seventeen days.

Monday morning's called meeting of the HRC was full of foreboding. "From now on," said a business member of the committee, "it's going to be even harder to get things done." On the previous evening, reported the police chief, at the Bessemer City Drive-In Theater, "two Negro boys were beaten up by three car loads of white teenagers." From north Gastonia there had been reported two explosions in the black neighborhood and also "a Swastika painted on the car of a Jewish man." No incidents of violence were reported in front of the theater, however. It was pointed out that according to the city code the demonstration was technically illegal, because no permit had been secured for it. At the urging of the mayor, members of the city council decided on Wednesday to make additional legal provision for keeping the demonstration nonviolent. The new local statute prohibited demonstrations without a permit, a march line of more than two persons abreast, blocking of sidewalks, and the like. One section of the law read: "No person shall physically interfere with or obstruct any lawful parade, demonstration, or march, nor address profane, indecent, abusive, or threatening language to or at any persons engaged in a demonstration or parade." The ordinance went on to permit police to block streets and parking places about to be used by marchers. "This may inconvenience some people," a police captain commented, "but it's for their safety that we do it." The structured enforcement of civil liberty at this point was not spectacular, but it was a long way from the days of the anti-sound truck and anti-leaflet ordinances of 1934. Among southern towns in 1963, it even had the look of unaccustomed liberalism.[119]

Monday night, in a front page "Appeal to Reason in a Troublesome Time," the *Gazette*, under the biblical quotation, "Blessed are the peacemakers," expressed "heartbreak" over the turn of events. It went on to ask "the good people of Gastonia to make doubly certain that Gastonia does not become another Birmingham." It is the right of Americans to protest and to march, the paper allowed, just as it is the right of a property-owner to manage his property as he pleases. Neither right, in the *Gazette's* opinion, is being wisely exercised in this instance, but both rights must be protected. A third right—the right of access to public facilities—ought to take a backseat to the rights of private property; but hopefully the theater manager will cease exercising this latter right, and Negroes will cease exercising their rights of demonstration as well. Out of it all, the editor reflected, good may yet come.

No town, city, or nation ever grew into maturity without a few disrupting troubles. No rosebush ever produced a thing of beauty without consequent thorns.

To all the people of Gastonia, we appeal for reason.

We are all brothers under one God. With that thought constant in our minds, let us be ever aware of the peacemakers.[120]

Though at least one reader criticized the *Gazette* for underplaying the rights of private property in this editorial,[121] a local white church leader chose to commend the paper for its timely word. He was the Director of Christian Social Concerns of the Gastonia District of the Methodist Church. His letter to the editor is one of the few examples from this era of a white clergyman's public comment during a current crisis on the issues of that crisis. He was not the pastor of a local church but a staff member of a local denominational body. What he added to the *Gazette's* account of the Sunday evening "Freedom Rally" at the St. Peter's Church was a note about its atmosphere. He had attended the rally, said the minister,

because I am anxious to acquire a better understanding of the Negro's aspirations and problems. Although the speaker's words were not calculated to raise the white man's self-esteem . . . the atmosphere was not of hatred, as might be expected, but one of hope and heroism.

Perhaps, he went on to say, "all of us in the 'favored majority' ought to share in a similar experience, or at least give more serious thought to the basic injustice of any system depriving people of the heritage of freedom for which their forefathers died."[122]

By midweek the number of demonstrators in front of the two theaters had stabilized, but the crowd of white spectators had begun to grow. It was the crowd of whites, said the police chief to the city council, that was most explosive.[123] As the demonstration entered its second week, it became apparent that the crowd of whites was swelling from the efforts of a newly organized group calling themselves a chapter of the National Association for the Advancement of White People. Most recruits to the organization were young, and its leader was a small-business owner. On the twelfth demonstration night, the NAAWP conducted a counter-demonstration in front of one theater, jostling the signs of black picketers and the flaring of some tempers.[124] Moreover, the leader of the white group

stood on the street before the movie house with a pocketful of change, buying movie tickets for any white person wanting one, and several took advantage of his offer. Some other whites bought tickets and tore them up in front of the colored people's faces.[125]

Police separated the groups of protesters, and no arrests were made that night. During the whole of the seventeen days, only one person was arrested, a white man charged with newly-illegal heckling.

At this point in the affair, political pressure and counterpressure between the white and black communities underwent a dynamic that had never been approached in Gastonia before. The focus of the political struggle was the group of seven ministers. An effort by white leaders to deprive the ministers of their constituents now gathered momentum: first privately, then in consultations of the HRC, and finally in the public press. One political issue at stake throughout the crisis was whether or not aggressive, demonstration-prone leadership in the black community could be legitimate and therefore negotiated with by the white community. Early in the discussions of the HRC, for example, one black member "suggested the possibility of having _____ in the picture now." The man in question was the new school candidate, recently defeated for city council, who had carried the black ward by a large margin.[126] Should the committee establish liaison with the aggressive elements of the black community who considered this politician its hero? Was aggressiveness to pay off in terms of power and influence? No, the majority of HRC members agreed, not if we can help it. To underscore this point, just as the demonstration was coming to an end, one of the seven ministers, up till now a member of the HRC, was fired from the Committee. After some holding back from actually participating in the demonstration, the minister had joined the picket line. The Commitee, by unanimous vote, with one abstention, requested the mayor to suspend him. "They said he couldn't be a demonstrator and a negotiator at the same time."[127]

In democratic politics the telltale sign of the real presence of power is the counterpower that it activates. All during the theater demonstration opponents of that strategy focused their criticism and their action increasingly upon "the ministers." "Mr. _____ reported that white sentiment seems to be crystalizing in favor of the theater manager, and some are offering him financial aid and urging him to hold out against the ministers."[128] At the first meeting of the committee after the end of the demonstration, its members discussed "the possible next move to be made by the ministers. No one knows what it will be, but some indications were that it might be a selective buying campaign."[129] With the exception of political maneuvers related to the issues of beverage alcohol legislation, it was probably the first time in the history of Gastonia that an influential group of citizens found themselves dealing with a body of professional church leaders in terms of the latter's apparent power directly to effect social change.[130]

The most available counterpower against any manuevers of the black community in Gastonia, as in other southern communities, had always been economic. "I'm getting my money from these white people," one church member said to his militant minister, "Leave them alone!"[131] Most leaders of the black community, however, reported afterwards that economic pressure was used sparingly by whites, and in one or two instances it backfired. A few of the younger demonstrators were threatened with loss of jobs. One was actually fired: "She was a girl who worked in a laundry near our church," said one black layman. "In three weeks that place went out of business from the loss of black customers. They tried to open up under a different name, but it didn't work."[132] The economic squeeze did not work on ministers either. At the height of the theater demonstration a prominent white member of the HRC—a non-Presbyterian—came privately to one of the seven activist ministers and said: "You know, the First Presbyterian Church gives your congregation $750 a year, and you wouldn't want anything to happen to that contribution." "I told him," reported the minister,

"that we didn't have to have that money (though since we have continued to get it). In fact, he was the only person who ever brought such pressure on me. They knew that I wouldn't give in on something like that, and they might even have feared that it would backfire on them if they tried. As one of my own church officers said, 'Let them have the money; we'll dig deeper into our own pockets.' "[133]

The growing economic independence of some parishioners was doubtless one factor in the support which the militants had already garnered in their own congregations. One influential black professional, his income relatively protected from direct white intervention, commented with obvious satisfaction: "When the idea of demonstrating was first getting going among the ministers, the chairman of the HRC came to see me thinking that I was the man behind our minister. But I wasn't. I was paying almost 10% of the budget of the church, but I refused to raise one hand to mess with those ministers. . . . By then the Negro members of the HRC were against the ministers, and they still are, not realizing that they are out of step with the Negro community."[134]

Other varieties of power were invoked against the seven ministers before the crisis cleared. Much to the later dismay of six of them, the local police had the "goods on" one of the seven in terms of information about a personal scandal. It was in their arm-twisting threat to use this information to discredit the minister that the black community first got wind of this scandal. "We first found out about the trouble _____ was getting into in connection with the demonstration. The police tried to get the ministers to call it off by threatening to pull out the 'rap' they already had on him. But the rest refused to call it off."[135] The most public, direct attempt to erode support from the seven, however, was a pair of *Gazette* editorials aimed at traditional black conservatism. On successive afternoons the paper cried:

(Rev. Cox and the CORE leaders) must have had trouble engendering support among our citizens for they had to find it with the Gaston County Interdenominational Ministerial Alliance, an organization composed of only seven Negro churches out of the dozens in our town. But they got it and we had marches.[136]

We know for a fact that the seven Negro ministers who have fallen in with Mr. Cox do not have their congregations behind them. We know for a fact that even now the seven ministers are divided.

You Negroes of our city, if you are truly interested in restoring harmony here, you will let these seven ministers know it soon.

You will tell them how you feel—in whatever way you think best, as long as it is peaceful and within the law. Certainly, you ought to do this now.

. . . Let's get our city back where it was, back to making progress peacefully.

We've been set back. But with the help of God and the understanding that comes with men working together, we'll be able to start all over again and act like citizens of the city ought to act.[137]

Two black readers quickly responded to this appeal with a pair of letters. One writer was negative to the demonstrators and expressed her gratitude to "white friends" for the support they had long given to church-related schools in the black community. The other said that in his opinion

. . . the only one who has the spunk to stand up for the right is some of our ministers, and I thank God for them. I don't know who told you that their congregations are not behind them. They are just telling the wrong thing, because we are. Of course the two-face ones are not. And remember, if we don't get what we want now, we will get it later as we are going to die fighting to get freedom for our children, whether you or the others like it or not.[138]

Two years later, a knowledgeable new school leader said confidently: "Only a handful of Negroes objected to the demonstration."[139]

Did the theater demonstration accomplish anything for the improvement of race relations in Gastonia? Afterwards a vocal set of white leaders continued to reply no. The demonstrations, if they did anything, set back progress, or brought it to a standstill.[140] Two years later, the opinion was still being voiced that Rev. Cox, the "intruder," had interrupted "normal good feeling" between the races.[141] But even among the white residents of the town, answers to the question would vary for years to come. Substantial numbers of whites as well as blacks apparently came to believe that changes in race relations require some kind of "pressure."[142]

Blacks were most aware of this; and two years later even the old school leaders of the black community had concluded that, on the whole, inside and outside pressures, demonstrations and near-demonstrations, had been beneficial to blacks in Gastonia. "Though the demonstration was a flop in terms of its immediate objective," said an old school black leader in 1965, "it did some good." The particular good it did, said a young participant in the event, was to dramatize to black people the hope that they could do something to change their lot. "Gastonia has been slow to change. We have lots of people who say, 'Things can't get better, so why try?' Things began to change for us in 1963 because we began to exert pressure to make it change." As one young black politician summarized his evaluation of the event:

Without the demonstrations that we did have, we would have had wildcat demonstrations and riots. I personally stopped several such wildcat affairs among young people in the black community. The white man does not realize that the Negro answers questions about how well things are going according to the impression he will make in the white person's eyes. The demonstrations helped from the Negro standpoint. Things are seething, building up, and ready to explode. The demonstration let a lot of pentup feelings out. It said: "You see, Mr. White Man, we were not afraid to demonstrate." It declared who we were. We were no longer leading a double life. . . . Some whites developed bitterness towards the Negro ministers, but that is about gone now. The businessmen never penalized the Negro churches through defaulting on building contracts and service needs. And after the demonstrations, white people recognized Negro people as people—there was less walking over you. And they would talk about the problem. Of course during the demonstration we were on the verge of a breakdown; then the atmosphere got better.

Or as the reputedly most conservative of Gastonia's black leaders put the dynamic principle of the matter: "One pulls apart and then gets back together with your opponent in politics, don't you?"[143]

Demonstration Aftermaths: Schools, Churches, Mills

The crisis over desegregation continued to simmer in Gastonia, as it did in the United States as a whole, all during the sixties. The downtown theater owner did not integrate his theater until he was forced to do so by the Civil Rights Law of 1964.[144] The work of the HRC continued, at a slower pace, chiefly in the area of increasing employment opportunity for blacks. School desegregation expanded without incident. In 1965 the number of blacks in a new senior high school greatly increased; in 1966 the all-black and all-white

high schools in Gastonia were merged; and in 1968, by county-wide referendum, Gaston voted to merge three administrative school systems into one,
with bonds and a tax increase to facilitate the merger. One result was the
achievement, over the next seven years, of a degree of racial integration in local
public education unmatched in some more urbanized areas of the United States.
By that year every school in Gaston County had some black students—though
the mark of the old segregated pattern peeped out in the fact that four of the
fifty-five county schools had less than ten such students. No school had a
majority of black students; virtually none had more than 20% or less than 5%
black professional staff. Racial distribution in the system as a whole was as
follows in 1975, according to the Gaston County Board of Education:[145]

%Black Students	No. Schools	%Black Professionals	No. Schools
(Low: .3%)0–5%	6	(Low:5.1%) 0–5%	0
5–10%	14	5–10%	28
10–15%	15	10–15%	19
15–20%	6	15–20%	7
20–25%	2	(High:22.2%)20–25%	1
25–30%	8	25–30%	0
(High:43.9%)+30%	4	+30%	0
	‒‒		‒‒
	55		55

Such figures bespeak an irregular achievement of "total" school desegregation.
They portray dramatically the total breakup of the black school system, with all
the human ambiguities implicit in such a breakup. Federal education authorities
must have viewed these statistics as close to the letter of the desegregation law
in a county with a black school population of only 15%. The statistics, of
course, did not tell much about the intra-schoolroom reality of educational
integration. (One testimony to that inner reality came at the end of the 1973-74
school year from a 19-year old exchange student from Peru, who, after a year at
a Gastonia high school commented to a *Gazette* reporter: "Something terrible
separates [the races] all the time: in classrooms, in the halls, at lunch, during
activities. You can just feel it, though everyone denies it." Peru, she said, was
different: there, the races are so many and so long mixed that "there is hardly
any recognizable division."[146])

In the meantime, the county and its cities continued to accumulate some
historic "firsts" in the public arenas of race relations: in 1970, seventeen years
after the precedent of Gastonia, the town council in Belmont appointed its first
black member to a vacancy in its ranks.[147] By 1971 the 76-man Gastonia police

force had 8 black members or 11.6%—a record among the cities of North Carolina.[148] A Gastonia junior high school, still largely white, in that same year elected a black student as student body president.[149] In the summer of 1974, the Gastonia-Gaston Human Relations Commission hired its first paid director, a twenty-eight-year-old black professional from nearby York, South Carolina.[150] Finally, a local Baptist church began actively to recruit members from the black community, and Mrs. Myrtle Hoffman accepted the invitation, becoming perhaps the first black in several decades of Gaston history to join an "all white" church.

To this foreground of change was occasionally added the background of reversion to the old ways in race relations: reported knifings in two public schools, leading to expulsions of black and white students; rallies and demonstrations by the Mount Holly chapter of the Ku Klux Klan, whose leaders were seeking a new nonviolent image for their organization; and countless private acclamations of the segregationist tradition—such as the plan of one suburban organization to construct a community park with a swimming pool, tennis court, and a picnic area for "carefully screened members," i.e., all-white.[154]

Evidence of the former type would be heavily relied upon to sustain the judgment of some Gastonians that in the seventies the county was still a "pace-maker" in race relations. The latter evidence would as easily sustain the judgment of one recently arrived minister who believes that "Gastonia and Gaston County should be recognized for their outstanding performance of tokenism."[152] But the most important, undeniable change in the 1964-74 period was in black employment in the mills.

Writing in 1952, Donald Dewey observed that the classic exclusion of the southern black from the textile mills was, if anything, more absolute by 1940s than it had been earlier in the century[153] "Among the 400,000-odd textile workers in Virginia, North Carolina, and South Carolina there is, apparently, not a single Negro employed as a weaver, spinner, or loom-fixer."[154] Nothing suggests that the situation was any different in Gastonia up to the early nineteen-sixties. In 1960, federal sources calculated that 3.3% of the national textile work force in the country was black.[155] But within five years dramatic changes occurred throughout the industry. First there was the civil rights movement; then the Civil Rights Bills of 1964 and 1965; and finally the upwardly mobile southern white textile worker—who since 1945 has steadily worked his way into skilled and managerial jobs in new industries in places like Marietta, Huntsville, Raleigh, and Gastonia. Among other things, "industrial diversification" all over the South meant mill jobs quit by whites for better jobs.

It was an irresistible combination of forces for ushering in the day of "fair employment" in the textile industry: by 1966 in North Carolina, the level of black employment had risen to 8% in the state's textile mills and to 11% in the metropolitan areas.[156] By 1970, the percentage would climb to 14.3% for the American textile industry as a whole; some southern textile leaders would be proudly claiming that the level in the South was 20%—double the national average of black employment in manufacturing for 1970.[157]* By 1974 black employment in Gastonia's mills averaged 20%, according to the executive vice-president of the local Chamber of Commerce.[158]

Few complaints of race-connected friction between the new black and the old white workers resulted from these changes. Subsequent interviews with mill executives suggested that integration went smoothly in the mills because management had decided it would be that way. Within a few months, in many a Gastonia mill, some version of this incident (from another part of the South) must have occurred:

"I called my workers together . . . and told them, 'Look, we need to hire some Negroes in production. If we don't we might have to close. And the Federal government is going to make us hire them anyway. I need your help to make it work out.' "[159]*

Several executives in Gastonia said that "the word was passed" down the management line that no fights, arguments, or other overt conflicts would be tolerated between workers; such conflict would be grounds for the loss of jobs. Did management count on this threat or on a sense of fair play in their white workers? The balance between the two leverages for change is impossible to calculate, but managers in various parts of the industry confessed to some surprise that so few incidents of racial conflict actually occurred in the '65-'66 changeover. Said one executive of a Burlington plant in another North Carolina city, "I think the greatest surprise some of our managers had at first was the acceptance by whites of the Negroes."[160]

By the mid-seventies, such acceptance was beginning to register in terms of union-organization success in various parts of the South. The situation was promising, said TWUA regional director Scott Hoyman, because the new economic and political power of southern blacks was at least being perceived by many working-class whites as potentially beneficial to them as well.

"In spite of the fantastic economic inertia of the southern textile industry, I believe that the people of the industry will now start organizing. It won't be a cataclysmic move-ment, but the forces are moving in this direction. Take the political dimension: recently in Andrews and Lane, South Carolina, the TWUA won because blacks in those counties were so well registered to vote that our picket line was not harassed. We had a *peaceful* six-month strike without ever having an injunction from the courts. All the officials respected the political clout of blacks. The sheriff and state troopers were much more respectful of the rights of strikers than in most previous strike situations in the Carolinas. And in both states, this same political shift was felt in the Congressional elections of 1974. Two anti-union congressmen in North Carolina were defeated, and in each case black votes made a difference. Our campaign strategy in '74 focused on the bills which incumbents had voted against— especially minimum wage legislation. The wage bill of 1973 was the first on which a sizable proportion of North and South Carolina congressmen voted *for* a raise. Even the congressman from the district that includes Gaston County voted for it."[161]

In sum, as survey data below will also substantiate, in his transition to integrated employment the much-touted prejudices of the "poor white" textile worker have been subjected to a detection-test. For a long time, populist critics of the South have suspected that the classic southern upper-class analysis of "our race problem" (the impossibility of combining prejudiced poor whites in the same organization with blacks) is a stereotype, a self-confirming prophecy, and an ideological instrument for the perpetuation of elitist control of industrial institutions. Both events and our survey data seem to confirm Reese Cleghorn's speculation that "businessmen . . . have more difficulty than the mills' white workers in accepting the idea that Negroes can be integrated-and-equal production workers." The problem of employment integration, at least, is not necessarily centered in the "Rufus Crosses" of southern society:

> Rufus Cross is the kind of man who often is called a "cracker" and presumed to be living evidence that another generation must pass before Southern poor whites accept poor Negroes as equals. . . . What seems most arresting, however, is his almost casual acceptance of the change.
>
> It may be that Rufus Cross is the kind of man who, ultimately, must "get along" if whites and blacks are to work tthings out together at the bottom of the industrial ladder. They have been deprived together.[162]

Community Perception of Change and Its Leaders

In our account of the relation of religious organization, ideology, and the labor union issue in Gastonia, the fit of the historical and the sociological-survey data was relatively straightforward and predictable.[163] Not so, the fit between the two sorts of data on race relations: set against the background of the narrative just concluded our survey of a cross section of Gastonians in the 1965-67 period yields as many puzzles as confirmations of the narrative's suggestions of how change has come to this community.

1. Perceptions of change. • A community long imbued with the "spirit of

Progress" is by definition a community whose members are predisposed to at least some kinds of ongoing social change. We have seen that, among most Gastonians, the labor union has not yet acquired status as an element of Progress; but clearly for black Gastonians and ambiguously for whites, changes in patterns of race relations apparently resonate with the attitudes of important segments of the public.

Our inquiry into this matter was structured on three levels of questions: what did a sample of residents think about change in general? what particular recent changes in Gastonia did they feel to be the most important? whom did they believe to be the leaders in the making of those changes?

One section of our survey probed for the respondent's general views about the importance of "changing things" versus "keeping things as they are." The data in Table 6.1 indicate that most of our interviewees expressed pro-change attitudes. Men tended to be more pro-change than women in answers to questions about the validity of tradition. A large majority of both sexes agreed with statements concerning satisfaction with things as they are, but a majority also agreed that everyone should think about needed changes. Few striking differences associated with race appear in the data. While such data do not provide much information about specific changes, they suggest an openness to change among the population in the community.

Mere change is one thing; a "good" change may be something else, so we asked: "What do you think is the most important (single) improvement in Gastonia in recent years?" From Table 6.2, it is evident that various groups differ considerably in their choice of improvements in the community. As expected, a larger proportion of blacks identified racial integration as the most important improvement, while economic growth and public facilities were most important to whites. Changes in housing and employment did not rank as changes of first-priority for these respondents, but it is possible that for blacks "integration" covered employment-integration and for whites "economic growth" covered the same. The rather uniform responses among the four groups to the importance of both "education" and "economic growth," however, suggest that these two indexes to "progress" are widely affirmed in the Gastonia population at large. (Since the inquiry was an open-ended question that asked for only the "most important" improvement, no judgments can be made here about how the respondents would have ranked a total list of such items. The data do not necessarily mean, therefore, that whites opposed integration.)

This survey occurred some four years after the upsurge of the civil rights movement and other assertions of power by the black community in Gastonia, so we were especially curious to know what perceptions of the local "power structure" prevailed among Gastonians and if these perceptions extended, from

Table 6.1
PROPORTION OF RESPONDENTS HAVING PRO-CHANGE ATTITUDES BY RACE AND SEX IN PERCENT

Question	Black		White	
	Male	Female	Male	Female
Everybody should be thinking seriously about changes needed in the community (Agree)	88.6 (61)	88.9 (72)	91.0 (177)	85.7 (91)
We could save ourselves a lot of trouble by doing things the way they have always been done (Disagree)	65.6 (61)	44.4 (72)	76.8 (177)	68.1 (91)
We have to learn to live with the world as it is (Disagree)	27.9 (61)	11.3 (71)	29.9 (177)	33.0 (91)
Usually things improve only when someone dares to be different (Agree)	58.3 (60)	50.7 (71)	59.0 (173)	54.9 (91)
One is usually better off putting his confidence in things that have stood the test of time (Disagree)	31.1 (61)	15.3 (72)	22.0 (177)	11.0 (90)
I wish older people would be as open to change as young people seem to be (Agree)	78.7 (61)	74.3 (70)	59.2 (174)	64.8 (88)
A man can get too satisfied with things as they are (Agree)	92.9 (61)	88.9 (72)	85.8 (176)	81.3 (91)
Good seldom comes from conflict and disagreement (Disagree)	45.9 (61)	25.4 (71)	45.5 (176)	27.8 (90)
My ideas about what is good for the community have changed considerably in recent years (Agree)	75.4 (61)	59.2 (71)	50.9 (173)	43.8 (89)

Table 6.2

RESPONDENTS WHO IDENTIFIED VARIOUS CHANGES AS MOST
IMPORTANT IMPROVEMENTS IN GASTONIA, BY RACE
AND SOCIAL-RESIDENTIAL GROUPS

| | | Race and Neighborhood | | |
| | | | White | |
Improvement	Black	Mill Village	Old Suburban	New Suburban
Integration	24.6	–	3.6	3.0
Employment	7.5	8.0	1.2	3.0
Economic Growth	10.4	21.2	23.8	27.3
Housing	7.5	7.1	14.3	3.0
Education	11.9	11.5	11.9	10.6
Government	2.2	–	2.4	3.0
Public Facilities	3.0	17.7	23.8	21.2
Number of Cases	134	113	84	66

(Percentages do not total 100 because each figure is the proportion of all possible
respondents who identified that improvement.)

either side, across the interracial boundary. Our question was: "Suppose some
new project were being considered for the community—a new park, a new
hospital, or the like. Who are four or five people who would be most influential
in getting the community to support the project?" The resulting answers were
not far from the findings of other more elaborate studies of power and influence
in American communities: the leaders most frequently mentioned were local
economic and government leaders. Even concerning the change to integration,
only one respondent mentioned a nonlocal person. The proportion of people
who could identify any leader was small, however: only eighteen of the
thirty-three blacks who felt integration was an improvement could identify at
least one of its leaders, and similar results obtained for whites. Among whites
only the upper middle class mentioned specific individuals with regularity
—largely because many of these respondents were themselves involved with
the leaders in effecting the changes.

Most significant as a test of public perceptions of community leadership
patterns were the actual names given in answer to this question.

Table 6.3

IMPROVEMENTS AND NUMBER OF TIMES EACH TYPE OF LEADERSHIP
INVOLVED WAS IDENTIFIED BY RESPONDENTS, BY RACE AND
SOCIO-RESIDENTIAL GROUPS

Improvement and Leadership	Black	White		
		Mill Village	Old Suburban	New Suburban
Integration				
Federal Government	1	—	—	—
Local Government	63	—	2	—
Private Individuals	13	—	1	—
Ministers	17	—	—	—
Economic Leaders	11	—	—	6
Employment				
Local Government	11	—	—	—
Ministers	1	—	—	—
Economic Leaders	14	4	—	2
Economic Growth				
Local Government	3	3	7	1
Economic Leaders	6	1	11	17
Housing				
Local Government	10	—	—	—
Private Individuals	—	—	6	2
Ministers	1	1	6	2
Economic Leaders	—	2	—	—
Education				
Local Government	3	1	3	2
Private Individuals	—	1	—	—
Ministers	2	1	—	—
Economic Leaders	—	2	4	4
Government				
Local Government	1	—	2	2
Public Facilities				
Local Government	5	5	8	2
Private Individuals	—	—	2	3
Ministers	1	—	—	—
Economic Leaders	9	—	3	9

In occupational terms, the leaders mentioned by whites come overwhelmingly from industry and business, but whites are little aware of the leaders of either race in the integration issue. In one issue—housing—whites believe that ministers have exercised major influence, but virtually in no other areas. Only in the area of public facilities do whites perceive government leadership as very important for a change that has occurred.

Most significant of all, perhaps, are the data of Table 6.4, especially the *absences* in the data: *Blacks and whites are unable to identify leaders in each other's communities, and very few local persons related to a non-local government or industry are perceived as having large local influence.* The politics of racial integration and the economics of industrial diversification to the contrary, Gastonians white and black are profoundly unaware of the identity of particular persons in the community who are (1) leaders of a racial group not their own, (2) leaders of an economic or political enterprise not locally based. The first finding, perhaps, is not surprising; it suggests vividly the continuing

Table 6.4

PERSONS MENTIONED AS INFLUENTIALS AND NUMBER OF TIMES MENTIONED BY RACE AND SOCIO-RESIDENTIAL GROUP

Influentials	Total	Black	Mill Village	Old Suburban	New Suburban
			White		
Banker*	29	28	—	1	—
Banker	29	—	—	4	25
Dentist*	21	21	—	—	—
Minister*	19	19	—	—	—
Publisher, Editor	17	—	3	5	9
School Principal*	15	15	—	—	—
Textile Executive	15	—	1	3	9
Textile Executive	13	—	—	2	11
Bank Vice-President	12	—	—	2	10
Textile Executive	12	—	—	6	6
Publisher	10	—	2	4	4
Textile Executive	10	—	1	3	6

*Black

legacy of segregation in the experience of most whites and blacks in American communities; *leaders* of the two communities get to know each other through their negotiations on community problems involving both races, but awareness so acquired is not widely shared in the respective racial communities. Among other things this means that corporate relationships between whites and blacks in Gastonia remain highly mediated through leaders who are not publicly identifiable as a total group.

For different reasons, the absence from the list of a person related to a non-locally-owned industry is equally striking. We know from the history already recorded above, for example, that the executive heads of the local Firestone and Burlington plants could be persons of considerable influence on certain issues in that history. But the picture which most white citizens in 1967 apparently had of the local "power stucture" was little different from the one that they might well have had twenty years before. Only one of the seven executives named is a post-1945 newcomer to Gastonia, and five out of seven are related to Textiles, Inc. or the local bank closely associate with that corporation. Assessments of these perceptions are subject to many different interpretations, but one minimal interpretation has to be that as of 1967 Gastonians had little sense of change in the structure of "white power" in the community during the past two decades. In particular (since we allowed our respondents to identify a leader in terms of an organization), few are aware of people exercising *actual* power in the community whose power *base* is outside Gastonia. Like citizens of many another urban region, they are in fact subject to an increasing diffusion of the locus of organized power influencing their lives, but they have fewer and fewer names and faces in their minds to associate with that power. The problems growing out of this diffusion, for the Gastonias of America, are many. As one student of the subject summarizes it:

While their economic position has made the managers seem to be the appropriate and duty-bound incumbent of top local civic statuses, their lack of family legitimacy and enduring local residence identification in the community makes them more the representatives of a foreign power than the rightful chiefs of the local tribe. . . . Re-establishing a valued legitimate elite structure in the local community is a major and possibly insoluble task.[164]

2. Church participation, social class, and racial attitudes.   A puzzling relationship between historical and sociological data emerged from our study of the often-researched question of possible correlations between social class, religious orientation, and race-related attitudes in Gastonia. The findings of much recent research on this question have themselves been somewhat inconsistent. Lack of conclusive evidence may derive in part from the inadequacy of measures of class, often defined too broadly to include a wide range of objective, discrete variables.[165] In our social survey of 1966-67, we chose to focus on three major components of social class—occupation, income, and education. In addition religious factors such as participation, type of congregation, and beliefs were examined.

A number of investigations have found an inverse relationship between education and prejudice.[166] The negative relationship between education and prejudice may be explained by personality factors which are related, in turn, to both of these variables. On the other hand, several studies suggest that people with white collar occupations are more fearful of neighborhood integration than those with blue-collar occupations,[167] but this is only one expression of the prejudicial attitude.

Methodological variations—such as different measures of religiosity and racial attitudes—may also partially explain inconsistencies in findings concerning religious commitment and prejudice. This conclusion is supported by a recent review of numerous studies which also reports other pertinent findings:[168] the average, moderately active church member "is more prejudiced than the average nonmember"; however, the highly active were generally "more tolerant."

It appeared that holding a strong value position which allowed one to stand outside of the value traditions of society at large was crucial in adopting a nonprejudicial position and was typical of both nonreligious and highly religious people.

No position can be currently drawn about the role of the institutional church in developing or reducing prejudice.[169]

Our data on Gastonia suggest that the relationship between racial attitudes and socio-economic status in *this* community is more complex than might be predicted from the findings of certain of these other studies. In order to examine these relationships locally, the investigators utilized two Likert-type attitude questions, to compare answers within various social categories. The attitude-questions were:

(1) "The church should have been the first organization to open its doors to Negroes."
(2) "Race should not have anything to do with getting a job."

A majority of our respondents agreed with both of these items. White ministers were more liberal in their attitudes toward racial integration and opportunities for minorities than the laity, as Jeffrey Hadden has suggested.[170] Ninety-five percent of the thirty-seven clergymen who were asked endorsed these statements.

When respondents' education, occupation and income were related to attitudes toward race, the data, as presented in tables 6.5 and 6.6, indicated different patterns for males and females and variations according to the class index being used. The *least* educated white males were most willing to open the church doors to blacks; but the same must be said for high-white-collar males when the occupational index is employed. Moreover, about four-fifths (81.3%) of the white female high school graduates and three-fourths (73.7%) of the college-educated white females favored the integration of the church, compared to slightly over half of their male counterparts. High-school-educated females and high-blue-collar males were the groups most likely to favor the elimination of job discrimination. The relationship between income and racial attitudes appears to be indirect at best: those with annual family incomes less than $4,000 were least likely to favor integration and the elimination of job discrimination. If one judges from these items and this sample, social class, as measured here, seems to be a rather unreliable predictor of racial attitudes in Gastonia.

What about the factors of church participation, denomination or type of congregation attended? Here the intergroup comparisons yield no clear pattern, but this in itself helps break the alleged stereotypical association between sectarian religion, low social class, and racial prejudice among southern whites. Using the same questions—"The church should have been the first organization to open its doors to Negroes" and "Race should have nothing to do with getting a job"—our findings are consistent with those of some other researchers. Data in Table 6.7 suggest that whites who participate in church most actively through weekly attendance and participation in some church organization are most likely to agree with both statements. However, the apparent influence of church participation is clearer for the church integration item. (In terms of denominational or organizational categories, it is of some interest that Methodists are least likely to feel that the church should have led in integration. Considerably fewer Methodists agreed with both statements than any other denomination, including sectarians.) Again, such data raise the questions regarding the association of social factors and prejudice, particularly the suggestion that it is the sectarians who are most likely to be prejudiced against blacks.

One more salient datum is worth noting here: *in virtually every case respondent support for equal job opportunity was stronger than the conviction that the church should have been the first institution to integrate.* This preference for economic over religious-institutional integration is itself intriguing in the Gastonia context, and for some readers it will be part of the puzzle which these statistics pose for the historical-sociological understanding of the

Table 6.5

PROPORTION OF LAITY AGREEING THAT "THE CHURCH SHOULD HAVE
BEEN THE FIRST ORGANIZATION TO OPEN ITS DOORS TO NEGROES"
BY RACE, SEX, AND SOCIAL CHARACTERISTICS

| | Race and Sex | | | | | | | |
| | Black | | | | White | | | |
Social Characteristics	Male Percent	N	Female Percent	N	Male Percent	N	Female Percent	N
Total *	88.5	61	90.1	71	54.9	175	61.5	91
Income								
Less than $4,000	90.5	21	92.3	26	38.9	18	48.3	29
$4,000-$6,999[a]	87.5	16	(66.7)	(6)	56.7	67	67.9	28
$7,000-$9,999[b]	—	—	—	—	72.2	18	(77.8)	(9)
$10,000 and over	—	—	—	—	56.6	53	—	—
Occupation								
High white collar[c]	(100.0)	(8)	—	—	63.2	57	(85.7)	(7)
Low white collar	—	—	—	—	23.8	21	66.7	27
High blue collar[d]	85.8	49	76.2	51	57.9	19	48.1	31
Low blue collar	—	—	—	—	54.7	64	—	—
Education								
8 years or less	91.4	35	92.9	42	61.2	49	47.4	38
9-11 years	85.8	14	80.0	15	43.9	41	58.8	17
High school grad[e]	80.0	10	92.9	14	60.0	35	81.3	16
Some college or more	—	—	—	—	53.1	49	73.7	19
Age								
College students[f]	—	—	—	—	62.9	27	—	—
39 or less	66.7	12	94.4	18	46.1	52	65.6	32
40-49	95.0	20	77.8	18	62.5	48	60.9	23
50-59	92.9	14	100.0	13	65.2	46	63.1	19
60 and over	100.0	13	91.7	12	37.5	24	56.3	16
Length of Residence								
Less than 20 years	(100.0)	(7)	92.3	13	45.8	57	64.3	28
20 years or more	88.9	54	89.7	58	59.3	118	60.3	63

*Does not include students

a. For blacks, $4,000 and over
b. For white females, $7,000 and over
c. For blacks, white collar respondents are combined
d. For blacks and white females, blue collar respondents are combined
e. For blacks, high school grad or more
f. There were too few college students in our sample to subdivide according to sex.
   Age categories which follow refer to adults.

Table 6.6

PROPORTION OF LAITY AGREEING THAT "RACE SHOULD NOT HAVE ANYTHING TO DO WITH GETTING A JOB" BY SOCIAL CHARACTERISTICS

Social Characteristics	Race and Sex							
	Black				White			
	Male Percent	N	Female Percent	N	Male Percent	N	Female Percent	N
Total *	100.0	61	94.4	71	74.0	177	74.7	91
Income								
Less than $4,000	100.0	21	92.3	26	50.0	18	65.5	29
$4,000-$6,999[a]	100.0	16	100.0	12	80.6	67	82.1	28
$7,000-$9,999[b]	—	—	—	—	77.8	18	(66.7)	(9)
$10,000 and over	—	—	—	—	79.7	54	(88.9)	(9)
Occupation								
High white collar[c]	(100.0)	(8)	(100.0)	(3)	81.0	58	(85.7)	(7)
Low white collar	—	—	—	—	54.5	22	85.2	27
High blue collar[d]	100.0	48	96.1	51	89.5	19	64.6	31
Low blue collar	—	—	—	—	70.3	64	—	—
Education								
8 years or less	100.0	37	97.6	41	75.5	49	68.8	38
9-11 years	100.0	14	87.5	16	63.4	41	58.8	17
High school grad[e]	100.0	10	100.0	14	80.5	36	93.7	16
Some college or more	—	—	—	—	76.0	50	84.2	19
Age								
College students[f]	—	—	—	—	74.0	27	—	—
39 or less	100.0	12	100.0	18	67.9	53	64.4	32
40-49	100.0	20	100.0	18	73.4	49	69.6	23
50-59	100.0	14	100.0	13	80.4	46	68.4	19
60 and over	100.0	13	83.3	12	75.0	24	68.8	16
Length of Residence								
Less than 20 years	(100.0)	(7)	92.3	13	70.1	57	82.1	28
20 years or more	100.0	54	94.8	58	75.8	120	71.4	63

*Does not include students

a. For blacks, $4,000 and over

b. For white females, $7,000 and over

c. For blacks, white collar respondents are combined

d. For blacks and white females, blue collar respondents are combined

e. For blacks, high school grad or more

f. There were too few college students in our sample to subdivide according to sex.
   Age categories which follow refer to adults.

Table 6.7

PROPORTION OF LAITY AGREEING WITH STATEMENTS ABOUT
RACE, BY RELIGIOUS PREFERENCE AND PARTICIPATION

Race and Religious Preference and Participation	Statements			
	Church Open First		Race Have Nothing To Do With Job	
	Percent	N	Percent	N
Denominational Preference				
White				
Baptist	73.8	122	83.7	123
Methodist	56.7	60	81.7	60
Presbyterian	84.6	39	92.3	39
Sect	78.4	19	84.2	19
Other	86.2	29	90.0	30
Black				
Baptist	66.3	80	77.5	80
Methodist and				
Presbyterian	40.0	35	71.4	35
Other	57.1	14	64.3	14
Type of Congregation Attended				
White				
Uptown	55.9	59	73.8	61
Transitional	54.3	81	71.6	81
Middle Class	73.5	34	85.3	34
Sect	55.6	18	88.9	18
Black				
Uptown	91.8	61	98.4	61
Sect	84.6	13	84.6	13
Sect-Church Beliefs				
White				
Sect type	63.8	58	86.2	58
2	47.4	38	65.8	38
3	78.0	77	87.0	77
Church type	74.2	58	82.8	58
Black				
Sect type	67.8	28	71.4	28
2	47.4	38	65.8	38
3	61.7	34	73.6	34
Church type	46.4	28	75.0	28
Index of Participation				
White				
High	80.2	93	87.3	94
2	66.7	21	85.7	21
3	65.1	43	86.4	44
4	66.7	21	85.7	21
Low	70.4	91	81.5	92
Black				
High	56.2	73	72.6	73
2	57.1	28	82.2	28
Low	67.9	28	71.4	28

community's way of behaving on the race issue. All these data, in fact, call for some understanding in a larger framework of interpretation than is inherent in the data themselves—such a framework as we endeavor to set forth below.

Summary and Conclusion

We can claim few clear answers to the question: have the churches made positive contributions to the change of attitudes and behavior in race relations in Gastonia? But the clearest positive answer for both attitude and behavior emerges from our investigation of the *black* churches. In terms of apparent attitudes, white churchmen cast a majority vote for a desegregated church, and white clergy cast an overwhelming vote for the same. But a large majority of almost all groups believe that the time has come to eliminate discrimination by race in the labor market. As a priority, economic integration is viewed as more important than religious integration. Whether religious conviction and training have contributed to a sense of marketplace justice, whether a belated sense of the "American dream" reinforced by government decree has recently influenced our respondents, or whether these values continue to be abstractions only worth recording in an interview, are questions subject to diverse judgments. It has been our judgment here, based on the judgments of Gastonians themselves, that the churches, albeit fitfully, have been influences for change in this region of the community's life.

Table 6.8

PROPORTION OF RESPONDENTS WHO AGREE THAT "WHITE PEOPLE TEND TO NOTICE THE NEGRO ONLY WHEN HE ORGANIZES AND PUTS THE PRESSURE ON," BY RACE AND SEX

Race and Sex	Percent Agreeing	Number of Cases
Whites		
Male	40.1	177
Female	42.9	91
Black		
Male	68.9	62
Female	56.9	72
College Students	37.0	27
Ministers: White only	57.9	38

Table 6.9

PROPORTION OF RESPONDENTS WHO BELIEVE THAT THERE SHOULD
BE DISCUSSIONS OF SOCIAL AND POLITICAL ISSUES IN THEIR CHURCHES,
BY RACE, SEX, AND SOCIAL CHARACTERISTICS

Social Characteristics	Race and Sex							
	Black				White			
	Male Percent	N	Female Percent	N	Male Percent	N	Female Percent	N
Income								
Less than $4,000	81.3	16	64.7	17	38.5	13	65.4	26
$4,000-$6,999[a]	81.3	16	(66.7)	(6)	64.7	51	81.3	16
$7,000-$9,999[b]	–	–	–	–	83.3	18	(62.5)	(8)
$10,000 and over	–	–	–	–	71.7	46	(55.6)	(9)
Occupation								
High white collar[c]	–	–	(33.3)	(3)	70.6	51	(71.4)	(7)
Low white collar	–	–	–	–	73.7	19	78.3	23
High blue collar[d]	70.7	41	57.9	38	66.7	15	60.7	28
Low blue collar	–	–	–	–	56.3	48	–	–
Education								
8 years or less	70.4	27	53.3	30	59.0	39	64.5	31
9-11 years	76.9	13	53.8	13	54.8	31	57.1	14
High school grad[e]	(77.8)	(9)	(88.9)	(9)	78.6	14	84.6	13
Some college or more	–	–	–	–	65.9	41	70.0	20
Age								
College students[f]	–	–	–	–	95.7	23	–	–
39 or less	(77.8)	(9)	78.6	14	61.4	44	78.6	28
40-49	88.9	18	62.5	16	76.9	39	63.6	22
50-59	66.7	12	(44.4)	(9)	61.1	36	56.3	16
60 and over	(55.6)	(9)	(50.0)	(8)	50.0	22	75.0	12
Length of Residence								
Less than 20 years	(87.5)	(8)	69.2	13	63.3	49	61.5	26
20 years or more	72.1	43	60.0	25	65.3	98	72.2	54

a. For blacks, $4,000 and over.
b. For white females, $7,000 and over.
c. For blacks, white collar respondents are combined.
d. For blacks and white females, blue collar respondents are combined
e. For blacks, high school grad or more
f. There were too few college students in our sample to subdivide according to sex.
  Age categories which follow refer to adults.

Table 6.10

PROPORTION OF RESPONDENTS AWARE OF DENOMINATIONAL STANDS ON SOCIAL ISSUES BY RACE, SEX, AND SOCIAL CHARACTERISTICS

Social Characteristics	Race and Sex							
	Black				White			
	Male Percent	N	Female Percent	N	Male Percent	N	Female Percent	N
Income								
Less than $4,000	28.6	21	16.0	25	0	16	13.8	29
$4,000-$6,999[a]	18.8	16	(0)	(7)	28.6	63	18.8	16
$7,000-$9,999[b]	–	–	–	–	38.9	18	(22.2)	(9)
$10,000 and over	–	–	–	–	45.8	48	(66.7)	(9)
Occupation								
High white collar[c]	–	–	(33.3)	(3)	51.9	52	(57.1)	(7)
Low white collar	–	–	–	–	31.8	22	37.0	27
High blue collar[d]	27.7	47	16.0	50	22.2	18	12.9	31
Low blue collar	–	–	–	–	15.5	58	–	–
Education								
8 years or less	26.5	34	10.0	40	24.4	45	18.4	38
9-11 years	7.1	14	7.7	13	26.3	38	0	16
High school grad[e]	60.0	10	50.0	16	17.1	35	26.7	15
Some college or more	–	–	–	–	52.3	44	65.0	20
Age								
College students[f]	–	–	–	–	56.5	23	–	–
39 or less	25.0	12	27.8	18	20.4	49	31.3	32
40-49	26.3	19	10.0	20	4.7	43	43.5	23
50-59	33.3	15	25.0	12	34.9	43	10.5	19
60 and over	25.0	12	9.1	11	26.1	23	13.3	15
Length of Residence								
Less than 20 years	30.0	10	6.3	16	25.5	51	34.5	29
20 years or more	26.4	53	19.0	58	32.2	115	23.8	63

a. For blacks, $4,000 and over.

b. For white females, $7,000 and over.

c. For blacks, white collar respondents are combined.

d. For blacks and white females, blue collar respondents are combined.

e. For blacks, high school grad or more.

f. There were too few college students in our sample to subdivide according to sex. Age categories which follow refer to adults.

We may clarify our own interpretation of the historical and sociological evidence if we conclude with a bit of explicit agreement and gentle debate with certain other sociologists who have written on this subject. Three of them are especially important for our dealing with these data: Liston Pope, J. Milton Yinger, and Jeffrey Hadden.

1. Our study of institutional relationships in Gastonia has reaffirmed, with Pope, the impressive influence of gross economic and political forces over human behavior. Again and again the "moral" factors in social change have waited for the strong assist of these "self-interest" factors. Pope was eminently realistic when he called attention in his study to the tendency of church leaders to jump on the bandwagons of change once the latter had gathered momentum in society at large. Pope notes that:

Ministers who had not been concerned previously with the application of moral judgments to the particular issue in question, suddenly see its new relevance and sanction the change as being for the general welfare of the community.[171]

Elimination of children in the mills was effected only when economic advantage reinforced considerations of moral and social welfare to decree their dismissal.[172]

Our only disagreement with the implications of such observations by Pope and others is that the power of a "two-factor" push for change must still be counted as larger than a single-factored push. It is worth remembering, in the context of the civil rights movement, that the economic *dis*advantages of the segregated system were an insufficient condition to rouse large numbers of black Americans to join public demonstrations against civil injustices. One of the added ingredients that galvanized them into new activity on behalf of their own economic interests was the ingredient of moral conviction. And, if one accepts no less than a double-motivation theory of the social behavior of some blacks in recent American history, one is bound also to accept it in connection with the social behavior of some whites. It is too easy to dismiss even the employment integration issue with the observation that economic profit at last overwhelmed discriminatory employment policies in Gastonia industries. The absence of crisis in this transition is itself an event requiring a more subtle, complementary set of explanations. Among the latter, we recall again a feature of the southern Piedmont culture—the mutedness of its antagonism against blacks—and the features of the "Gastonia ideology"—Progress and Harmony—that are vital ingredients to the choice between economic growth and racial discrimination: when Gastonians "really want" the one over the other, that very preference is suffused with cultural as well as dollars-and-cents logic. As is demonstrated by the case of some textile plants in the south whose managers preferred closing to unionization, people may be willing to pay (or lose) various amounts of money as "tribute" to their social-political convictions. For a century the southern wage worker has been paying such tribute to his racial prejudices, but the analytical-interpretative principle here is again one indebted to Hannah Arendt and Max Weber: power-relations between subgroups in a society are more likely to change quickly and permanently when "cultural" reasons and "coercive" reasons are combined. It is the elective affinity of philosophical politics and *realpolitik* that, in the end, is the most powerful politics of all. Some of Pope's perspectives on the Gastonia of the thirties tended to denigrate this perspective; we think that a more critical, Weberian balance in his analysis would have improved it.

2. J. Milton Yinger makes much the same point as does Pope when he observes in *The Scientific Study of Religion*:

> If it took two decades after the beginning of serious industrial conflict—expressive of the problems faced by workers in a new industrial society—before American churchmen began to give more than passing attention to the issue, it was four or five decades after the first stirrings of the civil rights movement before a significant number of churchmen began to struggle with the problems faced by black Americans.[173]

In this study we have met many leaders of the Gastonia churches who would oppose Yinger's perspective at a very basic value-concept level: what he would be likely to call "paternalism" in the churches and in the culture of southern industrial communities, these church leaders would advance as a way of recognizing and dealing with the problems of both industrial workers and blacks. The reply would not be utterly off the target of sociological interest, either, because—if our conclusions about the church and labor unionism in Gastonia are correct—just this conceptual system underlies the powerful resistance to unions and civil rights organizations in the local culture.

Our caveat with Yinger is not so philosophical; it is more strategic: does he not implicitly have a moral expectation of institutions *generally* that little in their history gives us grounds to entertain? Institutions are characteristically changed, if at all, by small numbers of people, certainly at the beginning of movements for their change. Moreover, certain social evils—such as child labor—are supported by an interlaced network of relationships among various institutions. This has always been part of the wisdom of Marxian analysis, but even Marx did not expect "great" institutions to reform themselves without being shaken by large external forces or subverted from within by a disciplined cadre of revolutionaries. One of Marx's critical mistakes, of course, was his failure to grapple profoundly enough with the problems of the corruptibility of the institutions founded by revolutionaries, but of the conservatism and the interlocking injustices of most historic institutional arrangements, he was profoundly conscious. That consciousness is appropriate even for us who analyze religious institutions and their relationship to other institutions. Put another way, our reply to Yinger is merely that the injustices of slavery and the subsequent injustices of industrialism in American history were cancers at the roots, pathologies infecting the *spectrum*, of institutions in American society. The minority of persons who came forward at last to fight these injustices often had to form *new* institutions—typically voluntary associations—because in *all* of their current institutional affiliations they were discouraged from attending to these controversial issues. What single American institution should be granted a clean bill of health on the matter of slavery? From the beginning of the nation, government, surely, was no model institution for real justice for black Americans. Eleven years after the Declaration of Independence some of its very authors helped contrive an institution of government that officially recognized slavery and even temporarily recognized the slave trade. The contradiction between ideal and material interests, so strange an inconsistency in this Constitution (strange to moralists and logicians, not to politicians) was to become a central theme and bone of contention in American history. Yet one cannot explain American history without recognizing the combined powers of: the ideals in the Declaration, the economic interests written into the Constitution, and the longterm conflict between the two in the 200 years of this nation's political existence. Such was Gunnar Myrdal's thesis over 30 years ago, a thesis still very useful for interpreting American political history as a whole.[174]

This dynamic in American politics has analogies in many other American institutions—most certainly in the churches. Indeed, in every society where religious organizations are rather closely identified with a large proportion of citizenry or a wide cross section of them, the structure of the religious organization will *incorporate* much of the structure of the whole society. In this sense the churches, because they still number in their ranks something like a majority of Americans are as likely and as unlikely a place to "fight evil" as any other institutional sector of the society. Only a sectarian, moriastic idealism will expect any historic religious organization to be composed primarily of saints and martyrs—a tiny minority of human beings, often the creative minority who bring change to a society after much struggle. Sometimes these saints and martyrs find their inspiration in "ordinary" religious organizations from which they separate themselves as prophets. But the prophet is a rare person, and no institution has a monopoly on the power to produce such persons.

To speak this way, of course, is to distinguish between the many "levels" of what an institution is: majorities and minorities; voluntary and involuntary arrangements; values that apparently transcend the best of human effort and that plainly sit in judgment upon the worst; laws and rules "more honor'd in the breach than the observance" but not absolutely dishonored. A sociological

observation of this sort, of course, is no justification or excuse for the hypoc-
risies that attend all or some men's institution-building and institution-main-
tenance. But it does put churches on a sociological par with all other institutions; and it suggests that theologian D. T. Jenkins is sociologically correct in
saying that "as an institution, the Church is as secular as any other."[175] In the
context of the foregoing analysis, it may also be said that other institutions are
as "holy" as the church—in that other institutions have their inevitable negotiations with values, norms, ideological standards of excellence, that transcend
their performance. They too fall short of behaving in conformity with their own
culture; so that holiness, which may be ascribed to the culture, is not ascribed to
the performance. In this sense, textile companies that render approximate
obedience to federal fair employment standards are both as secular and as holy
as the churches. The theological side of D. T. Jenkins' mind would probably
add that holiness has never, in the Christian tradition, inhered in any institution
whatsoever, certainly not in the church, nor in the political state nor in the
business corporation, indeed, in nothing human at all.

3. A final word of dialogue with a recent writer on the subject of the church
and race relations: Jeffrey Hadden. Seldom pretending to a completely "value-
free" stance towards the church in its record of opposition to racism in modern
America, Hadden is frank to introduce his empirical survey of the matter with
the judgment:

> Of all the areas of criticism, the lack of aggressive action in race relations has
> emerged as the most critical indicator of the church's commitment to the status quo. The
> picture of eleven o'clock on Sunday morning as the most racially segregated hour in
> America has flashed across the nation and around the world as a symbol of American
> religion.[176]

The gist of our dialogue with Hadden is this: that there is more politics and
more social ethics in the segregated church hour in America than usually meets
the moralist's eye. If one wanted merely to defend the churches on a "could-
be-worse" basis, of course, one could make a good empirical case for the
counter-aphorism that the most segregated hour in America is the country-club
cocktail hour—in the mid-sixties this was literally the case in Gastonia. But
with more pertinence one could point out also that at noncongregational levels
the denominations of Protestantism have labored hard in the past twenty years
to overcome segregation in the supra-congregational organization of themselves. That some major Protestant bodies (the Methodists for example) have
only completed their official self-integration as late as 1972, provides only one
more example of how the problems of behaviorally achieving the charter-ideals
of church bodies are strictly analogous to the problem in the other institutions of

the society. Yet because of such halting efforts, some southern Protestants testify that their first meaningful touch with an "integrated society" was in denominational church meetings. One can find this particular testimony in Gastonia.[177]

The picture of "progress" on the interracial front, however, is fitful at best in the churches; and the sluggishness of this progress is an appropriate target for the church leader's own moral criticism—no more and no less an appropriate target than is the American Constitution in light of the Declaration of Independence. As Hadden's and our own data show clearly, the large majority of clergy are aware of the discrepancy between the ethical demands of the Christian religion and the institutional segregation of the churches.[178] But the discrepancy is not absolute; indeed, from the standpoint of *some* of the ethical demands of the religion, the current state of segregatedness has positive justification. Premature moralizing about segregated hours of worship can easily overlook the meaning of the fact that few black church leaders in Gastonia or anywhere else in American during the sixties devoted much energy to the cause of integrating congregations and denominations. The very formation of black congregations and denominations, as is well known, grew out of black Christians' desire to control their religious associations and thereby to acquire the power which accrues to any organized social group. American blacks have jealously guarded the independence of their churches—for more than a century what other organized social entity belonged to them? And what is true of blacks in American church history has been just as obviously true of disadvantaged whites, as Liston Pope and other chroniclers of sectarianism have demonstrated. In an exceedingly rugged, political sense, therefore, what church membership means to members of "oppressed classes" in American society is likely to constitute a strong deterrent to hasty desegregation of that prolix mixture of small religious fellowships called local churches in cities like Gastonia. Most of those churches have less than 200 members. From mill-village times onward, many served as places for psychological retreat from worldly care; and for this function the small, homogeneous-class membership pattern was well fitted. Many served unwittingly as training grounds for the socialization of marginal and semimarginal persons whose only experience of "leadership" was in a church.[179] It would not be *these* persons, in short, who could be counted on to think most kindly of any change in ecclesiastical membership patterns that might undermine this social function of the church.

To be sure, blacks in considerably larger proportions than whites in Gastonia believe that the (white church) should have been "the first organization to open its doors to Negroes." Though it is a belated sociological hypothesis (too late to be included in our survey), a smaller proportion of black respondents would probably have been enthusiastic about the companion proposition: "The black church should welcome into its membership any number of whites who sincerely want to join." Until the day when racial prejudice is truly a thing of the past in American society at large, the self-interest of the black community may have much to lose from any such over-integration of the churches. Black churchmen are typically clear-minded on the non-racial nature of the *normative theological* church, but they are as typically realistic about the importance of maintaining for the American present a black church base for assisting *the politics of social justice* in this society. There are strain and tension between this theological and this ethical-political view of ecclesiastical policy, but it is not inconsistent in human terms. People build institutions for more than one purpose, and measure their efficacy according to more than one criterion —there are, after all, ten commandments in the Judeo-Christian tradition. Further, in the fitful pursuit of their own institutional charter-ideals, human beings distinguish between an ideal that is desirable ultimately and one that takes active priority now. Gastonian churchpeople, black and white, seem to agree that economic justice takes priority for now over ecclesiastical integration. If pressed, they might even articulate some form of the insight that a segregated church, in the grey social world of mixed good and evil, does a kind of justice to the needs of some oppressed people—all the while ironically serving to fortify injustice by perpetuating the illusion of racial superiority among some of these same people. Even while affirming the proximate use of a segregated church, therefore, such churchpeople might affirm its ultimate dispensability.

It is a moralistic rather than a socio-political understanding, in short, that abandons the segregated churches of Gastonia to the darkness of hypocrisy while applauding the political and economic forces that may now be bringing new human opportunity to black people in the same society. Had it not been for a segregated black church, some of that opportunity might be missing in today's Gastonia. This is not to disagree with Hadden's counsel to ministers and other church leaders that, especially in relation to racist attitudes among whites, "mechanisms of rationalization" for those attitudes must be patiently "stripped away." Our own parallel counsel is merely: no person or institution should have a rationalization stripped away before the *use* of that rationalization to him, to her, to it has been well understood. It is the first office of the social sciences, perhaps, to assist in that understanding.

NOTES

1. Cf. *MP*, Preface, p. x: "Of 12,392 Negroes in the county in 1930, less than 400 were employed in cotton mills, and even these were marginal workers."

2. *Population and Economy: Gaston County: Projected to 1990*, Traffic and Planning Associates, Hickory, North Carolina, (n.d., c. 1967), p. 11.

3. Cf. above, p. 65.

4. As early as 1940, for example, race-related editorials in the *GG* were calling for an abolition of "two kinds of justice, one for the man with pull or money and the other for the man without a friend at court." And in the same year the editor chastized the white community for not doing its part in the "heroic effort" of the black community "to advance their position." (*GG*, January 19, 1940; April 10, 1940)

5. *GG*, September 5, 1942. The editorial went on to ask the "fine, intelligent, conservative Negro leaders . . . the teachers and the preachers, the Scout leaders" to "counteract these unsafe and unreasonable rumors" of organized protest against the local wage scale.

6. *GG*, July 29, 1943.

7. *GG*, July 17, 1944.

8. Published as part of Ben E. Atkins' weekly column, *GG*, May 31, 1947. Such a setting gave this letter considerably more prominence than it would have had as an ordinary letter to the editor and showed Atkins' basic sympathy with the letter's point of view.

9. Howard W. Odum, *Race and Rumors of Race* (Chapel Hill: University of North Carolina Press, 1943), p. 171, as quoted by George B. Tindall, *The Emergence of the New South* (Baton Rouge: Louisiana State University Press, 1967), p. 716.

10. *GG*, October 17, 1950.

11. *GG*, November 21, 1943.

12. *GG*, March 14, 1945.

13. Cf. *GG*, November 8, 1955. The most prestigious private golf course in the community, at the Gaston Country Club, was another matter.

14. *GG*, September 23, 1952; June 8, 1954.

15. *GG*, June 4, June 16, August 20, September 23, 1949.

16. One of the hospitals, the largest, was county-government supported; the other was a private hospital.

17. *GG*, June 6, 1950.

18. *GG*, March 30, 1950.

19. Interview, June 1966.

20. Though it formally voted to admit black doctors to its membership in 1955, the Gaston County Medical Society claimed no such members as late as 1963. By that date, local black doctors were lodging formal requests to be allowed to practice in Gaston Memorial Hospital in the wake of that hospital's use of funds under the Hill-Burton Act and, in that same year, in a bow to financial, political, and professional realism, Gaston Memorial Hospital hired its first three black nurses. From precisely this same time the upsurge of black employment in the local textile mills took its beginnings. *GG*, June 7, 1955; November 15, 1963; April 3, 1963.

21. *GG*, June 5, 1951.

22. *GG*, December 2, 1953.

23. *GG*, October 17, 1950.

24. *GG*, April 29, 1947. The range of votes for the five victorious uptowners was 1347 to 1054. The No. 6 vote dropped to 664, the No. 7—and east Gastonian—to 632; and the other five candidates drew from 420 to 97 votes.

25. *GG*, December 7, 1948.

26. LeGette Blythe, *Robert Lee Stowe: Pioneer in Textiles*, (Belmont: North Carolina, 1965), p. 237.

27. Interview with resident of Belmont, March 1971. Stowe died in 1963 at the age of

ninety-six. His record for long-term office-holding was in Belmont's First Presbyterian Church, which he served as treasurer for seventy years. Cf. Blythe, *op. cit.*, pp. 151-153.

28. An uneventful council election in 1949 drew 1,241 voters, about 5% of the population. A local utility-bond election, requiring a special registration, had 586 participants, while a school board election that same spring, which in previous years had drawn as few as 100 voters, turned out a "heavy vote" of 919. The school board election in the spring of 1953, on the other hand, apparently overshadowed by the council election of that year, saw participation of a grand total of 57. *GG*, April 2, 1951; March 5, 1951; March 7, 1951.

29. A state bond issue election for schools and mental hospitals in 1951, on the other hand, drew just under 2000 voters from the county population of 110,000.

30. *GG*, advertisement, April 20, 1951.

31. *GG*, April 23, 1951. The newspaper published the current registration list of all 10,000 names, asking citizens to check for their own names. Some of the new registrations came from sections of the city recently annexed.

32. *GG*, April 25, 1951, on the authority of the City Clerk.

33. One of the Yancey-team trio failed to be elected, and David Gillespie, a fourth independent—independent of the Independents—took the second spot in the election returns, 300 votes behind Yancey. The two "establishment" candidates ran third and fifth in the field, with 2205 and 2087 votes respectively.

34. *GG*, May 1, 1951. In the 1950-60 period some 8,000 blacks were residents of Gastonia Township, out of its population of 49,000. An estimated 5,000 of these lived in the City of Gastonia, out of its population of 23,000. Cf. *Population and Economy: Gaston County*, pp. 2, 12.

35. Yancey's teammate Gillespie was a staff member of the newspaper; the third independent was an automobile dealer while the two conservatives were a downtown stationery store owner and an official of the Citizens National Bank.

36. *GG*, May 9, 1951.

37. *GG*, July 11, 1952.

38. Quoted in an editorial column of the *Gazette*, February 5, 1952. *GG*, June 30, 1974 lists assets of $1.9 million.

39. This prompted the editors of *Life* to send a reporter to Gastonia in early 1955 to discover what manner of change was going on in this little town, these twenty-five years after its infamous strike. *GG*, April 13, 1955.

40. *GG*, March 18, 1953. At one point in the spring campaign, the pro- and anti-ward forces fought each other in terms of the choice of a white or a black public school as the site of a public debate on the ward issue. Candidate Barber and a group of three ministers petitioned the school board to change the site of one meeting from a black to a white school to avoid "injecting the racial issue into the debate." In the furor surrounding the affair, one incumbent city councilman accused Yancey of trying to "grab power" by inciting textile workers against millowners, blacks against whites, and one section of the city against another.

41. Early in his second term of office Mayor Yancey attempted to sweep out a large number of "old guard" administrators and other employees in the city government, and for this he lost the support of many crucial leaders in the town, including most of the city council and the newspaper. In the fall of 1953, his enemies brought court proceedings against him for illegal practice as an architect without the required legal licenses. This ruined his business. At this juncture he revealed some of his affinities for the problems addressed by the Populists by attempting to found a People's Credit Union, which would provide its working-class share-holders with free life insurance. *GG*, October 31, 1953.

42. *GG*, May 2, 1953.

43. *GG*, May 4, 1953.

44. *GG*, August 29, 1951.

45. *GG*, December 2, 1953. The plaintiffs made it clear that they were seeking a new school, not the desegregation of the school system but that very demand, the county school superintendent reminded the public, posed severe financial problems. Cf. above, pp. 241-242.

46. *GG*, September 2, 1954.

47. *GG*, September 2, 1954.

48. *GG*, August 26, 1955.

49. *GG*, September 6, 1955.

50. Cf. above, p. 45. (Introduction)

52. Interview, July 9, 1965. This latter minister was first in Gastonia 1953-1959, and was largely responsible for integrating the local Ministerial Association in 1963, during a second term as pastor of a local church.

52. *GG*, May 17, 1954.

53. *GG*, May 21, 1954. The program being filmed was Edward R. Murrow's "See It Now." Yancey's refusal to appear before the cameras was surely motivated in part by the fact that he was so much embroiled in a personal political crisis that he had little to gain politically from appearing on television in connection with this very controversial issue. Nevertheless, his talk about "democracy" on this same occasion suggested that he was ready to go along with the decision: he could not, at any rate, have openly opposed the decision and remained very consistent with his collaboration since 1951 with the local black community.

54. GG, June 4, 1955.

55. In North Carolina, public school policy and financing are centralized rather heavily in the State Department of Public Instruction; and so, especially in contrast with the attempts of other southern state governments to *forbid* localities to desegregate their schools, the Pearsall Plan had about it a show of democratic compromise. A leading state official of this period, interviewed in 1965, observed that the Pearsall Plan was devised as a temporary outlet for citizen frustration. Few of its architects expected it to serve the state's long-range educational needs or to survive the test of the Federal Courts.

56. Two such groups, which both resolved against the plan in the spring of 1956, were the state chapter of the NAACP and the state convention of the National Baptist Church.

57. The North Carolina NAACP immediately after the September 8, 1956 referendum, filed suit against the plan as being unconstitutional, which it was duly declared later by the Supreme Court.

58. It was during the Eisenhower Administration that the Republican Party showed its first signs of consistent strength in Gaston County, as it carried the county for Eisenhower successively by 1,371 votes (1952) and 2,498 votes (1956) in a state which gave its majority both years to Stevenson. Republicans first ran a full slate of local candidates in 1962.

59. *GG*, June 13, 1957.

60. This again is Shriver's impression. During his three years of residing in Gastonia, 1956-59, conversations about impending school desegregation were exceedingly rare. Very few white people seemed to believe that the new law of the land would ever get enforced. Not a single black child in 1960 was attending a white school.

61. Cf. above, pp. 206-210 on the breaks in the latter amity in 1958-59. Gastonia's, first Jewish mayor, a department store owner, was elected in 1955, along with second-term councilman Nathaniel Barber, who managed to maintain his support in the black community while making alliances with a "Good Government" ticket that represented a return to power by the more traditional uptown forces in Gastonia. Both Barber and Marshall Rauch came to enjoy cordial

relations with the "return to normalcy" business leadership that dominated local politics in the 1955-60 period. Barber had some opposition for his seat on the Council in 1955 from Charles S. Hall, pastor of a local Baptist Church, whose members split with some intensity over his candidacy. (The opposition claimed that politics was affecting his church work and that "religion and politics don't mix." *GG*, April 14, 1955.) In 1959, after serving six years on the local council, Barber stepped aside in favor of J. Q. Falls, also a businessman, whose easy election in 1959 and 1961 suggested that Gastonia white voters had come to recognize the utility of having at least one black councilman. One or two white candidates did offer themselves for the predominantly black ward council seat during these years and under the modified ward system requiring all voters to vote on a total slate, these candidates could have been elected. In 1953, Barber was one of three blacks elected to local public office in North Carolina; in 1959-60, Falls was one of eight. Cf. *GG*, October 21, 1961.

62. Williston was a physician. As front page news, the *Gazette* published an account of the backing of his candidacy by the national NAACP. A delegation led by the president of the local NAACP (a minister) demanded a retraction of this news story, claiming that the initiative for the voter registration drive was wholly local. The retraction was granted, on the front page. *GG*, February 28; March 2, 1959.

63. *GG*, February 28 and March 4, 1959. Williston thus got only 23% of the vote. If not quite all black voters voted for him, almost half of the 881 votes were cast by whites. That would have meant one in seven white voters who wanted black representation on their school board.

64. This theme was whistled editorially by the *Gazette* on the occasion of a dinner, attended by 300 local citizens, in honor of Nathaniel Barber's retirement from his six years on the City Council. J. Q. Falls had just been elected to take his place, but the presence of a deep split in white-black attitudes on school integration was now out in the open as never before in the five years since 1954. The Stanley protest had now arrived in the city of Gastonia.

65. *GG*, February 24, 1960.

66. *GG*, September 26, 1960.

67. In the 1960 campaign Lake consistently denied that he favored such a policy. The record showed that in the spring of 1956—when Lake was an assistant attorney general and the state legislature was in the process of passing its "voluntary segregation plan" (the Pearsall Plan) he had indicated in a speech to an Asheboro civic club that if necessary he would favor closing the schools over desegregating them. By 1960 he had either changed his mind or saw such a view as politically unacceptable to the voters of the state, who for many years had been taught by their politicians that education was North Carolina's highroad to "progress." The Sanford forces exploited the 1956 speech to raise doubts about Lake's real devotion to the public school system. (Interviews with two Sanford campaign leaders, April 1965 and February 1972.)

68. As quoted by Graham Jones, "Terry Sanford," in *Messages, Addresses, and Public Papaers of Terry Sanford, Governor of North Carolina, 1961-65*, ed. Memory F. Mitchell (Raleigh: Council of State, 1966), pp. xxiv-xxv. In an interview (January 14, 1972) Jones stated that the closest Sanford ever came in the campaign to using apparently anti-black rhetoric was a remark he took care to make especially in textile communities: "I know how to handle the NAACP!" After election as Governor, Jones relates, one of the rival campaign leaders said, with an exaggeration that testified to Sanford's in-office image as a friend of blacks: "We didn't know that when he said, 'I can handle the NAACP' he meant he'd appoint them to half of the offices in state government."

69. He also became the only southern governor to back John F. Kennedy for the presidential nomination. Only twelve of North Carolina's sixty-odd delegates to the 1960 Los Angeles Convention voted with Sanford for Kennedy. Jones, *ibid.*, p. xxv.

70. *GG*, November 9, 1960. It was in these early 1960s that the Republican Party in Gaston County would mount its first full slate of local candidates. In 1968 it would join with several adjoining counties to elect a Republican congressman.

71. Jones, *Messages*, pp. 277-278. During 1962 North Carolina's relative position actually fell from 42nd to 44th, in spite of a 4% climb in the actual level of income—a fact that Sanford likewise called to the attention of students at North Carolina Agricultural and Technical College in Greensboro. Some of these very students had been the originators of the lunchcounter sit-in movement in the spring of 1960. *Ibid.*, p. 331.

72. Minutes of the Mayor's Committee on Human Relations, October 5, 1960; in the following, notes to be referred to simply as HRC Minutes. For making these minutes and other documents related to the 1960-65 desegregation crisis available, the writers are indebted to the committee, several of whose members have supplemented the following with their own comments in interviews that took place in the years 1965-67.

73. HRC Minutes, May 3, 1962. The only other grievance that the committee apparently discussed was the hiring policy for bus drivers at the local bus company. The committee requested the mayor to inquire with the bus company manager about the hiring of "one or more Negro bus drivers," with the understanding that "no pressure (is) implied in this motion" and that upon objection by the manager "this matter should be dropped." There was objection, and the matter was dropped.

74. *GG*, February 13, 1963. A similar letter followed from a local black college graduate on February 16.

75. Cf. above, footnote 64. Elected to succeed Nathaniel Barber in 1959, black councilman J. Q. Falls shared his sense of Progress in Gastonia at a 1961 meeting of civic leaders in Minneapolis, Minnesota: "How many Negroes do you have on your city council?" he asked rhetorically. The answer was "none."

76. The *GG* went out of its way, just prior to the council election, to editorialize on the excellence of the establishment candidate, whom it commended as a "quiet unassuming man who sets about the task of being a good citizen in an unobtrusive manner," who had served on the mayor's committee for three years, who as president of the local black credit union had "learned the importance of fiscal responsibility and proper business planning," and who— contrary to the wishes of "extreme racists"—would never bow to their demands. On the contrary, "he has . . . worked steadily and continually for the progress of his race." *GG*, May 6, 1963.

77. Interview, June 25, 1965. Though the Jewish community in the South has never been large and though traditional southern race prejudice has focused on the Negro, anti-semitic prejudice has been real enough in the region, of a piece with prejudice against Roman Catholics. Again, the ease with which this small southern Piedmont town apparently avoided or put off some dimensions of race prejudice in its political life is little short of remarkable. Though statistics on Jewish members of city councils in cities of 30,000 in the contemporary South are hard to secure, it seems fair to say that in the 1950s, a city that had two blacks and two Jews successively elected to its council was a real rarity in the South. An official of the Anti-Defamation League expressed his opinion on the matter of Rauch's appointment as chairman of the newly constituted Human Relations Committee, in a letter to another local Jewish industrial leader in July 1963, as follows: ". . . very few of the chairmen in the South . . . are Jewish. I have a feeling that Gastonia will not become the pressure cooker in race relations like Birmingham, Montgomery, Jackson, or many other cities. Therefore, I think Mr. Rauch will be able to play a very constructive role without becoming a prisoner of a crisis situation."

78. All during the early sixties editorials in the *GG* had intoned the rituals of "friendly race relations" that traditionally had prevailed in the town. Great alarm and hostility characterized the newspaper's response to the subject of freedom riders. "Some of them are the scum of the earth,

professional agitators who delight in chaos and confusion. . . . The rumblings can be heard as near as Charlotte. The feeling of interdependence and mutual respect which has long existed between the races is gradually crumbling . . . God forbid that it should ever happen here—and, we don't believe it will." (*GG*, May 29, 1961.)

79. HRC Minutes, June 8, 1963.

80. *Ibid.* Theoretical questions about the urgency of the local race relations crisis were not permitted in this meeting to obscure other agenda items that were to become very practical problems for the committee during the ensuing six months: "colored" signs at the local municipal golf course which had been open to black citizens since 1951; the bus company's continued lack of black bus drivers; the low wages paid most black employees of the city government; the still-segregated theaters; the low quality of health care available at the Gaston County Negro Hospital; and the continued segregation of hotels, motels, and restaurants.

81. Martin Luther King, "Letter from Birmingham City Jail," (Philadelphia: American Friends Service Committee, 1963), p. 9.

82. *GG*, June 11, 1963.

83. The seven-point demand, as communicated to the committee chairman, was:

1. Remove all signs of discrimination and segregation in the court house, play grounds, and all public property.

2. Hire persons based on qualifications and not race in government and private business.

3. Desegregate the police department.

4. Desegregate all facilities (such as hotels, theaters, motels, cafes, restaurants, all eating establishments, and recreational facilities).

5. Desegregate public schools.

6. Desegregate hospitals.

7. In-service training for Negroes in mills for technical and skilled jobs.

84. This and the following statements are based on interviews recorded in more detail in Part II of this volume.

85. *GG*, June 12, 1963.

86. *GG*, May 10, 1963.

87. *GG*, June 22, 1963.

88. Emil Brunner in the introduction of his theological ethics, *The Divine Imperative* (London: Lutterworth Press, 1937) spoke about the "demand for ethics" in the contemporary church. The idea is reminiscent of Max Weber's contention that cultural values, including religion may not fix the "tracks" of social change, but on occasion a society requires values as "switching points" to direct the society down one track or another. Cf. Weber, "The Social Psychology of the World Religions," in Hans H. Gerth and C. Wright Mills, eds., *From Max Weber: Essays in Sociology* (New York: Oxford University Press, 1946) p. 280.

89. The First Methodist Church Administrative Board, on June 27; the First Presbyterian Session on September 9; the First Baptist and the Episcopal Churches, October 21.

90. Interview with minister of First Presbyterian Church, July 2, 1965, and his statement in *GG*, September 21, 1963.

91. Cf. HRC Minutes, July 8, 1963 on one such meeting in Bessemer City.

92. Interview, July 24, 1965. That the King letter was actually distributed to the HRC is partly confirmed by the presence of a copy of the publication in the HRC files.

93. Interview, September 21, 1965. This respondent was a layman from one of the black churches, a member of the HRC, and a member of the "establishment" black leadership group that became established by breaking into Gastonia politics in 1953. Ten years later, it was this group of leaders that was to be under fire from younger elements within the black community.

94. Another black professional informed the researchers that during the first meeting of the first HRC (September 1960) the subject of local lunchcounter desegregation was about to be totally ignored when Moffett's predecessor, James Huggins, the minister of the First Methodist Church, asked the committee to consider the subject. From this small agenda-input, the committee moved rapidly to schedule discussions with all the lunchcounter owners in town. Interview, August 18, 1965.

95. The term "uptown" has only an analogous meaning applied to the black churches, but the analogy is not fanciful. As noted above, the ministers who furnished leadership of the civil rights movement were pastors of the larger, more middle class denominations.

96. HRC Minutes, July 1, and July 8, 1963.

97. *GG*, August 1, 1963. Asked how he thought the city government avoided paying the federal minimum wage to its laborers, a local black minister replied that the city could keep its wages low by "delays in upgrading the worker and by using rehabilitation prisoners." Interview, July 24, 1965. Even the $1.05 hourly wage was only paid to the garbage worker after one year on the job.

98. HRC Minutes July 15, August 5, August 19, October 29, November 11, December 2, 1963; and a succession of other such notations well into 1965. On August 5 the HRC discussed the formation of a Subcommittee on Employment. The Committee concluded that among its members there would have to be "a representative of the power structure of the textile industry . . . possibly Mr. Albert Myers, Jr. and Mr. Allen Sims." Mr. Myers, the Committee noted, "speaks for 16 mills." By December 2 this subcommittee reported that some ten or twelve of these mills now had blacks in new or upgraded jobs.

99. Interview, September 21, 1965.

100. *GG*, August 6, 1963.

101. *The Charlotte Observer*, August 6, 1963. School integration (nine years after the 1954 Supreme Court decision) began in Gastonia with four high school students transferred from black schools, after parents of the four students applied to the local city and county school boards. Interviews two years later in the black community made it clear that ministers of the black churches played a major role in initiating this application. Two of the four students were the children of a local AME Zion minister.

102. *GG*, September 16, 1963. The appeal to religion is palpable and literal in this editorial. The phrase "interrupting a successful building program" comes straight out of the in-house talk of the local uptown Methodist church, to which the editor belonged.

103. The other major holdout was the manager of a local unit of a national motel chain. The theater manager's no to the phalanx of uptown business leaders evidently had a source in something more than immediate fears of losing customers. One of our knowledgeable informants stated that "all of Main Street, including the *Gazette,* was pushing (the theater owner), including the attorneys for the city and bankers. He was fighting Main Street, really because the _____ Bank had refused to lend him some money not long ago." Interview, July 28, 1965. Substantiating this interpretation is the fact that in the summer of 1963 Charlotte theaters desegregated without incident, and Charlotte's example has always tended to set the pace in business in Gastonia.

104. HRC Minutes, September 12, 1963.

105. Interview with black leader, September 21, 1965.

106. These two designations of the older and younger leadership styles were made by one of the activist black ministers. Interview, July 15, 1965.

107. Interview, July 24, 1965. The oscillating use of "we" and "they" in this interview is worthy of note. In a profound sense, the question of which pronoun the black citizen of Gastonia was justified in using, was the whole issue of the civil rights struggle. "They" were the ones who had the strike in 1929; but "we" were trying to get the All America City award. This respondent, in

fact, was one of the two activist black ministers who were interviewed by representatives of *Look* in connection with the All America City contest of 1963. The other minister who gave us this latter information, was much more ambivalent on the All America City issue. "While we were demonstrating in 1963 a local newspaperman came to me to say 'I hope that his demonstrating will not keep us from getting the All America City award.' I told him, 'As far as I can see, this is not an American city.' And I was thinking about the poor whites, too. They suffer as well as the Negroes." Interview, July 15, 1965.

108. Interview, September 21, 1965.

109. Interview, August 8, 1965.

110. Interview, July 28, 1965.

111. Interview, July 15, 1965.

112. Interview, July 24, 1965.

113. *Ibid.*

114. *Ibid.* In this very autumn the Gastonia Ministerial Association was engaged in a debate over its own integration. Since 1953 the Association had been officially open to ministers from the Jewish, Catholic and black Protestant churches. (Interview with Wesleyan Methodist Minister. July 9, 1965.) But the parallel organization of black ministers, the Gaston County Ministerial Alliance, had remained intact, and in this latter group of black ministers the activist push in civil rights was now originating. At a mid-fall meeting, with a show of bad timing that seemed to show bad faith with the cause of integration, the white-dominated Ministerial Association voted to ask the Alliance to integrate "fully" with the larger organization—i.e. to disband. In the debate a young white minister "raised the question of Association support of theater picketing," as a way of showing that the interests of the black community would not get drowned in the proposed consolidation. "But the answer of the Association president was that such support could only be forthcoming by a majority vote, and at this the members of the Alliance decided not to disband their organization." (Interview September 20, 1965 with this white minister.) As the events of the fall unfolded, the Ministerial Association was one of the last community-wide groups in town to offer public support to the work of the Human Relations Committee, following in the train of several local congregations and most of the civic clubs. (The Association resolution backing the HRC was published on January 11, 1964.)

115. Interview, September 21, 1965. He went on to say: "Through history the church has always been an integral part of our way of life, though perhaps that is not as true today as it used to be. Once the church was all we had to turn to." This respondent, as well as some of his peers on the old school leadership team, was not enthusiastic about the demonstration itself. Major criticisms of the demonstration, from their point of view, were that it was ill-timed in relation to the efforts of the HRC and ill-targeted as well. "The older folk thought that it was terrible for a demonstration against a *movie* house to be led by *ministers*. Though I questioned the timing, I supported the purpose of the demonstration. Many of our churches felt strongly about our minister's part in it. It seems we all have different concepts of what our ministers should be." The dismay of the older black parishioners was not helped by the fact that the particular movie to be picketed was entitled "Wives and Lovers," and starred Van Johnson! On the similar variety of ascribed role-definitions largely duplicated in the white churches, but in different proportions of constituency opinion, cf. below, Chapter Seven.

116. HRC Minutes, October 14, 1963.

117. *GG*, October 14, 1963.

118. *GG*, October 14, 1963.

119. *GG*, October 17, 1963. It was some further evidence of a dogged, formal local adherence to the American civil-liberty tradition. The text of the law took pains to point out that peaceful parading, demonstrating, and marching were "valid exercises of the rights of citizens"; that

marchers were entitled to protection; and intimidating comments by bystanders were subject to arrest for a misdemeanor.

120. *GG*, October 14, 1963.

121. Interview July 15, 1965. A careful reading of this "appeal to reason" leaves no doubt that the rights of private property were awarded policy-priority by the *Gazette*, in conformity with a large body of business-oriented opinion prior to the passage of the 1964 federal Civil Rights Bill. But this not-so-careful reader chastised the statement for its "undercurrent theme that the theater owner should relinquish his right to operate his business as he sees fit. Could it be possible that you advocate appeasement in place of Free Enterprise?" "No," the *Gazette* replied indignantly, "in no manner should the theater owner's choice be taken from him . . . right or wrong, we recognize his right to make that choice, and contrary to certain politicians, would never advocate legislation depriving him of that right. If you are familiar with our paper, you realize that we have been and remain staunch advocates of the free enterprise system. The free-spending new frontiersmen (of the Kennedy administration) may have captured some portion of the press, but never here if we can help it." *GG*, October 22, 1963.

122. *GG*, October 16, 1963.

123. *GG*, October 17, 1963.

124. *GG*, October 25, 1963.

125. *Ibid*.

126. Cf. above, p.252.

127. Interview, July 24, 1965 and HRC Minutes October 29, 1963. The man in question was a relative newcomer to Gastonia, having been pastor of one of the larger black Baptist churches for little more than a year. One knowledgeable respondent said that this minister early sought to align himself with the traditional leadership of the black community, and thus was chosen as the one black minister for the HRC. One of these leaders, also a member of the HRC, told us that the minister's very experience in a demonstration-crisis in Columbia, S.C., was a factor in his appointment. "We wanted to capitalize on the fact that he had gone through a demonstration." As a Baptist, this minister probably had more trouble securing the support of his constituency than any other of the seven activists. Both the relative non-militance of other black Baptist ministers in town and the comments of others about this minister's brief career in Gastonia suggest that this is so. His successor as pastor of the Baptist church in question said to us: "My congregation will probably be the last stronghold of the old school. In spite of this, I must do what I know to be right. There are many times when I must stand alone, though there may be some in the congregation who would stand with me." This same respondent did not agree that his predecessor was moved to leave his post for reasons of militancy. "There is nothing to support that theory. He was offered a better church in Birmingham, Alabama, where he is carrying-on the same cause." Interview, July 27, 1965.

128. HRC Minutes, October 21, 1963.

129. HRC Minutes, November 11, 1963.

130. The HRC discussion of November 11 was the occasion for a number of strategy suggestions for committee coping with the militant clergymen: "Approach them in humbleness and ask their help . . . ask one of them to serve on the committee . . . try to regain the initiative . . . make a breakthrough in jobs for women as an answer to the ministers. . . ."

131. Interview, July 15, 1965.

132. Interview, July 28, 1965.

133. Interview, July 15, 1965.

134. Interview July 28, 1965. The respondent was the defeated candidate for the city council in 1963. He went on to say, "My business and income do not depend upon my getting elected to

things, and I will stay in politics only as long as I can stand up for what I think is right. Otherwise I'd lose my integrity."

135. Interview, July 28, 1965. Several months later, accusations against the man in question—no essential part of this narrative—escalated from scandal to murder. All our respondents in the black community who mentioned this incident reflected a profound sense of shame. "It really rocked this community," confided one respondent, "but it didn't hurt the race relations cause," because the cause was clearly and critically distinguishable from the conduct of one of its leaders. Little public use was made of this apparent blot on the cause by the local newspaper but one can speculate on how many times "I told you so" went the rounds of Gastonia supper tables on the weekend of the murder. It was on this same spring weekend that the news came of Gastonia's selection as an All America City. *GG*, March 27, 1964.

136. *GG*, October 25, 1963.

137. *GG*, October 26, 1963. This editorial, on the front page, was entitled, "Go Home Mr. Cox. We'll Settle Our Own Problems." In addition to reciting again the story of Gastonia's progress over the past decade in race relations, the editor excoriated Cox as having come to Gastonia precisely because "we have done more here in Gastonia . . . than any of those cities which you brought to a throbbing standstill."

138. *GG*, October 29, 1963.

139. Interview July 28, 1965.

140. Cf. editorial, *GG*, October 30, 1963.

141. *GG*, September 22, 1965.

142. Cf. above, p. 283, Table 6.8, on survey results in 1965-67 that support this statement.

143. The writers are aware that we must be careful not to adopt uncritically the ideological classifications which our black respondents often made of each other. To call the latter respondent a conservative or an old school politican is not to do justice to a side of his political outlook that is decidedly "confrontationalist." He told us, for example, how a man one generation younger than himself had tested a local truck-stop restaurant during the summer of '63 and had been asked belligerantly by the proprietor, "What do you want, boy?" The younger man reported than in anger he had stalked out of the restaurant. "I told him that he should have stayed in there and replied, 'a cup of coffee, boy!' and waited to see what would happen!"

144. By that time he had obtained his $12,000 loan from the local bank and cheerfully announced that in spite of integration he was now proceeding to redecorate his theaters. *GG*, June 1964.

145. Information supplied the writers by Gaston County Board of Education, January 1975.

146. *GG*, June 22, 1974.

147. *GG*, November 10, 1970.

148. *GG*, August 17, 1971.

149. *GG*, January 10, 1971. The ratio of blacks to whites in this school was 230 to 1,185.

150. *GG*, June 29, 1974.

151. The latter interpretation is part of a personal communication on the subject from a resident of the community in question, in the fall of 1971. No large attention has been given in this study to the one or two chapters of the still surviving KKK in Gaston County. In spite of some renewed public activity in recent years, this organization shows many signs of being beleaguered. Gaston blacks conducted open counter-demonstrations against one demonstration of the Klan in Mount Holly in 1971 (*GG*, June 6, 1971); and one local Klan leader complained bitterly in 1970 that Klan membership was so unpopular now that a known member stood to lose his job in the county's mills. "When an employer learns an employee has joined the Klan, the worker often gets an ultimatum: get out of the Klan or get another job. This happened recently in Charlotte when two policemen

joined the Klan. I think these people are being discriminated against. . . . It looksmto me like they have a gripe under the civil rights act." On the "new image" of the Klan, the same leader commented that as for blowing up school buses, "we don't do things like that." (*GG*, October 12, 1970) In fact, the only explosion associated with the KKK in Gaston County recently was the one which destroyed the Klan clubhouse in Cherryville, an incident which Grand Dragon Robert Jones attributed to intra-Klan splinter group rivalries. (*GG*, October 19, 1971).

152. Interview, July 1972.

153. Donald Dewey, "Negro Employment in Southern Industry," *The Journal of Political Economy*, Vol. LX, No. 4 (August 1952), 279-93. Used by permission of the publisher, University of Chicago Press. Dewey concludes that the position of the southern black industrial worker actually deteriorated in the 50 years before World War II. "In South Carolina textiles 9 percent of all workers were Negro in 1918; yet, although employment in the industry more than doubled in South Carolina over the next twenty-two years, the Negro's share of work was down to 4 percent in 1940." *Ibid.*, p. 282. Dewey's statistics come from the *Fifth Annual Report of the South Carolina Department of Labor*.

154. *Ibid.*, p. 285.

155. Reese Cleghorn, "The Mill: A Giant Step for the Southern Negro," *New York Times Magazine* (November 9, 1969), p. 35. © 1969 by The New York Times Company. Reprinted by permission.

156. "Percent Employment of Negroes in the Textile Industry by Selected States, 1966," *Equal Employment Opportunity Commission*, in a study of 80% of the mills in these states.

157. "Textiles: Blacks in the Mills," *Newsweek*, Vol. LXXVI, No. 18 (November 2, 1970) p. 88.

158. Statistics on the exact proportions of black workers employed in all Gaston County industries (as distinguished from employment in textiles) are hard to uncover. A leading Gastonia business-related person, interviewed March 2, 1972, who had reason to know, reported to us that in the late sixties officials from local industries frequently went out of their way to ascertain the census-figures on Gastonia's black population, presumably because federal government inspectors were careful to ask if the particular industry had black employees proportionate to blacks in the local population. In 1960, the county-wide figures was 13.1%, and 14.1% for the City of Gastonia. (North Carolina had a black population of 25.4% in 1960). The 1970 census showed 12% blacks in the county, 17% in the city, and 22% in the state.

159. *Newsweek*, November 2, 1970, p. 88.

160. Reese Cleghorn, *New York Times Magazine*, November 9, 1969, p. 35. Another South Carolina executive said: " 'All of us have been really amazed at the high degree of acceptance by both black and white.' " *Newsweek,* November 2, 1970, p. 88.

161. Interview, April 24, 1975. The congressman in question was James Broyhill, who, in a shift of multi-county district-boundaries, defeated Gaston native Basil Whitener in 1968, to become that county's first Republican congressman in forty years. Broyhill won reelection in November 1974 over Jack Rhyne, the Democratic nominee, whose political career to that date had itself been a striking sign of local political change. A former resident of a mill village in Belmont, Rhyne got himself elected successively Mayor of Belmont, state representative, state senator, and nominee for Congress, all on a power-base as close to "populist" as any modern Gaston politician could claim. The Democratically-auspicious post-Watergate mood of 1974 was insufficient, however, to carry Rhyne into office. He even failed, by a narrow margin, to carry Gaston County.

162. Cleghorn, *op. cit.*, p. 147. Scott Hoyman confirms Cleghorn's perspective in the late sixties with some data from the mid-seventies: "Black employment industry-wide is about 18%, but in some Piedmont counties it is as high as 40%. We find that blacks are not so much the victims of paternalistic attitudes as whites have been. Blacks are personally more aggressive in terms of

wanting a higher standard of living. Furthermore, the civil rights movement taught them not to be afraid of trying to change society and its institutions. We even have situations in which white workers boast, 'we're going to win this strike because we have the black workers with us.' This is most likely to happen in a crisis, like a strike. For example, in the Fieldcrest campaign in Columbus, Georgia recently, many white workers were driving in from their homes in Alabama with Wallace stickers on their cars; but they joined blacks to support the union." Interview, April 24, 1975.

163. Cf. above, p. 210.

164. Norton E. Long, "The Corporation, Its Satellites, and the Local Community," in Edward S. Mason, ed., *The Corporation in Modern Society* (Cambridge: Harvard University Press, 1961), pp. 214-217. Long finds that national corporation executive is drawn into local political roles that are merely ceremonial, dutiful, and episodic. Vulnerable to the local demand that they exercise power, such executives have little organizational or self-interest in becoming enough involved to exercise *real* power.

165. See, e.g., Harold M. Hodges, Jr., *Social Stratification* (Cambridge, Massachusetts: Schenkman Publishing Co., 1964), p. 13. Hodges defines classes as "the blended product of shared and analogous occupational orientations, educational backgrounds, economic wherewithal, and life experiences."

166. See for example, Donald L. Noel and Alphonso Pickney, "Correlates of Prejudice: Some Racial Differences and Similarities," *American Journal of Sociology*, Vol. LXIX, No. 6 (May 1964), pp. 609-22 and John D. Photiadis and Jeanne Biggar, "Religiosity, Education, and Ethnic Distance," *American Journal of Sociology*, Vol. LXVII, No. 6 (May 1962) pp. 666-672.

167. See for example, Noel and Pinkney, *op. cit.* and Frank Westie and Margaret Westie, "The Social-Distance Pyramid: Relationships Between Caste and Class," *American Journal of Sociology*, Vol. LXIII, No. 2 (September 1957) pp. 190-96.

168. Richard L. Gorsuch and Daniel Aleshire, "Christian Faith and Ethnic Prejudice: A Review and Interpretation of Research," *Journal for the Scientific Study of Religion*, Vol. XIII (September 1974), pp. 281-307.

169. *Ibid.*, p. 281-307.

169. *Ibid.*, p. 281.

170. Jeffrey Hadden, *The Gathering Storm in the Churches* (Garden City, N.Y.: Doubleday and Company, Anchor Books 1969), pp. 155-157.

171. *MP*, p. 195.

172. *Ibid.*, p. 197.

173. J. Milton Yinger, *The Scientific Study of Religion* (London: Collier-Macmillan Limited, 1970), p. 371.

174. Gunnar Myrdal, with the assistance of Richard Sterner and Arnold Rose, *An American Dilemma* (New York: Harper and Row, 1944).

175. Daniel T. Jenkins, *Beyond Religion* (Philadelphia: The Westminster Press, 1962), p. 83.

176. Hadden, *op. cit.*, p. 7.

177. Cf. above, Preface, p. 18.

178. Almost three quarters of the ministers in Hadden's sample agreed that " 'For the most part, the churches have been woefully inadequate in facing up to the civil rights issue.' " (Hadden, p. 118.) And approximately 90% agreed that " 'Many whites pretend to be very Christian while in reality their racial attitudes demonstrate their lack of or misunderstanding of Christianity.' " (*Ibid.*, p. 119.)

179. Cf. above, p. 150. (Barger)

Chapter Seven

The Future of the Churches in Gastonia: *Some Untended Agendas*

Truth, not use, is the test of science. We will have served the scientific goal of this study, therefore, if we have accurately rendered the portrait of religion and social change in the most recent generation of Gastonians. But we have dedicated our book "to the next generation of Gastonians" in a hope that should have at least second-order legitimacy in the sociological profession: that the results of research will be useful as well as true. (A certain philosophical as well as post-Watergate political insight urges us to believe that the usefulness of our findings are indivisible from their truth.) In so dedicating the book, we do not imagine that either this or the Pope volume could serve as a guidebook for anyone's decisions about his or her participation in the future of churches, industries, governments, or other social institutions. But we do imagine that such studies as this can make a contribution to the clarification of the analytical, the decisional, and the policy-making *agendas* of such institutions. Surely the study will be of merely academic interest if it does not offer Gastonians, in particular, food for thought about their own roles in the future of their community.

The Critical Fact of Structural Differentiation

We have seen that a generation of change has posed some new problems and social contexts for such thought. To bring the problems and contexts into focus, we need now to deal systematically with a concept that has entered the foregoing analysis from time to time and whose importance for this study two of our sociological colleagues perceptively predicted ten years ago. In their Introduction to the 1965 edition of *Millhands and Preachers*, Richard A. Peterson and Nicholas J. Demerath, III[1] suggested that the evolving relation between Gastonia churches and American society should be carefully viewed in light of *social-structural differentiation*. In this chapter we want to affirm this Peterson-Demerath perspective and to demonstrate its pertinence, not only for understanding the foregoing narrative but also for identifying the future agendas of churches in places like Gastonia. Peterson and Demerath summarize the nature of structural differentiation as a process wherein

institutions are pulled out of the close articulation that characterizes the undifferentiated community. Politics, education, the family, the economy, and even religion become more specialized and more autonomous. The possibility of one dominating another grows more remote as each becomes an island unto itself. Each institution is likely to have more contact with its national affiliates than with different institutions in the same community.[2]

Illustrations abound from the foregoing narrative: industrial consolidation, the "managerial revolution," unionism, the civil rights movement, the bureaucratization of church denominations, and the internationalization of commerce all testify to the import of structural differentiation in Gaston County in the 1940-75 period. In the Cherryville incident, for example, a national union leader, two national denominational officials, a national governmental board, and even the local textile management successively criticized or deserted the cause of seven local ministers. And since Cherryville was one of some three towns in the county least changed since the mill-village days of Pope's time, the situation in the economically more dynamic town of Gastonia, *a fortiori*, was even less hospitable to open incursions by church leadership into direct influence on economic policy. This incident offered poignant, concrete confirmation of the pertinence of the questions which Peterson and Demerath go on to raise about the impact of structural differentiation upon the potential role of religious organizations:

. . . in nondifferentiated communities the church is frequently forced to take sides whenever conflict occurs. Moreover, it is generally necessary for it to side with the dominant party, whether this is the feudal nobility, the rising bourgeoisie, the industrial entrepreneurs at the end of the nineteenth century, or the Gastonia mill management. But differentiation conduces to a new neutrality. In an age of specialization, the church is often ignorant of the intricacies of conflict in other areas. In an age of bureaucratization, this conflict is generally resolved at the highest reaches of bureaucracies that are impenetrable to church influence.

For all these reasons, the church is often put in the position of commentator rather than combatant. Once relegated to the periphery, it both gains and loses. We are not asserting that the church is better off in either the differentiated or the non-differentiated community. Is it preferable to be the captive of the dominant forces or to be defined as irrelevant? Is it better to pay the price of vassalage for the prize of community involvement or to pay the price of irrelevance for the prize ideological freedom? The point is not that there is no longer a dilemma but that the nature of the dilemma has changed.[3]

To put it very simply: if you are a minister in Gastonia now, you can disagree with local management and keep your job. So the vital pragmatic-theoretical question now is: can the minister and other church leaders discover in their own religious heritage any provocations to *use* "the prize of ideological freedom" in ways that avoid the twin dangers of (1) presumption on the competence of other institutions and (2) irrelevance to the latter's problems? The two conditions for churchly contribution to "economic regulation," Pope concluded at the very end of his book, were "larger structural independence and cultural transcendence of the economic institutions in the county."[4] Now the society, unasked, has provided the first condition; will the churches provide the second? And if they don't, will the churches decline increasingly into the status of some other victims of evolutionary differentiation: the status of vestigial remainders?

A second, related observation is provoked by Peterson and Demerath's reference, in this same context, to another classic community-study, *Middletown*, by Robert and Helen Lynd.

The dominant theme of the Lynds' study is that of "secularization"—the decline of traditional values and an increasing willingness to subject any value to dispassionate criticism and innovation. Since religion crystallizes much of tradition, it is especially vulnerable.[5]

This interpretation of religion, however, omits one of its major historic themes: the subjection of human values to the judgment of a Power believed to be the ultimate *source* of good, right, and proper "criticism and innovation." Seasoned theologians among church leaders are not likely to confuse themselves with that Power; their own theology—or even a leaf from the writings of Karl Mannheim[6]—will suggest that the allegedly secular demand for "dispassionate criticism" of "traditional values" harks back to the authority of some other value, criterion, or *functionally* transcendent standard. Both axiomatically and demonstrably in this study, *society* has its functional transcendents; and debate over the content of these transcendents is often the key conflict in social crises. Thus religion in Gastonia is now thrown, willy nilly, into a situation where it will either get into the business of defining a religiously transcendent social ethic for their community's life, or *qua* religion, it may just go out of business; for Peter Berger's word about the function of "theology" in the church applies equally to the function of the church itself in a highly differentiated society:

Theology provides criteria by which Christian churches can judge themselves. If these criteria are lost, the Christian faith becomes the night in which all cats are grey.[7]

Religion, Ideology, and Social Change: Four Summary Events

That is the pivotal conclusion toward which this second-generation book in Gastonia has to tend. It is a conclusion close to Pope's—but infused with new data suggestive of a more threatening crisis for the Gaston churches than any they faced in the early pioneer days or in the Great Strike of '29. To be sure, for those theologians and sociologists who agree that the survival of the churches as institutions does not depend upon their "relevance" to social change or social stability, the structural differentiation question does not face the churches with any crisis at all. Having survived in the past either through sheer dogged faith—a possible theological view—or through that very retreat from society which attracts the conservative and the marginal person to religion—a popular sociological view—the churches are perhaps fit as ever for survival. On either view the churches can expect to have less and less intentional relation to social change and social order; both the ideas and the power to effect either will increasingly belong to other institutions than the churches.

To argue a preference for another mode of relation between the church and its social community is no necessary task for the completion of this study. We would be remiss, however, if we failed here at the end to make clear what a church-society relationship in the "irrelevance" mode will mean in terms of *costs*—to certain values and interests in American communities like Gastonia. And, instead of clarifying such costs only by further excursions into sociological theory, it may sharpen the relevance of the above conclusion if we mesh our theory yet again with some data on several events, from recent Gastonian history, which we find illuminating. Historians and sociologists betray their own values in the events they find "illuminating." Often enough have we betrayed our own in the selection of events scrutinized in this book. But precisely against the background of these previous choices, we detect in the foreground some signals of a possible future social agenda for the churches of Gastonia. Below we have chosen four occasions which seem to emit such signals—occasions when the churches themselves were, so to speak, standing on the frontier of their own future relation to society. Two of these occasions were very national: the assassination of one American president, the resignation of another. The two others were very local: an award to Gastonia as an "All-America City" and a management change in the city newspaper. Together the four events touch upon the four themes of the local ideology as we have described it above; all show the marks of the social-structural differentiation that grows apace in Gastonia now; and all at once illustrate the possibility, the pertinence, the costs, and the difficulty of future churchly forays into "criticism and innovation" *vis à vis* this society.

1. The All-America City Award: progress and the social relevance of forgiveness.   Until its demise in the early seventies, *Look Magazine* annually awarded to ten American locales the kudos, "All-America City."[8] Main criterion for the award was demonstrated effort "by private citizens to solve major community problems."[9] Among other cities, Louisville, Kentucky, achieved the award in 1964; Aztec, New Mexico; Seward, Alaska—and Gastonia, North Carolina.

In every sense the distinction had to be achieved: citizen-committees made application for it, and finalist-candidates sent delegations to appear before the *Look* jury during the fall preceding the spring announcement of winners. On November 18, 1963, Gastonia's delegation, headed by the local newspaper editor, presented to the jury a 1300-word statement highlighting three recent accomplishments of the community: industrial expansion, made possible through the city's 1963 annexation of seven square miles of neighboring rural territory; the upgrading of local higher education, through the founding of Gaston Community College and a vote for local taxes to support it; and, finally, the opening up of public accommodations and jobs for Gastonia's black citizens, through voluntary citizen compliance with the work of a Human Relations Committee. A description of the last area of "progress" occupied the largest section of the statement, and a fifth of the total account concerned the disappointment of many local citizens over their inability to avoid racial demonstrations, which, said the spokesman, had finally been stirred up by a "dissident group which sought power among our colored citizens" and which had "called in an outsider" to aid its quest for power. But the opening and the closing of the presentation touched most deeply upon the ideological current in "Gastonia's story." That story, in a word, had been the story of Progress.

Long the "red-headed stepchild" of the state, Gastonia could neither find her place among the tradition-steeped antiquities of eastern North Carolina, nor among the great urban centers of the Piedmont. She had industry, but little commerce. She lacked the age to have much history.[10]

So her leaders set out to make a history in the only direction in which it was accessible—the future. Hence the expansion of industry, the building of new educational facilities, the advance in opportunity for blacks, and numerous other additions to community well-being, including the new sanctuary of the First Presbyterian Church, built at a cost of $1,400,000. Never a "dead town" since its beginning less than a century ago, Gastonia was nonetheless a town whose "progress was sporadic. It now has a steady heartbeat. Where growth came in spurts, it is now planned and orderly." Gastonians, said the statement, are of a mind to keep growing in that way.

It is a city where the people believe in the future and believe in working to get there.[11]

Impressed, the *Look* jury voted for Gastonia. To headline the Gastonia story in an April issue of the magazine, its editor put in bold type the word Gastonians themselves preferred to describe their city:

"PROGRESS, to serve a community, must be continuous and creative."[12]

More interesting than what they did to get the award, however, was what Gastonians said in response to its announcement. The local newspaper took occasion not only to rejoice in the new distinction but to identify points in local history of which citizens could hardly be proud:

There already have been some people who have had a tendency to back up and say, "I didn't know we were that good."

Then, they would go on and recite instances where, years ago, they'd be traveling through the Far West or North and meet some individual who almost recoiled upon learning that the traveler was from Gastonia. "Oh, yes, I've heard of Gastonia," the person would say, "You folks sure have your share of violence down there."

This we admit. Things like the Loray Strike and a mother drowning her three children on Easter Sunday and a preacher raping his granddaughter have a tendency to linger on. Time is slow in washing such from memory.

These days are gone, and with vigilance, they shall never return. They were poison to the system of a city's people, and they erupted in violence that seemed to come from an inventive mind.

We still have violence. We still have conditions that condone the unusual. But the situation has improved immeasurably, and, the citizenry willing, our new acclaim will be the impetus to make this city as clean as it possibly can be made.[13]

As these words were written, the local theater was still segregated; the slum housing of the black community and the deteriorated former mill villages still lined many a street of the town; and jobs for blacks in textile mills had only begun to increase. Much was still wrong with the city, if you looked at it from some points of view. But one contemporary local black leader, whatever his reservations about the degree of progress in race relations in Gastonia, expressed complete understanding of the mood and motive behind such editorializing. Said he in an interview in 1965:

In the back of their minds there are people here who really want to put this town on the map, and though some of them may personally be against some of these things, they'll let this take secondary place to their ambition for the town. As late as 1958 a rival city for an industry tried to use the 1929 Red Scare to swing an industry to another town rather than Gastonia. Once that Red dot gets on you, you have to do a lot to get it off!

Or as a young textile executive said, somewhat plaintively, two years later: "The fact that we made All-America City shows the progress that was made."[14] The "All-America" medallions on the local police uniforms, the new signs at the city limits, and the stickers in merchants' windows—many a Gastonian in 1964 must have found it a peculiarly satisfying accolade.

Doubtless many citizens of the other All-America cities of 1964 found it the same. One would have to know their local histories to know just what differences the towns displayed in their public response to the award. Knowing Gastonia's history, one readily asks what relevance *religion* had to it all. On the surface, religion had little or nothing to do with it. Yet, the mood and tone of religion infuse the language that surrounded the occasion: How "good" a city it is now, how threatened once with evil "from an inventive mind"; how much some memories need "washing" away, how much impetus we now have to make the town "as clean as it possibly can be . . ."; children drowned by their mother at *eastertime*; a *preacher* committing incest . . . the language itself resonates with the mood and mystery of the ultimate concerns of evangelical Protestant religion, especially its concern with judgment upon evil and a deliverance from that evil variously called "salvation" and "the forgiveness of sins." It takes no stretch of sociological imagination to discern again in Gastonia culture the social good news of a "whence" more convincingly left behind and a "whither" more hopefully reaffirmed.[15] One has to conclude, in short, that for many a prominent Gastonian "putting this town on the map" meant getting absolved from what first put the town on the map for many an extra-Gastonia American: the Loray Strike and all the misery that could, justly or unjustly, be associated with it.

It was absolution from afar. But what about absolution from near-at-hand? We know from a variety of clues[16] that "things like the Loray Strike" were not food for frequent public or private conversation in post-1929 Gaston society. In general the people and the institutions of the town, including the churches, avoided saying much about the event. Usually it became a topic of open attention in the midst of some painful crisis alleged to resemble that of 1929.[17] But the All-America City award demonstrated eloquently that wanting to be delivered from the shadow of the Loray Strike was a slumbering social-therapeutic need of this local society. Of course it is risky, intellectually speaking, to make casual analogy from individual trauma to social trauma; one cannot speak of a social illness in just the sense one speaks of a personal illness. But educated intuition strongly suggests that a social form of "the return of the repressed" was occurring here; some unacknowledged "hangup" with the past was getting released and some social-personal liberation was occurring that deserved to be called a muted version of the forgiveness of sins.

In the religious context, this All-America City Award was thus a great irony: no doctrine more regularly resounds from the pulpits of Gaston churches than the forgiveness of sins; but how often in the thirty-five years since 1929 had the sermons, the Sunday school classes, the revival meetings, or any other institutional expression of religion engaged in some form of explicit therapy concerning traumatic, "sinful" *social* events? It is a truism of psychiatry that verbalizing an old pain is essential to the process of emotional-mental healing. A form of such therapy is needed in every society from time to time on all levels—families, cities, nations, once torn apart, require putting back together again, if their constituents are to relate to each other in more than crippled fashion. The *social utility* of the Christian belief in the forgiveness of sins is easily seen in this light—as Robert Frost (not a self-confessed Christian) suggested in his line: "To be social, is to be forgiving." The "cultural reintegration" that Pope saw the churches helping to effect in Gastonia of the thirties had this valid internal legitimation in their theology: in the push and shove of social conflict, the injury that some people do other people requires some form of coming-to-peace with past evils. Psychiatry calls it acceptance. But the traumatic ruptures of personal and social pasts can be neither accepted nor forgiven unless they are *acknowledged* in personal or social consciousness. Until acknowledged, "things like the Loray Strike and a mother drowning her three children on Easter" do indeed "have a tendency to linger on"—viciously. The question is: by their own official doctrine, do the churches have any way to cut short such lingering? If the "progress" of persons and communities is significantly retarded by neurotic attachments to the past, can religion make its peculiar contribution to progress without dealing openly with the sources of the neurosis?

Cool observers, little identified with the tribulations of small towns like Gastonia, may dismiss the whole All-America City affair as a subject for satirical humor. But the pastors of churches in Gastonia, forbidden by their own principles to ignore any form of human distress, are not likely to chuckle over the accusation being leveled at them here: over the years since 1929, they have (as Jeremiah might say)[18] healed the wounds of the Gaston community lightly; for as a group they have collaborated with the tendency of the community as a whole to bury a past before its traumatic power was killed. The very same analysis can be made of many another trauma in the history of social conflict —the white man's treatment of the American Indian, the scandal of slavery, and the tragedy of Vietnam, to name three American examples. Religion, in other words, can be *historically relevant* in terms of how it deals with its constituents' *reorientation to their social past* not only in terms of how it deals with the contemporary. Indeed, there are some dimensions of the future that individuals and communities cannot be free to explore, until they are freed from the baleful tyranny of certain memories. In this sense, the religious notion of forgiveness contributes to social change by making the past genuinely past, the future a genuinely new possibility. And thus the Greek words *symbol* and *diabol* are strictly, literally pertinent to social-historical reality: For lack of appropriate symbols that "throw" a society back "together," the society falls prey to the diabolic—it is "thrown apart," losing its integrity. For some social disruptions, only a symbol will do for healing.[19]

2. *The Kennedy assassination: harmony and tension between faith and values.*   Four days after Gastonians made their pitch for the All-America City award, the thirty-fifth president of the United States was assassinated in another southern city. Superficial observers may well have associated Gastonia with Dallas: political murder had been done in both places. But the resemblance of the two might have been tagged in the more sophisticated terms of ideology. If Dallas represented the spirit of southern economic Progress on a large scale, Gastonia represented the same on a small scale. The damage done to the image of that Texas city by violence must have been well understood by Gastonia's business community.

Data on local response to the assassination is rare. Presumably Gastonians, like other Americans, were caught up in the national grief that television facilitated that weekend. For some it must have been a grief with traces of religious feeling in it.[20] More certainly, the assassination of a president poses serious political and constitutional questions for the American people as a whole; for an American president is an official of enormous administrative and symbolic power. When he is elected, inaugurated, impeached, or assassinated, his constituents are reminded of some very basic political assumptions which are in every sense "constitutional" for the nation. A theoretical word about the relation of religion, political constitution, and social change in the American-Gastonian context, therefore, is in order for introducing below one dimension of the Gastonia response to Kennedy's death.

Over a thirty-year period, both the labor union and the civil rights struggles in Gastonia were often centered on questions of the institutional-constitutional *rules* that serviced or failed to service certain subgroup interests. Assumed here is the empirical generalization that most socially institutionalized rules have coercion behind them for implementation, but the authority of rules (typically at the time when institutions are first conceived) is at some historical point intrinsic for those who accept them. If one wants to change the ways in which institutions are arranged and function, one must reckon eventually with change in the rule-level of the institutions.

Common experience in society teaches that there is often great discrepancy between the formal and the functioning rules of institutions. The rule "last-hired and and first-fired" has had a terrible reality in the lives of black people in America for many years in their relations with the nation's economic institutions. This rule was seldom if ever written down in the operating manuals of employers, but it was nonetheless one of the operating rules. To the change of a whole category of such rules the civil rights movement in the early sixties devoted most of its energies. The strategy for the change was two-fold: on the one hand, the movement threatened—even if ever so mildly—certain material interests of the white majority that were precious enough in the latter's eyes to be worth some concessions on other interests served by discriminatory rules —the "ideal" interest of segregationist sentiment, for example. The threat of public demonstrations to Gastonia's economic prosperity was an example of this strategy. On the other hand, the movement was appealing for a change in some operating institutional rules in the name of other rules already occupying some place in the total society. Specifically, the movement invokes the Constitution of the United States over against the legal and informal segregationist rules of many American institutions. More specifically yet, it invoked some parts of the Constitution—notably those believed to relate to equality—over against certain other parts—notably those believed to relate to individual rights of property. Thus, one aim of the movement was to overturn some legal rules and to institute other rules more consistent, it believed, with the general rules of the Constitution.

At a level of symbolic-legal generality higher than the concept of national Constitution, however, the movement also invoked principles of conscience, and its representatives often expressed these principles in terms of the Christian religious traditions of its adherents. As it appealed to the conscience of white people and white Christians, the movement was thus banking on the possibility that allegiance to a religiously grounded ethic could yield support for change in segregation rules. They were counting on the pragmatic realism of an assumption stated early in this book: in politics, the power of coercion needs the power of justification. As Hannah Arendt says, the power of coercion is not really powerful until it acquires justification.[21]

The key test of this theory locally, as we saw in Chapter Six, was the *threat* of violence in the civil rights struggle of 1963. Gastonians of all categories —white and black, rich and poor, elite and non-elite—shared an overt consensus on the illegitimacy of violence as a means of achieving social change. The non-violent norm of the theater demonstrators and the city council's ordinance for protecting the rights of peaceful protest were clear evidence of that in 1963. Though journalists, organized white rightists, and militant young blacks may have waved the rhetoric of violence before their respective constituencies, the question of violence entered this incident largely as something which all major parties felt obligated to avoid. It was a "power struggle," all right; but the power consisted chiefly in a complex of physically noncoercive leverages on both sides. Among these leverages were a set of institutional rules in conflict with each other or with opposing group interests. Fundamentally the social argument was over which of these rules had *priority* importance for the behavior of all parties to the dispute.

A set of questions very old but still alive in American social history was thus rising to the surface of public discourse—in Gastonia and many other communities that experienced the civil rights controversies of the early sixties. Though few participants may have so conceptualized it at the time, the struggle was integrally related to similar arguments which had led the country into civil war a century before. Freedom of speech, the rights of private property, the requirements of justice, and the benefits of civil peace have been values long present in the laws and institutions of the United States. But which of these should be given practical priority, and whether these values alone sufficiently define the interest of a given social group—these are questions not likely to be settled permanently in the American or any other human society. Indeed, for the provisional settlement of such questions, citizens ordinarily first make appeal—not to violence—but to justifications or legitimacies that may or may not have formal constitutional basis, as the example of the Declaration of Independence suggests. In groups seeking to use their power to achieve social change related to their self-interest, the resort to such argument may be supremely practical. To them in particular will be evident the truth of the sociological dictum that no society institutionalizes all its values; and in making appeal to values more reached-for than grasped-by the society, reformers often rise on tiptoe, so to speak, to bring down to their cause justifications high on the shelves of generality. As we noted in the opening pages of this book, it is on those top shelves that religion ordinarily finds its roomiest place in the scale of justification. Both the weakness and the power of religion as a contributor to social change are related to this locus. Apart from law and its enforcement in the life of a society, talk about "brotherhood" is likely to sound hollow and irrelevant in most citizens' ears. Yet, when questions of *changes* in laws and law-enforcement are abroad in a society, the resort to talk about higher laws may acquire new interest among a variety of constituencies, for the only orderly way to revise old norms is to have on hand some new norms by which to identify and to remedy the deficiency of the old. "Old" and "new" in this statement must be taken in the very historical-sociological sense that a value remains "new" in a society so long as it is not institutionalized. In this sense, certain elements of the U.S. Constitution remain new ideas for many people in American society, and certain elements of the Christian religion remain newer yet. It could be said, in fact, that the idea of the supremacy of divine purpose in human affairs and the ultimate social norm of universal brotherhood are ideas incapable of institutionalization in any society, including the church. At best, even for the religious believer, relative approaches to social embodiment of these articles of faith are all that can be expected. If he or she does expect at least *that*, however, the believer may have a critically important contribution to make to the process of social change: one may justify a change in a "lower" law by arguing from a "higher" one. Such argument, on occasion, does move people to action; and such action, on occasion, does lead to institutionalized social change. Thomas Jefferson knew that; so did William Lloyd Garrison; and so did Martin Luther King, Jr.[22]

The clearest example of churchly contribution to change in this story is the example of the black churches in the civil rights struggle of 1963, but the drama of this example should not be permitted to obscure its implications for a general theory of actual and possible religious contributions to social change. As social institutions whose rationale for being makes their leaders specialize in talk about higher laws, the churches are not fundamentally charged, by the gist of their own charters, with the promotion or administration of all categories of social change. Hardly ever in the Western tradition have churchpeople claimed that the religious institution as such was charged with all the tasks of government, the economy, the family, etc. But the shaping of general critiques—or ethics—for all institutional sectors of the society has in fact been a self-assumed intellectual task of some churchpeople. Only the most sectarian "spirituals" in church history have divested themselves of all responsibility for providing society with "guidance and justification" concerning "the end it pursues."[23] Especially in a relatively stable society, this highly general guidance and justification of church people may strike their neighbors in either of two ways, both of which betoken irrelevance. The guidance may seem like (a) an old-familiar generalization that "everybody knows" and which everybody may allegedly observe; or (b) a high ideal that few people can afford to take seriously because it transcends ordinary human social achievement. The former reaction is what H. Richard Niebuhr used to call "cultural religion"; the latter, what he called "dualism" or, in another form, "synthesis."[24] The same person in different circumstances may inconsistently disparage religion successively on both counts: so often religious exhortations seem ordinary; so often they seem impossibly idealistic. But for any person or group in a society with axes to grind and changes to propose for that society's dealings with their interests, the religious institution may cut a different, more relevant picture. To them the high-minded guidance of religion may be (c) an ideal *familiar* enough to a segment of citizens to claim their allegiance, and (d) in critical *tension* enough with their actual behavior to function as a lure to different behavior. It is this notion of religion's potential relation to social change that the social reformer, inside or outside of the church, openly or implicitly affirms. (To this view of the relation of a religion to the rest of culture, H. Richard Niebuhr accorded the term "transformationist.")

In brief, as in the crisis of 1929, Gastonians in 1963 were having to wrestle with "basic truths" that underlay their existence as a society. Such junctures in social history are by definition the points where religion—the most general value-commitments that "bind-together" the body-politic—may have its peculiar opportunity to move from latent to manifest contribution to social change. In the fall of 1963, it was a group of seven black ministers who were most aware of this possibility. They were the ones who managed to combine (1) an appeal to the religious norm of brotherhood with (2) an appeal to neglected values of the national constitution with (3) a program of remedies to specific ills suffered by a minority interest group with (4) leadership in corporate action for these ends.

No such rich, viable combination of religion with the other ingredients of social change can be reported of a comparable group of white church leaders in the same period. We have observed, however, the leadership of certain white ministers and laity in helping to shape agendas for decision-making in the local white power structure; and one example of such a leader was the pastor of the affluent First Presbyterian Church, Harry M. Moffett. As it happens, late in 1963, soon after the most active time of his service on the Human Relations Committee, Moffett was asked by the Gaston County Democratic Party to deliver a eulogy to the late John F. Kennedy. Something important about the local culture was being stated in the fact that a political organization looked to a clergyman, not only to say a prayer at its meeting, but to discourse on the meaning of Kennedy's life in face of its tragic end. "Numerous requests" came to the local newspaper for reprints of Moffett's address to the assembled Democrats, who must have gone back to home and work talking about it. The full text was published in the newspaper just before Christmas.[25]

Conflict, tension, the unresolvable ambiguity of politics were Moffett's major themes. Read closely, the address was thus an implicitly religious commentary on the ancient theme of Harmony in the Gastonia Ideology. The aim of his statement, said he in his introduction, was to express "something of my faith and conviction about our American democratic process." This was an orthodox enough beginning for traditional civic club addresses by local clergy;

indeed, some of Moffett's paragraphs had the ring of the religion-tinged politics of World War II: the mission of America to protect freedom in the world, its great economic wealth and responsibility for the world's poor, and other like echoes of the Kennedy-version of American global paternalism. More prominent in the speech, however, was Moffett's effort to portray the positive contributions of *disharmony* to the well-being of human societies. This was a relatively original note to be struck by a Gastonia minister: were ministers not the epitome of the local society's hope for ultimate harmony and reconciliation?[26] Calling his audience's attention to another sort of relation between religious faith and social order, Moffett identified three healthy tensions which he saw embodied in the career of the late President:

(a) The tension between two or more human values. The American Constitution, said Moffett, sets a high standard for human social achievement by insisting on "two equally important and essential but often conflicting principles of political truth": rights associated with the private ownership of property, and rights associated with personal liberty. "In every community—in every county and state—in both political parties—the conflict between the claims of property rights and privileges as against the extension or protection of personal rights is in constant tension and debate—and this tension I believe to be the major source of our strength, our progress, and our liberties."[27]

(b) The tension between contesting political groups. Many Americans, Moffett went on to say, are distrustful of a political process that involves the apparent erosion of a politician's devotion to principle through his having to fight in the political arena for power. Many Americans distrusted Kennedy because he was so obviously a manipulator of power.

But no man can emerge as president of this country until he has been subjected to all the practical pressures, the sectional schisms, the public partisanship that creates the fierce intraparty strife and political will that is inherent in our system. No man can emerge from this fierce fight without being marked and scarred by the ordeal through which he has passed . . . The very toughness of the pragmatic political battle that brought (Kennedy) victory raised questions among many Americans as to the readiness of his mind, his spirit, sometimes even his deep commitment to the great ideals and principles that are imbedded in our nation's strength and unity.

Yet, said Moffett, in these very conflicts between large factions of people was located the opportunity to serve these very principles. Democratic politicians, he implied, serve property rights, personal rights, and other principles of human welfare in the way they confront and handle conflict, not in their success in avoiding it. And the most salient domestic example of Kennedy's attempt to see conflict as opportunity rather than threat was in the area of civil rights for a

. . . historically discriminated-against racial minority. Held in subtle bondage to poverty, through limited educational and economic opportunity and discriminatory laws, their plight is supported by a vast complex of entrenched fears and privileges, of submerged guilt and open hate, of deep frustrations and accepted prejudices. Here, in this conflict, the fundamental principles of our constitutional democratic government are locked in a deadly struggle in which, not only our national respect for law, order and justice but our influence and leadership of the peoples and nations struggling for life and liberty in our world is in serious jeopardy.

While I do not for one moment ask or demand your entire approval of his approach to this problem, I am confident you will join me in honoring his courage and his commitment to the basic but difficult principles and ideals of our American dedication to liberty and justice for all men everywhere, as he saw them, and for his willingness to risk his political future in a bold confrontation of the problem; for he sought to create through law a broader area in legal and civil justice by which he hoped to establish an atmosphere in which the subtle, more personal and intangible difficulties of racial desegregation could be confronted and adjusted in peace and order.

(c) The tension between institutional loyalties.   Though he did not relate his idea of tension directly to conflict between institutions, Moffett drew towards the close of the speech affirming what few Gastonia clergymen since 1960 had affirmed: a belief that a Roman Catholic Christian could be loyal to his church, loyal to the office of the presidency, and loyal to God.[28] "Kennedy was loyal to his church and to his creed. At the same time, he was equally and fully committed to the vital American principle of religious liberty and the separation of church and state." But again, Moffett implied, that is not to be understood apart from a view of the relation of God, the church, and the state to each other in the mode of tension. There are no smooth harmonies in or between the worlds of ideas, social groups, institutions and persons.

Out of this conceptual framework Moffett could move with impressive consistency to call, at the conclusion of his statement to the Gaston Democrats, for more "honest, forthright, courageous debate" among partisans of differing public and private interests; and "a condemnation and repudiation of vituperation, of threats, of malicious unsupported attacks on the integrity and loyalty of those we oppose." In this sense, he concluded, as citizens we should "awaken to the vital importance of personal and community standards of high moral integrity, of respect for law and the rights of others."

It was a singularly rare, intellectually complex, and politically sensitive view of the uses and abuses of disharmony in human social affairs. It was also unique in the spareness of its theological nomenclature, as if Moffett respected the secular nature of his setting too much to confuse it with his Sunday pulpit. Yet it is hard to imagine that the statement could have been framed by a mind unaccustomed to thinking about the transcendence of God and the universality of the religiously defined human community. Furthermore, it is hard to imagine that the statement was unconditioned by his recent experience of the theater demonstrations.[29]

In effect, this church leader was bringing into focus his notions as a theologian, as an American, and as a citizen of Gastonia. Among churchpeople in Gastonia throughout the 1940-75 era such a speech was a rarity. It was nonetheless a speech well targeted on the practical-intellectual deficiencies of an overly simple appeal to the ideology of Progress, Harmony, and Liberty; and one is driven to conclude that Moffett was able to take critical aim at some features of the Gastonia ideology because he stood on ground apart from the target: the ground of a religion and its associated ethical priorities. Of the human importance of such targeting and such grounding, we have more to say in connection with two more "illuminating occasions" below.

3. The Gazette management change: the free person in a free society. Seldom do small town newspapers, say some students of city politics, fail to reflect the general consensus of opinion in their communities. We have assumed as much in making generous use of *The Gastonia Gazette* in this study. But our third illuminating occasion constitutes an exception to this generalization. It also suggests something of the human cost that such an exception may exact from a community.

From 1906 to August 1968, the *Gazette* was owned by a single Gastonia family headed by the elder James Atkins. After his death in 1961, his nephew, James H. Atkins, a lawyer, took over the job of editor for most of the nineteen-sixties. During this period he was as active as his uncle had been in Gastonia affairs, including the Human Relations Committee, of which he was chairman in the late sixties.

In August 1968, with no public announcement,[30] the *Gazette* underwent a management change. D. R. Segal, one of the principal owners of Freedom Newspapers, Inc., became the new publisher. An examination of the list of names and addresses of the stockholders of Freedom Newspapers shows that half lived in the vicinity of Orange County, California; one fourth lived in Texas.[31]

The new publisher had spent most of his journalistic career in these two locales. Atkins chose to remain actively associated with the newspaper, but in January 1969 he abruptly announced his resignation from the staff for reasons of "ideological differences with Freedom Newspapers." Declining to elaborate, Atkins said that he was returning to the practice of law. In the next two years he launched a political career, first by changing his voting registration from Democratic to Republican, then by getting nominated for the State Senate on the Republican ticket, and finally by getting elected in November 1970 as Gaston County's first Republican representative in the state legislature.[32]

In fact, these successes offered the community some elaboration of Atkins' "ideological differences with Freedom Newspapers"; for, among other negative items in the journalistic creed of the new owners was a hyperindividualistic philosophy of government. Publisher Segal put that philosophy in words like these:

[Government] is best when it is smallest. It will be even better when we have learned to do without it.[33]

It is easy to be my congressman. The watchword is DON'T.[34]

The Gazette believes each person would get more satisfaction in the long run if he were permitted to spend what he earns on a voluntary basis rather than having any part of it distributed involuntarily.[35]

No person ideologically at home with these statements could be a candidate for the state legislature or anything but a principled opponent of organized government. This was radical "libertarianism," so named by the publisher, who dubbed it the "fastest growing movement" in America.[36]

Such single-hearted devotion to individual freedom, over the next two years, took some Gastonians by surprise. The surprise turned to anger for some, especially certain public officials; and to an unnamed anxiety for others, especially certain government-workers charged with the delivery of services to the community. In the name of freedom one could be opposed in principle to all "community organization." Not only unions, civil rights organizations, and protest groups of poor people were under attack but school boards, county commissioners, and churches.

A ready, plausible explanation of all this ideological lather was that Freedom Newspapers had long ago discovered that Harmony is not a virtue in the news business because circulation rates thrive on controversy. The paper's circulation did rise sharply by the end of 1971,[37] but there was more to be learned about Gastonia from this event than was encompassed by the renewed economic vigor of its daily paper. Wherever its papers are published, said the new publisher a year after coming to Gastonia, Freedom Newspapers make two sorts of organizations angry: unions and school boards. The latter was a distinct addition to the category of suspect organizations in Gaston County. School boards are constantly working to raise teacher pay, he observed; they propose bond issues and spend other monies on schools, but they cannot improve the school system: the only real improvement would be the system's total abolition.[38]

County School board members, some eighteen months later, discovered that opinions such as these, regularly spread around the local community in a newspaper, constituted no idle philosophizing. The paper contributed, they said, to a deterioration of the relationship of the Board and its tax-paying constituents.[39]

It was the first time in most Gastonians' memory when attention had been paid by anyone but a small minority of liberals to the ideological orientation of the local press. It was as if the editorials and editorizalized news of the old *Gazette* had been so much in accord with long-established local consensus that few officials had ever experienced the slings and arrows of a news medium fundamentally at odds with public policy. The sharpness of the conflict was underscored in the spring of 1971 in a politically heated controversy over the right of the county commissioners to regulate the ambulance services of local funeral homes. The "state is trying to take over private enterprise," cried the *Gazette*. Not at all, said the chairman of the commissioners; we don't mean to put anyone out of business, but only to be sure that ambulances have proper insurance and the like. Just this sort of regulating, retorted the *Gazette*, is a step on the road to socialism. Grumbled one of the commissioners in reply: "I don't appreciate being called a Communist." When in all Gaston history had anyone made such a suggestion about county commissioners?[40]

The phenomenon was rich with evidence for the thesis that ideological change is on occasion a power for social change—for social disturbance at least. For decades the champions of organized social justice in Gastonia had had (in common with the traditional champions of Progress, Harmony, and Liberty) a pluralistic set of values prescribed for the "good society." In Freedom Newspapers, Inc., both ideological parties were confronted with a single-minded social philosophy which was so rationally simple, so astutely promoted, so well financed, and related to public issues in a way so oblivious of long-standing social mores, that this philosophy was suddenly a formidable ideological irritation.

The irritation was all the more powerful for being socially and financially independent of the Gastonia community and its particular history. When articulated at all, shock at the new editorial policies was explained locally in terms of this "foreignness." Since the buying of the local newspaper was part of the national movement toward financial consolidation of smalltown dailies, the local impact was formally similar to that of the national industrial chains: the break of organic relations between local company power and the history of the community. In this sense the Gastonia newspaper had for long been "conservative" in the original, Burkean sense of the term; and the ideological position of Freedom Newspapers was "liberal" in the original, rationalistic-Jeffersonian sense of the term. Economic determinists would argue that the California-based newspaper chain could "afford" any ideology that would sell papers; and there was resonance enough for radical libertariansim in Gastonia to do that.

But radical, rational singlemindedness is not only unconservative in the Burkean sense; on a practical level, it can be a great hindrance to the tasks of institution-building and social leadership, as many leaders and staff members of governmental institutions in Gastonia found to their sorrow. They were better served by an ideology of Liberty *and* Progress, Liberty *and* Harmony, than they were ever served by an ideology of Liberty alone.[41] The *mills* were an organized, not an individual, artifact; so also were even the *Baptist* churches!

This is one way of describing the persuasive sense of threat which many Gastonians, who otherwise thought of themselves as conservative, felt in the management change at the *Gazette*. At a meeting of representatives of a broad cross section of staff members from the social-service agencies of the county in the fall of 1971, attended by one of the authors, the sense of bewilderment, danger, and anxiety over these matters was striking and unmistakable. Somehow, the canopy under which this community went about its daily business had suffered structural damage. The idea of government was being strangely undermined by the idea of freedom.[42]

The churches, it turned out, were eventually caught up in the crisis through the newspaper's aggressive animosity towards the "social gospel." The result was a rare example of open conflict between religion and ideology in Gastonia. Ironically, the social gospel was one area of solid agreement between the new and old *Gazette* publishers. In the very month of his resignation from the newspaper, James H. Atkins had appeared before the Gaston Ministerial Association to advise the local clergy to "stay out of politics." Echoing the sentiment of an editorial which he had apparently written the previous November—"[The minister] should be the last to become involved in petitioning the abundant life from politicians"[43]—Atkins handed the political task over to the laity. Some ministers present reacted negatively to the speech. A leading antagonist in the discussion, the Roman Catholic priest, veteran of some thirty years of residence in the county, protested: "You are asking us to put God in a box and get him out Saturday night and put him back on Sunday." "No," replied Atkins, "the layman has to get out and participate."[44] *At issue, however, was the deeper question of whether religion itself was a ground and provocation for even the layperson's organized participation in the political process.* It was basically a question of theology and theological ethics—a level of discourse at which the Catholic priest was instinctively ready to engage Atkins. It is inconsistent, the priest suggested, to claim a citizenship role for the Christian as such and to deny it to the Christian who happens to be ordained.

By the end of the month Atkins had resigned from the paper, evidently with the determination to follow his own advice. (He was a member of the First Methodist Church.) But the debate between the ministerial association and the local newspaper was picked up in April in the same setting with hardly a suggestion that in the meantime the face of journalistic leadership had changed. No records of the new publisher's speech are at hand; but the thrust of his views on the nonpolitical nature of the church and its clergy was spelled out clearly in the columns of the paper over the next several years. His views on the church, while more colorfully expressed and more plainly radical, matched Atkins' views rather closely. Favorite bad example for both was the National Council of Churches.

They make statements that take the church out of its priestly role and place it squarely in the prophetic role . . . For many people, this just doesn't seem right.[45]

It was a way of putting the theological question as clearly as the director of the local anti-poverty agency put the social-philosophy question when, later in the year, he distinguished sharply between "helping people" and "social change."[46] Over against the prophet, Segal asked, "Has anybody seen the preacher-pastor?"

He was a people-to-people man, unhurried, untroubled and at ease in a vocation which he felt the Lord had counseled him to follow.

His modern counterpart often is half-organizer, half money-raiser, and half social reformer. If that makes one and a half to you, it makes less than one to me. . . .

My complaint is not with the preacher, though. Apparently most people want their pastors to be "active in community affairs" . . . A church, in my view, should have pillars and stained glass and a very big organ. It should be quiet, rather dark (not dismal) and it ought to smell churchy. Just sitting for awhile in a place like that has some therapeutic value. But sitting in a conversation piece and hearing a political sermon preached from a pulpit—well.[47]

Added to the pages of the *Gazette* during these months, a rash of syndicated columnists intoned similar sentiments about the evils of the Social Gospel.[48] Clergy replies to these statements took several forms: letters-to-the-editor, guest-editorials,[49] and Sunday morning sermons. The overall effect was an unprecedented heightening of both the public and the in-church discussion of two questions, one clearly ideological and the other clearly religious: what is freedom? what is the role of the church in a "free" society?

Among the prominent participants in this debate was the pastor of the uptown Episcopal church. In the context of regular dialogue with various groups in the congregation, said he in 1970, he had tried to educate himself about local political and social issues ever since his coming to town in 1967. His active involvement covered a broad range of concrete issues: a petition to the county commissioners for electoral reapportionment, a study of the community's need for comprehensive health services, the development of the local anti-poverty agency, and the scandal of Gastonia's dozen gateless railroad crossings. In a *Gazette* "guest editorial" he stated his rationale for this dimension of the ministry:

> It's not enough today for the people to say they have to support the church because it's there, but rather they support it because it's doing something. . . . If I expect my parishioners to participate in civic affairs, I have to also. But I do it first because I'm a citizen—it's an expression of what I am. . . . Any man can exercise the Christian ministry by being a responsible citizen. I hope my people are community oriented. The first and foremost ministry for [them] in Gastonia is Gastonia. . . . If the churches do not become actively involved in the community, they will become little more than museums.[50]

Can/should human beings be "free" apart from "active involvement" in *some* community? The question—which was at once empirical and ethical——continued to agitate the minds of some Gastonians well into the early 1970s, which saw no retreat from single-minded libertarianism in the editorial pages of the paper.[51] One rather eloquent sign that the debate over the meaning of liberty still simmers, as this is written, among laity as well as clergy, was a series of paid advertisements published in 1974 by McNeill Industries, Inc., a Bessemer City textile firm. The ads consisted in long commentary on a variety of commercial, civic, religious, and philosophical topics under the authorship of the company president, W. Allen McNeill, an active Baptist.[52] One obvious purpose of the ads was to aid the company's search for prospective employees; but in commending his company to them, McNeill took occasion to debate with the *Gastonia Gazette* such issues as public utility rate changes and the human meaning of liberty. On two separate occasions in 1974 he wrote:

> . . . we need to sit down to try to find some sense in all the noise we hear about our individual rights and our personal freedom that floods our country . . . Think of the chaos that would result on Franklin Avenue beween 4 p.m. and 6 p.m. with every motorist ignoring traffic lights and driving as he pleased! This applies to all the rest of our relationships.

> . . . every successful person received a lot of help from others. So many times successful people forget they received help . . . A fallacy that we run into quite often in our society is this: "Behind every good man is a woman." The truth of the matter is that for every successful woman or man there was someone beside them. . . .[53]

Such statements suggest that a sort of "critique of ideology" is beginning to thrive in Gastonia, if only because some ordinary human experience and some very traditional local values are affronted by a cheerfully radical free enterprise philosophy spread abroad almost daily in a local print medium. It is a critique whose time has inevitably come, not only in the logic of the matter but in the growing clash between the diverse power bases of the community. Do the churches have a growing or a declining role to play in the development of such a critique? The future, of course, will tell. What can be told now is the possibility that the theology and ethics of the churches have conceptual resources for understanding personal and social life in richer, more complex, and more ordinary ways than clear-minded abstract libertarianism is likely to provide. And, if this conclusion about the *Gazette* crisis seems biased by an implicit evaluation of the churches' conceptual heritage, this minimum empirical conclusion must still be urged: pervasive anxiety and stress can fill the minds and the institutions of citizens when their long-held values are suddenly subjected to disparagement and domination by one value ripped out of its previous context and offered, with seductive simplicity, as the salvation of self and society. Such a master-value, by our earlier definition, is inherently religious, because it is the measure of all other things. Whether their faith in God has something to do with a more pluralistic, perhaps more human vision of social values, the churches must decide.

4. Watergate:"government founded on truth and justice."   Early in this book, one of us asked the question: how can the churches as organizations have influence on broad social affairs when so much activity in the churches centers on personal religion? And the kindred question: how can the church contribute to "civic consciousness" if the drift away from civic-discussion in Shriver's church of 1959 was typical of the community at large?[54] The data now before us supply a collage of answers to these questions, and our final "illuminating event" offers a chance to focus and summarize these answers.

This book was virtually on its way to the presses when, in the summer of 1974, there occurred an event which living Americans will remember at least as long as they will remember the assassination of President John F. Kennedy: the resignation of President Richard M. Nixon. Surely, the three of us said to ourselves, Watergate presents us with another momentous occasion for inquiring about the possible relevance or irrelevance of Gastonia churches to the affairs of their society. Watergate was an affair for all of American society; how the churches ignored it or addressed it, would be a matter of curiosity for anyone interested in the social meaning of religion in any American locale.

The outcome of this curiosity was a brief questionnaire, mailed to almost all the ministers of Gaston County, asking about their behavior related to the events of Watergate, especially in the traumatic presidential summer of 1974. The questionnaire was mailed to 242 local ministers. Replies were received from 88 of these ministers. or some 36%.[55] Why did two-thirds of the ministers of the county decline to give any data to us on this subject? Our speculative answers are three: (1) we are becoming an over-questionnaired society, (2) giving information to outsiders about the relation of a controversial issue to religion is still a matter that most Gastonia ministers shy away from, and (3) a significant proportion of the ministers in fact gave very little attention to the Watergate affair in prayers, sermons, or other church-connected ways. A questionnaire which asks about such matters communicates the built-in value presumption that such attention might be a "plus." Most professionals hesitate to give other professionals data which the latter are likely to interpret negatively. One exception to this third speculation was a minister of the Jehovah's Witnesses who was patient enough to explain to his sociological correspondent that the viewpoint of his faith forbids any real concern for such a matter:

My first tendency was to ignore the questionnaire, as Jehovah's Witnesses are completely neutral with regard to political issues. However, I thought it may be helpful for your survey to have some background in the view we take of such matters. We are by no means surprised at such events occurring . . . We expect to see shortly a rule, not by Democrats, Republicans, or any other form of human government, but by the government of God, in the hands of Christ Jesus. Any reference we make to Watergate, then, is basically to contrast human rule to Divine rule, and to show that it is high time for something better.

This was consistent classic anti-worldly sectarianism. The replies of most of the eighty-seven other ministers who participated in our survey were apparently grounded in other theologies.

The questionnaire was designed to probe for three different dimensions of minister-response on the Watergate issue: (a) *Occasion*, (b) *Timing*, and (c) *Idea-content*.

(a) Occasion. When asked about their "main attempts to relate to Watergate," respondents indicated that the two most popular occasions were prayer in worship services (90%) and conversation with people in the church (86%). Sermons were a principal occasion for 58%, discussion with community leaders for 44%, and Sunday School classes or other group meetings for 39%. Most striking here is the widely shared sense, in this sub-group of the county's ministers, that Watergate was an eminently appropriate time for public prayer. Prayer in a liturgy is a very "religious" element in it, for the symbols of prayer presuppose a direct communication of the believer and God. In this light, Watergate for these ministers was an occasion when religion and politics profoundly mixed. Equally interesting is the similarly high percentage of ministers who report that conversation with people in the congregation was a major occasion for references to the crisis. These two responses together span the spectrum from highly formal "vertical"-religious attention to highly informal "horizontal"-social attention. Even this subgroup of ministers, evi-

dently, found praying and conversing about Watergate more appropriate than preaching about it.

(b) Timing. We explicitly asked for responses in the summer of 1974 related to the pre-resignation, post-resignation, and post-pardon periods. Three weeks prior to the resignation, 95% of the eighty-eight ministers mentioned some aspect of the crisis at least once in public prayers; and most made more than two references. Eighty percent made sermonic references, which declined to 71% after the resignation and to 54% after the pardon. References in public prayers also declined after the resignation and after the pardon; but even in the latter priod, 62% made at least one reference. Plainly the pre-resignation period of political tension, when actions against the President were rapidly accumulating, was the time when these ministers felt the most reason for paying attention to Watergate. Given all the questions of law and amnesty, judgment and forgiveness, connected with both the theology of the churches and the presidential pardon of September 7, 1974, it is somewhat surprising that this latter event seemed to command so much less attention than did the events of July and August. But on the other hand, the true political crisis came to its climax in early August, and the data may suggest a certain sense of political proportion among the respondents here.

(c) Idea-content. Five general themes dominated the replies of some sixty-eight ministers in response to this inquiry:[56] (1) The individual Christian has a civic responsibility as a citizen or office holder; the society needs politicians of high ethical standards. (21 respondents.) (2) The failings manifested by government officials are not peculiar to them but rather symptomatic of a more widespread human problem—sinfulness; we are all, in some sense, guilty or culpable. (21 respondents.) (3) We must not forget God's love, mercy, grace and forgiveness.[57] (13 respondents.) (4) We must pray for government officials, for the leadership of God in public affairs, for obedience to God's laws or seek God's assistance. (13 respondents.) (5) Sin will not go undetected or unpunished by suffering, sorrow, heartache; truth cannot be concealed. (11 respondents.)

A sample of the individual responses on which the above summary is based:

(The main ideas I have tried to get across to my congregation about the Watergate crisis have been:)

That Christians must not withdraw from leadership roles in civil life but rather seize every opportunity to bear a Christian witness. (Minister of First Wesleyan Church, Gastonia.)

Integrity of government leaders is a mandatory expectation. The sham of "court religion"—a la Billy Graham and the parade of White House preachers. The necessity for public officials to know who they are, to have a moral conscience, to be able to

Table 7.1

THE WATERGATE CRISIS

Responses from Ministers of Gaston County
(Data on 88 out of 273 Possible Respondents)

1. "My main attempt to relate to the Watergate crisis"

N	%	
77	90.0	Prayers in worship services
73	85.9	Conversation with people in the church
49	57.6	Sermons
37	43.5	Conversation with community leaders
33	38.8	Talks or other discussions in groups like Sunday school classes
9	10.6	Other attempts (e.g. letters to Congressmen, newspapers)

(N=85)

2. Timing and frequency of liturgical references, July 15-September 30, 1974.

		Before the Resignation (July 15-August 7)		After the Resignation (August 8-30)			After the Pardon (September 7-30)		
		N	%		N	%		N	%
Public Prayers:	No mention	4	5.2	No mention	4	5.3	No mention	27	38.0
	Once	9	11.7	Once	17	22.7	Once	14	19.7
	Twice	9	11.7	Twice	14	18.7	Twice	8	11.3
	More	55	71.4	More	40	53.3	More	22	31.0
	(N=77)			(N=75)			(N=71)		
Sermons:	No mention	15	19.7	No mention	21	29.2	No mention	32	45.7
	Some	58	76.3	Some	49	68.1	Some	37	52.9
	A lot	3	3.9	A lot	2	2.8	A lot	1	1.4
	(N=76)			(N=72)			(N=70)		

3. "The main ideas I have tried to get across to my congregation about the Watergate crisis have been:"

	No. of references to this theme:*
(1) Individual Christian responsibility in government, civic affairs	21
(2) Guilt for Watergate shared by us all	21
(3) Forgiveness as well as judgment must apply	13
(4) Prayer for God's assistance to government	13
(5) Sin, truth cannot be concealed	11

*Sixty-eight out of 88 respondents supplied information on these themes, some giving more than one theme.

distinguish truth from error. The horror of Watergate is a reflection of the ominous scenes of George Orwell's *1984*. It's time for real persons in government and not synthetic "Madison Avenue" figures.
(Minister of First Baptist Church, Gastonia.)

Why try to remove a speck of sawdust from someone's eye while there is a log protruding from your own? I'm a Democrat, and sick from the top of my head to the tip of my toes from hearing so much about this. However if this continues, I will definitely change parties and become one of the most dedicated Republicans in the world.
(Minister, Southside Baptist Mission, Gastonia.)

As ordinary citizens we are co-conspirators in Watergate due to our letting it happen, turning it into a partisan issue, and not seeing our own "little Watergates." Watergate is God's judgment on the United States and its life.
(Minister of Lutheran Church, Stanley.)

(1) The culpability is not limited to the White House—all of us share in the blame. (2) Freedom demands eternal vigilance—we must not be so involved in pursuing our personal goals that we lose sight of our corporate goals. (3) To judge or condemn others self-righteously is not Christian. (4) Democracy is only possible when citizenry participates in the democratic process. (5) God can use these crises to bring renewal.
(Minister of West Avenue Presbyterian Church, Gastonia.)

It was an example of misdirected trust through the setting up of a presidential god.
(St. Paul's Missouri Synod Lutheran Church, Gastonia.)

Two general observations, one predictable and the other surprising, can be made from the gist of these quotations: predictably, the Watergate crisis resonated deeply with that sense of the critical importance of the *responsible individual* in the local religious ethos. Not so predictably, the crisis produced in the ministers a striking reaffirmation of the importance of government, politics, and the participation of Christians therein. In the absence of comparable data from 1940, one cannot be sure, but one suspects that in Gastonia now are a larger number of ministers who perceive religious issues at stake in political institutions. This one third of the county's ministers, at any rate, showed little inclination to dismiss the Watergate affair with the old Protestant saw, "Politics is dirty business." Politics is so important, many seemed to say, that religious people, at least as individuals, must do their best to make it cleaner.

Two ministers among the eighty-eight took the survey itself to task —from a much different angle than did the Jehovah's Witness quoted above. One was the Presbyterian minister in Cherryville:

My main emphasis on the Watergate affair was in 1973. I consciously refrained from this during the period which you are studying—everyone was on the bandwagon then. I like to think I was a prophetic voice last year. This seems so true of the church. We speak out vigorously *after* the fact, not before it. I first noted this in 1954 about racial integration, and have seen it happen many times since.[58]

And the Reverend C. Peter Setzer, minister of the Holy Trinity Lutheran Church in Gastonia, said in a similar vein:

I had said so much previous to July 15 on the question of Watergate that the events of the summer did not precipitate a new rash of pulpit commentary. I hesitated to enjoy saying, "I told you so!"

As it happens, we know some things that Mr. Setzer said previous to July 15. We asked all our respondents to send us copies of sermons or prayers or any other material written by them about Watergate, and Mr. Setzer's sermon of May 17, 1973 was one of two sermons sent. (This was the Sunday soon after Mr. Nixon's dismissal of Mr. Haldeman and Mr. Erlichman from the White House staff.) Like the address of Dr. Harry Moffett to the County Democratic Party in 1963, this sermon is an example—as notable as exceptional—of how religiously-grounded political commentary occasionally sounds from a Gastonia church leader.[59] The sermon is all the more interesting in light of the fact that one of Mr. Setzer's parishioners was the editor and chief editorial writer of the *Gastonia Gazette*.[60] Having already written critically of Mr. Nixon in the paper prior to May 17, the editor testified to Setzer and to us concerning the impact of the sermon:

At the time, President Nixon still enjoyed wide popularity in this area, and many of the things said by Rev. Setzer might not have set too well with some members of his congregation. Still, they needed to be said in order to get the congregation to think about this vital issue. . . . This sermon had as much impact on me and my family as any we had heard him preach. . . . I believe that the sermon and editorials worked hand-in-hand to help change the thinking of some members of the congregation.[61]

When you're sledding downhill, it's a big help to get a shove from someone going the same way.[62]

Setzer himself said:

There was more adverse citicism than any other sermon I had preached before or since, but at the same time there was more positive comment than usual. The positive comments outweighed the negative. One person said, "If I wanted to hear about politics I would have gone to the court house and not to church this morning!" . . . The sermon was "popular" in that it was widely discussed, "unpopular" in that there were a few strongly opposed to the message.[63]

One remembers that the "message" of Watergate was a long way from seizing the imagination of a majority of the American people in May of 1973. The Senate hearings of that summer and the House Judiciary Committee impeachment deliberation of 1974 were still over the horizon, when, taking a text from the prophet Nehemiah,[64] this Lutheran minister delivered himself as follows:

He began by describing the rededication of the Hebrew people, recently returned from captivity in Babylon, to their ancient legal codes. For them it was a time of "national repentance," he said, and such a time has arrived in modern America. Repentance consists of two human experiences, both necessary for the health of persons and societies: the pain of telling the truth, and the joy of recovering it.

The sermon then spoke a word to four groups of people in American society who seemed resistant to both sides of political repentance: (1) The *cynics*, who, like some people polled recently in Charlotte, N. C., "see Watergate . . . as merely the kind of behavior politicians routinely engage in. . . . If the majority of the American people are reasonably well informed about the scandal and still believe that, then our political system is deathly sick, and we need not only repentant leaders; we need repentant citizens." (2) the *pragmatists*, who characteristically argue: "What if Babylon and Egypt find out about our failures? Would it not appear to them as a weakness and thus reduce our bargaining power with them?" (3) the *super-patriots*, who in Nehemiah's time "held an idealistic, starry-eyed conception of the king. For them, the king could do no wrong. He was incorruptible, deserving absolute trust and loyalty." On the contrary, "the biblical witness makes manifestly clear that every human being is twisted into a predisposition toward self-service and abuse of power. High office has *never* served as a cure for self-centeredness. . . . The prophets were aware of this; they insisted that only the God of Abraham, Isaac, and Jacob was to be given absolute trust and loyalty." (4) the *defenders of national virtue,* who believe, as did Nehemiah, that their nation "has something the other nations did not have." Perhaps the United States does have such virtue, said Setzer, but "what makes our system superior to other political systems is our capacity to live with the Truth about ourselves."

Shifting to positive analysis, he went on to proclaim some of the connections he saw between the biblical injunction against lying and the health of a human political community.

The Ten Commandments were not intended for just the religious people. They are the moral laws built into the very fabric of the universe. When they are broken, man suffers the consequences . . . The Eighth Commandment requires man to tell the truth, and yet we are faced with a series of wholesale deceptions on the part of this Administration: official denials that are reversed later, forgeries, thefts . . . leaving us now in the position of questioning the integrity of every White House utterance.

It is not the beginning of "official lying" in the White House, Setzer cautioned. Eisenhower, Kennedy, and Johnson before him provided this precedent for Nixon. All such lying, of course, was done in the name of national self-interest. But this is an argument that can turn against itself:

If it is justifiable to lie to the enemy, then on similar grounds it is justifiable to lie to the citizenry.

At stake here is an integral, rather than a superficial, relation between religious ethics and political ethics:

In spite of the well-advertized Presidential Prayer Breakfasts of the past six years and the passionate sermons of Billy Graham calling for personal righteousness, the law of God forbidding lying was patently ignored, or scoffed at as naive or dismissed as out-dated and politically impractical.

At stake also is what a person and a society can do to extricate themselves from the deteriorating consequences of systematic lying. Whatever secular solutions might be recommended, said Setzer, the biblical solution is repentance. Here King David is the instructive example. Having used his power to kill an innocent man, David was brought to the moral dock by a prophet who convinced him "that unless he confessed, his guilt would destroy him." So David confessed, and not only was he not destroyed but "the Hebrew nation did not fall apart" either. "The King's confession became an example of humility to every citizen, and the nation experienced a great spiritual revival. . . . It is better to hear the king's confession than serve under one who cultivates the illusion of righteousness and regards the appearance of honesty more important than the practice of honesty."

The personal-social-human result of such confession, concluded Setzer, can be a great rejoicing.

Why be dejected and sad? With each disclosure of the bitter truth God's law is being vindicated. Truth is coming to light. Justice is being done. The people are getting their priorities in the correct order. . . . Far from undermining our confidence in the ability of men to govern other men in justice and honor, the exposure of this scandal in the White House renews our confidence in constitutional government, where the highest officials in the land are also subject to the Law. It renews our confidence in the democratic system, with its delicate balance of powers between the Executive, Judicial and Legislative branches. We can even rejoice that a free press has ferreted out so much of the truth, that an aroused public has a conscience to be smitten . . . The bruising impact of this scandal draws forth from this great nation a reaffirmation that *deception is not necessary for national survival*. We can build a viable nation on *truth*; and we reaffirm our basic confidence that the political system will work because God is alive in the hearts of enough of our people to make it work. So finally we rejoice that we have a God who is so gracious as to guide and empower sinful mortals in the pursuit of good government founded on truth and justice.

If the Moffett discourse on the Kennedy assassination tells us what a religious "critique of ideology" sounds like outside the pulpit in Gastonia, the Setzer discourse on the Watergate scandal tells us what it sounds like inside the pulpit. One can readily imagine that such a sermon was "an unpopular position" in Gastonia—and who knows how many other American communities in May of 1973? Less readily can we imagine what religion, ideology, social order, and social change might have been in the minds of church-going Gastonians if such sermons had been their Sunday staple during all thirty-five years of history treated in this book. Are Gastonia churches on their way to addressing broad social questions with religious imagination and practical effect? Do they contribute in discernible ways to civic consciousness? Our aggregated, quantitative data on Watergate seem to answer: "Not very directly, in most quarters; yes, in some." But an exceptional, qualitatively significant event like this sermon seems also to say: "Emphatically yes, in a few churches."

NOTES

1. (New Haven and London: Yale University Press, 1965) pp. xvii-xlix.

2. *Ibid.*, p. xxvii.

3. *Ibid.*, p. xxix.

4. *MP*, p. 334.

5. Petersen and Demerath, *op. cit.*, p. xxx, quoting from Robert Lynd and Helen Lynd, *Middletown*, p. 350.

6. Cf. Introduction, above, p. 42, and Karl Mannheim's *Ideology and Utopia: An Introduction to the Sociology of Knowledge*, translated Louis Wirth and Edward Shils (New York: Harcourt, Brace and Company, Harvest Books, 1936.) In a series of crucial passages on pp. 88-90 of this classic volume, Mannheim claims that every thought-system has its "horizon within which lies (the) world of reality" of the thinker. He is speaking of himself and his own book, therefore, as he goes on to say: "The exposure of ideological and utopian elements in thought is effective in destroying only those ideas with which we ourselves are not too intimately identified. Thus it may be asked whether under certain circumstances, while we are destroying the validity of certain ideas by means of ideological analysis, we are not, at the same time, erecting a new construction . . . ." (Page 88, note 24.)

7. Peter L. Berger, *The Noise of Solemn Assemblies* (Garden City: Doubleday, 1961), p. 125.

8. Chaired by George H. Gallup and composed of ten other nationally prominent persons, plus the publisher of the magazine. *Look Magazine*, April 21, 1964.

9. *GG*, March 26, 1964.

10. *GG*, April 5, 1964.

11. *Ibid.*

12. *Look*, April 21, 1964, Vol. 28, No. 8, p. 93.

13. *GG*, March 28, 1964.

14. A comment made during the conversation quoted at the beginning of this book, Preface, p. 13 above.

15. Cf. above, Chapter One, p. 65, note 33.

16. For example, cf. above. Preface, p. 17 and Chapter Five, pp. 217-220.

17. Cf. above, Chapter Five, pp. 180, 184-185, 210, and Chapter Six, pp. 257-258.

18. Cf. Jeremiah 6:14.

19. Our impressionistic evidence on the avoidance of a reading of *Millhands and Preachers* by Gastonians in the forties and fifties further confirms the interpretation here. By the mid-sixties, said the local county librarian to us in an interview, local readers of *MP* were growing, especially among high school students. By contrast and by chance one of the authors encountered in the fall of 1974 a young woman born in Gastonia in the early forties whose father was an executive in a local textile mill. After hearing the above narrative about the All-America City award, she volunteered the comment: "The Loray Strike was never a topic of conversation in our home in the forties and fifties; I didn't know anything about it until I went off to college. But I think that I'll read the Liston Pope book soon. I've just about worked up the courage to do so." The idea that it takes "courage" to read a book about one's own hometown, written thirty-three years ago about an event that took place forty-five years ago, will strike many people outside Gastonia as odd indeed. But this woman's comment resonates deeply with Gastonia culture as we know it.

20. Cf. Robert N. Bellah, "Civil Religion in America," Chapter Nine in Bellah, *Beyond Belief: Essays on Religion in a Post-Traditional World* (New York: Harper and Row, 1970), and a collection of sermons preached after the assassination by a score of clergymen around the country, *A Man Named John F. Kennedy: Sermons on His Assassination*, eds. C. J. Stewart and Bruce Kendall (Glen Rock, N. J.: Paulist Press, 1964.)

21. Cf. above p. 37, and Arendt, *On Violence* (New York: Harcourt, Brace & World, Inc., 1970), p. 49, where the logic of her position is implicit in the sentence: "Everything depends on the power behind the violence."

22. The speeches of Martin Luther King were full of this escalating logic of justification. An early example was his speech to a Montgomery black audience at the beginning of the Montgomery bus boycott, reckoned by most students of the civil rights movement as its inaugural event. Said King in one part of the speech (December 5, 1955):

"If we are wrong, the Supreme Court of the United States is wrong.

If we are wrong, the Constitution of the United State is wrong.

If we are wrong, God Almighty is wrong.

If we are wrong, then Jesus of Nazareth was just a utopian dreamer."

23. Hannah Arendt, *op.cit.*, pp. 51-53.

24. H. Richard Niebuhr, *Christ and Culture*, (New York: Harper, 1951).

25. *GG*, December 23, 1963.

26. Cf. above, pp. 164-165.

27. *GG*, *op. cit.*

28. The dispute over Kennedy's Catholicism raged in Gastonia in 1960 as hotly as it did in many other predominantly Protestant communities. One of Moffett's uptown church peers, the pastor of the First Baptist Church, was leader of a statewide movement among clergymen to raise public question over the appropriateness of a Catholic in the White House. Moffett's lack of support for this viewpoint was apparently well known to the members of the First Presbyterian Church, but no publicly recorded statement to the effect is available from 1960.

29. In his position on the HRC he had probably seen more tension and conflict at first hand in Gastonia than he had seen since his arrival in the city in 1952. At least one fellow Presbyterian minister in town believed that "Moffett underwent a rapid change during 1963" in the civil rights crisis.

30. If an announcement was published in the paper in August, these researchers missed it.

31. "Statement of Ownership, Management, Circulation, etc. of the *Gastonia Gazette*," *GG*, September 28, 1969. This listing of stock and bondholders owning 1% or more of the investment of the company contains some 108 names; which are divided geographically as follows: California,

55; Texas, 24; Colorado, 14; Ohio, 12; New Mexico, 2; Gastonia, 1—the editor himself. Freedom Newspapers, Inc., is headquartered in Santa Ana, where the largest number of stockholders (27) live. Nineteen others live in Orange, Balboa, and Anaheim.

32. In 1928 and in 1968 the county was part of a congressional district that voted for Republican congressmen.

33. *GG,* Editorial, January 15, 1969.

34. *GG,* May 9, 1969.

35. *GG,* October 5, 1969.

36. *GG,* March 28, 1971. The masthead-creed of Freedom Newspapers, as published September 8, 1969, consisted of some 125 words, six of which were the words "freedom" or "free." The text of the creed is as follows:

Let Peace Begin With Me!

This newspaper is dedicated to furnishing information to our readers so that they can better promote and preserve their own freedom and encourage others to see its blessings. For only when man understands freedom and is free to control himself and all he produces can he develop to his utmost capabilities.

We believe that all men are equally endowed by their Creator and not by a government, with the right to take moral action to preserve their life and property and secure more freedom and keep it for themselves and others. Freedom is self-control, no more, no less.

To discharge this responsibility, free men, to the best of their ability, must understand and apply to daily living the great moral guide expressed in the Coveting Commandment.

37. In the two and a half years that ended in June 1971, *Gazette* circulation rose 19%—a gain of 5,060 copies of the paper. During the eleven years that ended on the same date, the neighboring *Charlotte Observer,* one of the state's major newspapers, had its circulation rise by only 7%, according to a *Gazette* account of the matter, June 2, 1971. Circulation in mid-1974 totaled some 33,000—according to a publication of that year from the Gaston County Chamber of Commerce. (*Gaston County, North Carolina.* Woodland Hills, Calif., Windsor Publications, 1974.)

38. *GG,* November 30, 1969.

39. The Board's view of the matter came to light in the spring of 1971 in its public discussion with an outside public relations consultant. Apprised of the conflict in philosophy between the board and the newspaper, the consultant commented that the need for an additional outlet for information was particularly acute in an area such as Gastonia where information given the people comes mostly from one source. In response to this, the chairman of the board said that in his opinion the basic philosophy supported by the owners of the *Gazette* was against public education in general. . . . [He] expressed concern because the *Gazette* was not locally owned and word from the top was hard to come by. . . . "I think it would be unhealthy for everybody to be in agreement all the time," he said. "You're talking about a publisher that must be pretty far to the right," [the consultant] said at one point in the discussion. "That's putting it mildly," [the board chairman] replied.

40. *GG,* March 21, 1971. An astonishingly large public fracas eventuated from the ambulance affair. During this same month a petition, alleged to have 15,000 local names, went with a "busload" of citizens to the state legislature in Raleigh to support the right of the funeral home's ambulance service to continue its operation, and in connection with the same dispute 5,000 other citizens petitioned for the ouster of the long-popular sheriff.

41. In openly relishing the stir of community controversy, the new management was obviously little moved by the old southern virtue of Harmony; and in an early editorial he went out of his way

to take a shot at the much-touted, locally celebrated notion of Progress. *GG*, February 16, 1969. It is fair to say that progress for the new editor was to be measured strictly in terms of the increase of personal wealth and personal freedom.

42. One of the researchers was present for this meeting, reporting on the findings of this research; and, though no survey was taken of the forty social-service-agency workers, there was all but unanimous agreement in the discussions that, however suspicious the "old" *Gazette* had been, on occasion, of the social-welfare functions of government, it had been a constructive community influence.

43. *GG*, November 21, 1968.

44. *GG*, January 7, 1969.

45. The words were a quotation from the director of the Dallas, Texas, Council of Churches, in an editorial commending this view, *GG*, August 9, 1969.

46. *GG*, October 25, 1969.

47. *GG*, October 26, 1969.

48. The new syndicated columns introduced by the new *Gazette* editor included Al Capp, S. C. Hayakawa, David Poling, and George Crane. David Lawrence and Paul Harvey had for long appeared in the paper, but with these and other additions, few newspapers in North Carolina now rivaled the *Gazette* in demonstrated "carrying capacity" for conservative columnists. One of the new columnists, Morris Ryskind, wrote a column in 1969 in praise of Joseph McCarthy; and one of the guest editorial writers—a farmer living on the outskirts of Gastonia—wrote at length about the "left-wing political activities and pressures put on Congress by the National Council of Churches," e.g., through the 1965 testimony of Dr. J. Edward Carothers before the Labor Committee of the House in 1965, on Section 14-b of the Taft-Hartley law. *GG*, February 7, 1971.

49. This new *Gazette* feature in these months was written by local residents who were invited by the new editor to contribute their opinions on any subject they wished. Many occupations and viewpoints were represented in the group of twenty or so persons. At least two were ministers, one of them very active in community affairs and in developing the social ministry of his downtown congregation.

50. Interview, "Church Can't Be 20th Century Luxury," *GG*, September 17, 1969. Included in the interview were quotations from this minister's analysis of the local political structure in terms of the imbalance between town population and their power to vote for county commissioners, "When this base is equalized, the trust of the people will go up and the men who serve will enjoy what they're doing more." It was a rare example of clergy analysis of a political problem from the double standpoint of the empirical social structure and a critique of the structure based in a certain social value—in this case, justice.

51. Editorials on the subject of freedom in the summer of 1974 included statements like these: "Government at best is a necessary evil." (August 9, 1974). "What this country needs is a good five-cent evangelist . . . a person who would go across the length and breadth of this land preaching the gospel of do-unto-self-that-which-self-can-do." (August 29, 1974). "On this Labor Day, when men of all kinds of employment relax and reflect, it would be wise to reflect on the unusual dignity of hard work . . . and the indignity of able-bodied, healthy humans living off the sweat and toil of someone else." (September 2, 1974).

52. He is a member of the Flint Groves Baptist Church in Gastonia.

53. *GG*, August 23, 1974; May 26, 1974.

54. Cf. above, pp. 28-29.

55. As mail questionnaire returns go, this was an acceptable rate of return. Sixty-five were returned from the first mailing, 23 more after a follow-up request which went out to 181 of the ministers. Sixteen of these 181 indicated by return card that they would return the questionnaire, and all 16 did so. But 21 more took occasion to return the card saying that they did not want to

participate. The questionnaire and accompanying letter were so framed as to make it maximally easy for a minister to participate: the questionnaire could be filled out in as little as two or three minutes, and a stamped envelope facilitated return. Names were secured from the current (1974) city directory, telephone directory, and lists used in our earlier research of 1965-69. The approximate distribution and returns of the questionnaires by denomination was as follows:

Denomination	Questionnaires sent (N=242)	No. of returns (Total=88)	% returns
Baptist	104* *(82 affiliated with S.B.C.)	34** **(all but one S.B.C.)	32.7
Methodist	28	16	57.1
Presbyterian	17	9	52.9
Lutheran	10	8	80.0
Sectarian	61	13	21.3
Miscellaneous	22	8	36.4

56. These themes represent a composite view. No one minister's reply embodied all of these elements or themes. A total of 68 ministers provided the information on which this summary is based.

57. But one of these respondents noted the "importance of confession and repentance before absolution/forgiveness."

58. This minister went on later to add parenthetically: "I re-read Pope's *Millhands and Preachers* not long ago and found it surprisingly pertinent." Letter, October 1974.

59. Setzer came to Gastonia in 1970. In 1973 he was thirty-five years old. Born in Brunswick, Georgia, he was brought up in several southern and midwestern cities where his father was a Lutheran pastor. He graduated from Lutheran Theological Seminary in Columbia, S. C. in 1965. He reports that this Gastonia church has, on other occasions, addressed political issues as part of its educational program, and that "our Lutheran Church of America Church School Curriculum provides a good balance of biblical and political studies." (Letter to authors, February 26, 1975.)

60. This editor is not the publisher-owner prominent in the above description of the *Gazette* management change. Watergate-related editorials of this period showed, at most, the muted impact of the liberatarianism in Mr. Segal's by-lined columns. But, consistently enough, a September 4, 1974 editorial tagged "the most valuable lesson" of Watergate as "the error . . . of a political machine" which takes over "the business of living from individual responsibility."

61. Letter from editor to authors, February 25, 1975.

62. Comment quoted from letter by Setzer to authors, February 26, 1975.

63. *Ibid.*

64. Cf. Nehemiah Chaps. 8, 9, 10. This text must have been used by many American ministers in 1973-74 because of the irresistible coincidence that, according to Nehemiah 8:1, the event described here took place "in the front of the Water Gate" of ancient Jerusalem.

CONCLUSION

Conclusion

What, then, is the summary impact of religious institutions upon the rest of the institutional fabric of Gaston County in the generation subsequent to the Liston Pope study? We may draw together our answers to this master-question in four generalizations:

1. Religion and the churches persist as major elements of local social life. In the early days of Gaston history, as Pope demonstrated, the churches and the mills were the chief institutions of the community. Since then, and especially since World War II, the county has undergone the raft of changes often called "urbanization." The local economy remains heavily invested in textile or textile-related industries. Business interests still loom large in the affairs of the community. But the economic structure is more diversified than ever, and the old textile elite increasingly feels the intrusion of other economic and political powers. The latter includes the federal government, an organized black community, the remote-controllers of national and multinational corporations, nearby and faraway business competitors for workers, the mass communications industry, and all those other structures of contemporary society that fuzz the boundaries of experience, function, and culture between the local and the global.

This steady development of a more differentiated society has had great impact on Gastonian churches. In the old single-industry economy, the churches were for the mill worker largely a refuge from the stresses of life; for the mill owners, a fortifier of harmonious relations between all classes of people in the community; and for the missionary-minded church leader, a social instrument for effecting individual religious salvation. Social differentiation has reshaped these functions of the churches. Many Gastonians still see the church as a refuge from stress, but that image is not peculiarly present in particular classes of local citizens. A more dynamic competitive society has apparently brought its share of new stresses to a cross-section of people.[1] Correlatively, as a means of "stress management," the churches now have competitors, rare in the twenties and thirties, such as automobiles, television, trips to the beach—for some locals an effective substitute for the elixir of revival meetings. At the same time, the churches have also lost their obvious serviceability as protectors of social harmony. The industrial personnel move-

341

ment; the new private and governmental social service agencies; and the kaleidoscopic breakup of the old residential, political, and ecclesiastical tags of the local workforce, all lessen the ability of the church, or any other institution, to function unilaterally as a "mode of social control."

From one viewpoint therefore, the churches—once located in the main trunk of the society—now find themselves shoved to the outer branches. Who needs the church anymore to run a society? But that viewpoint is deceptively simple. The churches not only endure in Gastonia; they flourish. By almost any social measure—budget, assets, proportion of population on the membership rolls, private and public deference—religion and churches persist vigorously. Apparently they provide many individual members a sense of meaning and personal status not supplied in other sectors of their lives. Typically in congregations of one to five hundred members, they offer an opportunity for socialization and training in the art of group leadership. In the work of pastors and subcongregational groups, they are a chief source of interpersonal support for individuals undergoing the crises of sickness, death, and other pain. In their "preaching services" and other liturgical occasions, they regularly celebrate the meaning of human life from a variety of theological perspectives; and, in these and other symbolic ways, religion touches, shapes, and is shaped by the ideological themes of local social life. Religion and ideology in Gastonia show many degrees of conformity and non-conformity, but there seems little doubt that what Gastonians believe about ultimate good continues to permeate what they believe about the social good.

2. *The relation of the churches to other institutions is no longer settled and predictable.* The new, relative structural independence of the churches has given their leaders two new options in relation to the other institutions of the community: (1) The new situation permits the church to "mind its own business" of preaching, converting, organizing, and caring for its own members. (2) It also permits the church to mind the business of the whole community. The repertory of behaviors that can now be associated with the minister's role is emblematic of the change here. Hardly anyone can "finger" the minister in Gastonia now as deftly as did that South Carolina mill executive quoted in one of Liston Pope's few hilarious footnotes: " 'We had a young fellow from an Eastern seminary down here as pastor a few years ago, and the young fool went around saying that we helped pay the preachers' salaries in order to control them. That was a damn lie—and we got rid of him.' "[2] Though the burden of industrial paternalism still hangs over a few towns in the county, the minister in suburban Gastonia is relatively free to make pro-union statements from the pulpit; for the power to get him fired resides less and less in any non-church structure. The churches and the industries of the community are both pulling away from an image that stresses their mutual threat or promise to each other's

existence. If some persons on either side still feel them, the pressures of such an image reside increasingly in the realm of idea, ideology, and symbol.

Our research indicates that few ministers and other church leaders are making frequent use of this new liberty as evaluators of the local social scene. A growing number of congregations, however, are undertaking forms of social action largely lacking a generation ago: recreation projects, day care centers, chapters of Alcoholics Anonymous, and collaborative programs with some local social service agencies. A few congregations have ministers and members seriously devoted to the development of a social ethic informed by religious faith; but the large, middle-group of Gaston church leaders still believe that the highroad to social salvation is the saved, spirit-filled individual, who more or less automatically expresses the faith in society. Here the change from a generation ago may simply be that questions of individual responsibility in society are more likely to appear in sermons, church school literature, and conversation in the churches. Whether or not the church as congregation, denomination, or ecumenical organization should take public positions on social questions, or take public action, remains in genuine dispute in and outside the churches.

Even that dispute is a change. Thirty years ago the churches had a widely-agreed-upon "place" in the lore and life of the community. Who can be certain anymore what the place of the church is? And even if one is certain, one encounters the growing presence of other, contrary certainties among one's local peers. The community, in short, may be ready for some re-definitions of the social role of the church as never before in local history.

3. The functions of religious organizations have both decreased and multiplied. This conclusion seems contradictory. Insofar as the churches have adapted to a more complex society, however, it might be expected that they would reflect this complexity in their very adaptation. More than the congregation of thirty years ago, a local church in the city of Gastonia may now include Gaston natives and non-natives, northerners and southerners, workers and at least lower-level managers, college graduates and high-school graduates, government employees and service-industry wage-earners. One may predict that a large number of these people will continue to opt for traditional personal-religion in the church, but a growing number are asking for a religion which encompasses their relation to non-church structures.

In the future, therefore, a strategic question for many churches may be how to build a multiple-function organization that interrelates these various people. A contrary possibility is that particular congregations will attract members in terms of specialized reputations as havens for either "personal" or "social" religion. But we think this highly unlikely. More likely is an emerging pattern of church programming that seeks to deal simultaneously with questions of individual and social values. Such programming would erode the popular southern Protestant distinction between personal and social gospels. This is somewhat speculative. Not speculative is the presence of a group of ministers and parishioners in Gastonia who do not expect the church of the future to offer its members simple replays of oldstyle revivalist religion. Even the new *Gazette* publisher concedes that "apparently most people want their pastors to be 'active in community affairs.' "[3] As one observer of this sort of church constituency described it to us:

Volunteers in organizations outside the church tend to be made up of people who are most active in their respective churches. This suggests to me that the talents and resources of persons within churches are not being fully utilized and that there are those who feel the need to become involved in some type of ministry in addition to their immediate church involvement. This again suggests to me that there are those within the church who do not feel that the church has been broadening its concept of ministry as it should.

As a member of the Board of Directors of (one) local organization I have observed that of the approximate membership of 60 we probably represent as many as 50 congregations and 6 or more denominations. There is a great deal of concern among the membership of this group for the increased involvement of their churches in meeting the needs of people.[4]

Such persons are not likely to applaud the distinction between personal and social religion, nor the distinction between the action of converted persons and the action of religious institutions in society. They are more likely to expect from their churches (a) help from like-minded peers in the active service of social causes legitimated, in their eyes, by their religion; and (b) some parallel help in clarifying the relation of religion to these causes—what our informant calls a "concept of ministry." Not social action or personal faith, but the uncertain relation between the two, would seem to be a frontier that these churchpeople want somehow to explore.

4. *The churches continue to be potential contributors to social change, but that task is more exacting and subtle than before.* We have seen that over the past thirty years the black churches have tested and raised the tolerance-levels of the community for discussion, conflict, and change in the structures of race relations. They have not done so, to be sure, in isolation from other institutional forces such as law and economics. The white churches, we conclude, have contributed to this same change by symbolic readying of their members for the breakdown of racially segregated society. An opposite but nonetheless powerful influence has emanated from the churches in the matter of labor unionization. By their silences, their participation in the baleful local memory of 1929,

their ratification of the conflict-shyness of southern culture, and their preferences for an individual rather than organized search for social justice, the churches have functioned largely as they did in the nineteen-twenties: inhibitors of the labor movement. Even here, however, we conclude that their role has been increasingly in the realm of symbolic culture: Progress, Harmony, and Liberty have had their echo and fortification in religiously similar concepts of salvation, love, and freedom. Neither the ideology nor the religion has stressed a socially relevant concept of justice.

Throughout our study we have assumed that social symbols are the lenses or screens through which persons and groups perceive issues of value and value-conflict in their surroundings. The recent evidence from Gaston County suggests that such issues, in some local fields of vision, are multiplying. In the old Gastonia, only a few issues of social change or continuity qualified as "moral issues" in the perspective of the churches. Prohibition was preeminently such an issue. But this old, single-exception to the adage, "Religion and politics don't mix," appears odd to some younger people in the churches. These are the constituents for ministers in the early seventies who were detecting moral issues in fields as traditionally remote from religion as voting reapportionment and job-retraining programs for the poor. Here William McLean's boundary-confusion may be an emblem of his generation: "I'm at a loss to know how to separate the moral and non-moral aspects of politics."

On the other hand, the churches of Gastonia participated, in 1974, in a judgment often made that year in national magazine articles: "people are backing down from the activism they once demanded of their churches"; instead, they desire "to return to the fundamental tenets . . . of the faith."[5] But this judgment is doubly questionable when applied to Gastonian churchpeople. Never in great numbers have *they* "demanded activism" in their churches; moreover, those who want a church culture that attends to social issues do not seem to be asking merely for more "action." Sound instinct may have moved the restless church members, described above, who have joined local voluntary associations to render some social service or to achieve some social change. Such associations may be better instruments than the churches for organized action on a highly focused issue of change. Both the prohibition movement and the civil rights movement illustrated that. And a similarly sound instinct may have moved the proponents of "non-political" religion to ask for something humanly more profound than short-range political perspective when they worship. Both groups are likely to agree that mindless, unreflective participation in social change is as empty and frustrating as utopian dreaming unexpressed in the world of everyday life. *At stake, in short, is not the choice between a religion of action and a religion of fundamental convictions—but the relation of the one to the other in a time of social-cultural change.*

This study and Pope's offer profuse illustrations of the pertinence of this way of defining the issue: the Loray Strike, the union struggles of the forties, the groundshifts in race relations in the fifties, the overt interracial tension of the sixties, industrial diversification, and the recent shadow of depression have all been occasions when decisions of personal and group behavior entailed questions of value, conviction, meaning. Like other crises in the experience of other people in the modern world, these issues in Gaston society called for some new "fit" between facts and values. In each crisis old and new fact was calling for interpretation through old and new value: the *combinations* appropriate to the present had to be somewhat different from those appropriate to the past.

Where, if not in the churches, are Gastonians to find the room in time, space, and organization to search for such new combinations? To be sure, there are substitutes for churches as groups wherein people may consider together the basic meaning of their life in a changing society. Families might serve the function; clubs, lodges, gatherings of friends. But one guesses that the issues of meaning here are too general, too complex, and too important to be grappled-with satisfactorily in groups making no claim to grounding in religion as such. The likelihood that many Gastonians will soon have substitutes for churches is remote. Religiously-grounded "order in the brawl"[6] of contemporary life they are apt to seek in some church-on-the-corner.

When they seek such order, they will be seeking to combine variables like those which we have sought to combine in this book: sociology, history, ideology, ethics, and theology. Surely the quest for integrity in the relation of all these dimensions of thought is not reserved for academic people. Whether they use such names or not, Gastonians ask many of the questions which sociologists and ethicists ask. An example of such question-asking, growing directly out of church-attendance, was offered late in 1971 by a businessman in the county who wrote a "guest editorial" for the local paper. Riding home from the Sunday sermon, he said, he had a disturbing thought:

With all those fine thoughts and eloquent words, I still know in the back of my mind that the Ku Klux Klan was scheduled to have another meeting in my community last night. Now that I am home from church, I wonder: Why is the Klan hanging around Mount Holly? What does the Klan derive from my community? What is in my town that the Klan thrives on? Are the words I have heard all my life empty words? Do I miss their meaning?[7]

Such questions are at once scientific and moral. They call for a style of communal religious life as devoted to inquiry as to proclamation. We have seen often, in this and the Pope study, that, for lack of coherent perceptions of scientific-historical fact in some ideological-religious perspective, the symbolic proclamations of the churches have sounded hollow and unworldly. The "two-world" theory of religion and society is one possible theory; but crisis——personal and social—is hard on that theory in human terms. Sober reflection on everyday life is equally hard on it: human beings seem not to live by religion alone, ideology, money, votes or bread alone. In fact they live by all of these things in some sort of wholeness. Out of their belief in the possibility of such wholeness, the institutions of religion presumably justify their continued existence.

NOTES

1. The evidence for this statement is scattered throughout the data above on religious activities, social attitudes, church membership and styles of church life. No consistency was found among sectarians, when classified either by religious attitudes or membership, regarding social attitudes or the role of the church in community life. Similar comments are appropriate for church members. Indeed, membership in a sectarian group may not be predictive of sectarian-type social attitudes; similarly, many attitudes found to be associated with sectarianism in other communities are held by members in large, denominational churches in Gastonia. In short, our findings are similar to those of Pope, in that stress and religious responses to it are not concentrated in any one identifiable religious or social category. Cf *MP*, pp. 126-140.

2. *MP*, pp. 159-160, note 15.

3. Cf. above, Chapter Seven, p. 323.

4. Personal communication, October 21, 1971.

5. Along with other statements from other local pastors to this same effect, these particular comments were made to a *Gazette* reporter by the associate pastor of the Gastonia First Presbyterian Church in mid-1974. *GG*, June 2, 1974.

6. The phrase is from H. Richard Niebuhr, *The Meaning of Revelation* (New York: The Macmillan Company, 1941), p. 109.

7. *GG*, October 17, 1971.

Appendix A
Bibliography

Adams, James Luther. "Religion and the Ideologies" *Confluence*, Vol. 4, No. 1 (April 1, 1955).

Allport, G. W. and Ross, J. M. "Personal Religious Orientation and Prejudice." *Journal of Personality and Social Psychology* Vol. 5 (April 1967): 432-443.

American Textile Manufacturers Institute, Inc., *Textile Hi-Lights*. Charlotte, N.C. (1947-1974).

Andrews, Mildred B. "Textile Industry Aids State's Sociological Development." *Employment Security Commission Quarterly* Vol. 10 (Summer-Fall 1953): 76.

Arendt, Hannah. *On Violence*. New York: Harcourt, Brace & World, 1970.

Bachman, Jules and Gainsbrugh, M. R. *Economics of the Cotton Textile Industry*. New York: National Industrial Conference Board, Inc., 1946.

Beal, Fred E. *Proletarian Journey*. New York: Da Copo Press, 1971.

Bellah, Robert N. *Beyond Belief: Essays on Religion on a Post-Traditional World*. New York: Harper and Row, 1970.

Berger, Peter. *The Noise of Solemn Assemblies*. Garden City, N.Y.: Doubleday, 1961.

Berger, Peter. *The Sacred Canopy: Elements of a Sociological Theory of Religion*. Garden City, N.Y.: Doubleday and Co., 1967.

Berger, Peter. "Sectarianism and Religious Sociation." *American Journal of Sociology* Vol. 64 (July 1958): 41-44.

Berger, Peter and Luckmann, Thomas. *The Social Construction of Reality*. Garden City, New York: Doubleday and Company, Anchor Books, 1967.

Birnbaum, Norman. *The Sociological Study of Ideology: A Trend Report and Bibliography*. Oxford: Basil Blackwell, 1962. Originally issued as Vol. IX, No. 2 of *Current Sociology*, 1960.

Blauner, Robert. *Alienation and Freedom: The Factory Worker and His Industry*. Chicago: University of Chicago Press, 1964.

Blizzard, Samuel. "The Minister's Dilemma." *The Christian Century*, Vol. 73 (April 25, 1956).

Blythe, LeGette. *Robert Lee Stowe: Pioneer in Textiles*. Belmont, N.C.: 1965.

Bodo, John R. "The Pastor and Social Conflict" in *Religion and Social Conflict*, edited by Lee, Robert and Marty, Martin. New York: Oxford University Press, 1964.

Boling, T. Edwin. *Factors Related to Congruous and Incongruous Membership in White Protestant Religious Organizations*. Unpublished Ph.D. thesis, The Ohio State University, 1968.

348

Broom, Leonard and Selznick, Philip. *Sociology*. New York: Harper and Row, 1968.

Brunner, Emil. *The Divine Imperative*. Translated by Olive Wyon. London: Lutterworth, 1937.

Campbell, Thomas and Fukuyama, Yoshia. *The Fragmented Layman*. Philadelphia: United Church Press, 1970.

Cater, Douglass. "Labor's Long Trial in Henderson, N.C." *The Reporter*, (September 14, 1961), pp. 36-40.

Chambers, Frank P., Harris, Christian P., and Bayley, Charles C. *This Age of Conflict*. New York: Harcourt, Brace and Company, 1950.

Cleghorn, Reese. "The Mill: A Giant Step for the Southern Negro." *New York Times Magazine*, (November 9, 1969) p. 34.

Cohen, Sanford. *Labor in the United States*. Second Edition, Columbus, Ohio: Charles E. Merrill, 1966.

Coleman, John A. "Church-Sect Typology and Organizational Precariousness." *Sociological Analysis* Vol. 29 (Summer 1968): 50-68.

Coser, Lewis A. *The Functions of Social Conflict*. New York: Free Press, 1964.

Dabbs, James M. *The Southern Heritage*. New York: Alfred A. Knopf, 1958.

Dabbs, James M. *Who Speaks for the South?* New York: Funk & Wagnalls, Co., 1964.

Dahl, Robert. *Who Governs?* New Haven: Yale University Press, 1961.

Demerath, Nicholas J. "Social Stratification and Church Involvement: The Church-Sect Distinction Applied to Individual Participation." *Review of Religious Research* Vol. 2 (Spring 1961): 146-154.

Dewey, Donald. "Negro Employment in Southern Industry." *The Journal of Political Economy* Vol. 60 (August 1952): 279-293.

Dynes, Russell R. "Church-Sect Typology and Socio-Economic Status." *American Sociological Review* Vol. 20 (October 1955): 555-560.

Dynes, Russell R. "The Consequences of Sectarianism for Social Participation." *Social Forces* Vol. 35 (May 1957): 331-334.

Eister, Allan W. "Toward a Radical Critique of Church-Sect Typologizing: Comment on 'Some Critical Observations on the Church-Sect Dimension.' " *Journal for the Scientific Study of Religion* Vol. 6 (Spring 1967): 85-90.

The Employment Security Commission Quarterly Vol. 10, No. 3-4 (Summer-Fall 1952). Raleigh, N.C.: Employment Security Commission.

Equal Employment Opportunity Commission, "Percent Employment of Negroes in the Textile Industry by Selected States, 1966."

Gaston County Historical Bulletin Vol. 7, No. 1 (March 1961).

Gaston, Paul M. "The South and the Quest for Equality." *New South* Vol. 27, No. 2 (Spring 1972): 12-13.

Gastonia Gazette, Gastonia, N.C., Issues from January 1940 through September 1974.

Gerlach, Luther and Hine, Virginia. "Five Factors Crucial to the Growth and Spread of a Modern Religious Movement." *Journal for the Scientific Study of Religion* Vol. 7 (Spring 1968): 23-40.

Glock, Charles Y. and Stark, Rodney. *Religion and Society in Tension*. Chicago: Rand McNally and Co., 1965.

Goode, Erich. "Some Critical Observations on the Church-Sect Dimension." *Journal for the Scientific Study of Religion* Vol. 6 (Spring 1967): 69-77.

Gorsuch, Richard L. and Aleshire, Daniel. "Christian Faith and Ethnic Prejudice: A Review and Interpretation of Research." *Journal for the Scientific Study of Religion* Vol. 13 (September 1974): 281-307.

Gustafson, James M. *Treasure in Earthen Vessels: The Church as a Human Community.* New York: Harper and Brothers, 1961.

Gustafson, Paul. "UO-US-PS-PO: A Restatement of Troeltsch's Church-Sect Typology." *Journal for the Scientific Study of Religion* Vol. 6 (Spring 1967): 64-68.

Haas, Ben. *The Chandler Heritage.* New York: Simon and Schuster, 1971.

Hadden, Jeffrey K. *The Gathering Storm in the Churches.* Garden City, N.Y.: Doubleday and Co., Anchor Books, 1969.

Hammond, Phillip E. and Mitchell, Robert E. "Segmentation of Radicalism—the Case of the Protestant Campus Minister." *American Journal of Sociology* Vol. 71 (September 1965): 133-143.

Hill, Samuel S., Jr. *Southern Churches in Crisis.* Boston: Beacon Press, 1966.

Hodges, Harold M., Jr. *Social Stratification.* Cambridge, Mass.: Schenkman Publishing Co., 1964.

Hoover, Calvin B. and Ratchford, B. U. *Economic Resources and Policies of the South.* New York: The Macmillan Company, 1951.

Hunter, Floyd. *Community Power Structure.* Garden City, N.Y.: Doubleday and Co., 1963.

Jenkins, D. T. *Beyond Religion.* Philadelphia: The Westminster Press, 1962.

Johnson, Benton. "A Critical Appraisal of the Church-Sect Typology." *American Sociological Review* Vol. 22 (February 1957): 88-92.

Johnson, Benton. "Do Holiness Sects Socialize in Dominant Values?" *Social Forces* Vol. 39 (May 1961): 309-316.

Johnson, Benton. "On Church and Sect." *American Sociological Review* Vol. 28 (August 1963): 539-549.

Jones, Graham. "Terry Sanford," in *Messages, Addresses and Public Papers of Terry Sanford, Governor of North Carolina, 1961-1965.* Edited by Memory F. Mitchell. Raleigh: Council of State, 1966.

Kelley, Dean M. *Why Conservative Churches are Growing: A Study in Sociology of Religion.* New York: Harper & Row, 1972.

King, Martin Luther, "Letter from Birmingham City Jail." Philadelphia: American Friends Service Committee, 1963.

Lenski, Gerhard. *The Religious Factor.* Garden City, N.Y.: Doubleday and Co., 1961.

Long, Norton E. "The Corporation, Its Satellites, and the Local Community" in *The Corporation in Modern Society*, edited by Mason, Edward S. Cambridge: Harvard University Press, 1961.

Lynd, Robert S. and Lynd, Helen Merrell. *Middletown: A Study in Contemporary American Culture.* New York: Harcourt, Brace and Co., 1929.

Lynd, Robert S. and Lynd, Helen Merrell. *Middletown in Transition: A Study in Cultural Conflicts.* New York: Harcourt, Brace and Co., 1937.

Mannheim, Karl. *Ideology and Utopia: An Introduction to the Sociology of Knowledge*. Translated by Louis Wirth and Edward Shils. New York: Harcourt Brace and Company, Harvest Books, 1960.

The Manufacturers Record. May 1952.

Marshall, F. Ray. *Labor in the South*. Cambridge: Harvard University Press, 1967.

Martin, David. "The Denomination." *British Journal of Sociology* Vol. 13 (March 1962): 1-14.

Mayor's Committee on Human Relations, Gastonia, "Minutes." July 15, 1963; August 5, 1963; August 19, 1963; October 29, 1963; November 11, 1963; December 2, 1963; September 12, 1963; October 14, 1963; October 21, 1963; October 5, 1960; May 3, 1962; June 2, 1963; July 8, 1963.

McKinney, John C. and Thompson, Edgar T., editors. *The South in Continuity and Change*. Durham: Duke University Press, 1965.

Merton, Robert K. and Rossi, Alice S. "Contributions to the Theory of Reference Group Behavior" in Robert K. Merton, *Social Theory and Social Structure*, Revised Edition. New York: Free Press, 1957, pp. 225-280.

Miller, Perry. *The New England Mind: The Seventeenth Century*. Cambridge: Harvard University Press, 1954.

Myrdal, Gunnar with the assistance of Sterner, Richard and Rose, Arnold. *An American Dilemma*. New York: Harper and Row, 1944.

Neal, Sister Marie Augusta. *Values and Interests in Social Change*. Englewood Cliffs, N.J.: Prentice-Hall, Inc., 1965.

The News and Observer, Raleigh, N.C. March 6, 1947; March 11, 1947; March 14, 1947; December 24, 1967; June 28, 1971.

Niebuhr, H. Richard. *Christ and Culture*. New York: Harper & Row, 1951.

Niebuhr, H. Richard. *The Meaning of Revelation*. New York: The Macmillan Company, 1941.

Niebuhr, Reinhold. *Moral Man and Immoral Society*. New York: Charles Scribners Sons, 1932.

Noel, Donald L. and Pinkney, Alphonso. "Correlates of Prejudice: Some Racial Differences and Similarities." *American Journal of Sociology*, Vol. 69 (May 1964): 609-622.

Photiadis, John and Biggar, Jeanne. "Religiosity, Education, and Ethnic Distance." *American Journal of Sociology* Vol. 67 (May 1962): 666-672.

Pope, Liston, *Millhands and Preachers: A Study of Gastonia*. New Haven: Yale University Press, 1942.

Population and Economy: Gaston County: Projected to 1990. Hickory, North Carolina: Traffic and Planning Associates, n.d. (*circa* 1967).

Rand, Ayn. *Atlas Shrugged*. New York: New American Library, Signet Books, 1957.

Scanzoni, John. "A Note on Method for the Church-Sect Typology." *Sociological Analysis* Vol. 26 (Winter 1965): 189-202.

Schwartz, Gary. *Sect Ideologies and Social Status*. Chicago: University of Chicago Press, 1970.

Shriver, Donald W., Jr. "Business Ethics and Religious Ethics." *Religion in Life*, Vol. 37, No. 3 (Autumn 1968).

Shriver, Donald W., Jr. and Robinson, Ralph S., Jr. "The Case of the Constant Customers." *Harvard Business Review* Vol. 46 (July-August 1968).

Shriver, Donald W., Jr., editor. *The Unsilent South*. Richmond: John Knox Press, 1965.

Spinrad, William. "Correlates of Trade Union Participation: A Summary of the Literature." *American Sociological Review* Vol. 25 (April 1960): 237-244.

Stark, Werner. *The Sociology of Religion: A Study of Christendom:* Vol. 2, *Sectarian Religion*. New York: Fordham University Press, 1967.

Stewart, C. J. and Kendall, Bruce, editors. *A Man Named John F. Kennedy: Sermons on His Assassination*. Glen Rock, N.J.: Paulist Press, 1964.

"Textiles: Blacks in the Mills." *Newsweek* Vol. 76, No. 18 (November 2, 1970): 88.

Textile Worker's Union of America 1948, *Building a Textile Union*. New York: TWUA.

Textile Worker's Union of America. *Textile Labor*. Vol. 35, No. 9 (September 1974), Vol. 36, No. 6 (June 1975).

Tindall, George B. *The Emergence of the New South, 1913-1945*. Baton Rouge: Louisiana State University Press, 1967.

Troeltsch, Ernst. *The Social Teaching of the Christian Churches*. Vol. I and II. Translated by Olive Wyon. New York: Harper Torchbook, 1960.

Underwood, Kenneth W. *Protestant and Catholic: Religious and Social Interaction in an Industrial Community*. Boston: Beacon Press, 1957.

U.S. Bureau of Census. U.S. Census of Housing for 1940, 1950, 1960, and 1970. General Housing Characteristics, N.C.

U.S. Department of Commerce, *County Business Patterns, 1945, 1960, 1970*.

U.S. Department of Commerce, *Historical Statistics of the United States: Colonial Times to 1957*.

U.S. Department of Commerce, *Statistical Abstract of the United States, 1974*.

U.S. Department of Labor, *Handbook of Labor Statistics* 1973.

U.S. Department of Labor, *Monthly Labor Review*, 1940-1946.

U.S. Department of Labor, *Monthly Labor Review*, January 1975.

Vidich, Arthur J. and Bensman, Joseph. *Small Town in Mass Society: Class, Power and Religion in a Rural Community*. Garden City, N.Y.: Doubleday, 1958.

Warner, W. Lloyd. *Yankee City*. New Haven: Yale University Press, 1963.

Weber, Max. "The Social Psychology of the World Religions" in Gerth, Hans H. and Mills, C. Wright, editors. *From Max Weber: Essays in Sociology*. New York: Oxford University Press, 1946.

Westie, Frank and Westie, Margaret. "The Social-Distance Pyramid: Relationships Between Caste and Class." *American Journal of Sociology* Vol. 63, (September 1957): 190-196.

Winter, Gibson. *Elements for a Social Ethic: Scientific and Ethical Perspectives on Social Process*. New York: The Macmillan Company, 1966.

Winter, J. Alan. "The Attitudes of Societally-Oriented and Parish-Oriented Clergy: An Empirical Comparison." *Journal for the Scientific Study of Religion* Vol. 9 (Spring 1970): 59-66.

Winter, J. Alan and Mills, Edgar, Jr. *Relationships Among the Activities and Attitudes of Some Christian Clergymen: A Preliminary Report*. Washington, D.C.: Ministry Studies Board, Report 201, mimeo.

Yearbook of American Churches. New York: Council Press, 1969.

Yinger, J. Milton. *The Scientific Study of Religion*, London: Collier-Macmillan, 1970.

Appendix B
Data as a Social Variable

I. Introduction

Social research inevitably reflects, both in the focus of the research and the nature of the investigation, the concerns and interests of the researchers. Despite the obvious truth of this statement, its implications have often been ignored and unexamined, a fact that in no way diminishes the significance of these factors for the research itself. It is to the effects of such interests and concerns of the three primary investigators that the present inquiry is directed, in an effort to identify not only the consequences but the *process* of social research, and in this case, the process of research in a community which had been studied before.

In community studies, questions of reliability, validity, and objectivity have special significance. However, other, more serious problems also inhere in such studies, including problems that cannot be resolved in advance of the field work and the data analysis due to the nature of the research itself. New foci for study, new questions and new types of questions, new understandings of the nature of community life, developing identifications with the community itself, and the sheer complexity of urban communities challenge the planning and the application of traditional methodologies and, in fact, many of the traditional conceptions upon which much social research is based. As eloquently stated in the preface to *Reflections on Community Studies* edited by Arthur Vidich:

> . . . [There is] an intimate connection between the investigator, his methods of investigation, his results, and his own future intellectual development. . . . There is no way to disentangle the research method from the investigator himself.
>
> Anyone who studies a community is as much changed by his work, even while in the midst of it, as the community he studies. During the research and his personal experience of it, the investigator is led into interests and problems that were initially outside the scope of his imagination, so that only with the passage of time does his own work inevitably become fairly sharply defined. (vii)

Nothing in our experiences in restudying Gastonia would contradict these statements. What began for at least two of us as an effort to apply the traditional methods of survey research to a community has resulted in a project of considerable complexity, in which traditional methods could not be consistently applied. The experience of the third

354

researcher has been documented in the Preface, demonstrating the process of gradual understanding of this city and its people. Out of our experience has come a joint realization that social research is a process, requiring alterations of plans, redefinitions of issues, and immediate decisions about various facets of a study, a fact that was not so apparent to us before our work in Gastonia.

Throughout the study, the earlier work by Pope increased the significance of each research decision; indeed, the focus of our study—the relationship of religious institutions and other social institutions in Gastonia—was derived from his study. Unlike the work of Pope, however, our research occurred during the maturing of social research methods, and hopefully reflects the growing sophistication of the social sciences. Thus, while our constant awareness of the earlier study provided insights and clues to the character of the interrelationships we studied, the fact of changes in research, in the community, and in the research personnel precludes a precise replication of the earlier work.

It is to the issues raised by these differences that we now turn in an effort to reconstruct the research process as explicitly as possible. Analytically, it is possible to distinguish data collection from data analysis, a procedure we shall follow here. Such distinctions are difficult in the actual process of community studies, however, and these stages do not coincide with the reality of the study itself, a fact which will soon become apparent to the reader.

II. The Equivocal Character of Fact:
General Issues in Project Planning and Data Collection

The basic issues that have been raised during our research are numerous, though most of them are interrelated with wide-ranging consequences for community level research. Certain modes of analysis presuppose certain types of data, while the methods of data collection may preclude some types of analysis. These issues themselves are the general focus of this statement on methodology and have some unique features; because it is a restudy, their significance extends beyond Gastonia to community studies generally.

A. The Problem of Changing Methodologies

During the past third of a century since Pope's work, social research has changed dramatically. Increased sophistication in sampling techniques, in methods of data collection, and in the analysis of data has created a sociology at once more scientific and more self-conscious. Because of the relatively undeveloped state of social science in 1938—only a few years after the Literary Digest debacle—Pope was unspecific about many methodological issues; in fact many of the problems in methodology about which we have become conscious have emerged out of the turmoil surrounding the growth of the social sciences in the years following World War II. It is obvious that no explicit analysis of comparability in methods is possible under such circumstances; however, it is equally apparent that no researcher in the 1970s can neglect, either for himself or for his present and future colleagues, a statement of the techniques utilized in the study. In an effort to provide a precise picture of our total research effort, we shall delineate the methods used in the data gathering phase of the research project, methods which further illustrate the uniquely social and variable nature of data in a community study.

1. The Study of the General Population

Modern Gastonia presented an interesting problem of obtaining a representative sample of the residents in the community. Housing areas formed a patchwork pattern, typically comprised of mill villages joined together by several blocks of better, more recently built houses. Few residential areas, especially those of pre-World War II origin, were of uniform quality or value, while the houses constructed in newer suburban areas were consistently larger and more expensive, characteristics which tended to emphasize the economic differences between the occupants of these residences.

To obtain a sample representative of the entire population, residential areas were classified in terms of racial and socio-economic characteristics. Personal visits were made to all parts of the city, and areas were delineated in which houses tended to be of relative homogeneous quality and type. As a result, four general sampling categories were developed: black, mill village, old suburban, and new suburban.

The black sample was drawn from an area containing 140 blocks in north Gastonia. From the larger area, a random sample of 16 blocks containing 183 addresses was selected as the basic sample. One additional block was later added to this sample specifically for the purpose of including some high income black family units.

The white samples were similarly drawn from a large pool of blocks. Five widely scattered areas, with a total of 155 blocks comprised the mill village population, from which eighteen blocks containing 218 addresses were randomly selected. The residences in the mill village sample were, almost without exception, houses that were built by mills for their workers in earlier years.

The old suburban area, comprised of houses constructed prior to or shortly after World War II, was located in southwest Gastonia. The entire area contained 110 blocks, from which eleven blocks with 185 addresses were randomly selected for sampling.

Finally, the new suburban area included 106 blocks in the southeastern part of the city. Virtually all of the houses in the area selected were constructed after 1950, and most during the 1960s. Eleven blocks, containing 201 addresses, were drawn from this area.

Addresses and names of residents for all dwelling units in each sampling block were obtained from the Gastonia City Directory. One resident in each household, the adult male head, or the female head if an adult male head was not present, was designated as the desired respondent. Substitutions of other adults in the household for the desired respondent were permitted only if the desired respondent either was not available for interviewing at a convenient time, or had moved to a different address, or was uncooperative. Under no other circumstances were substitutions allowed. About one third of the females included in the sample were substitutes for the desired male household head (e.g., wives or new residents); conversely, fewer than one in twenty of the males in the final sample was a substitute for a female head of household (e.g., new residents or adult sons). For houses that had been demolished or were no longer inhabited, no substitution was permitted; instead, additional addresses (i.e., blocks) were added from the sampling pool.

Interviews among the general population were conducted between April 1 and July 15, 1966. The interview schedule used is included in Appendix B. Students or faculty members involved in social science courses at nearby colleges and the principal investigators and their research assistants comprised the interviewing teams. Two training sessions were held for the student interviewers prior to the interviewing in Gastonia. The first session preceded a period of practice interviewing in Charlotte and Belmont, and the second was held immediately before undertaking the interviews in Gastonia. A third session with the interviewers was conducted approximately two weeks after the interviewing began to answer questions and offer advice to the interviewers.

Interviewers from the colleges were matched for race with respondents and were given a nominal payment for each completed interview. All 135 black interviews finally used in the study were conducted by these students. All 67 of the New Suburban, three-fourths of the Old Suburban and one-third of the Mill Village interviews were conducted by the principal investigators or their graduate research assistants. The total sample of the general population, excluding those removed from the sample due to questionable validity, includes 135 blacks and 271 whites.

Certain standard checks were made to verify the interviews themselves and to assess the quality of the interviewing. Contacts were made by telephone to several persons who had been claimed as respondents by interviewers. The information obtained from these contacts raised serious questions about the authenticity of some of the interviews, with the result that all 14 interviews reportedly done by one student were discarded. Examination of other interviews resulted in the elimination of ten additional interviews done by another student when the responses were compared and appeared to be of questionable validity.

Interviewers also were asked to indicate their evaluation of the respondent's attitude during the interview and to indicate the length of time involved. Both of these items were designed to give some measure of the degree of rapport established with the respondent. About 84% of the interviews were described as "frank, honest, and conscientious"; about 8% of the respondents were classified in each of two categories: "careless and inattentive" or "distorted his true feelings and attitudes." Comparisons among these groups failed to indicate any systematic or consistent differences in responses and no interviews were discarded because of interviewer evaluation of the respondents' attitude. The other 8% were eliminated from the sample as unacceptable. Average lengths of the interviews were compared among interviewers, again without any consistent patterns of differences. Median interview time reported was fifty-six minutes for blacks ($Q_1 = 47$ and $Q_3 = 66$) and sixty-two minutes for whites ($Q_1 = 47$ and $Q_3 = 71$). Median lengths of interviews done by the principal investigators among comparable white samples were identical to those reported by the student interviewers.

A final effort to estimate the quality of the data obtained from interviews involved an examination of the refusal rates. No consistent pattern of refusals emerged, though white student interviewers reported somewhat more frequent refusals than did the principal investigators. Only seven requests for interviews were rejected by blacks, about 5% of those contacted. For other categories, the proportions refusing were: Mill Village—18%, Old Suburban—23%, and New Suburban—18%.

Table B-1

COMPARISONS OF GASTONIA POPULATION, U.S. CENSUS 1960 AND 1970,
WITH STUDY SAMPLE, BY RACE

	Race					
	White			Black		
	Gastonia (1970)	Gastonia (1960)	Sample	Gastonia (1970)	Gastonia (1960)	Sample
Number	39,015	30,610	271	8,105	6,666	135
Age[1]						
19	2.2	2.1	0.4	3.2	2.5	0.8
20-29	21.6	21.7	10.9	23.6	19.9	9.0
30-39	18.1	24.1	21.4	16.8	22.7	14.8
40-49	21.0	20.7	27.1	19.2	23.1	32.0
50-59	16.9	16.3	24.4	17.8	18.0	23.0
60-69	12.3	9.3	12.0	12.6	9.1	15.6
70 and over	7.9	5.7	3.8	6.8	4.8	4.9
Total %	100.0	99.9	100.0	100.0	100.1	100.1
Occupation[2]						
High white coll.	21.8	18.0	28.7	5.7	4.8	5.0
Low white coll.	21.0	21.6	21.3	7.2	2.7	5.9
High blue coll.	14.2	13.1	8.3	5.1	7.2	5.0
Low blue coll.	43.0	47.3	41.7	82.0	85.3	84.2
Total %	100.0	100.0	100.0	100.0	100.0	100.1
Education: Median years[3]						
Females	10.0	8.7	9.4	9.3	7.1	7.0
Males	10.2	8.5	8.9	8.9	7.1	6.7

1. Persons under age 19 are not included in either the Gastonia population or the sample in order to make the comparisons meaningful. Figures for age and occupation are in percentages.

2. High white-collar includes "professional and semi-professional workers" and "proprietors, managers, and officials, except farm"; low white-collar includes "clerical and kindred workers" and "salesmen and saleswomen"; high blue-collar includes "craftsmen, foremen, and kindred workers"; low blue-collar includes "operatives and kindred workers," all "service workers," and "laborers except farm and mine." Farmers and farm workers and unemployed persons are not included in the computations.

3. Education for blacks in Gastonia for 1960 was not available by sex; 7.1 is the median education for the entire black population. The 1970 median education for white Gastonians is the figure for the total population.

Some indication of the degree to which our sample is representative of the entire Gastonia population can be seen in Table B-1. Blacks were oversampled intentionally to obtain sufficient numbers of males for detailed analysis, and as a result blacks comprise one-third of the total sample, though only 22% of the population in Gastonia. In general our respondents reflect the composition of the larger population rather well, with some minor differences. The whites in the sample tended to be older, better educated, and disproportionately employed in high status occupations compared to whites in Gastonia at large. Blacks in the sample also tended to be older, but were less well-educated than blacks in the general population, though there were only slight variations in the proportions employed in various occupational levels.

Through the cooperation of instructors at Gaston College, an additional twenty-seven interview schedules were completed by students during the spring of 1968. No control was exercised by the primary investigators over the administration of these instruments, and except for comparisons at certain points in the data analysis, these respondents are not considered as a part of the total sample.

2. The Study of Clergymen

Approximately 150 clergymen were residents of Greater Gastonia in the mid-1960s, nearly all of whom were pastors of local congregations. Sixty-six of these ministers, 57 whites and 9 blacks, were interviewed by the principal investigators during 1965 and 1966. The schedule used for these interviews is Appendix C.

The black clergy were selected from varied types of congregations, including both sects and denominational bodies. The white clergymen represented a broad range of denominational affiliations: fifteen Baptist, eight Presbyterian, seven Methodist, four Church of God, three Holiness, three Lutheran, and two Episcopal pastors included. The remaining fifteen white clergymen were primarily sectarian ministers. For the most part, the congregation served by each of these fifteen men was the only one of that sect in Gastonia. In terms of comprehensiveness, the clergy interviews include data from over one-third of all clergymen in Gastonia, and at least one minister from every denomination or sect in Gastonia was included in the sample.

The selection of these ministers, both black and white, was based upon two factors: relative importance of the congregation in the community and the concern for inclusiveness, including all types of sects and religious organizations in the community. Thus, in an effort to assure that the attitudes of these men are representative of all ministers, the entire range of organizational types, of denominations, and of socio-economic levels has been included in the sample of both black and white clergymen.

B. History and the Present

Though it is a truism that history shapes the present it does not negate the fact that any effort to reconstruct the social history of a community is a complicated and difficult process. The past is always viewed in terms of the present and the significance of current events is evaluated by the understanding of the past (e.g., see Preface above, p. 16). As a result, one's conception and interpretation of the past, and also of the present, is partial, selective, and tentative, molded by the public and the personal understanding held of the present. Social research inevitably is subject to such limitations; any historically-oriented research faces the dual questions of validity and comprehensiveness in conceptualizing or defining those factors that are relevant for the later study. In this context, though several problems might be mentioned, we will focus upon only three aspects of the dilemma.

1. The Problem of Change and Continuity

An understanding of change and/or continuity presents a two-faceted challenge. First, it is necessary to develop a definition or conceptualization of change, i.e., what is meant by change, and second, the methods of measurement to document change, i.e., indicators that will be used to identify or document these changes must be identified. Changes such as economic growth or recession, growth in size and number of churches, population expansion, industrial diversification and consolidation, and other such shifts which involve readily quantifiable data pose few problems of definition and documentation. Somewhat less easily observed and less easily verified are changes involving racial desegregation, shifts in labor union membership, growth in the proportions of positive sentiments toward organized labor among workers, or altered conditions and patterns of housing. Even more difficult to conceptualize and adequately document are shifts in the attitudes of the population toward certain issues, or the changing patterns of influence in decision-making in the community. Not only are such changes often imperceptible or undocumentable with traditional social research methodologies (e.g., see Preface above, pp. 17-18). In addition, the relationships of these factors to individual behavior or to institutional patterns are vague and also are subject to instability over a generation, presenting a difficult problem even with the best of research designs. The very meaning of "institutional pattern" is hard to specify exactly and consistently in research-design terms. And, in particular, a concern for "institutional legitimacies" (Introduction, p. 44) compels the researcher to use an approximate and broad definitional net, at the expense of precision, if he is not to exclude from consideration social realities which some fine nets (e.g., mathematical) cannot as yet catch. There are no precise ways to measure the "pull" of an institutional norm upon individual behavior.

Our recognition that theoretical models and research foci shape both data collection and later analysis forced us to undertake a careful, though necessarily superficial, consideration of community issues that might be studied. Variations in the speed of change and in the sources of influence for change or continuity (the latter an obvious interest because of the earlier study by Pope) were the bases for our initial selection of four issues: housing, liquor, labor unions, and race relations. These issues were chosen as a focus for identifying the processes of decision-making and the patterns of influence through comparing the contexts, leadership, and community involvement in resolution of these problems.

Even in such issues, where organizational or physical change could be documented, the conceptual problem is not entirely resolved (e.g., see Introduction, p. 51). Though the liquor issue represented a case of rapid change, race relations moderate change, and housing conditions and labor unionization relatively little change, our indicators of change were inadequate to measure the degree to which public action represented change in behaviors of Gastonians. Thus questions concerning the nature of change remained. Does the legalization of alcoholic beverage sales in the county mean a change in drinking habits of Gastonians? Does the official action of desegregation of schools permit an interpretation of data which suggests that race relations in Gastonia are "good"? Does the persistent failure of labor unions in Gastonia reflect a satisfied labor force? In the attempt to answer such questions, the definitions and conceptions of change became a crucial factor, both in collecting data and in analyzing it.

2. The Problem of Defining Relevant Issues

Pope researched Gastonia in the post-strike era, concentrating his attention upon the structures which had emerged after and in response to the 1929 strike. No such dramatic incident has involved the attention and passions of the community in the ensuing years, a fact which limited both direct comparisons with earlier years and detailed analysis of the processes involved in maintaining community life in a time of serious crisis. Indeed, only scattered community level issues could be found which involved a sizeable proportion of the community and which we hoped would permit us to elaborate the recent social, religious, political, and economic interrelationships in a manner similar to that by Pope in the 1930s. Of the four we identified, two were later found to be largely irrelevant to institutional life and to the concerns of our respondents. Housing conditions continued to be ignored, despite both visual and written documented evidence of its inadequacy, raising an additional issue of the factors which lead to the recognition of a problem in the community. In a different manner of resolution, the liquor issue was settled by a vote to change Gaston County from "dry" to "wet," (in part because the solid front of church opposition was broken) and then largely forgotten as a public concern. These two issues, despite their apparent relevance for examining decision-making in Gastonia, had to be eliminated as basic foci for analysis because our initial information regarding their significance proved to be incorrect. (See Shriver's own statement about similar misconceptions in Preface above, pp. 20-21).

Our focus, therefore, has of necessity been directed to the resolution of issues somewhat narrower in community impact than was the 1929 strike. But even our selection may be in error: an issue of relevance to churches may not be of significance to business; an issue of importance to government may be defined by churches as an area of illegitimate involvement. It is only with detailed historical understanding that the knowledge of critical issues emerges; this fact is an inherent problem for social research because the participation which permits the historical understanding may also preclude objectivity in interpretation.

3. The Problem of Identifying the Relevant Data Unit

A third issue of history is that of the data unit itself. In much sociological research, the individual and/or his attitudes and behavior toward some object constitute the basic unit of data. However, for a study focusing upon community issues and continuity and change in institutional interrelationships, data obtained at one time period from or about individuals alone are not adequate to identify the processes or factors in change. Unfortunately, the methodology of social research is underdeveloped in dealing with institutional and organizational level interrelationships. (Cf. Introduction, pp. 45-47.)

To resolve the problems posed by the limitations inherent in the cross-sectional method of data collection, data of several types and from a variety of sources were obtained. Our interviews with city residents provided an opportunity to assess the degree of awareness of issues and of support or involvement for changes at one specific time in the thirty year period under consideration. Additional data, especially clues and insights regarding other sources of information were gained because of the significance of the positions held by some individuals in our sample. Laypersons from various socio-economic levels and ministers provided evidence of the existence of varied perspectives concerning the role of the church in community life, both historically and ideally.

Other data were not obtained from individuals, but included official records of community organizations when available to us, historical records of the community —especially the *Gastonia Gazette,* church membership lists, minutes of various meetings, demographic data, and personal reports of the researchers as participants. As expected, the available data on institutional level units often were neither gathered for our purposes nor, for the most part, complete in the detail we desired. As a result, our interpretations necessarily are based upon multiple types of data from several sources, woven together to provide the most adequate description of the processes of change and decisionmaking concerning the issues under consideration.

C. Comparability of Data: The Problems of Community Size and Complexity

The size and complexity of the community has made the examination of institutional patterns in Gastonia far more difficult in 1970 than in 1940. The issues upon which we decided to focus our attention were relatively narrower in impact though they may have involved more persons within Gastonia than did the 1929 strike. During the three decades following Pope's study, the changes that can be documented with quantified data offer considerable evidence about growth, but little direct information concerning change in institutional interrelationships.

The problem of comparability can be illustrated by some specific examples. In 1940, about 50 churches existed in Greater Gastonia; by 1970 the total number of churches exceeded 160—an increase of 320%, a rate of growth nearly twice that of the growth of population in the area. Unfortunately, such data offer little information concerning the meaning of religion or the significance of religious institutions for Gastonians now, as compared to 1940. Similarly, since 1940 the range of occupations available to residents of Gastonia and Gaston County has developed along the pattern of that in the United States generally, with a consistent decline in the number of operatives and blue collar workers and clerical and sales workers. Such changes are important because of the significance of occupational roles in shaping the perceptions of persons toward life and the community. In Gastonia in the 1960s, the fact that work experiences occurred in a general occupational context quite different from that of persons living there in the 1940s makes it difficult to compare the meaning of such experiences to those of a generation later (e.g., see Preface above, pp. 23-24).

At best, comparisons of time periods are guided by well defined measures of the phenomena under study and well developed hypotheses or theoretical perspectives. Few specific hypotheses are adequate to specify the nature of institutional relationships in a community at two time periods, however; neither can the same measures of institutional interrelationships be applied in two time periods without distortion. In short, it was necessary to utilize a model more general and more tentative than that of Pope, while other measures of institutional control and interrelationships had to be used (e.g., see

Introduction, pp. 34-36). For example, diversification of the industrial base of the community represents a shift from total control of labor policies by textile interests to an environment of competition with other types of industry for labor, resulting in shifts in labor relations policies.

While the fact of changing industrial conditions is readily documented, its significance is less easily verified. The problems of data analysis, as compared to data collection are most directly involved with this issue, and it is to these concerns that we now turn.

III. The Fragile Inference: Problems of Data Analysis

The desire of the principal researchers to make causal inferences, rather than simply to identify correlates, introduced additional issues into the research design and analysis. Elaboration of such relationships rests upon the nature of answers to certain questions about individual attitudes, individual behavior, institutional patterns, and their interrelationships. In addition to those questions concerning such issues during data collection, other, more specific problems emerged during the analysis of the data: what is the significance of various attitudes toward the community issues, and what is the relationship between attitudes of people and change or continuity in community life? What activities of individuals are relevant for an understanding of the community? What are the techniques of analysis by which behavior can be interpreted, since meaning is nearly always involved in behavior? How can the significance of institutions in the total life of the community be assessed? And, most difficult question of all, how shall the meaning and human impact of *symbols* be assessed? (Cf. Introduction, pp. 49-50.)

These concerns, by the very nature of the data available to us, are focused upon three general issues. First, the data concerning attitudes and personal information provided by the over 400 interviews offer insight into the ideological-value dimensions of social life, especially as these relate to the larger institutional structures of Gastonia. Second, the data concerning individual behaviors, based upon case studies, interviews, or participant observation, permit an analysis of the differential impact of various individuals' behaviors upon community institutions. Institutional changes and continuities identified by observation and historical records, offer a third focal point for elaborating the nature of social relationships in Gastonia.

A. Individual Attitudes and Individual Behavior

Attitudes can be measured; behavior can be described or defined by observation. Unfortunately, however, the relationship between attitudes, as identified through survey research techniques, and behaviors is not easily determined. Religious or ethical attitudes regarding race relations do not always mean behavior consistent with these attitudes; a vote for legalizing the sale of alcohol does not necessarily mean that the person personally desires to purchase such beverages or is in favor of "drinking"; attendance at church may or may not indicate a high level of religious belief or commitment.

Indeed, an adequate interpretation of such data involves several types of analysis. The objective relationship, i.e., the correlation of attitudinal responses and behavior, provides evidence of community wide patterns of thought and action, as in the case of the close correlation of religious beliefs and church attendance (see Introduction, pp. 49-50).

One dramatic example of this consistency occurred during the field survey. One of the principal investigators was interviewing a white sectarian minister, recently moved from rural South Carolina, having a third grade education and having spent twenty-five years in the mills or on the farm. As the question concerning the best path for future race relations was being read, his teenage daughter walked through the room, and he responded, albeit somewhat sadly, that "Jesus sees no differences in races," and so "if she decided to marry a black man, I guess I'd have to let her do so."

More difficult to interpret, however, is the lack of any significant correlation, as in the case of sectarian religious beliefs and social attitudes.

In such cases, a central problem to much social research emerges, that of the meaning of attitudes and/or behavior. Specifically, the question is that of WHY, or the relationship which the respondent himself perceives between his attitudes and his behavior. The symbolic nature of much religious behavior complicates the examination of this relationship, as in that belief system which presupposes certain behaviors, e.g., a patriot who believes that a good American attends church, prays, and participates in religious activities, whether or not he sees them as intrinsically meaningful.

Unfortunately, the information required to elaborate this relationship is too detailed to be feasible in most social research, including our own study. Inferences of necessity are made in an effort to interpret the significance of beliefs as factors in behavior, without the benefit of longitudinal data as a measure of the validity of such inferences.

B. Individual Attitudes and Behaviors and Institutional Patterns

The relationship of the individual to social institutions remains a significant focus of social research; similarly the relationship between the Christian church and the Christian individual—our focus in Gastonia—is structured and defined by the dominant culture of the community. For our purposes, an examination of the role of individual beliefs in shaping social institutions involved comparisons of beliefs and actions of Christians and non-Christians in non-religious institutional life or a consideration of the basic structure of social relations in the community (e.g., see Introduction, pp. 46-49). The impact of various individuals upon institutional patterns remains an open question, however, despite our focus upon this question (e. g., see Preface above, p. 27).

Our interviews asked about community leaders for various issues; only a minority of respondents could identify persons whose influence in the community extended beyond the informal, interpersonal level. Information concerning the impact of individuals upon institutions is drawn instead from observation of the community; thus the data must be indirect rather than direct and dependent upon the interpretation of their meaning by the researcher rather than focused upon the meaning held by the respondent or actor.

An example of this difficulty in Gastonia involved a consideration of power in community decision-making. One of the principal investigators attended a public meeting of the Gastonia Urban Redevelopment Commission, at which time construction of a pedestrian mall down Main Street was proposed and discussed. After some statements by people supporting the proposal and some by others in opposition to it, one member of the audience announced that the plan would render useless the recently constructed drive-in windows of a downtown establishment. Though never identified by name during the meeting, the existence of this business in the downtown area precluded further discussion of the mall and the plan was dropped. No person directly associated with the affected business spoke at the meeting; indeed, its president was among those present, but he sat in the back row, said nothing, and left before the discussion was terminated, apparently satisfied that there was no danger to their recent investment in drive-in facilities.

A similar problem exists in the examination of the effect of institutions upon individual behavior or attitudes. Because institutions are temporally antecedent to individuals they structure social situations that impinge upon the individuals' behavior. Changes in institutional patterns, e.g., the elimination of racial segregation or the change from non-union work relationships to labor unionization, generate a different pattern of behaviors which are reinterpreted or rationalized by the development of a belief system to accommodate the new behaviors. Obviously this statement oversimplifies the process. However, without detailed, precise longitudinal data, inferences about causality must reflect most clearly our basic sociological perspectives concerning the sources and order of changes.

C. Institutional Interrelationships

As with Pope, our focus upon institutions and their interrelationships quickly led us to identify the economic organization as the basic source of continuity and change in the community. As such, causal inferences depend upon defining relationships between the demands of economic institutions, e.g., honesty, efficiency, responsibility, and the demands of other institutions, such as the family, the church, or government.

Basically the issue involves the level at which relationships are accepted as documented. Data from individuals provided information that is subject to several limitations, including the factors of personal perception and interpretation (see Introduction, pp. 45-46). Direct information concerning institutional influence, e.g., the sponsorship of a church by an economic organization, is largely lacking; case studies and privileged information would be necessary to show such relationships. The scarcity of actual data demands that inferences be made from indirect data, such as demographic information or statistical measures of economic power.

The case for religious institutions as agents for social change also deserves close scrutiny; influence from religious organizations appears to have been indirect through the individuals. The individuals have not acted in concert, however, with some supporting change in the structures of community life, some supporting the status quo, and some viewing such interchange as invalid.

What is at stake in these issues is the validity of our inferences. Causal inferences require a consideration of factors that cannot be examined adequately without varied sources of information and without multiple tools of analysis. No single method of research or analysis is capable of providing enough information to justify causal inferences. It is in recognition of this fact that we have utilized questionnaires, interviews, demographic data, issue analysis, case studies, and, perhaps most importantly, participant observation to support our interpretations.

Appendix C

Interview Schedule: General Population Sample

ADDRESS _____ NUMBER _____
NAME _____
BLOC NO. _____
CATEGORY: UMC _____
LMC _____
MV _____

PREFERENCE IN RESPONDENT: HUSBAND _____ ; WIFE _____
 If preferred respondent is not available, is a substitute acceptable?
 If substitution is made:
 Wife for husband _____ (widow _____ ; divorcee _____ ; other _____
—specify relationship _____)

 Child for parent _____ (son _____ ; daughter _____ ; other _____
—specify relationship _____)

 Good afternoon (evening). My name is _____ and I'm from Belmont Abbey College. Along with some other students, I'm doing some interviewing on this block as a part of a study of people's attitudes about work, religion, and life—and about Gastonia in general. Your address was chosen at random and I'd like to ask you some questions. I'm not selling anything, and anything you say will not be repeated to anyone in Gastonia so that you will ever be identified. May I come in?

Time: 45 minutes to an hour
Use of information: by persons outside the city to see what changes have occurred in the
 attitudes of people over the last few years
Confidentiality: the individual will not be identified in any way at any time
Project: registered with the Chamber of Commerce and supported by religious, educa-
 tional, and philanthropic agencies

TO BE COMPLETED *AFTER* LEAVING THE HOUSE:
 1. Refusals: a. Person who talked to you (if known) _____
   b. Reason offered for refusing _____

366

c. Your evaluation of the person's reasons:
_____ (1) objects to all interviews
_____ (2) too busy
_____ (3) didn't want to be bothered
_____ (4) generally hostile during our conversation
_____ (5) other: _____

2. Date of Interview:
1st attempt: _____ (Completed _____ ; Refused _____ ; Not at home _____)
2nd attempt: _____ (Completed _____ ; Refused _____ ; Not at home _____)
3rd attempt: _____ (Completed _____ ; Refused _____ ; Not at home _____)
3. Length of interview: _____ hours _____ minutes
4. Evaluation of the interview: How would you rate the information given?
_____ In general, the respondent was frank, conscientious, and cooperative
_____ The respondent probably consciously distorted his true feelings and attitudes
_____ The respondent was generally careless and inattentive during the interview
_____ Other: _____

5. Name of interviewer: _____ (Signature)

1. One of the first things we are interested in is the kind of work people in Gastonia do. *What is your job at the present time*? (Get similar information for both *wife* and *husband*)
Self: Spouse:
1a. (If R. gives place of work) What do you do there?
Self: Spouse:
1b. (If not already answered) Do you work for yourself, or are you employed by another person or by a company?
Self: ____ self-employed   Spouse: ____ self-employed
____ employed by another person   ____ employed by another person
____ employed by company   ____ employed by company

2. (If R or spouse does not work now) Have you (Has your wife, husband) ever held a full-time job outside the home?

Self: _____ yes   Spouse: _____ yes
_____ no   _____ no
2a. (If yes) What type of work:
Self: Spouse:

3. Would you tell me which of these things on this card you most prefer in a job? (would want most in your husband's job?) . . . next? . . . third? . . . least? (Note order: most-1, next-2, third-3, least-5) SHOW CARD A.
_____ High income
_____ No danger of being fired
_____ Working hours short, lots of free time
_____ Chances for advancement
_____ The work is important and gives a feeling of accomplishment
_____ Other:

4. Some people say that they couldn't really be happy unless they were working at some job (or keeping house). But others say they would be a lot happier if they didn't

have to work and could take life easy. How do you feel about this?

_____ work

_____ take life easy

4a. Why is that?

5. Do you think every family should save a part of its income every month or not?

    _____ yes

    _____ no

    5a. (If yes) How important is this? Should people save even if they have to go without things they would really like to have, or should they save only when they can do it without any trouble?

    _____ even without things they would really like to have

    _____ without any trouble

6. Let's change the subject a bit. I'd like to ask you some questions about yourself. How long have you lived in Gastonia?

    _____ 1. Less than one year

    _____ 2. 1-2 years

    _____ 3. 3-5 years

    _____ 4. 6-10 years

    _____ 5. 11-19 years

    _____ 6. 20 years and over

    _____ 7. All my life.

7. Where were you born?

8. Where did you spent most of your childhood?

9. What is the highest grade in school you completed? (Circle)

    1   2   3   4   5   6   7   8   9   10   11   12   13   14   15   16   16 +

10. What type of work did your father do?

11. In what year were you born?

12. What was your total family income in 1965? (Furnish Card B)

    _____ 1. 0-999

    _____ 2. 1,000-1,999

    _____ 3. 2,000-2,999

    _____ 4. 3,000-3,999

    _____ 5. 4,000-4,999

    _____ 6. 5,000-6,999

    _____ 7. 7,000-9,999

    _____ 8. 10,000- and over

    _____ 9. Don't know

    _____ 10. Won't answer

13. Let's change the subject a bit. What are some of the things that you particularly like about Gastonia?

    13a. Are there things about Gastonia that you don't like?

14. Most communities have some problems. What do you consider the main problems facing Gastonia?

14a. What do you think has been the most important improvement in Gastonia in recent years?

14b. Who were the leaders in this change? (Give names and community positions, when possible)

14c. Do you know of any people who opposed this change?

14d. Did church leaders, including ministers, take part in making this change possible?

15. Suppose some new project were being considered for the community—a new park, a new hospital, or the like—who are four or five people who would be the most influential in getting the community to support the project?

16. There are a lot of textile mills in Gastonia and Gaston County. What is there about this city or county that makes favorable conditions for the textile industry?

17. Would you favor a minimum wage law?
    _____ yes
    _____ no   (If he says why—note it)
    17a. Do you think most Gastonians would favor it?
        _____ yes
        _____ no   (If he says why—note it)

18. North Carolina has a law which allows a man to work in a unionized plant without joining the union. Do you approve of this law?
    _____ yes
    _____ no   (If he says why—note it)
    18a. Do you think most Gastonians would approve of this law?
        _____ yes
        _____ no
    18b. How do you feel about labor unions in general?
    18c. Does Gastonia need labor unions?
    18d. What reasons do you think the average mill worker in Gastonia would give *for* joining a union?
    18e. What reasons do you think the average mill worker in Gastonia would give *against* joining a union?

19. Are wages here high or low compared to the rest of the country?
    _____ high
    _____ low
    _____ about the same

20. What changes have come recently in working conditions in mills in Gastonia?
    20a. What changes in working conditions would you like to see in the mills?

21. Is poor housing a problem in Gastonia?
    _____ yes
    _____ no   (If no, skip to 21c.)
    21a. (If yes) What has led to this problem?
    21b. Who should take the responsibility for solving the housing problem?
    21c. Is the selling of the mill villages a good thing or not?
        _____ a good thing
        _____ a bad thing

21d. Why do you feel this way?

22. In the last few years there have been some changes in relations between the races. What changes have you noticed in Gastonia?
(If none, skip to question 23)

22a. Have these changes been good or bad?
_____ good
_____ bad

22b. Did local Negroes push for these changes?

22c. Would these changes have been made without pressure from the national government?
_____ yes
_____ no

22d. What do you think is the best path toward race relations in the future?

23. Now I'd like to ask you some questions about your attitude toward religion and your interest in the church. About how often have you attended church in the last year?
_____ once a week or more
_____ two or three times a month
_____ once a month
_____ less than once a month
_____ never

24. When you attend church, what are the main reasons for going?

25. a. What things do you like best about your church?
b. What improvements would you like to see in your church?

26. When you do not attend church, what is the main reason for not going?

27. What church organizations do you take part in?

28. a. Would you say that you attend services more often, about the same, or less often than you did ten or fifteen years ago?
_____ more often
_____ less often   (If more or less often, ask 28b.)
_____ about as often
b. What has been the reason for the change?

29. Do you think the Bible influences people today more, just as much, or less than it did ten or fifteen years ago?

_____ more
_____ less
_____ just as much

30. What is your religious preference or denomination?
_____ Protestant (Please specify denomination: _____)
_____ Catholic
_____ Jewish
_____ None

30a. (If none) Have you ever had a preference?

_____ yes (please specify: _____)

_____ no (if no skip to 31.)

30b. (If R. has a preference) What local church do you attend?

30c. Are you a member?

_____ yes

_____ no

30d. Have you always belonged to this denomination?

_____ yes

_____ no

30e. (If no to 30d.) What was your former denomination?

31. What was your father's denomination?

32. What was your mother's denomination?

33. Would you say that your father was more, less, or about as religious as you are?

_____ more

_____ less

_____ about as religious

34. Are you more or less interested in religion than you were ten or fifteen years ago?

_____ more

_____ less

_____ about the same

35. If you were a member of a committee looking for a new minister, what kind of man would you look for?

36. a. Do you think that a minister should be different from other Christian people in town?

_____ yes

_____ no

b. (If yes) In what ways should he be different?

37. a. Do you think a minister should be informed about such present-day problems as politics, race, the schools, and U.S. foreign policy?

_____ yes

_____ no

b. Why do you feel this way?

38. Do you know of any social questions on which your denomination has taken a stand, such as war, race relations, labor-management relations, or politics?

_____ yes

_____ no

38a. (If yes) What issues?

38b. What was the stand your denomination took?

39. In recent years have local churches or church leaders had any influence on any of the following:

elections?
_____ yes (If yes) What?
_____ no
housing?
_____ yes (If yes) What?
_____ no
labor-management relations?
_____ yes (If yes) What?
_____ no
alcohol?
_____ yes (If yes) What?
_____ no
race relations?
_____ yes (If yes) What?
_____ no

40. In your local church has there been any discussion of matters like those?
_____ yes   (If yes, ask the following three questions, 40a., 40b., and 40c.)
_____ no
40a. What kinds of discussions? (READ LIST)
_____ sermons
_____ Sunday School class
_____ informal group discussions
_____ church officer meetings
_____ specially called meetings
_____ other (Please specify _____)
40b. Do you feel that there should be such discussions in your church?
_____ yes
_____ no
40c. Do you feel that there should be *more* such discussions in your church?
_____ yes
_____ no

This has been a rather long discussion already, but we are almost finished. I want to read some statements. Would you say whether you:
    strongly agree with the statement,
    strongly disagree with it,
    agree with it (but don't feel strongly about it)
    disagree with it (but don't strongly disagree)
    or are undecided?

(Respondent may need some prompting at the beginning here. Give him CARD C with the five answers. If he says, "Agree," check his answer with a comment like, "You agree, but not strongly, right?")

SA A U D SD   41. Everybody should be thinking seriously about changes needed
                        in the community.

SA A U D SD   42. We could save ourselves a lot of trouble by doing things the way
                        they have always been done.

SA A U D SD 43. White people tend to notice the Negro only when he organizes and puts the pressure on.

SA A U D SD 44. All men are equal in the eyes of God.

SA A U D SD 45. People seldom do the right thing because it's right but because it benefits them in some way.

SA A U D ·SD 46. We have to learn to live with the world as it is.

SA A U D SD 47. Usually things improve only when someone dares to be different.

SA A U D SD 48. The church should have been the first organization to open its doors to Negroes.

SA A U D SD 49. One is usually better off putting his confidence in things that have stood the test of time.

SA A U D SD 50. Race should *not* have anything to do with getting a job.

SA A U D SD 51. I wish older people would be as open to change as young people seem to be.

SA A U D SD 52. The best way to improve the world is to improve yourself.

SA A U D SD 53. A man can get too satisfied with things as they are.

SA A U D SD 54. A stronger two-party system in North Carolina would help the whole state.

SA A U D SD 55. It's only natural for a man to look out for himself first.

SA A U D SD 56. Good seldom comes from conflict and disagreement.

SA A U D SD 57. A man should stand up for his convictions no matter how many people disagree with him.

SA A U D SD 58. A worker or businessman should always be loyal to his company.

SA A U D SD 59. Religion doesn't need to change because its truths are eternal.

SA A U D SD 60. My ideas about what is good for the community have changed considerably in recent years..

SA A U D SD 61. All the miracles in the Bible are true.

SA A U D SD 62. A person should "feel" his religion before he joins a church.

SA A U D SD 63. It is more important to live a good life now than to bother about life after death.

SA A U D SD 64. A congregation should encourage the minister during his sermon by saying "Amen."

SA A U D SD 65. In church, I would rather sing the hymns myself than hear the choir sing.

SA A U D SD 66. Churches should have more revivals.

SA A U D SD 67. We should emphasize education in religion and not conversion.

SA A U D SD   68. Testifying about one's religious experience should be a part of regular church services.

SA A U D SD   69. A person who is not willing to follow all the rules of the church should not be allowed to belong.

SA A U D SD   70. Churches don't do enough about saving souls.

The rest of the statements call for answers just like the ones you have given, but they all concern your opinions about the kind of leader a minister should be. For example: (Read the first case and check again on the "agree"—"strongly disagree" distinction.).

71. A city election is approaching, and the candidates disagree mostly on whether or not taxes should be raised to improve the local schools. If he believes the taxes should be raised, what should a minister of a local church do?.

SA A U D SD   —He should present his views privately to people with whom he is acquainted.

SA A U D SD   —The Sunday before the election, without mentioning schools, he should offer a prayer of thanksgiving for the privilege of voting.

SA A U D SD   —He should feel free to speak out in a sermon for the school taxes, and he should get involved in a political organization supporting that side.

SA A U D SD   —He shoud give a talk at a church supper, presenting both sides of the question, seeking not to take a side himself.

72. A local company has just announced its intention of closing down its plant because of business competition. This decision means a serious loss to the city. What should a local minister consider doing?

SA A U D SD   —He should think about organizing food basket distribution and a clothing collection to help those who may soon be without work.

SA A U D SD   —He should write a letter to the company president, asking him to reconsider. If the answer is "no," he should take no further action.

SA A U D SD   —He should remind the congregation and others that the company leaders are doing what they have to do, from a business point of view.

SA A U D SD   —He should point out in a sermon that the free enterprise system does not always benefit everybody connected with it.

73. A certain busy street corner near a church has no traffic light. One day a school child from a church family is killed by a car at this corner. In this situation, what should the minister do?

SA A U D SD   —He should conduct the funeral service, remembering to ask forgiveness for everyone responsible for the death of the child.

SA   A   U   D   SD   —He should investigate the need for a traffic light, should consult with the proper officials, and, if necessary, should lead a community-action group for bringing pressure upon the officials.

SA   A   U   D   SD   —He should appeal to his congregation and others to become safer drivers, and to school children to be more careful crossing streets.

SA   A   U   D   SD   —He should visit with the family of the child and with the driver of the car to help them get over their grief and guilt.

Conclusion of Interview:

That's the end, and you have been very helpful. We certainly thank you for your cooperation and for your time.

Ministers Interview Schedule

Date _____

Personal and Church Data:

Name _____

Congregation _____

Age _____ Family _____

Born _____ Childhood and youth spent in _____

Schooling: College:
                Seminary:

Pastorates served:	*Place*	*Church*	*Dates*
	Gastonia		—present

Congregational Data:

Number of members: _____   Year church was founded: _____

Major occupations of members:

Major occupations of church officers:

Members drawn from what sections of town?

Have you ever read any books on Gastonia or Gaston County?

Introduction:
1. Purpose of the interview: to understand the relationships of the churches of Gaston County to the community.
2. Confidential nature of the interview.

A. Gastonia: The Community
1. What are some things which you *like* about this community?
2. What do you see as the main *problems* of the community?
3. What would you say were the main reasons for Gastonia's award as an All-America City?

    3a. What do you regard as the most important improvement in the community in recent years?

    3b. What made it possible for this change to occur?

    3c. Who were the leaders in this change?

    3d. Do you know of any groups or persons who were vocal in their opposition to this change? (Any who opposed it even if not vocally?)

    3e. Did church leaders, including ministers, have a part in making the change possible?

3f. Suppose some new project were being considered for the community—a park, a hospital, or the like—what four or five persons would be most helpful in gaining community-wide acceptance of the project?

4. In recent years has the interest of industrial leaders in community affairs
( ) increased   ( ) decreased, or   ( ) remained about the same?

4a. Do executives of the large or the small companies take the greater interest in the community?

4b. How do you account for their interest in the community?

5. Has the decrease in family-owned mills changed the community in any way?

B. Specific Issues

1. What is there about Gaston County that makes for favorable conditions for the textile industry?

1a. Would you favor a minimum wage law? _____

1b. Would most Gastonians favor it? _____

1c. Do you favor the so-called right-to-work law?

1d. Do most Gastonians favor it?

1e. How do you feel about unions in general?

1f. Does Gastonia need unions?

What reasons, in your opinion, would the average mill worker in Gastonia give *for* or *against* joining the union?

1g. *For:*

   Against:

1i. Are wages here high or low compared to the rest of the country?

2. Is housing a serious problem in Gaston County?

2a. What has led to this problem?

2b. What would be a good approach to remedying the housing problem?

2c. Is the decline of the old mill village a good development or not?

2d. Has it affected company-worker relationships?

2e. Has it affected the church?

3. What factors have led to interracial progress in Gastonia?

3a. Was there any pressure from the Negro community for this progress?

3b. Would the progress have been made without the pressure?

3c. What would you regard as the path toward better race relations in the years just ahead?

C. The church.

1. What do you consider to be the proper role of the church in relation to economic and political affairs?

2. Are there many people in Gastonia who feel that the church should *not* concern itself with political and economic affairs?   (Who?)

3. People in Gastonia sometimes speak of the church as one of the assets of the community. Do the churches perform any services to the industries of the community? Do they help industry in any way?

4. Have churches or church leaders done anything recently to *help* or to *hurt* labor-management relationships?

5. Have industrial leaders done anything to help or to hurt labor-management relationships?

6. How about unions? Have they done anything to help or to hurt?

7. Suppose some member of your church worked in a textile mill and were having a problem in his work—difficulty with his supervisor, or felt he were being underpaid or overworked. What alternative ways would you consider for trying to help him with this problem?

8. Do the mills and other industries help the churches in any way? (Do they give the churches direct financial support? Other kinds of support?)

D. The minister.

1. How good do you consider communication to be between leaders of industry and the ministers of the community?

   1a. How does such communication take place?

   1b. Does it need to be improved?   (If so, how?)

2. In the period of time that you have been in Gastonia, do you notice any changes in the religious life of the people? Are they more religious, less so, about the same, or what?

3. What kind of a minister do you think most people in the community like?

   3a. How would the average mill worker rank the importance of his minister being

       ( ) a good pastor

       ( ) a good preacher

       ( ) a good community leader

       ( ) a good church administrator (Rank 1, 2, 3, 4)

   3b. How would the average industrial executive rank these abilities?

       ( ) a good pastor

       ( ) a good preacher

       ( ) a good community leader

       ( ) a good administrator (Rank 1, 2, 3, 4)

   3c. How would *you* rank these four?

       ( ) a good pastor

       ( ) a good preacher

       ( ) a good community leader

       ( ) a good administrator

   3d. Are there any other qualities you particularly like to see in a minister?

4. What kinds of community leadership do you feel to be appropriate for a minister to undertake?

5. In your church have there been any discussions of the matters touched on in our discussion—race relations, labor relations, housing, politics, and the like?

   5a. Do you feel that more such discussions should be held in churches?

   5b. Do you see any dangers in such discussions in the church?

6. What do you see as the reasons for the tendency in some churches for the minister to bring social issues into his sermons?

7. As you think about your congregation, why do people keep coming to church? What brings them here?

Index

Adams, Daisie Hasson, 239-240
African Methodist Episcopalian (AME) Zion, 118, 141, 260, 261
Albright, R. Mayne, 193-194
Alcoholic Beverage Control (ABC), 136, 138, 148, 159, 171 ff., 264; Prohibition, 345
Alcoholics Anonymous, 343
All America City Award, 259, 307, 308, 310, 311, 312
American Federation of Labor (AFL), 177, 178, 183
Anti-poverty agency, 323-324
Arbitration, 180, 181
Arendt, Hannah, 37, 287, 313
Assembly of God, 127
Atkins, Ben E., 182, 195, 196, 198
Atkins, James H., 319, 320, 322-323
Atkins, James Sr., 319
Baptist Church (National), 140
Barber, Nathaniel, 244-246
Beal, Fred, 58
Bellah, Robert, 46
Belmont, N.C., 86, 132, 149, 150, 248, 268, 357
Berger, Peter, 306-307
Berger, Peter and Thomas Luckman, 39, 40, 43, 44, 45, 46, 48, 60
Bessemer City, N.C., 262, 324
Bittner, Van, 178
"Branchhead boys," 193
Broughton, J. Melville, 195
Bulwinkle (Congressman), 194
Bureaucracy, 305
Burkean conservatism, 321-322
Burlington Mills, 78, 87, 88, 90, 139, 182, 187, 191, 270, 277
Byssinosis (brown lung disease), 190
Cannon Mills, 184
Chamber of Commerce, 19, 21, 82, 86, 270
Charlotte Observer, 79, 257
Cherry, R. Gregg, 62, 101, 173, 180, 193
Cherryville incident, 199-206, 217, 221, 305
Church of God, 129, 130
Churches:
  Attendance, 18,103 ff.; and economic class, 148; and economic issues, 154-157, 160; and elections, 171 ff.; financial contributions of members, 103 ff.; functions of, 343-344; growth, 101-105; and industry, 33-35,
199-205; membership and attitudes toward labor unions, 216, 217, 220; racial composition, 107; and social change, 341-342; 344-347; and social class, 107 ff.; and social control, 341-342; and social issues, 19, 27-29, 52, 134-135, 136, 137-138, 143-144, 147-150, 151 ff., 245-248, 253-255, 257 ff., 304 ff., 341 ff., 342-343; and stress, 341
Churches, black, 118-119, 139-144, 221-222, 257 ff., 290-291, 344
Churches, middle class, 114-115
Churches, mill, 33, 34, 44, 107, 114, 115, 132, 135
Churches, rural, 107
Churches, transitional, 112-114
Churches, uptown, 107, 110-112
Cleghorn, Reese, 271
Clara-Dunn-Armstrong Mills, 179-183
Clergy, See minister's role of ministers and labor unions
Cohen, Sanford, 192
Communism, 184, 195, 196, 198, 208
Cone Mills, 207
Congress of Racial Equality (CORE), 260, 266
Congress of Industrial Organizations (CIO), 177, 178, 184, 185, 201
Constitution, U.S., 288, 290, 315
Counts, Dorothy, 20
Cox, B. Elton, 260-261, 266
Cramerton, N.C., 199
Cramerton Mills, 23, 78-79, 87, 89, 184
Crime, 174
Culture, 35-36, 46; and anti-union attitudes, 217-220; and constraint, 157; southern, 131; transcendence by churches, 305-306; and the uptown church, 112
Dabbs, James M., 20
Dallas, N.C., 199, 247
Daniels, Josephus, 64
Day Care centers, 343
Declaration of Independence, 288, 290
Dellinger, Kenneth E., 196
Demerath, Nicholas J., III, 304-306
Democratic Party, 16, 316, 318, 330; 1948 Primary for Governor, 193-194; 1950 Primary for Senator, 194-199 See also Elections
DeTocqueville, Alexis, 37
Dewey, Donald, 269